EXAM✓CRAM

MCTS 70-642
Windows Server 2008 Network Infrastructure, Configuring

Patrick Regan

D1067247

MCTS 70-642 Exam Cram
Windows Server 2008 Network Infrastructure, Configuring

ISBN-13: 978-0-7897-3818-9
ISBN-10: 0-7897-3818-x

Library of Congress Cataloging-in-Publication Data

Regan, Patrick E.

MCTS 70-642 exam cram : Windows server 2008 network infrastructure, configuring / Patrick Regan.

p. cm.

ISBN 978-0-7897-3818-9 (pbk. w/cd)

1. Electronic data processing personnel--Certification. 2. Microsoft software--Examinations--Study guides. 3. Computer networks--Examinations--Study guides. 4. Microsoft Windows server. I. Title.

QA76.3.R45556 2008

005.4'476--dc22

2008041604

Printed in the United States on America

First Printing: November 2008

Trademarks

Warning and Disclaimer

Bulk Sales

Que Publishing offers excellent discounts on this book when ordered in quantity for bulk purchases or special sales. For more information, please contact

U.S. Corporate and Government Sales
1-800-382-3419
corpsales@pearsontechgroup.com

For sales outside of the U.S., please contact

International Sales
international@pearsoned.com

Associate Publisher
David Dusthimer

Executive Editor
Betsy Brown

Development Editor
Box Twelve Communications, Inc.

Technical Editor
David Camardella

Managing Editor
Patrick Kanouse

Senior Project Editor
San Dee Phillips

Copy Editor
Margo Catts

Indexer
Heather McNeill
Tim Wright

Proofreader
Sheri Cain

Publishing Coordinator
Vanessa Evans

Multimedia Developer
Dan Scherf

Cover and Interior Designer
Gary Adair

Page Layout
Louisa Adair

Contents at a Glance

Table of Contents

About the Author

Patrick Regan has been a PC technician, network administrator/engineer, design architect, and security analyst for the past 16 years after graduating with a bachelor's degree in physics from the University of Akron. He has taught many computer and network classes at Sacramento local colleges (Heald Colleges and MTI Colleges), and participated in and led many projects (Heald Colleges, Intel Corporation, Miles Consulting Corporation, and Pacific Coast Companies). For his teaching accomplishments, he received the Teacher of the Year award from Heald Colleges and he has received several recognition awards from Intel. Previously, he worked as a product support engineer for Intel Corporation Customer Service, as a senior network engineer for Virtual Alert supporting the BioTerrorism Readiness suite, and as a senior design architect/engineer and training coordinator for Miles Consulting Corp (MCC), a premiere Microsoft Gold partner and consulting firm. He is currently a senior network engineer at Pacific Coast Companies supporting a large enterprise network.

He holds many certifications, including the Microsoft MCSE, MCSA, MCT; MCITP CompTIA's A+, Network+, Server+, Linux+, Security+ and CTT+; Cisco CCNA; and Novell's CNE and CWNP Certified Wireless Network Administrator (CWNA).

Over the last several years, he has written several textbooks for Prentice-Hall Publisher, including *Troubleshooting the PC*, *Networking with Windows 2000 and 2003*, *Linux*, *Local Area Networks*, *Wide Area Networks*, and the Acing Series (*Acing the A+*, *Acing the Network+*, *Acing the Security+*, and *Acing the Linux+*). He has also co-authored *ExamCram 70-290 MCSA/MCSE Managing and Maintaining a Microsoft Windows Server 2003 Environment, 2nd Edition Exam Cram*, has written *70-620 MCSA/MCSE TS: Microsoft Windows Vista, Configuring* and is currently writing *Exam Cram 70-643: Windows Server 2008 Application Platform, Configuring*. In addition, he has completed the study guides for the A+ certification exams for Cisco Press.

You can write with questions and comments to the author at Patrick_Regan@hotmail.com. (Because of the high volume of mail, every message might not receive a reply).

Dedication

I dedicate this book to Lidia, the woman that I am going to marry.

We Want to Hear from You!

As the reader of this book, *you* are our most important critic and commentator. We value your opinion and want to know what we're doing right, what we could do better, in what areas you'd like to see us publish, and any other words of wisdom you're willing to pass our way.

As the Associate Publisher for Que Publishing, I welcome your comments. You can email or write me directly to let me know what you did or didn't like about this book—as well as what we can do to make our books better.

Please note that I cannot help you with technical problems related to the topic of this book. We do have a User Services group, however, where I will forward specific technical questions related to the book.

When you write, please be sure to include this book's title and author, as well as your name, email address, and phone number. I will carefully review your comments and share them with the author and editors who worked on the book.

Email: feedback@quepublishing.com

Mail: Dave Dusthimer
            Associate Publisher
            Que Publishing
            800 East 96th Street
            Indianapolis, IN 46240 USA

Reader Services

Visit our website and register this book at www.quepublishing.com/register for convenient access to any updates, downloads, or errata that might be available for this book.

Introduction

Welcome to the 70-642 Exam Cram! Whether this book is your first or your 15th Exam Cram series book, you'll find information here that will help ensure your success as you pursue knowledge, experience, and certification. This book aims to help you get ready to take and pass the Microsoft certification exam "TS: Windows Server 2008 Network Infrastructure, Configuring" (Exam 70-642). After you pass this exam, you will earn the Microsoft Certified Technology Specialist: Windows Server 2008 Applications certification.

This introduction explains Microsoft's certification programs in general and talks about how the Exam Cram series can help you prepare for Microsoft's latest certification exams. Chapters 1 through 9 are designed to remind you of everything you'll need to know to pass the 70-642 certification exam. The two sample tests at the end of the book should give you a reasonably accurate assessment of your knowledge and, yes, we've provided the answers and their explanations for these sample tests. Read the book, understand the material, and you'll stand a very good chance of passing the real test.

Exam Cram books help you understand and appreciate the subjects and materials you need to know to pass Microsoft certification exams. Exam Cram books are aimed strictly at test preparation and review. They do not teach you everything you need to know about a subject. Instead, the author streamlines and highlights the pertinent information by presenting and dissecting the questions and problems he's discovered that you're likely to encounter on a Microsoft test.

Nevertheless, to completely prepare yourself for any Microsoft test, we recommend that you begin by taking the Self-Assessment that is included in this book, immediately following this introduction. The self-assessment tool helps you evaluate your knowledge base against the requirements for becoming a Microsoft Certified Technology Specialist (MCTS) and will be the first step in earning more advanced certifications, including Microsoft's IT Professional and Professional Developer (MCITP and MCPD) and Architect (MCA).

Based on what you learn from the self-assessment, you might decide to begin your studies with classroom training or some background reading. On the other hand, you might decide to pick up and read one of the many study guides available from Microsoft or third-party vendors. We also recommend that you supplement your study program with visits to http://www.examcram.com to receive additional practice questions, get advice, and track the Windows certification programs.

This book also offers you an added bonus of access to Exam Cram practice tests online. This software simulates the Microsoft testing environment with similar types of questions to those you're likely to see on the actual Microsoft exam. We also strongly recommend that you install, configure, and play around with the Microsoft Windows Vista and Windows Server 2008 operating systems. Nothing beats hands-on experience and familiarity when it comes to understanding the questions you're likely to encounter on a certification test. Book learning is essential, but without a doubt, hands-on experience is the best teacher of all!

The Microsoft Certification Program

Microsoft currently offers multiple certification titles, each of which boasts its own special abbreviation. (As a certification candidate and computer professional, you need to have a high tolerance for acronyms.)

The certification for end users is

▶ **Microsoft Office Specialists:** For professionals recognized for demonstrating advanced skills with Microsoft desktop software (including Microsoft Office).

The older certifications associated with the Windows Server 2003 operating system and related network infrastructure are

▶ **Microsoft Certified Professional (MCP):** For professionals who have the skills to successfully implement Microsoft products (such as Windows XP or Windows Server 2003) or technology as part of a business solution in an organization.

▶ **Microsoft Certified Desktop Support Technician (MCDST):** For professionals who have the technical and customer service skills to troubleshoot hardware and software operation issues in Microsoft Windows environments.

▶ **Microsoft Certified Systems Administrators (MCSAs):** For professionals who administer network and systems environments based on the Microsoft Windows operating systems. Specializations include MCSA: Messaging and MCSA: Security.

▶ **Microsoft Certified Systems Engineer (MCSE):** For professionals who design and implement an infrastructure solution that is based on the Windows operating system and Microsoft Windows Server System software. Specializations include MCSE: Messaging and MCSE: Security.

The newer certifications based on Windows Vista, Windows Server 2008, and related server products are

▶ **Microsoft Certified Technology Specialist (MCTS):** For professionals who target specific technologies and distinguish themselves by demonstrating in-depth knowledge and expertise in the various Microsoft specialized technologies. The MCTS is a replacement for the MCP program.

▶ **Microsoft Certified IT Professional (MCITP):** For professionals who demonstrate comprehensive skills in planning, deploying, supporting, maintaining, and optimizing IT infrastructures. The MCITP is a replacement for the MCSA and MCSE programs.

▶ **Microsoft Certified Architect (MCA):** For professionals who are identified as top industry experts in IT architecture and who use multiple technologies to solve business problems and provide business metrics and measurements. Candidates for the MCA program are required to present to a review board—consisting of previously certified architects—to earn the certification.

For those who want to become or who are database professionals, the following certifications are based on the Microsoft SQL Server products:

▶ **Microsoft Certified Database Administrators (MCDBAs):** For professionals who design, implement, and administer Microsoft SQL Server databases.

For developers and programmers, the following certifications are based on the Microsoft .NET Framework and Visual Studio products:

▶ **Microsoft Certified Professional Developer (MCPD):** For professionals who are recognized as expert Windows Application Developers, Web Application Developers, or Enterprise Applications Developers. They demonstrate that you can build rich applications that target a variety of platforms such as the Microsoft .NET Framework 2.0.

▶ **Microsoft Certified Application Developers (MCADs):** For professionals who use Microsoft technologies to develop and maintain department-level applications, components, web or desktop clients, or back-end data services.

For trainers and curriculum developers, the following certifications are available:

- ▶ **Microsoft Certified Trainer (MCT):** For qualified instructors who are certified by Microsoft to deliver Microsoft training courses to IT professionals and developers.

- ▶ **Microsoft Certified Learning Consultant (MCLC):** Recognizes MCTs whose job roles have grown to include frequent consultative engagements with their customers and who are experts in delivering customized learning solutions that positively affect customer return on investment (ROI).

In 2008, Microsoft introduced two advanced certifications. The Master certifications identify individuals with the deepest technical skills available on a particular Microsoft product, such as Windows Server 2008, Exchange 2007, and SQL Server 2008. To achieve Master certification, candidates must attend several required sessions, successfully complete all in-class exams (written and lab), and successfully complete a qualification lab exam.

The highest-level certification is the Microsoft Certified Architect (MCA) program, focusing on IT architecture. Microsoft Certified Architects have proven experience with delivering solutions and can communicate effectively with business, architecture, and technology professionals. These professionals have three or more years of advanced IT architecture experience and possess strong technical and leadership skills. Candidates are required to pass a rigorous Review Board interview conducted by a panel of experts.

The best place to keep tabs on all Microsoft certifications is the following website:

http://www.microsoft.com/learning/default.mspx.

Microsoft changes their website often, so if this URL does not work in the future, you should use the Search tool on Microsoft's site to find more information on a particular certification.

Microsoft Certified Technology Specialist (MCTS)

Technology Specialist certifications enable professionals to target specific technologies and to distinguish themselves by demonstrating in-depth knowledge and expertise in their specialized technologies. Microsoft Technology Specialists are consistently capable of implementing, building, troubleshooting, and debugging a particular Microsoft technology.

At the time of the writing of this book, there are 28 Microsoft Certified Technology Specialist (MCTS) certifications:

MCTS: SQL Server 2008, Business Intelligence Development and Maintenance

MCTS: SQL Server 2008, Database Development

MCTS: SQL Server 2008, Implementation and Maintenance

MCTS: .NET Framework 3.5, Windows Presentation Foundation Applications

MCTS: .NET Framework 3.5, Windows Communication Foundation Applications

MCTS: .NET Framework 3.5, Windows Workflow Foundation Applications

MCTS: .NET Framework 2.0 Web Applications

MCTS: .NET Framework 2.0 Windows Applications

MCTS: .NET Framework 2.0 Distributed Applications

MCTS: SQL Server 2005

MCTS: SQL Server 2005 Business Intelligence

MCTS: BizTalk Server 2006

MCTS: Enterprise Project Management with Microsoft Office Project Server 2007

MCTS: Managing Projects with Microsoft Office Project 2007

MCTS: Microsoft Office Live Communications Server 2005

MCTS: Microsoft Exchange Server 2007, Configuration

MCTS: Microsoft Office SharePoint Server 2007, Configuration

MCTS: Microsoft Office SharePoint Server 2007, Application Development

MCTS: Windows Mobile 5.0, Applications

MCTS: Windows Mobile 5.0, Implementing and Managing

MCTS: Windows Server 2003 Hosted Environments, Configuration, and Management

MCTS: Windows Server 2008 Active Directory Configuration

MCTS: Windows Server 2008 Network Infrastructure Configuration

MCTS: Windows Server 2008 Applications Infrastructure Configuration

MCTS: Windows SharePoint Services 3.0, Application Development

MCTS: Windows SharePoint Services 3.0, Configuration

MCTS: Windows Vista and 2007 Microsoft Office System Desktops,
Deploying and Maintaining

MCTS: Windows Vista, Configuration

Microsoft Certified IT Professional (MCITP)

The new Microsoft Certified IT Professional (MCITP) credential lets you highlight your specific area of expertise. Now you can easily distinguish yourself as an expert in database administration, database development, business intelligence, or support. At the time of this writing, the following Microsoft Certified IT Professional certifications exist:

IT Professional: Database Developer

IT Professional: Database Administrator

IT Professional: Business Intelligence Developer

IT Professional: Enterprise Support Technician

IT Professional: Consumer Support Technician

IT Professional: Database Developer 2008

IT Professional: Database Administrator 2008

IT Professional: Enterprise Messaging Administrator

IT Professional: Enterprise Project Management with Microsoft Office Project Server 2007

IT Professional: Enterprise Administrator

IT Professional: Server Administrator

At the time of this writing, details are just starting to be revealed on the Microsoft Certified Technology Specialist (MCTS) on Windows Server 2008. The MCTS on Windows Server 2008 helps you and your organization save time, reduce costs and take advantage of advanced server technology with the power to increase the flexibility of your server infrastructure,. Transition certifications are available today for Windows Server 2003 certified professionals, and full certification paths will be available soon after the Windows Server 2008 product release. For more details about these certifications, visit the following website:

http://www.microsoft.com/learning/mcp/windowsserver2008/default.mspx

If the URL is no longer available, don't forget to search for MCTS and Windows Server 2008 with the Microsoft search tool found on the Microsoft website.

Microsoft Certified Technology Specialist: Windows Server 2008 Applications Infrastructure

The Microsoft Certified Technology Specialist certifications enable professionals to target specific technologies and distinguish themselves by demonstrating in-depth knowledge and expertise in their specialized technologies. A Microsoft Certified Technology Specialist in Windows Vista, Configuration possesses the knowledge and skills to configure Windows Vista for optimal performance on the desktop, including installing, managing, and configuring the new security, network, and application features in Windows Vista.

To earn the Microsoft Certified Technology Specialist: Windows Server 2008 Network Infrastructure, Configuration certification, you must pass one exam that focuses on supporting end-user issues about network connectivity, security, applications installation and compatibility, and logon problems that include account issues and password resets:

Exam 70-642: TS: Windows Server 2008 Applications Infrastructure, Configuration

If you decide to take a Microsoft-recognized class, you would take several classes to cover all the material found on this exam. The preparation guide (including exam objectives) for Exam 70-642 TS: Windows Server 2008 Network Infrastructure, Configuring can be found at

http://www.microsoft.com/learning/exams/70-642.mspx

Taking a Certification Exam

After you prepare for your exam, you need to register with a testing center. At the time of this writing, the cost to take exam 70-642 is (U.S.) $125, and if you don't pass, you can take each again for an additional (U.S.) $125 for each attempt. In the United States and Canada, tests are administered by Prometric. Here's how you can contact them:

- ▶ **Prometric:** You can sign up for a test through the company's website, http://www.2test.com or http://www.prometric.com. Within the United States and Canada, you can register by phone at 800-755-3926. If you live outside this region, you should check the Prometric website for the appropriate phone number.

To sign up for a test, you must possess a valid credit card or contact Prometric for mailing instructions to send a check (in the United States). Only when payment is verified, or a check has cleared, can you actually register for a test.

To schedule an exam, you need to call the appropriate phone number or visit the Prometric websites at least one day in advance. To cancel or reschedule an exam in the United States or Canada, you must call before 3 p.m. Eastern time the day before the scheduled test time (or you might be charged, even if you don't show up to take the test). When you want to schedule a test, you should have the following information ready:

▶ Your name, organization, and mailing address.

▶ Your Microsoft test ID. (In the United States, this means your Social Security number; citizens of other countries should call ahead to find out what type of identification number is required to register for a test.)

▶ The name and number of the exam you want to take.

▶ A method of payment. (As mentioned previously, a credit card is the most convenient method, but alternate means can be arranged in advance, if necessary.)

After you sign up for a test, you are told when and where the test is scheduled. You should arrive at least 15 minutes early. You must supply two forms of identification— one of which must be a photo ID—to be admitted into the testing room.

Tracking Certification Status

As soon as you pass a qualified Microsoft exam and earn a professional certification, Microsoft generates transcripts that indicate which exams you have passed. You can view a copy of your transcript at any time by going to the MCP secured site (this site may change as the MCP is retired) and selecting the Transcript Tool. This tool enables you to print a copy of your current transcript and confirm your certification status.

After you pass the necessary set of exams, you are certified. Official certification is normally granted after six to eight weeks, so you shouldn't expect to get your credentials overnight. The package for official certification that arrives includes a Welcome Kit that contains a number of elements (see Microsoft's website for other benefits of specific certifications):

▶ A certificate that is suitable for framing, along with a wallet card and lapel pin.

- A license to use the related certification logo, which means you can use the logo in advertisements, promotions, and documents, and on letterhead, business cards, and so on. Along with the license comes a logo sheet, which includes camera-ready artwork. (Note that before you use any of the artwork, you must sign and return a licensing agreement that indicates you'll abide by its terms and conditions.)

- Access to the *Microsoft Certified Professional Magazine Online* website, which provides ongoing data about testing and certification activities, requirements, changes to the MCP program, and security-related information on Microsoft products.

Many people believe that the benefits of MCP certification go well beyond the perks that Microsoft provides to newly anointed members of this elite group. We're starting to see more job listings that request or require applicants to have Microsoft and other related certifications, and many individuals who complete Microsoft certification programs can qualify for increases in pay and responsibility. As an official recognition of hard work and broad knowledge, a certification credential is a badge of honor in many IT organizations.

About This Book

Each topical Exam Cram chapter follows a regular structure and contains graphical cues about important or useful information. Here's the structure of a typical chapter:

- **Opening hotlists:** Each chapter begins with a list of the terms, tools, and techniques that you must learn and understand before you can be fully conversant with that chapter's subject matter. The hotlists are followed with one or two introductory paragraphs to set the stage for the rest of the chapter.

- **Topical coverage:** After the opening hotlists and introductory text, each chapter covers a series of topics related to the chapter's subject. Throughout that section, we highlight topics or concepts that are likely to appear on a test, using a special element called an Exam Alert:

EXAM ALERT

This is what an Exam Alert looks like. Normally, an alert stresses concepts, terms, software, or activities that are likely to relate to one or more certification-test questions. For that reason, we think any information in an Exam Alert is worthy of unusual attentiveness on your part.

You should pay close attention to material flagged in Exam Alerts; although all the information in this book pertains to what you need to know to pass the exam, Exam Alerts contain information that is really important. You'll find what appears in the meat of each chapter to be worth knowing, too, when preparing for the test. Because this book's material is very condensed, we recommend that you use this book along with other resources to achieve the maximum benefit.

In addition to the Exam Alerts, we provide tips and notes that will help you build a better foundation for Windows Server 2008 knowledge. Although the information might not be on the exam, it is certainly related and it will help you become a better-informed test taker.

TIP

This is how tips are formatted. Keep your eyes open for these, and you'll become a Windows Server 2008 guru in no time!

NOTE

This is how notes are formatted. Notes direct your attention to important pieces of information that relate to Windows Server 2008 and Microsoft certification.

Each chapter contains the following:

▶ **Exam prep questions:** Although we talk about test questions and topics throughout the book, this section at the end of each chapter presents a series of mock test questions and explanations of both correct and incorrect answers.

▶ **Details and resources:** Every chapter ends with a section titled "Need to Know More?" That section provides direct pointers to Microsoft and third-party resources that offer more details on the chapter's subject. In addition, that section tries to rank or at least rate the quality and thoroughness of the topic's coverage by each resource. If you find a resource you like in that collection, you should use it, but you shouldn't feel compelled to use all the resources. On the other hand, we recommend only resources that we use on a regular basis, so none of our recommendations will be a waste of your time or money (but purchasing them all at once probably represents an expense that many network administrators and Microsoft certification candidates might find hard to justify).

The bulk of the book follows this chapter structure, but we'd like to point out a few other elements. Practice Exams #1 and #2—two practice exams and their answers (with detailed explanations)—help you assess your understanding of the material presented throughout the book to ensure that you're ready for the exam.

Finally, the tear-out Cram Sheet attached next to the inside front cover of this Exam Cram book represents a condensed collection of facts and tips that we think are essential for you to memorize before taking the test. Because you can dump this information out of your head onto a sheet of paper before taking the exam, you can master this information by brute force; you need to remember it only long enough to write it down when you walk into the testing room. You might even want to look at it in the car or in the lobby of the testing center just before you walk in to take the exam.

We've structured the topics in this book to build on one another. Therefore, some topics in later chapters make the most sense after you've read earlier chapters. That's why we suggest that you read this book from front to back for your initial test preparation. If you need to brush up on a topic or if you have to bone up for a second try, you can use the index or table of contents to go straight to the topics and questions that you need to study. Beyond helping you prepare for the test, we think you'll find this book useful as a tightly focused reference to some of the most important aspects of Windows Vista.

The book uses the following typographical conventions:

▶ Command-line strings that are meant to be typed into the computer are displayed in special font, such as

```
net use lpt1: \\print_server_name\printer_share_name
```

▶ *New terms* are introduced in italics.

Given all the book's elements and its specialized focus, we've tried to create a tool that will help you prepare for and pass Microsoft Exam 70-642. Please share with us your feedback on the book, especially if you have ideas about how we can improve it for future test takers. Send your questions or comments about this book via email to feedback@quepublishing.com. We'll consider everything you say carefully, and we'll respond to all suggestions. For more information on this book and other Que Certification titles, visit our website at http://www.quepublishing.com. You should also check out the new Exam Cram website at http://www.examcram.com, where you'll find information, updates, commentary, and certification information.

Exam Layout and Design

Historically, there have been six types of question formats on Microsoft certification exams. These types of questions continue to appear on current Microsoft tests, and they are discussed in the following sections:

- ▶ Multiple-choice, single answer
- ▶ Multiple-choice, multiple answers
- ▶ Build-list-and-reorder (list prioritization)
- ▶ Create-a-tree
- ▶ Drag-and-connect
- ▶ Select-and-place (drag-and-drop)

The Single-Answer and Multiple-Answer Multiple-Choice Question Formats

Some exam questions require you to select a single answer, whereas others ask you to select multiple correct answers. The following multiple-choice question requires you to select a single correct answer. Following the question is a brief summary of each potential answer and why it is either right or wrong.

1. You have three domains connected to an empty root domain under one contiguous domain name: `tutu.com`. This organization is formed into a forest arrangement, with a secondary domain called `frog.com`. How many schema masters exist for this arrangement?

   - ○ A. 1
   - ○ B. 2
   - ○ C. 3
   - ○ D. 4

1. The correct answer is A because only one schema master is necessary for a forest arrangement. The other answers (B, C, and D) are misleading because they try to make you believe that schema masters might be in each domain or perhaps that you should have one for each contiguous namespace domain.

This sample question format corresponds closely to the Microsoft certification exam format. The only difference is that on the exam, the questions are not followed by answers and their explanations. To select an answer, you position the cursor over the option button next to the answer you want to select. Then you click the mouse button to select the answer.

Let's examine a question for which one or more answers are possible. This type of question provides check boxes rather than option buttons for marking all appropriate selections.

2. What can you use to seize FSMO roles? (Choose two.)

○ A. The `ntdsutil.exe` utility

○ B. The Active Directory Users and Computers console

○ C. The `secedit.exe` utility

○ D. The `utilman.exe` utility

2. Answers A and B are correct. You can seize roles from a server that is still running through the Active Directory Users and Computers console, or in the case of a server failure, you can seize roles with the `ntdsutil.exe` utility. You use the `secedit.exe` utility to force group policies into play; therefore, Answer C is incorrect. The `utilman.exe` tool manages accessibility settings in Windows Server 2003; therefore, Answer D is incorrect.

This particular question requires two answers. Microsoft sometimes gives partial credit for partially correct answers. For Question 2, you have to mark the check boxes next to Answers A and B to obtain credit for a correct answer. Notice that to choose the right answers you also need to know why the other answers are wrong.

The Build-List-and-Reorder Question Format

Questions in the build-list-and-reorder format present two lists of items—one on the left and one on the right. To answer the question, you must move items from the list on the right to the list on the left. The final list must then be reordered into a specific sequence.

These questions generally sound like this: "From the following list of choices, pick the choices that answer the question. Arrange the list in a certain order." Question 3 shows an example of how these questions would look.

3. From the following list of famous people, choose those who have been elected president of the United States. Arrange the list in the order in which the presidents served.

○ Thomas Jefferson

○ Ben Franklin

○ Abe Lincoln

○ George Washington

○ Andrew Jackson

○ Paul Revere

3. The correct answer is

1. George Washington

2. Thomas Jefferson

3. Andrew Jackson

4. Abe Lincoln

On an actual exam, the entire list of famous people would initially appear in the list on the right. You would move the four correct answers to the list on the left and then reorder the list on the left. Notice that the answer to Question 3 does not include all the items from the initial list. However, that might not always be the case.

To move an item from the right list to the left list on the exam, you first select the item by clicking it, and then you click the Add button (left arrow). After you move an item from one list to the other, you can move the item back by first selecting the item and then clicking the appropriate button (either the Add button or the Remove button). After you move items to the left list, you can reorder an item by selecting the item and clicking the up or down arrow buttons.

The Create-a-Tree Question Format

Questions in the create-a-tree format also present two lists—one on the left side of the screen and one on the right side of the screen. The list on the right consists of individual items, and the list on the left consists of nodes in a tree. To answer the question, you must move items from the list on the right to the appropriate node in the tree.

These questions can best be characterized as simply a matching exercise. Items from the list on the right are placed under the appropriate category in the list on the left. Question 4 shows an example of how they would look.

4. The calendar year is divided into four seasons:

1. Winter

2. Spring

3. Summer

4. Fall

Identify the season during which each of the following holidays occurs:

- ○ Christmas

- ○ Fourth of July

- ○ Labor Day

- ○ Flag Day

- ○ Memorial Day

- ○ Washington's Birthday

- ○ Thanksgiving

- ○ Easter

4. The correct answers are

1. Winter

- ○ Christmas

- ○ Washington's Birthday

2. Spring

- ○ Flag Day

- ○ Memorial Day

- ○ Easter

3. Summer

- ○ Fourth of July

- ○ Labor Day

4. Fall

- ○ Thanksgiving

In this case, you use all the items in the list. However, that might not always be the case.

To move an item from the right list to its appropriate location in the tree, you must first select the appropriate tree node by clicking it. Then you select the item to be moved and click the Add button. After you add one or more items to a tree node, the node appears with a + icon to the left of the node name. You can click this icon to expand the node and view the items you have added. If you have added any item to the wrong tree node, you can remove it by selecting it and clicking the Remove button.

The Drag-and-Connect Question Format

Questions in the drag-and-connect format present a group of objects and a list of "connections." To answer the question, you must move the appropriate connections between the objects.

This type of question is best described with graphics. For this type of question, it isn't necessary to use every object, and you can use each connection multiple times.

The Select-and-Place Question Format

Questions in the select-and-place (drag-and-drop) format display a diagram with blank boxes and a list of labels that you need to drag to correctly fill in the blank boxes. To answer such a question, you must move the labels to their appropriate positions on the diagram. This type of question is best understood with graphics.

Special Exam Question Formats

Starting with the exams released for the Windows Server 2003 MCSE track, Microsoft introduced several new question types in addition to the more traditional types of questions that are still widely used on all Microsoft exams. These innovative question types have been highly researched and tested by Microsoft before they were chosen to be included in many of the "refreshed" exams for the MCSA/MCSE on the Windows 2000 track and for the new exams on the Windows Server 2003 and Windows Server 2008 track. These special question types are as follows:

▸ Hot area questions

▸ Active screen questions

▸ Drag-and-drop–type questions

▸ Simulation questions

Hot Area Question Types

Hot area questions ask you to indicate the correct answer by selecting one or more elements within a graphic. For example, you might be asked to select multiple objects within a list.

Active Screen Question Types

Active screen questions ask you to configure a dialog box by modifying one or more elements. These types of questions offer a realistic interface in which you must properly configure various settings, just as you would within the actual software product. For example, you might be asked to select the proper option within a drop-down list box.

Drag-and-Drop Question Types

New drag-and-drop questions ask you to drag source elements to their appropriate corresponding targets within a work area. These types of questions test your knowledge of specific concepts and their definitions or descriptions. For example, you might be asked to match a description of a computer program to the actual software application.

Simulation Question Types

Simulation questions ask you to indicate the correct answer by performing specific tasks, such as configuring and installing network adapters or drivers, configuring and controlling access to files, or troubleshooting hardware devices. Many of the tasks that systems administrators and systems engineers perform can be presented more accurately in simulations than in most traditional exam question types.

Microsoft's Testing Formats

Currently, Microsoft uses three different testing formats:

- ▶ Fixed length
- ▶ Short form
- ▶ Case study

Other Microsoft exams employ advanced testing capabilities that might not be immediately apparent. Although the questions that appear are primarily multiple choice, the logic that drives them is more complex than that in older Microsoft tests, which use a fixed sequence of questions, called a *fixed-length test*. Some questions employ a sophisticated user interface, which Microsoft calls a *simulation*, to test your knowledge of the software and systems under consideration in a more-or-less "live" environment that behaves just like the real thing. You should review the Microsoft Learning, Reference, and Certification Web pages at http://www.microsoft.com/learning/default.mspx for more detailed information.

In the future, Microsoft might choose to create exams using a well-known technique called *adaptive testing* to establish a test taker's level of knowledge and product competence. In general, adaptive exams might look the same as fixed-length exams, but they discover the level of difficulty at which an individual test taker can correctly answer questions. Test takers with differing levels of knowledge or ability therefore see different sets of questions; individuals with high levels of knowledge or ability are presented with a smaller set of more difficult questions, whereas individuals with lower levels of knowledge are presented with a larger set of easier questions. Two individuals might answer the same percentage of questions correctly, but the test taker with a higher knowledge or ability level scores higher because his or her questions are worth more. Also, the lower-level test taker is likely to answer more questions than his or her more knowledgeable colleague. This explains why adaptive tests use ranges of values to define the number of questions and the amount of time it takes to complete the test.

NOTE

Microsoft does *not* offer adaptive exams at the time of this book's publication.

Most adaptive tests work by evaluating the test taker's most recent answer. A correct answer leads to a more difficult question, and the test software's estimate of the test taker's knowledge and ability level is raised. An incorrect answer leads to a less difficult question, and the test software's estimate of the test taker's knowledge and ability level is lowered. This process continues until the test targets the test taker's true ability level. The exam ends when the test taker's level of accuracy meets a statistically acceptable value (in other words, when his or her performance demonstrates an acceptable level of knowledge and ability) or when the maximum number of items has been presented. (In which case, the test taker is almost certain to fail.)

Microsoft has also introduced a short-form test for its most popular tests. This test delivers 25 to 30 questions to its takers, giving them exactly 60 minutes to complete the exam. This type of exam is similar to a fixed-length test in that it allows readers to jump ahead or return to earlier questions and to cycle through the questions until the test is done. Microsoft does not use adaptive logic in short-form tests, but it claims that statistical analysis of the question pool is such that the 25 to 30 questions delivered during a short-form exam conclusively measure a test taker's knowledge of the subject matter in much the same way as an adaptive test. You can think of the short-form test as a kind of "greatest hits exam" (that is, it covers the most important questions) version of an adaptive exam on the same topic.

Because you won't know which form the Microsoft exam might take, you should be prepared for either a fixed-length or short-form exam. The layout is the same for both fixed-length and short-form tests—you are not penalized for guessing the correct answer(s) to questions, no matter how many questions you answer incorrectly.

The Fixed-Length and Short-Form Exam Strategy

One tactic that has worked well for many test takers is to answer each question as well as you can before time expires on the exam. Some questions you will undoubtedly feel better equipped to answer correctly than others; however, you should still select an answer to each question as you proceed through the exam. You should click the Mark for Review check box for any question of which you are unsure. In this way, at least you have answered all the questions in case you run out of time. Unanswered questions are automatically scored as incorrect; answers that are guessed have at least some chance of being scored as correct. If time permits, after you answer all questions you can revisit each question that you have marked for review. This strategy also enables you to possibly gain some insight into questions of which you are unsure by picking up some clues from the other questions on the exam.

TIP

Some people prefer to read over the exam completely before answering the trickier questions; sometimes, information supplied in later questions sheds more light on earlier questions. At other times, information you read in later questions might jog your memory about facts, figures, or behavior that helps you answer earlier questions. Either way, you could come out ahead if you answer only those questions on the first pass that you're absolutely confident about. However, be careful not to run out of time if you choose this strategy!

Fortunately, the Microsoft exam software for fixed-length and short-form tests makes the multiple-visit approach easy to implement. At the top-left corner of each question is a check box that permits you to mark that question for a later visit.

Here are some question-handling strategies that apply to fixed-length and short-form tests. Use them if you have the chance:

▶ When returning to a question after your initial read-through, read every word again; otherwise, your mind can miss important details. Sometimes, revisiting a question after turning your attention elsewhere lets you see something you missed, but the strong tendency is to see only what you've seen before. Avoid that tendency at all costs.

▶ If you return to a question more than twice, articulate to yourself what you don't understand about the question, why answers don't appear to make sense, or what appears to be missing. If you chew on the subject awhile, your subconscious might provide the missing details, or you might notice a "trick" that points to the right answer.

As you work your way through the exam, another counter that Microsoft provides will come in handy: the number of questions completed and questions outstanding. For fixed-length and short-form tests, it's wise to budget your time by making sure that you've completed one-quarter of the questions one-quarter of the way through the exam period and three-quarters of the questions three-quarters of the way through.

If you're not finished when only five minutes remain, use that time to guess your way through any remaining questions. Remember, guessing is potentially more valuable than not answering. Blank answers are always wrong, but a guess might turn out to be right. If you don't have a clue about any of the remaining questions, pick answers at random or choose all As, Bs, and so on. (Choosing the same answer for a series of question all but guarantees you'll get most of them wrong, but it also means you're more likely to get a small percentage of them correct.)

EXAM ALERT

At the very end of your exam period, you're better off guessing than leaving questions unanswered.

Question-Handling Strategies

For those questions that have only one right answer, usually two or three of the answers are obviously incorrect and two of the answers are plausible. Unless the answer leaps out at you (if it does, reread the question to look for a trick; sometimes those are the ones you're most likely to get wrong), begin the process of answering by eliminating those answers that are most obviously wrong.

You can usually immediately eliminate at least one answer out of the possible choices for a question because it matches one of these conditions:

- ▶ The answer does not apply to the situation.

- ▶ The answer describes a nonexistent issue, an invalid option, or an imaginary state.

After you eliminate all answers that are obviously wrong, you can apply your retained knowledge to eliminate further answers. You should look for items that sound correct but refer to actions, commands, or features that are not present or not available in the situation that the question describes.

If you're still faced with a blind guess among two or more potentially correct answers, reread the question. Picture how each of the possible remaining answers would alter the situation. Be especially sensitive to terminology; sometimes the choice of words (for example, "remove" instead of "disable") can make the difference between a right answer and a wrong one.

You should guess at an answer only after you've exhausted your ability to eliminate answers and you are still unclear about which of the remaining possibilities is correct. An unanswered question offers you no points, but guessing gives you at least some chance of getting a question right; just don't be too hasty when making a blind guess if you can eliminate one or two of the answers.

Numerous questions assume that the default behavior of a particular utility is in effect. If you know the defaults and understand what they mean, this knowledge will help you cut through many of the trickier questions. Simple "final" actions might be critical as well. If you must restart a utility before proposed changes take effect, a correct answer might require this step as well.

Mastering the Test-Taking Mindset

In the final analysis, knowledge breeds confidence, and confidence breeds success. If you study the materials in this book carefully and review all the practice questions at the end of each chapter, you should become aware of the areas where you need additional learning and study.

After you've worked your way through the book, take the practice exams in the back of the book. Taking these tests provides a reality check and helps you identify areas to study further. Make sure you follow up and review materials related to the questions you miss on the practice exams before scheduling a real exam. Don't schedule your exam appointment until after you've thoroughly studied the material and you feel comfortable with the whole scope of the practice exams. You should score 80% or better on the practice exams before proceeding to the real thing. (Otherwise, obtain some additional practice tests so that you can keep trying until you hit this magic number.)

> **TIP**
>
> If you take a practice exam and don't get at least 80% of the questions correct, keep practicing. Microsoft provides links to practice-exam providers and also self-assessment exams at http://www.microsoft.com/learning/mcpexams/prepare/default.asp.

Armed with the information in this book and with the determination to augment your knowledge, you should be able to pass the certification exam. However, you need to work at it, or you'll spend the exam fee more than once before you finally pass. If you prepare seriously, you should do well.

The next section covers other sources that you can use to prepare for Microsoft certification exams.

Additional Resources

A good source of information about Microsoft certification exams comes from Microsoft itself. Because its products and technologies—and the exams that go with them—change frequently, the best place to go for exam-related information is online.

Microsoft offers training, certification, and other learning-related information and links at the http://www.microsoft.com/learning web address. If you haven't already visited the Microsoft Training and Certification website, you should do so right now.

Coping with Change on the Web

Sooner or later, all the information we've shared with you about the Microsoft Certified Professional pages and the other web-based resources mentioned throughout the rest of this book will go stale or be replaced by newer information. In some cases, the URLs you find here might lead you to their replacements; in other cases, the URLs will go nowhere, leaving you with the dreaded "404 File not found" error message. When that happens, don't give up.

There's always a way to find what you want on the web if you're willing to invest some time and energy. Most large or complex websites—and Microsoft's qualifies on both counts—offer search engines. All of Microsoft's web pages have a Search button at the top edge of the page. As long as you can get to Microsoft's site (it should stay at http://www.microsoft.com for a long time), you can use the Search button to find what you need.

The more focused (or specific) that you can make a search request, the more likely the results will include information you can use. For example, you can search for the string

```
"training and certification"
```

to produce a lot of data about the subject in general, but if you're looking for the preparation guide for Exam 70-642, *Windows Server 2008 Network Infrastructure, Configuring*, you'll be more likely to get there quickly if you use a search string similar to the following:

```
"Exam 70-642" AND "preparation guide"
```

Likewise, if you want to find the Training and Certification downloads, you should try a search string such as this:

```
"training and certification" AND "download page"
```

Finally, you should feel free to use general search tools—such as http://www.google.com, http://www.yahoo.com, http://www.excite.com, and http://www.ask.com—to look for related information. Although Microsoft offers great information about its certification exams online, there are plenty of third-party sources of information and assistance that need not follow Microsoft's party line. Therefore, if you can't find something where the book says it lives, you should intensify your search.

Self-Assessment

We include a self-assessment to help you evaluate your readiness to tackle Microsoft certifications. It should also help you to understand what you need to know to master the 70-642 exam. You might also want to check out the Microsoft Skills Assessment Home web page (http://www.microsoft.com/learning/assessment) on the Microsoft Training and Certification website. But, before you tackle this self-assessment, let's talk about concerns you might face when pursuing a Microsoft certification credential on Windows and what an ideal Microsoft certification candidate might look like.

Microsoft Certification in the Real World

In this section, you'll learn about the ideal Microsoft certified candidate, knowing full well that only a few candidates meet that ideal. In fact, our description of those ideal candidates might seem downright scary, especially with the changes that have been made to the Microsoft certifications to support Windows. But take heart: Although the requirements to obtain the advanced Microsoft certification might seem formidable, they are by no means impossible to meet. However, you need to be keenly aware that getting through the process takes time, involves some expense, and requires real effort.

Increasing numbers of people are attaining Microsoft certifications. You can get all the real-world motivation you need from knowing that many others have gone before, so you will be able to follow in their footsteps. If you're willing to take the process seriously and do what it takes to obtain the necessary experience and knowledge, you can take and pass all the certification tests involved in obtaining the credentials. In fact, at Que Publishing, we've designed the Exam Cram series and the Exam Prep series to make it as easy for you as possible to prepare for these exams. We've also greatly expanded our website, http://www.examcram.com, to provide a host of resources to help you prepare for the complexities of the Windows exams.

The Ideal Microsoft Certification Candidate

To give you an idea of what an ideal Microsoft certification candidate is like, here are some relevant statistics about the background and experience such an individual might have:

> **NOTE**
>
> Don't worry if you don't meet these qualifications or even come very close. This world is far from ideal, and where you fall short is simply where you have more work to do.

- ▶ Academic or professional training in network theory, concepts, and operations. This area includes everything from networking media and transmission techniques through network operating systems, services, and applications.

- ▶ Two or more years of professional networking experience, including experience with Ethernet, DSL routers, cable modems, and other networking media. This experience must include installation, configuration, upgrading, and troubleshooting experience.

> **NOTE**
>
> Although all certifications really need some hands-on experience if you want to become certified, some of the more advanced exams require you to solve real-world case studies and network design issues—so the more hands-on experience you have, the better.

- ▶ Two or more years in a networked environment that includes hands-on experience with Windows Server 2008, Windows Vista, Windows Server 2003, Windows 2000 Server, or Windows 2000/XP Professional. A solid understanding of the system's architecture, installation, configuration, maintenance, and troubleshooting is essential.

- ▶ Knowledge of the various methods for installing Windows Vista, including manual and unattended installations, features of the different editions of Vista, and overcoming installation problems.

- ▶ Knowledge of how to resolve post-installation issues, including configuring Windows Aero, administrative versus standard user accounts, and configuring permissions.

▶ A good working understanding of optimizing performance for and configuration of Windows Media Player, Media Center, and connectivity with mobile devices.

▶ A thorough understanding of key networking protocols, addressing, and name resolution, including Transmission Control Protocol/Internet Protocol (TCP/IP), TCP/IP utilities and services, Dynamic Host Configuration Protocol (DHCP), Domain Name System (DNS), and Remote Desktop Connection.

▶ An understanding of how to implement security for the Windows Vista operating system and home office network, including IE security, Windows Firewall, Windows Defender, Parental Controls, User Account Control, and Windows Backup.

▶ A good working understanding of disaster recovery techniques, including Safe Mode, Last Known Good Configuration, Restore Points and System Restore, Complete PC Backup and Restore, and RegEdit utilities.

To meet all these qualifications, you would need a bachelor's degree in computer science plus three year's work experience in PC networking design, installation, administration, and troubleshooting. Don't be concerned if you don't have all of these qualifications. Fewer than half of all Microsoft certification candidates meet these requirements. This self-assessment is designed to show you what you already know and to prepare you for the topics that you need to learn.

Put Yourself to the Test

The following series of questions and observations is designed to help you figure out how much work you must do to pursue Microsoft certification and what kinds of resources you can consult on your quest. Be absolutely honest in your answers, or you'll end up wasting money on exams that you're not yet ready to take. There are no right or wrong answers—only steps along the path to certification. Only you can decide where you really belong in the broad spectrum of aspiring candidates. Two things should be clear from the outset, however:

▶ Even a modest background in computer science is helpful.

▶ Hands-on experience with Microsoft products and technologies is an essential ingredient in certification success.

Educational Background

The following questions concern your level of technical computer experience and training. Depending upon your answers to these questions, you might need to review some additional resources to get your knowledge up to speed for the types of questions that you will encounter on Microsoft certification exams:

1. Have you ever taken any computer-related classes? (Yes or No)

   If Yes, proceed to Question 2; if No, proceed to Question 3.

2. Have you taken any classes on computer operating systems? (Yes or No)

   If Yes, you will probably be able to handle Microsoft's architecture and system component discussions. If you're rusty, you should brush up on basic operating system concepts, especially virtual memory, multitasking regimes, user-mode versus kernel-mode operation, and general computer security topics.

   If No, you should consider doing some basic reading in this area. We strongly recommend a good general operating systems book on Windows Vista, such as *Sams Teach Yourself Microsoft Windows Vista All in One* by Greg Perry (Sams). If this book doesn't appeal to you, check out reviews for other similar books at your favorite online bookstore.

3. Have you taken any networking concepts or technologies classes? (Yes or No)

   If Yes, you will probably be able to handle Microsoft's networking terminology, concepts, and technologies. (But brace yourself for frequent departures from normal usage.) If you're rusty, you should brush up on basic networking concepts and terminology, especially networking media, transmission types, the Open System Interconnection (OSI) reference model, and networking technologies, such as Ethernet, Token Ring, Fiber Distributed Data Interface (FDDI), and Wide Area Network (WAN) links.

   If No, you might want to read one or two books in this topic area. The three best books that we know are *Computer Networks* by Andrew S. Tanenbaum (Prentice-Hall), *Computer Networks and Internets* by Douglas E. Comer and Ralph E. Droms (Prentice-Hall), and *Local Area Networks* by Patrick Regan (Prentice-Hall).

Hands-On Experience

The most important key to success on all the Microsoft tests is hands-on experience, especially when it comes to Windows Server 2008, and the many features and add-on services and components around which so many of the Microsoft certification exams revolve. If we leave you with only one realization after you take this self-assessment, it should be that there's no substitute for time spent installing, configuring, and using the various Microsoft products on which you'll be tested. The more in-depth understanding you have of how these software products work, the better your chance in selecting the right answers on the exam. Therefore, ask yourself whether you have installed, configured, and worked with the following:

1. Windows Server 2003 or Windows Server 2008? (Yes or No)

   If No, you might want to obtain one or two machines and a copy of Windows Server 2008. (A trial version is available on the Microsoft website.) Pick up a well-written book to guide your activities and studies, or you can work straight from Microsoft's exam objectives, if you prefer.

> **NOTE**
>
> You can download objectives, practice exams, and other data about Microsoft exams from the Training and Certification page at http://www.microsoft.com/traincert. You can use the Exams link to obtain specific exam information.

2. Windows XP Professional? (Yes or No)

   If No, you might want to obtain a copy of Windows XP Professional and learn how to install, configure, and maintain it. Pick up a well-written book to guide your activities and studies (such as *MCSE Windows XP Professional Exam Cram*), or you can work straight from Microsoft's exam objectives, if you prefer.

3. Windows Vista? (Yes or No)

   If No, you should obtain a copy of Windows Vista and learn how to install, configure, and maintain it. Carefully read each page of this book while working in your copy of Windows Vista, and review Microsoft's exam objectives.

Use One Computer to Simulate Multiple Machines

If you own a powerful enough computer—one that has plenty of available disk space, a lot of RAM (at least 512MB), and a Pentium 4–compatible processor or better—you should check out the VMware and Virtual PC virtual-machine software products that are on the market. These software programs create an emulated computer environment within separate windows that are hosted by your computer's main operating system—Windows Server 2008, Windows Vista, Windows Server 2003, Windows XP, Windows 2000, and so on. With this tool, on a single computer you can have several different operating systems running simultaneously in different windows! You can run everything from DOS to Linux, from Windows 95, XP, or Vista to Windows Server 2008. Within a virtual-machine environment, you can "play" with the latest operating systems, including beta versions, without worrying about "blowing up" your main production computer and without having to buy an additional PC. VMware is published by VMware, Inc.; you can get more information from its website at http://www.vmware.com. Virtual PC is published by Microsoft Corporation; you can find out more information from the Virtual PC 2007 website at www.microsoft.com/windows/products/winfamily/virtualpc/default.mspx.

TIP

For any and all of these Microsoft operating systems exams, the Resource Kits for the topics involved always make good study resources. You can purchase the Resource Kits from Microsoft Press (you can search for them at http://microsoft.com/mspress), but they also appear on the TechNet CDs, DVDs, and website (http://www.microsoft.com/technet). Along with the Exam Cram books, we believe that the Resource Kits are among the best tools you can use to prepare for Microsoft exams. Take a look at the Windows Deployment and Resource Kits web page for more information: http://www.microsoft.com/windows/reskits/default.asp.

Before you even think about taking any Microsoft exam, you should make sure you've spent enough time with the related software to understand how to install and configure it, how to maintain such an installation, and how to troubleshoot the software when things go wrong. This time will help you in the exam—and in real life!

TIP

If you have the funds, or if your employer will pay your way, you should consider taking a class at a Microsoft Certified Training and Education Center (CTEC). In addition to classroom exposure to the topic of your choice, you get a copy of the software that is the focus of your course, along with a trial version of whatever operating system it needs, as part of the training materials for that class.

How to Prepare for an Exam

Preparing for any Microsoft certification test (including Exam 70-642) requires that you obtain and study materials designed to provide comprehensive information about the product and its capabilities that will appear on the specific exam for which you are preparing. The following list of materials can help you study and prepare:

- ▶ The Windows Server 2008 product DVD-ROM. This disk includes comprehensive online documentation and related materials; it should be one of your primary resources when you are preparing for the test.

- ▶ The exam preparation materials, practice tests, and self-assessment exams on the Microsoft Training and Certification site, at http://www.microsoft.com/learning/default.mspx. The Exam Resources link offers samples of the new question types on the Microsoft Certification track series of exams. You should find the materials, download them, and use them!

- ▶ The exam preparation advice, practice tests, questions of the day, and discussion groups on http://www.examcram.com.

In addition, you might find any or all of the following materials useful in your quest for Windows Vista expertise:

- ▶ **Microsoft training kits:** Microsoft Learning offers a training kit that specifically targets Exam 70-642. For more information, visit http://www.microsoft.com/learning/books/. This training kit contains information that you will find useful in preparing for the test.

- ▶ **Microsoft TechNet CD or DVD and website:** This monthly CD- or DVD-based publication delivers numerous electronic titles that include coverage of Windows operating systems and related topics on the Technical Information (TechNet) series on CD or DVD. Its offerings include product facts, technical notes, tools and utilities, and information on how to access the Seminars Online training materials for Windows operating systems and the Windows line of products. Visit http://technet.microsoft.com and check out the information for TechNet subscriptions. You can utilize a large portion of the TechNet website at no charge.

▶ **Study guides:** Several publishers—including Que Publishing—offer Windows Server 2008, Windows Server 2003, Windows Vista, and Windows XP titles. Que Publishing offers the following:

    ▶ **The Exam Cram series:** These books give you the insights about the material that you need to know to successfully pass the certification tests.

    ▶ **The Exam Prep series:** These books provide a greater level of detail than the Exam Cram books and are designed to teach you everything you need to know about the subject covered by an exam. Each book comes with a CD-ROM that contains interactive practice exams in a variety of testing formats.

    Together, these two series make a perfect pair.

▶ **Classroom training:** CTECs, online partners, and third-party training companies (such as Wave Technologies, New Horizons, and Global Knowledge) all offer classroom training on Windows Server 2008, Windows Server 2003, Windows Vista, and Windows XP. These companies aim to help you prepare to pass Exam 70-642, as well as several others. Although this type of training tends to be pricey, most of the individuals lucky enough to attend find this training to be quite worthwhile.

▶ **Other publications:** There's no shortage of materials available about Windows Vista. The "Need to Know More?" resource sections at the end of each chapter in this book give you an idea of where we think you should look for further discussion.

This set of required and recommended materials represents an unparalleled collection of sources and resources for Windows Vista and related topics. We anticipate that you'll find this book belongs in this company.

Studying for the Exam

Although many websites offer suggestions on *what* to study for a particular exam, few sites offer any on *how* you should study for an exam. The study process can be broken down into various stages. However, key to all these stages is the ability to concentrate. Concentration, or the lack thereof, plays a big part in the study process.

To be able to concentrate, you must remove all distractions. Although you should plan for study breaks, it is the unplanned breaks caused by distractions that do not allow you to concentrate on what you need to learn. Therefore, first, you need to create an environment that's conducive to studying or seek out an existing environment that meets these criteria, such as a library.

First, do not study with the TV on and do not have other people in the room. It is easy for the TV to break your concentration and grab your attention. In addition, if you have people in the room, you have to pretend that you are not there and that they are not causing distractions, including talking with other people. Last, there are varying opinions on whether it is better to study with or without music playing. Although some people need to have a little white noise in the background to study, if you do choose to have music, you should keep the volume on a low level and you listen to music without vocals in it.

After you find a place to study, you must schedule the time to study. This should take into consideration not studying on an empty stomach. You should also not study on a full stomach because it tends to make people drowsy. You may also consider having a glass of water near to sip on.

In addition, make sure that you are well rested so that you don't start dozing off when you start. Next, make sure that you find a position that is comfortable and that the furniture is also comfortable. Lastly, make sure that your study area is well lit. Natural light is best for fighting fatigue.

The first thing that you should when you study is to clear your mind of distractions. So take a minute or two, close your eyes and empty your mind.

When you prepare for an exam, the best place to start is to take the list of exam objectives and study it carefully for its scope. During this time, you then organize your study, keeping these objectives in mind. This narrows your focus area to an individual topic or subtopic. In addition, you need to understand and visualize the process as a whole. This helps in addressing practical problems in real environments as well as some unexpected questions.

In a multiple-choice–type exam, you do have one advantage: The answer or answers are already there and you have to simply choose the correct ones. Because the answers are already there, you can start eliminating the incorrect answers by using your knowledge and some logical thinking. One common mistake is to select the first obvious-looking answer without checking the other options, so always examine *all* the options, then think and choose the correct answer. Of course, with multiple-choice questions, you have to be exact and should be able to differentiate between very similar answers. This is where a peaceful place to study without distractions helps so that you can read between the lines and not miss key points.

Testing Your Exam Readiness

Whether you attend a formal class on a specific topic to get ready for an exam or use written materials to study on your own, some preparation for the Microsoft certification exams is essential. At $125 a pop—whether you pass or fail—you'll want to do everything you can to pass on your first try. That's where studying comes in.

We include two practice exams in this book, so if you don't score very well on these tests, you can study the practice exams more and then tackle the test again. We also have practice questions for which you can sign up online through http://www.examcram.com. The MeasureUp CD-ROM in the back of this book has sample questions to quiz you; you can purchase additional practice questions from http://www.measureup.com. If you still don't hit a score of at least 80% after practicing with these tests, you should investigate the other practice test resources that are mentioned in this section.

For any given subject, you should consider taking a class if you've tackled self-study materials, taken the test, and failed. The opportunity to interact with an instructor and fellow students can make all the difference in the world, if you can afford that luxury.

If you can't afford to take a class, you can visit the Training and Certification pages anyway because they include pointers to free practice exams and to Microsoft-approved study guides and other self-study tools. And even if you can't afford to spend much money at all, you should still invest in some low-cost practice exams from commercial vendors. The Microsoft Training and Certification "Assess Your Readiness" page at http://www.microsoft.com/train-cert/assessment offers several skills-assessment evaluations that you can take online to show you how far along you are in your certification preparation.

The next question deals with your personal testing experience. Microsoft certification exams have their own style and idiosyncrasies. The more acclimated that you become to the Microsoft testing environment, the better your chances will be to score well on the exams:

1. Have you taken a practice exam on your chosen test subject? (Yes or No)

   If Yes, and if you scored 80% or better, you're probably ready to tackle the real thing. If your score isn't above that threshold, you should keep at it until you break that barrier.

   If No, you should obtain all the free and low-budget practice tests you can find and get to work. You should keep at it until you can break the passing threshold comfortably.

> **TIP**
>
> When it comes to assessing your test readiness, there is no better way than to take a good-quality practice exam and pass with a score of 80% or better. When we're preparing ourselves, we shoot for 80% or higher, just to leave room for the "weirdness factor" that sometimes shows up on Microsoft exams.

Assessing Readiness for Exam 70-642

In addition to the general exam-readiness information in the previous section, there are several things you can do to prepare for the Exam 70-642. As you're getting ready for the exam, you should visit the Exam Cram website at http://www.examcram.com. We also suggest that you join an active MCSE/MCSA email list and email newsletter. Some of the best list servers and email newsletters are managed by Sunbelt Software. You can sign up at http://www.sunbelt-software.com.

Microsoft exam mavens also recommend that you check the Microsoft Knowledge Base (available on its own CD as part of the TechNet collection, and on the Microsoft website at http://support.microsoft.com) for "meaningful technical support issues" that relate to your exam's topics. Although we're not sure exactly what the quoted phrase means, we have also noticed some overlap between technical-support questions on particular products and troubleshooting questions on the exams for those products.

Day of the Exam

Before you take an exam, eat something light, even if you have no appetite. If you stomach is actively upset, try mild foods such as toast or crackers. Plain saltine crackers are great for settling a cranky stomach. Keep your caffeine and nicotine consumption to a minimum; excessive stimulants aren't exactly conducive to reducing stress. Plan to take a bottle of water or some hard candies such as lozenges with you to combat dry mouth.

Arrive at the testing center early. If you have never been to the testing center before, make sure that you know where it is. You may even consider taking a test drive. If you arrive between fifteen and thirty minutes early for any certification exam, it gives you

▶ Ample time for prayer, meditation, and/or breathing.

▶ Time to scan glossary terms, quick access tables, and the cram sheet before taking the exam so that you can get the intellectual juices flowing and build a little confidence.

▶ Time to practice physical relaxation techniques.

▶ Time to visit the washroom.

But don't arrive too early. Of course, when you take the exam, you should also dress comfortably.

When you are escorted into the testing chamber, you will be usually given two sheets of paper (or laminated paper) with pen (or wet erase pen). As soon as you hear the door close behind you, immediately unload bits of exam information that you need to quickly recall onto the paper. Then throughout the exam, you can refer to this information easily without thinking about it. This way, you can focus on answering the questions and use this information as reference. Before you actually start the exam, close your eyes and take deep breath to clear your mind of distractions.

Typically, the testing room is furnished with anywhere from one to six computers, and each workstation is separated from the others by dividers designed to keep anyone from seeing what's happening on someone else's computer screen. Most testing rooms feature a wall with a large picture window. This layout permits the exam coordinator to monitor the room, to prevent exam takers from talking to one another, and to observe anything out of the ordinary that might go on. The exam coordinator will have preloaded the appropriate Microsoft certification exam—for this book, that's Exam 70-642 TS: Windows Server 2008 Network Infrastructure, Configuring—and you are permitted to start as soon as you're seated in front of the computer.

EXAM ALERT

Always remember that the testing center's test coordinator is there to assist you in case you encounter some unusual problems, such as a malfunctioning test computer. If you need some assistance not related to the content of the exam itself, feel free to notify one of the test coordinators—after all, they are there to make your exam-taking experience as pleasant as possible.

All exams are completely closed book. In fact, you are not permitted to take anything with you into the testing area, but you receive a blank sheet of paper and a pen or, in some cases, an erasable plastic sheet and an erasable pen. We suggest that you immediately write down on that sheet of paper all the information you've memorized for the test. Then throughout the exam, you can refer to this information easily without thinking about it. This way, you can focus on answering the questions and use this information as reference. In Exam Cram books, this information appears on the Cram Sheet inside the front cover of the book. You are given some time to compose yourself, record this information, and take a sample orientation exam before you begin the real thing. We suggest that you take the orientation test before taking your first exam, but because all the certification exams are more or less identical in layout, behavior, and controls, you probably don't need to do so more than once.

All Microsoft certification exams allow a certain maximum testing time. (This time is indicated on the exam by an onscreen timer clock, so you can check the time remaining whenever you like.) All Microsoft certification exams are computer generated. In addition to multiple choice, most exams contain select–and–place (drag-and-drop), create-a-tree (categorization and prioritization), drag-and-connect, and build-list-and-reorder (list prioritization) types of questions. Although this format might sound quite simple, the questions are constructed not only to check your mastery of basic facts and figures about Windows Vista, but also to require you to evaluate one or more sets of circumstances or requirements. Often you are asked to give more than one answer to a question. Likewise, you might be asked to select the best or most effective solution to a problem from a range of choices—all of which are technically correct. Taking the exam is quite an adventure, and it involves real thinking and concentration. This book shows you what to expect and how to deal with the potential problems, puzzles, and predicaments.

Dealing with Test Anxiety

Because taking a certification exam costs money and preparation time, and failing an exam can be a blow to self-confidence, most people feel a certain amount of anxiety when they are about to take a certification exam. It is no wonder that most of us are a little sweaty in the palms when taking the exam. However, certain levels of stress can actually help you to raise your level of performance when taking an exam. This anxiety usually serves to help you focus your concentration and think clearly through a problem.

But for some individuals, exam anxiety is more than just a nuisance. For these people, exam anxiety is a debilitating condition that affects their performance with a negative impact on the exam results.

Exam anxiety reduction begins with the preparation process. The first thing that you should consider is that if you know the material, there should not be anything to be nervous about. It goes without saying that the better prepared you are for an exam, the less stress you will experience when taking it. Always give yourself plenty of time to prepare for an exam; don't place yourself under unreasonable deadlines. But again, make goals and make every effort to meet those goals. Procrastination and making excuses can be just as bad.

There is no hard and fast rule for how long it takes to prepare for an exam. The time required varies from student to student and depends on a number of different factors, including reading speed, access to study materials, personal commitments, and so on. In addition, don't compare yourself to peers, especially if doing so has a negative effect on your confidence.

For many students, practice exams are a great way to shed some of the fears that arise in the test center. Practice exams are best used near the end of the exam preparation, and be sure to use them as an assessment of your current knowledge, not as a method to try to memorize key concepts. When reviewing these questions, be sure you understand the question and all answers (right and wrong). Also be sure to set time limits on the practice exams.

If you know the material, don't plan on studying the day of your exam. You should end your studying the evening before the exam. In addition, don't make it a late night so that you can get a full good night's rest. Of course, you should be studying on a regular basis for at least a few weeks prior to the evening of the exam so that you should not need the last-minute cramming.

CHAPTER ONE

Managing Windows Server 2008

Terms you'll need to understand:

✓ Server roles

✓ Windows Features

✓ Server Core

✓ Control Panel

✓ Administrative tools

✓ Computer Management Console

✓ Server Manager Console

✓ Windows Reliability and Performance Monitor

✓ Services

✓ Event Collector

✓ Initial configuration tasks

✓ Microsoft Management Console (MMC)

✓ Event Viewer

✓ Microsoft Remote Server Administration Tools (RSAT)

Techniques/concepts you'll need to master:

✓ How to install roles and features in Windows Server 2008

✓ Manage and configure Windows Server 2008 with common configuration tools, including the Control Panel and the Administrative tools (including the Computer Management Console and the Server Manager Console).

✓ Utilize Windows Reliability and Performance Monitor to analyze a computer running Windows Server 2008 for problems and potential problems.

Windows Server 2008 is a network operating system and server that is the successor to the Windows Server 2003. The client version of Windows Server 2008 is Windows Vista, on which Windows Server 2008 is partially based. Because it shares the same architecture as Windows Vista, it also has a new and improved rewritten network stack (native IPv6, native wireless, improved performance, and improved security), improved diagnostics and monitoring, improved security including BitLocker, and improved Windows Firewall, .NET Framework 3.0, memory and file system improvements, Windows Internet Explorer 7, and Vista Aero Themes. In addition, Windows Server 2008 includes an improved Internet Information Server (IIS) 7.0, Service Core, greatly improved Windows Terminal Services, Windows Server Virtualization, self-healing NTFS, a Windows Server 2008 Server Manager, and Windows PowerShell.

Server Roles

A server is designed to provide services. Therefore, Windows Server 2008 has organized the most common services into *server roles*, in which a server role describes the function of the server. When you define a server role in Windows Server 2008 (see Table 1.1), you are installing and configuring a set of software programs that enable a computer to perform a specific function for multiple users or other computers within a network. To install roles, you would use the *Initial Configuration Tasks* window or the Server Manager console.

TABLE 1.1   Available Roles in Windows Server 2008

Role Name	Description
Active Directory Certificate Services	Provides service for creating and managing public key certificates used in software security systems that employ public key technologies to prove the identity of a person, device, or service, which can be used by secure mail, secure wireless networks, virtual private networks (VPN), Internet Protocol Security (IPSec), Encrypting File System (EFS), smart card logon, and others. For ease of use, the digital certificates interface with Microsoft's Active Directory.
Active Directory Domain Services	Used to transform a server into a domain controller to provide a directory service via Microsoft's Active Directory (AD), which stores information about users, computers, and other devices on the network. Active Directory helps administrators securely manage this information and facilitates resource sharing and collaboration between users. Active Directory is required for directory-enabled applications, such as Microsoft Exchange Server (email server), and to apply other Windows Server technologies, such as Group Policy.

TABLE 1.1 *Continued*

Role Name	Description
Active Directory Federation Services	Active Directory Federation Services provides web single-sign-on (SSO) technologies to authenticate a user to multiple web applications using a single user account.
Active Directory Lightweight Directory Services (ADLDS)	Provides a store for for application-specific data, for directory-enabled applications that do not require the infrastructure of Active Directory Domain Services. Multiple instances of AD LDS can exist on a single search, each of which can have its own schema.
Active Directory Rights Management (AD Services RMS)	Technology that works with Active Directory RMS–enabled applications to help safeguard digital information from unauthorized use by specifying who can use the information and what can be done with it (open, modify, print, forward, and/or take other actions with the information).
Application Server	Provides a complete solution for hosting and managing high-performance distributed business applications build around Microsoft .NET Framework 3.0, COM+, Message Queuing, web services, and Distributed Transactions.
Dynamic Host Configuration Protocol (DHCP) Server	Enables servers to assign, or lease, IP addresses to computers and other devices that are enabled as DHCP clients.
Domain Name System (DNS) Server	Provides a naming service that associates names with numeric Internet addresses. This makes it possible for users to refer to network computers by using easy-to-remember names instead of a long series of numbers. Windows DNS services can be integrated with Dynamic Host Configuration Protocol (DHCP) services on Windows, eliminating the need to add DNS records as computers are added to the network.
Fax Server	Sends and receives faxes and enables you to manage fax resources such as jobs, settings, reports, and fax devices on this computer or on the network.
File Services	Provides technologies for storage management, file replication, distributed namespace management, fast file searching, and streamlined client access to files.
Network Policy and Access Services	Delivers a variety of methods (including using VPN servers, dial-up servers, routers, and 802.11 protected wireless access points) to provide users with local and remote network connectivity, to connect network segments, and to allow network administrators to centrally manage network access and client health policies.

continues

TABLE 1.1 *Continued*

Role Name	Description
Print Services	Enables users to print to and manage centralized printers that are connected directly or indirectly to print servers.
Terminal Services	Enables users to connect to a terminal server to remotely run programs, use network resources, and access the Windows desktop on that server.
Universal Description, Discovery, and Integration (UDDI) Services	Provides capabilities to share information about web services within an organization's intranet, between business partners on an extranet, or on the Internet.
Web Server (IIS)	Enables sharing of information on the Internet, an intranet, or an extranet via a unified web platform that integrates Internet Information Server (IIS) 7.0 to provide web pages, File Transfer Protocol (FTP) services or newsgroups, ASP.NET, Windows Communication Foundation, and Windows SharePoint Services.
Windows Deployment Services	Used to install and configure Microsoft Windows operating systems remotely on computers with Pre-boot Execution Environment (PXE) boot ROMs.
Windows SharePoint Services	Helps organizations increase productivity by creating websites where users can collaborate on documents, tasks, and events and easily share contacts and other information. The environment is designed for flexible deployment, administration, and application development.
Windows Server Virtualization	Provides the services that you can use to create and manage virtual machines (virtualized computer system that operates in an isolated execution environment, which enables you to run multiple operating systems simultaneously) and their resources.

Windows Features

Features are software programs that are not directly part of a role, or can support or augment the functionality of one or more roles, or can enhance the functionality of the entire server. Table 1.2 shows the features that are included in Windows Server 2008. To install Windows Features, use the Initial Configuration Tasks window or the Server Manager console.

TABLE 1.2   Features Available in Windows Server 2008

Feature Name	Description
.NET Framework 3.0 Features	Combines .NET Framework 2.0 Application Programming Interface (API) to build applications with appealing user interfaces and provide various forms of security for those services.
BitLocker Drive Encryption	Helps protect data on disks by encrypting the entire volume.
BITS Server Extension	Short for Background Intelligence Service, enables a client computer to transfer files in the foreground or background asynchronously so that the responsiveness of other network applications is preserved.
Connection Manager Administration	Used to customize the remote connection experience for users on your network by creating pre-defined connections to remote servers and networks via a virtual private network (VPN) server.
Desktop Experience	Includes features of Windows Vista such as Windows Media Player, desktop themes, and photo management.
Failover Clustering	Enables multiple servers to work together to provide high availability of services and applications. If one server fails, a second server is available to take over its work.
Group Policy Management	A Microsoft Management Console snap-in that allows easy management of Active Directory Group Policies to secure or standardize a network environment.
Internet Printing Client	Enables clients to use Internet Printing Protocol (IPP) to connect and print to printers on the network or Internet.
Internet Storage Name Server	Provides discovery services for Internet Small Computer System Interface (iSCSI) storage area networks.
LPR Port Monitor	Enables the computer to print to printers that are shared using a Line Printer Daemon (LPD) service. LPD service is commonly used by UNIX-based computers and printer-sharing devices.
Message Queuing	Provides guaranteed message delivery, efficient routing, security, and priority-based messaging between applications.
Multipath I/O	Along with the Microsoft Device Specific Module (DSM) or a third-party DSM, provides support for using multiple data paths to a storage device on Windows.
Network Load Balancing	Distributes traffic across several servers, using the TCP/IP net working protocol. NLP is particularly useful for ensuring that stateless applications such as web servers running IIS are scalable, so that servers can be added as the load increases.

continues

TABLE 1.2 *Continued*

Feature Name	Description
Peer Name Resolution Protocol	Enables applications to register and resolve names on your computer so that other computers communicate with these applications.
Quality Windows Audio Video Experience	A networking platform for audio and video streaming applications on IP home networks.
Remote Assistance	Enables you or a support person to offer assistance to users with computer issues or questions.
Remote Differential Compression	Computes and transfers the differences between two objects over a network, using minimal bandwidth.
Remote Server Administration Tools	Includes a MMC snap-in and a command-line tool to remotely manage roles and features.
Removable Storage Manager	Manages and catalogs removable media and operates automated removable media devices.
RPC over HTTP Proxy	Relays RPC traffic from client applications over HTTP to the server as an alternative to clients accessing the server over a VPN connection.
Simple TCP/IP Services	Supports Character Generator, Daytime, Discard, Echo, and Quote of the Day TCP/IP services.
SMTP Server	Supports the transfer of email messages between email systems.
SNMP Services	Includes the SNMP service and SNMP WMI provider. SNMP is used in network management systems to monitor network-attached devices for conditions that warrant administrative attention.
Storage Manager for SANs	Helps create and manage logical unit numbers (LUNs) on Fibre Channel and iSCSI disk drive subsystems that support Virtual Disk Service (VDS)
Subsystem for UNIX-based Applications	Enables you to run UNIX-based programs and compile and run custom UNIX-based applications in the Windows environment.
Telnet Client	Uses the Telnet protocol to connect to a remote Telnet server and run applications on that server.
Telnet Server	Enables remote users to perform command-line administration and run programs using a Telnet client, including UNIX-based clients.
TFTP Client	Enables users to read files or write files to a remote Trivial FTP (TFTP) server.
Windows Internal Database	A relational data store that can be used only by Windows roles and features.
Windows PowerShell	A command-line shell and scripting language.

TABLE 1.2 *Continued*

Feature Name	Description
Windows Process Activation Service	Generalizes the IIS process model, removing the dependency on HTTP.
Windows Recovery Disc	Enables you to restore your computer using the system recovery options if you do not have a Windows installation disc or cannot access recovery options provided by your computer's manufacturer.
Windows Server Backup Features	Enables you to back up and recover your operating system, applications, and data.
Windows System Resource Manager	An administrative tool that can control how CPU and memory resources are allocated.
WINS Server	WINS, short for Windows Internet Naming Service, provides a distributed database for registering and querying dynamic mappings of NetBIOS names for computers and groups used on your network.
Wireless LAN Service	Configures and starts the WLAN AutoConfig service, regardless of whether the computer has any wireless adapters.

One feature that is included with Windows Server 2008 is the subsystem for UNIX-based Applications (SUA) to provide a complete UNIX-based environment. It includes supporting case-sensitive filenames, job control, compilation tools, and the use of over 300 UNIX commands, utilities, and shell scripts. It also provides a source-compatibility subsystem for compiling and running custom UNIX-based applications on the server that are based on Portable Operating System Interface (POSIX). You can make your UNIX applications fully interoperable with Windows in SUA with little or no change to your original source code. Because the subsystem installs separately from the Windows kernel, it offers true UNIX functionality without emulation. You can also download a package from Microsoft that includes a comprehensive set of scripting utilities and a software development kit (SDK) designed to fully support the development capabilities of SUA. Finally, the subsystem also includes a Database (OCI/ODBC) library connectivity that supports connectivity to Oracle and SQL Server from database applications by using the Oracle Call Interface (OCI) and the Open Database Connectivity (ODBC) standard and supports 64-bit applications.

Configuring and Managing Windows

To configure and manage Windows, you still use the standard tools that you find in Windows XP, Windows Vista, and Windows Server 2003:

▶ Control Panel

▶ Administrative Tools (which include Computer Management and Server Manager consoles)

Control Panel

The *Control Panel* is a graphical tool used to configure the Windows environment and hardware devices. To access the Control Panel, you can click the Start button on the taskbar and select Control Panel. You can also display Control Panel in any Windows Explorer view by clicking the leftmost option button in the address bar and then selecting Control Panel (see Figure 1.1).

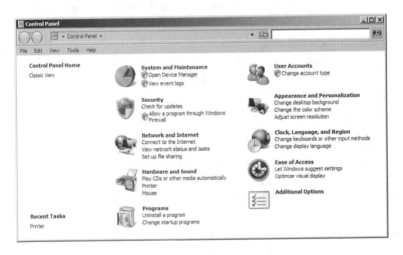

FIGURE 1.1 Window Server 2008 Control Panel in Category view.

Each of the 10 categories listed includes a top-level link, and under this link are several of the most frequently performed tasks for the category. Clicking a category link provides a list of utilities in that category. Each utility listed within a category includes a link to open the utility, and under this link are several of the most frequently performed tasks for the utility.

As with Windows XP and Windows Vista, you can change from the default category view to classic view. Control Panel in Windows Vista has two views:

Category view and Classic view. Category view is the default view, which provides access to system utilities by category and task. Classic view is an alternative view that provides the look and functionality of Control Panel in Windows 2000 and earlier versions of Windows (see Figure 1.2).

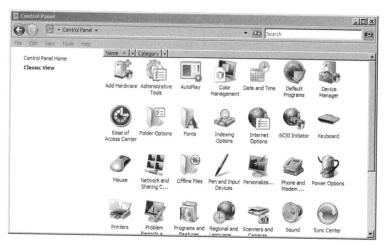

FIGURE 1.2 Windows Server 2008 Control Panel in Classic view.

Administrative Tools

Administrative Tools is a folder in Control Panel that contains tools for system administrators and advanced users. Many of the tools in this folder, such as *Computer Management*, are *Microsoft Management Console (MMC)* snap-ins that include their own help topics. To view specific help for an MMC tool, or to search for an MMC snap-in that you do not see in the following list, open the tool, click the Help menu, and then click Help Topics.

Open Administrative Tools by clicking Start, Control Panel, System and Maintenance, Administrative Tools. You can also find it on the Start menu.

Some common administrative tools in this folder include:

▸ **Computer Management**: Manage local or remote computers by using a single, consolidated desktop tool. Using Computer Management, you can perform many tasks, such as monitoring system events, configuring hard disks, and managing system performance (see Figure 1.3).

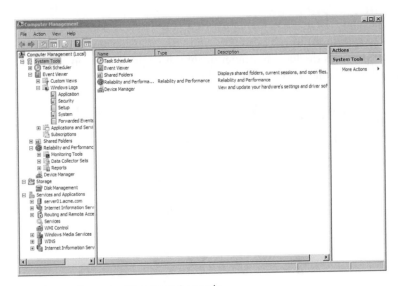

FIGURE 1.3 Computer Management console.

▶ **Data Sources (ODBC)**: Use Open Database Connectivity (ODBC) to move data from one type of database (a data source) to another.

▶ **Event Viewer**: View information about significant events, such as a program starting or stopping, or a security error, that are recorded in event logs.

NOTE

In Windows, the Event Viewer is a important tool that is often overlooked for troubleshooting many issues.

▶ **iSCSI Initiator**: Configure advanced connections between storage devices on a network.

▶ **Local Security Policy**: View and edit localhost policy security settings.

▶ **Memory Diagnostics Tool**: Check your computer's memory to see whether it is functioning properly.

▶ **Print Management**: Manage printers and print servers on a network and perform other administrative tasks.

▶ **Reliability and Performance Monitor**: View advanced system information about the central processing unit (CPU), memory, hard disk, and network performance.

▶ **Services**: Manage the different services that run in the background on your computer.

▶ **System Configuration**: Identify problems that might be preventing Windows from running correctly.

▶ **Task Scheduler**: Schedule programs or other tasks to run automatically.

▶ **Windows Firewall with Advanced Security**: Configure advanced firewall settings on both this computer and remote computers on your network.

▶ **Windows Server Backup**: Use to back up and restore the server. .

Server Manager Console

New to Windows Server 2008 is the *Server Manager console*, which is designed to simplify the task of managing and securing server roles (see Figure 1.4). It allows you to manage a server's identity, displaying current server status, identifying problems with server role configuration, and managing all roles designated for the server. To simplify these tasks, it often uses integrated wizards that step through adding and configuring server functions. While using these wizards, the Server Manager console performs all the necessary dependency checks and conflict resolutions so the server is stable, reliable, and secure. You have to run the Security Configuration Wizard after the role installation only if you need to modify the security defaults. It also has event viewer, performance and reliability monitors, device manager, task scheduler, services, local user and group administration, Windows server backup, and disk management.

FIGURE 1.4 Server Manager console.

Services

A *service* is a program, routine, or process that performs a specific system function to support other programs. To manage the services, use the Services console located under Administrative Tools or the MMC with the Services snap-in. The Services console is included in the Server Management console and the Computer Management console. To start, stop, pause, resume, or restart services, right-click the service and click the desired option. On the left of the service name is a description.

To configure a service, right-click the service and click Properties. On the General tab, under the start-up type pull-down option, set the following:

- ▶ **Automatic**: Specifies that the service should start automatically when the system starts.

- ▶ **Manual**: Specifies that a user or a dependent service can start the service. Services with manual start-up do not start automatically when the system starts.

- ▶ **Disable**: Prevents the service from being started by the system, a user, or any dependent service.

NOTE

Instead of disabling a service with which you are unfamiliar, you should consider stopping the service first so that you can test its effect.

Event Viewer

Event Viewer is a utility that is used to view and manage logs of system, application, and security events on a computer. Event Viewer gathers information about hardware and software problems and monitors Windows security events. You can execute Event Viewer by opening Administrative Tools and clicking Event Viewer or by adding it to the MMC. It is also part of the Computer Management console and the Server Manager console. You can also open it by executing `eventvwr.msc` at a command prompt or using the Run option.

EXAM ALERT

Most Windows and application errors are displayed in the Event Viewer, which can be accessed by itself or as part of the Computer Management or Server Manager console.

Default Logs

The preconfigured logs fall into two categories—Windows Logs and Applications and Services Logs. As you expand Applications and Services Logs, you will find multiple preconfigured event logs. These logs address specific services and features of the operating system and can be used to identify problems, before they start, as well as provide diagnostic and troubleshooting information after something unexpected has happened.

There are is also two more collections of logs which are hidden by default within the Event Viewer, analytic logs and debug logs. Analytic logs describe program operations and indicate problems that cannot be addressed with human intervention. Debug logs are used to help developers troubleshoot issues with their programs. They can be viewed by opening the view menu and selecting the Show Analytic and Debug Logs option.

Although there may be additional logs in the Event Viewer, you will always find the following:

▶ **Application**: The application log contains events logged by programs. For example, a database program might record a file error in the programs log. Program developers decide which events to monitor. The application log can be viewed by all users.

▶ **Security**: The security logs contain valid and invalid logon attempts as well as events related to resource use, such as creating, opening, or deleting files or other objects. For example, if you have enabled logon and logoff auditing, attempts to log on to the system are recorded in the security log. By default, security logging is turned off. To enable security logging, use Group Policies to set the audit policy or change the Registry. To audit files and folders, you must be logged on as the member of the Administrators group or have been granted the Manage Auditing and Security Log right in Group Policies. Security logs can be viewed only by administrators.

▶ **System**: The system log contains events that are logged by the Windows system components. For example, the failure of a driver or other system component to load during startup is recorded in the system log. The event types logged by system components are predetermined by Windows. The application log can be viewed by all users.

There are five types of events:

▶ **Error**: A significant problem occurs, such as loss of data or loss of functionality, for example when a service fails during startup.

▶ **Warning**: An event that is not necessarily significant, but may indicate a possible future problem. For example, when disk space is low, a warning is logged.

▶ **Information**: An event that describes the successful operations of an application, driver, or service. For example, when a network driver loads successfully, an information event is logged.

▶ **Success Audit**: An audited security access attempt that succeeds. For example, a user's successful attempt to log on to the system is logged as a success audit event.

▶ **Failure Audit**: An audited security access attempt that fails. The example, if a user tries to access a network drive and fails, the attempt is logged as a failure audit event.

When you double-click an event, the Event Properties window appears. The Event Properties can be divided into two parts: event header and event description. The event header information includes

▶ **Date**: The date the event occurred.

▶ **Time**: Local time the event occurred.

▶ **User**: Username on whose behalf the event occurred.

▶ **Computer**: Name of the computer where the event occurred. The computer name is usually the local computer unless you are viewing an event log on another Windows computer.

▶ **Event ID**: Number identifying the particular event type.

▶ **Source**: Software that logged the event, which can be either a program name, such as SQL Server, or a component of the system or of a large program, such as a driver name.

▶ **Type**: Classification of the event severity: error, information, or warning in the system and application logs; and success audit and failure audit in the security log.

▶ **Category**: Classification of the vent of by the event source.

Event Collector

One of the new features to Event Viewer is the capability to create and manage subscriptions to events that are placed in the Windows Event Viewer (locally and on remote computers) for devices and applications that support the WS-Management protocol. This can be a big benefit when you have a problem between two machines. By having the events go to one computer, you can then have an easier time in aligning on what is happening on each machine, hoping to discover how one machine affects the other.

EXAM ALERT

A new feature of the Event Viewer is the *Event Collector*, which can forward events from one Windows computer to another. Therefore, for the exam, you need to know how to enable and configure the Event Collector:

▶ You must configure the Windows Remote Management utility by running winrm on the source computers.

▶ You must configure the Windows Event Collector Utility by running wecutil on the Collector computer.

To create a subscription on the server to inject system log data from the client into the server's system log, follow these steps:

1. Open the Event Viewer.

2. Click the node for Subscriptions on the server.

3. When it asks to Automatically Start the Windows Event Collector Service Now and to Automatically Start the Service when the Server Restarts, click Yes. This service handles collecting Event Logs from your remote machines.

4. On the Actions menu, Create Subscription.

5. In the Subscription Name box, type a name of the subscription.

6. In the Description box, enter an optional description.

7. In the Destination Log box, select the log file where collected events are to be stored. By default, collected events are stored in the Event Viewer ForwardedEvents log.

8. Click Add and select the computers from which events are to be collected.

9. After adding a computer, you can test connectivity between it and the local computer by selecting the computer and clicking Test.

10. Click Select Events to display the Query Filter dialog box. Use the controls in the Query Filter dialog box to specify the criteria that events must meet to be collected.

11. Click OK on the Subscription Properties dialog box. The subscription is added to the Subscription pane and, if the operation was successful, the Status of the subscription is shown as Active.

If you click the Advanced button on the Subscription Properties dialog box, you can configure the account that will reads the log files and configure the bandwidth or latency options. In addition, you can also specify events to be forwarded using the HTTP protocol over port 80 (the default), or they can be transmitted securely using HTTPS, which is the HTTP protocol over a Secure Sockets Layer (SSL) tunnel. If you choose to use SSL, you will need a computer certificate.

To configure computers in a domain to forward and collect events, follow these steps:

1. Log on to all collector and source computers.

2. On each source computer execute the `winrm quickconfig` command.

3. On the collector computer, execute the `wecutil qc` command, which starts the Windows Event Collector service.

4. Add the computer account of the collector computer to the local Administrators group on each of the source computers.

5. Follow the steps in creating a new subscription to specify the events you want to have forwarded to the collector.

`wecutil.exe` is a Windows Event Collector utility that enables an administrator to create and manage subscriptions to events forwarded from remote event sources that support the WS-Management protocol. In addition to starting the Event Collector service, you can use `wecutil.exe` to set up multiple remote event source computers, using group policies and a configuration XML file to forward events to the event collector computer. To create the source initiated subscription, execute the following command:

```
wecutil cs configurationFile.xml
```

For more information on creating an XML file, visit:

http://msdn.microsoft.com/en-us/library/bb870973(VS.85).aspx

NOTE

If you receive a message that says The RPC Server Is Unavailable or The Interface Is Unknown when you try to run `wecutil`, then you need to start the Windows Event Collector service (`wecsvc`). To start `wecsvc`, at an elevated command prompt type **net start wecsvc**.

Windows Reliability and Performance Monitor

Windows Reliability and Performance Monitor is a Microsoft Management Console snap-in that provides tools for analyzing system performance. From a single console, you can monitor application and hardware performance in real time, customize what data you want to collect in logs, define thresholds for alerts and automatic actions, generate reports, and view past performance data in a variety of ways.

An important feature in Windows Reliability and Performance Monitor is the Data Collector Set (DCS), which groups data collectors into reusable elements. After a Data Collector Set is defined, you can schedule the collection of data with the DCS or see it in real time.

Windows Reliability and Performance Monitor consists of three monitoring tools:

▶ Resource View

▶ Performance Monitor

▶ Reliability Monitor

> **EXAM ALERT**
>
> The Reliability and Performance Monitor can be a powerful tool to help you diagnose and troubleshoot problems. Be sure to understand the three components, including the Resource View, Performance Monitor, and Reliability Monitor. In addition, be sure you understand how to establish a baseline using the Reliability and Performance Monitor so that you can compare it later when troubleshooting issues (so that you can understand how the system is running differently).

Resource View

Windows Reliability and Performance Monitor starts with the Resource Overview display (see Figure 1.5), which enables you to monitor the usage and performance of the major system subcomponents in real time: processors, disks, network, and memory resources. You can then click the Detail buttons (the small arrows shown in Figure 1.5) to see which processes are using which resources.

Detail Arrows

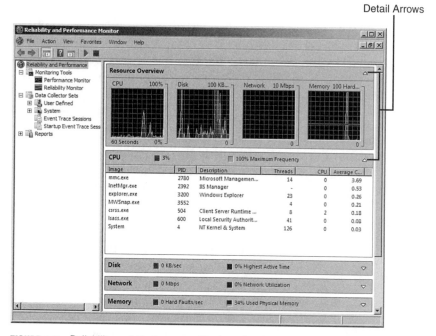

FIGURE 1.5 Reliability and Performance Monitor showing the Resource Overview.

Performance Monitor

Performance Monitor provides a visual display of built-in Windows performance counters, either in real time or as a way to review historical data. You can add performance counters to Performance Monitor by dragging and dropping, or by creating custom DCSs. It features multiple graph views that enable you to visually review performance log data. You can create custom views in Performance Monitor that can be expected as DCSs for use with performance and logging features.

The four systems that affect performance are

▶ Processors

▶ RAM

▶ Disk performance

▶ Network performance

For example, the computer is centered around the processor. Therefore, the performance of the computer is greatly affected by the performance of the processor. The `Processor:%Processor Time` measures how busy the processor is. Although the processor may jump to 100% processor usage, overall average is still important. If the processor is at 80% all the time, you should upgrade the processor (using a faster processor, or adding additional processors) or move some the services to other systems.

RAM is another important factor in server performance. You can use the Performance Monitor to view how much available memory you have or how much paging is being done. Paging is what's being done when the disk space is used like RAM (virtual memory) so that it can allow Windows to load more programs and data. If the performance monitor shows no or little available memory or has a high pages/sec (20 or higher), you should increase the memory.

The Performance Monitor can also benefit you because if the server has high processor utilization or high memory usage, you can determine which application is using most of the processor utilization or memory. Last, you can use Performance Monitor to set a baseline so that you know what is normal for the system. Then when you suspect poor performance, you can then use the Performance Monitor to compare to the baseline so that you can quickly determine where the system is slowing down (a bottleneck). Of course, you need to have a baseline before you run into issues.

You can create a custom Data Collector Set containing performance counters and configure alert activities based on the performance counters exceeding or dropping below limits you define. After creating the Data Collector Set, you must configure the actions the system will take when the alert criteria are met.

To create a Data Collector Set to monitor performance counters:

1. In the Windows Reliability and Performance Monitor navigation pane, expand Data Collector Sets, right-click User Defined, point to New, and click Data Collector Set. The Create New Data Collector Set Wizard starts.

2. Enter a name for your Data Collector Set.

3. Select the Create Manually option and click Next.

4. Select the Performance Counter Alert option and click Next.

5. Click Add to open the Add Counters dialog box. When you are finished adding counters, click OK to return to the wizard.

6. To define alerts based on the values of performance counters you have selected, from the list of performance counters select the counter to monitor and trigger an alert. From the Alert When drop-down, choose whether to alert when the performance counter value is above or below the limit. In the Limit box, enter the threshold value.

7. When you are finished defining alerts, click Next to continue configuration or Finish to exit and save the current configuration.

8. After clicking Next, you can configure the Data Collector Set to run as a particular user. Click the Change button to enter the username and password for a different user than the default listed.

9. Click Finish to return to the Windows Reliability and Performance Monitor.

To view the properties of the Data Collector Set or make additional changes, select Open Properties for This Data Collector Set. To start the Data Collector Set immediately, select Start This Data Collector Set Now. To save the Data Collector Set without starting collection, select Save and Close.

EXAM ALERT

You can configure scripts to execute automatically when an alert criteria is met.

Take these steps to configure alert actions:

1. Expand Reliability and Performance in the navigation pane.

2. Expand Data Collector Sets, expand User Defined, and click the name of the Data Collector Set with performance counter alerts.

3. In the console pane, right-click the name of a Data Collector whose type is Alert and click Properties.

4. On the Data Collector Properties page, click the Alerts tab. The data collectors and alerts already configured should appear.

5. Click the Alert Action tab to choose whether to write an entry to the application event log when the alert criteria are met. You can also start a Data Collector Set when the alert criteria are met.

6. Click the Alert Task tab to choose a Windows Management Interface (WMI) task and arguments to run when the alert criteria are met.

To open Windows Reliability and Performance Monitor, click Start, click in the Start Search box, type **perfmon**, and then click Enter.

Reliability Monitor

In addition to combing through the Event Viewer, you can use the Reliability Monitor to give you an overview of system stability and to view individual events that effect overall stability. Some of the events shown are software installation, operating system updates, and hardware failures.

Reliability Monitor calculates a System Stability Index that reflects whether unexpected problems have reduced the reliability of the system. A graph of the Stability Index over time quickly identifies dates when problems began to occur. The accompanying System Stability Report provides details to help troubleshoot the root cause of reduced reliability. By viewing changes to the system (installation or removal of applications, updates to the operating system, or addition or modification of drivers) side by side with failures (application failures, operating system crashes, or hardware failures), you can develop a strategy for addressing the issues quickly.

Initial Configuration Tasks

The Initial Configuration Tasks window (see Figure 1.6) is a new feature in Windows Server 2008 that is launched automatically after the installation of Windows Server 2008. As the name implies, it is designed to finish the setup and configuration of a new server, including performing many security-related tasks (such as setting the Administrator password, changing the name of the Administrator account, running Windows Updates, and configuring the Windows Firewall). It also enables you to add roles and features.

Some of the settings that you should change include the following:

▶ You should change the Administrator account password because it is initially set to blank by default.

▶ Servers are usually assigned static IP addresses, so you need to configure the IP addresses because all network connections are set to obtain IP addresses automatically through DHCP.

▶ If you need to, join the server to a domain. By default, it is joined to the common workgroup named WORKGROUP.

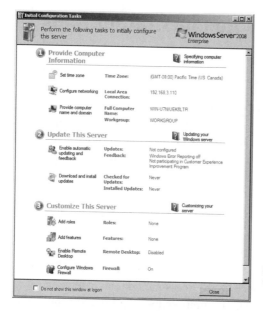

FIGURE 1.6 Initial Configuration Tasks window.

Microsoft Remote Server Administration Tools (RSAT)

Microsoft Remote Server Administration Tools (RSAT) enable administrators to remotely manage roles and features in Windows Server 2008 from a computer that is running Windows Vista with Service Pack 1 (SP1). It includes support for remote management of computers that are running either a Server Core installation option or a full installation option of Windows Server 2008. It provides similar functionality to the Windows Server 2003 Administration Tools Pack.

RSAT includes the following tools:

- ▶ Windows Server 2008 Administration Tools for Roles
- ▶ Windows Server 2008 Administration Tools for Features

Windows Server 2008 Administration Tools for Roles

The Windows Server 2008 Administration Tools for Roles include

- **Active Directory Certificate Services Tools**: Includes the Certification Authority, Certificate Templates, Enterprise PKI, and Online Responder Management snap-ins. Active Directory Certification Authority Tools includes the Certification Authority, Certificate Templates, and the Enterprise PKI snap-ins. Online Responder Tools includes the Online Responder Management snap-in.

- **Active Directory Domain Services (AD DS) Tools**: Includes Active Directory Users and Computers, Active Directory Domains and Trusts, Active Directory Sites and Services, and other snap-ins and command-line tools for remotely managing Active Directory Domain Services. Server for Network Information Service (NIS) Tools includes an extension to the Active Directory Users and Computers snap-in and the Ypclear.exe command-line tool.

- **Active Directory Lightweight Directory Services (AD LDS) Tools**: Includes Active Directory Sites and Services, Active Directory Services Interfaces (ADSI) Edit, Schema Manager, and other snap-ins and command-line tools for managing Active Directory Lightweight Directory Services.

- **DHCP Server Tools**: Includes the DHCP snap-in.

- **DNS Server Tools**: Includes the DNS Manager snap-in and the Dnscmd.exe command-line tool.

- **File Services Tools**: Includes the Storagemgmt.msc snap-in, the Distributed File System (DFS) Tools, and File Server Resource Manager Tools.

- **Network Policy and Access Services Tools**: Includes the Routing and Remote Access snap-in.

- **Terminal Services Tools**: Includes the Remote Desktops and Terminal Services Manager snap-ins.

- **Universal Description, Discovery, and Integration (UDDI) Services Tools**: Includes the UDDI Services snap-in.

Windows Server 2008 Administration Tools for Features

The Windows Server 2008 Administration Tools for Features include

- **BitLocker Drive Encryption Tools**: Includes the `Manage-bde.wsf` script.

- **Failover Clustering Tools**: Includes the Failover Cluster Manager snap-in and the `Cluster.exe` command-line tool.

- **Group Policy Management Tools**: Includes Group Policy Management Console, Group Policy Management Editor, and Group Policy Starter GPO Editor.

- **Network Load Balancing Tools**: Includes the Network Load Balancing Manager utility and the `Nlb.exe` and `Wlbs.exe` command-line tools.

- **SMTP Server Tools**: Includes the SMTP snap-in.

- **Storage Manager for SANs Tools**: Includes the Storage Manager for SANs snap-in, and the `ProvisionStorage.exe` command-line tool.

- **Windows System Resource Manager Tools**: Includes the Windows System Resource Manager snap-in and the `Wsrmc.exe` command-line tool.

Server Core

One of the notable new features of Windows Server 2008 is the introduction of the *Server Core*. Server Core installation provides a minimal environment with no Windows Explorer shell for running specific server roles and no Start button. Just about the only thing that you can see is a command prompt window to type in commands. Because the system has a minimal environment, the system runs more efficiently, reduces the maintenance and management requirements, and reduces the attack surface for those server roles (see Figure 1.7).

To discover the available server roles, open a command prompt and type **oclist**.

This command lists the server roles and optional features that are available for use with `Ocsetup.exe`. It also lists the server roles and optional features that are currently installed.

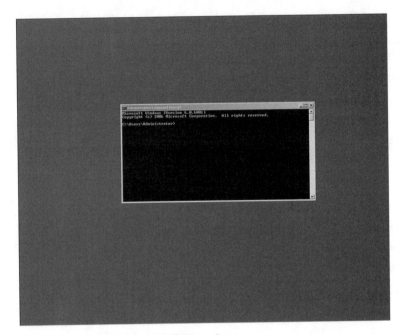

FIGURE 1.7 Windows Server 2008 Server Core.

Server Core Roles

A Server Core machine can be configured for the following roles:

▶ Active Directory Lightweight Directory Services (ADLDS)

▶ DHCP Server

▶ DNS Server

▶ Domain controller/Active Directory Domain Services

▶ File Services (including DFSR and NFS)

▶ IIS 7 web server (but does not include ASPNET, .NET Framework, IIS Management Console, IIS Legacy Snap-In, and IIS FTP Management)

▶ Print Services

▶ Streaming Media Services

▶ Terminal Services including Easy Print, TS Remote Programs, and TS Gateway

▶ Windows Server Virtualization

Server Core Features

A Server Core machine can be configured for the following features:

- Backup
- Bitlocker Drive Encryption
- Failover Clustering
- Multipath IO
- Network Load Balancing
- Removable Storage
- Simple Network Management Protocol (SNMP)
- Subsystem for UNIX-based applications
- Telnet client
- Windows Internet Name Service (WINS)

Running the Administrative Tools

Many of the administrative tools on a Server Core server can be accessed remotely, including those tools that are based on the Microsoft Management Console (MMC). To manage a Server Core server when using an MMC snap-in, follow these steps:

1. Log on to a remote computer.
2. Start an MMC snap-in, such as Computer Management.
3. In the left pane, right-click the top of the tree and click Connect to Another Computer. For example, in the Computer Management, right-click Computer Management (Local).
4. In Another Computer, type the computer name or IP address of the server running a Server Core installation and click OK (see Figure 1.8).

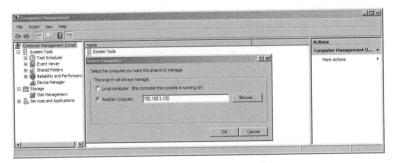

FIGURE 1.8 Connecting to another computer, using MMC.

5. You can now use the MMC snap-in to manage the server running a Server Core installation as you would any other computer running a Windows Server operating system.

NOTE

To use the Disk Management MMC snap-in remotely on a Server Core computer, you must start the Virtual Disk Service on the Server Core computer by typing the `net start` VDS command at the command prompt.

Exam Prep Questions

1. Which of the following would you use to enable to provide network services?

   ○ **A.** Server roles

   ○ **B.** Windows Features

   ○ **C.** Control Panel

   ○ **D.** Server Manager

2. What provides a bare minimum system that focuses on providing a particular network service?

   ○ **A.** Windows Explorer

   ○ **B.** Services Console

   ○ **C.** Windows Power Shell

   ○ **D.** Server Core

3. Which tool was added to Windows Server 2008 that enables you to manage and secure the server roles?

   ○ **A.** Computer Management Console

   ○ **B.** Server Management console

   ○ **C.** Reliability and Performance Monitor

   ○ **D.** Hyper-V

4. If you have a UNIX application that you would like to run in Windows Server 2008, what Windows feature would you install?

   ○ **A.** Windows Power Shell

   ○ **B.** .NET Framework

   ○ **C.** Subsystem for UNIX-based Applications

   ○ **D.** Windows Internal Database

5. You have a Windows Server 2008 Server Core loaded on a server. You just installed DHCP on the server. How do you configure the DHCP scopes?

   ○ **A.** You run the cscript dhcp.wsf script.

   ○ **B.** You modify the C:\windows\system32\etc\hosts file with Notepad.

    ○ **C.** You connect to the DHCP server with a DHCP MMC console, which connects to the DHCP server.

    ○ **D.** You don't need to configure DHCP because it is self configuring.

6. You have a Windows Server 2008 Server Core computer. You log on as a domain admin on your Windows Vista computer and open the Computer Management console on your Windows Vista computer. You then use the Computer Management console to connect to the Server Core computer. However, you are having trouble accessing the Disk Management MMC snap-in. What is the problem?

    ○ **A.** You are not running the updated Windows Server 2008 MMC on the Windows Vista computer.

    ○ **B.** You need to execute the `net start` VDS command at the command prompt on the Windows Server 2008 Server Core computer.

    ○ **C.** You are not logged in as an administrator for the Windows Server 2008 Server Core computer.

    ○ **D.** The Server Core computer needs to be added to the same domain as that of the Windows Vista computer.

7. You have a Windows Server 2008 computer that acts as a file and print server. Users are reporting slow performance when accessing documents from the server. When you connect to the server, you quickly discover that the processor is running at 100% processor utilization. What should you do?

    ○ **A.** Open the Event Viewer and view the system logs to find the problem.

    ○ **B.** Start the Windows Reliability and Performance Monitor to view the percentage of processor capacity used by each application.

    ○ **C.** Use the Event Viewer to configure a subscription that notifies you when the processor exceeds 80% processor utilization.

    ○ **D.** In the performance console, create a counter log to track processor usage.

8. You want to configure your Windows Server 2008 computer to automatically run a script when the hard disk is almost full. What do you need to do after you create a new Data Collector Set?

    ○ **A.** Create a subscription in the Event Viewer.

    ○ **B.** Add a performance counter alert.

    ○ **C.** Create a scheduled task.

    ○ **D.** Modify the startup script.

9. You have two Windows Server 2008 computers, Server1 and Server2. You create a new default subscription for Server2. You need to review the system events for Server2. Which event log should you select?

   ○ **A.** System log on Server1

   ○ **B.** System log on Server2

   ○ **C.** Forwarded Events on Server1

   ○ **D.** Forwarded Events on Server2

10. You have several Windows Server 2008 computers. You want the collector to be Server1. You want to ensure that the servers support Event Collectors. What actions do you need to perform?

    ○ **A.** Run the `wecutil qc` command on Server1. Run `winrm quickconfig` on all other Windows Server 2008 computers. The Add the Server1 account to the administrators group on each of the other Windows Server 2008 computers.

    ○ **B.** Run the `wecutil qc` command on the other Windows Server 2008 computers. Run `winrm quickconfig` on Server1. Add the Server1 account to the administrators group on each of the other Windows Server 2008 computers.

    ○ **C.** Right-click My Computer on each Windows Server 2008 computer except Server1. Click the Advanced tab. Specify Server1 in the Allow list.

    ○ **D.** Open the Services console on each Windows Server 2008 server and start the Windows Event Collector Service.

Answers to Exam Prep Questions

1. Answer A is correct. Server roles are those network applications that provide network services. Answer B is incorrect because Windows Features are software programs that are not directly part of a role. Answer C is incorrect because the Control Panel is used to configure the Windows environment. Answer D is incorrect because the Server Manager is a tool used to install and configure Server Roles and features and administer many of the server/network services.

2. Answer D is correct. The Server Core installation provides a minimal environment with no Windows Explorer shell for running specific server roles. Answer A is the shell that provides file management for Windows. Answer B is incorrect because the Services console is used to enable or disable services running on a Windows computer. Answer C is incorrect because the Windows Power Shell is a powerful scripting language.

3. Answer B is correct. The Server Management console is used to manage and secure server roles. Answer A is incorrect because the Computer Management console can be used to manage some server roles but it is not new to Windows Server 2008. Answer C is incorrect because the Reliability and Performance Monitor is used to monitor the reliability and performance of your Windows Server 2008 system. Answer D is incorrect because Hyper-V is the technology that provides virtualization to Windows Server 2008.

4. Answer C is correct because the subsystem for UNIX-Based Applications provides a kernel that enables the UNIX applications to run. Answer A is incorrect because the Windows Power Shell is a powerful command prompt/scripting environment. Answer B is incorrect because the .NET Framework provides an interface for programming applications. Answer D is incorrect because the Windows Internal Database provides a relational data store that can be used for Windows roles and features.

5. Answer C is correct. You would have to load administrative tools on your local PC or another server. You would then connect to the Windows Server 2008 Server Core. Answer A is incorrect because there is no dhcp.wsf script on the server. Answer B is incorrect because the host file is used for name resolution (hostname to IP addresses) but not to configure the DHCP scopes. Answer D is incorrect because DHCP is not self-configuring.

6. Answer B is correct because you must run the net start VDS command at the command prompt on the Windows Server 2008 Server Core. Answer A is incorrect because you can still access disk management with a Windows Vista MMC. Answer C is incorrect because you are logging in as a domain admin. Although that computer may not be part of the domain, you can still access the computer management from other computers that are not in the same domain or as part of a workgroup. Answer D is incorrect because the computer does not have to be part of the same domain to access the Windows Vista computer.

7. Answer B is correct. You need to determine which application is utilizing most of the processor. Answer A is incorrect because performance problems are not displayed in the system logs. Answer C is incorrect because the Event Viewer does not show processor utilization. Answer D is incorrect because creating a counter to track processor usage does not fix the problem. You need to determine what is utilizing the processor so you know where to focus on fixing the problem.

8. Answer B is correct. After the DCS is created, you need to create a performance counter alert. When the counter reaches the designated threshold, you can have a script execute. Answer A is incorrect because a subscription does not trigger a script to execute when a performance threshold is met. Answer C is incorrect because scheduled tasks are meant to execute tasks based on a day and time, not a performance counter. Answer D is incorrect because the startup script executes when Windows starts, not when a performance threshold is met.

9. Answer C is correct. You configure a subscription on Server2 so that events appear in the Forwarded Events on Server1. Answers A and B are incorrect because Server2's system events are not in the system log; they are in the Forwarded Events. Answer D is incorrect because the Forwarded Events are on Server1, not Server2.

10. Answer A is correct. You need to run `wecutil qc` on the collecting server and `winrm quickconfig` on each of the servers that are to forward the events. You also need to add the computer account of the sending computers to the local administrators group. Answer B is incorrect because the receiving collecting computer should have the `wecutil qc` command and each of the other servers should have `winrm quickconfig`. Answer C is incorrect because the Advanced tab in the System Properties does not give you the option to specify which computers are allowed to forward events. Answer D is incorrect because you need to do more then just start the Windows Event Collector Service.

Need to Know More?

To find out more information about Windows Server 2008, visit the following websites:

▶ http://www.microsoft.com/servers/default.mspx

▶ http://www.microsoft.com/windowsserver2008/en/us/product-information.aspx

To find more information about the configuring Server Core, open the Server Core Installation Option of Windows Server 2008 Step-By-Step Guide, which can be found at:

▶ http://technet2.microsoft.com/windowsserver2008/en/library/47a23a74-e13c-46de-8d30-ad0afb1eaffc1033.mspx?mfr=true

For more information about the event collector and the `wecutil.exe` command, visit the following websites:

▶ http://technet2.microsoft.com/windowsserver/en/library/30757b93-7291-4254-b15e-f0aa5f45ac541033.mspx?mfr=true

▶ http://technet2.microsoft.com/windowsserver2008/en/library/0c82a6cb-d652-429c-9c3d-0f568c78d54b1033.mspx?mfr=true

CHAPTER TWO

IP Addressing

Terms you'll need to understand:

- ✓ TCP/IP
- ✓ IP address
- ✓ IPv4
- ✓ IPv6
- ✓ Subnet mask
- ✓ Default gateway
- ✓ Domain Name System (DNS)
- ✓ Ping command
- ✓ Ipconfig command
- ✓ Address Resolution Protocol (ARP)
- ✓ Host
- ✓ Classful address
- ✓ Private network
- ✓ Subnet

- ✓ Netbits
- ✓ Hostbits
- ✓ Teredo address
- ✓ Classless Interdomain Routing (CIDR)
- ✓ Network address translation (NAT)
- ✓ Proxy server
- ✓ Global unicast addresses
- ✓ Link local unicast addresses
- ✓ Unicast
- ✓ Broadcast
- ✓ Multicast
- ✓ Anycast
- ✓ Port

Techniques/concepts you'll need to master:

- ✓ Compare and differentiate an IPv4 addressing to IPv6 addressing.
- ✓ List the private addresses used in an IPv4 addressing scheme.
- ✓ Configure a Windows Server 2008 computer to use a given IP address (IPv4 and IPv6), subnet mask, default gateway, and DNS server, using the GUI interface and the command prompt.

- ✓ Given a network connectivity problem, troubleshoot and correct the problem.

A network is two or more computers connected to share resources (such as files or printers). To function, a network requires a service to share (such as file or print sharing) and access to a common medium or pathway. Today, most computers connect to a wired network with an Ethernet adapter, which in turn connects to a switch or a set of switches via a twisted-pair cable, or the computers connect to a wireless network with a wireless adapter connected to a wireless switch. To bring it all together, protocols give the entire system common communication rules. Today, virtually all networks use the TCP/IP protocol suite, the same protocol that the Internet runs.

TCP/IP (Transmission Control Protocol/Internet Protocol) is an industry suite of protocols on which the Internet is based. It is supported by most versions of Windows and virtually all modern operating systems.

The lowest protocol within the TCP/IP suite is the Internet Protocol (IP), which is primarily responsible for addressing and routing packets between hosts. Each connection on a TCP/IP address is called a *host* (a computer or other network device that is connected to a TCP/IP network) and is assigned a unique IP address. A host is any network interface, including each network's interface cards or a network printer that connects directly onto the network. When you send or receive data, the data is divided into little chunks called packets. Each of these packets contains both the sender's TCP/IP address and the receiver's TCP/IP address.

Windows Server 2008 supports both IPv4 and IPv6 through a dual-IP-layer architecture and enables both by default. This architecture enables you to tunnel IPv6 traffic across an IPv4 network in addition to IPv4 traffic across an IPv6 network.

Physical Addresses, Logical Addresses, and Logical Names

When communicating on today's modern networks, there are three levels of addressing:

- ▶ Physical addresses (MAC addresses)
- ▶ Logical addresses (IP addresses)
- ▶ Logical names (domain names and hostnames)

Because many network devices share the same transmission channel, each node on the network must have some way to identify itself from the other nodes. The physical device address or media access control (MAC) address is a unique hardware address (unique on the LAN) burned onto a ROM chip assigned by the hardware vendors.

The MAC address is 48 bits (6 bytes) in length and is usually represented in hexadecimal format. The first 24 bits of a MAC address are referred to as the organizationally unique identifier or OUI. OUIs are sold and assigned to network hardware vendors by the Institute of Electrical and Electronics Engineers (IEEE). The last 24 bits are assigned by the individual vendor. A MAC address is ordinarily expressed as six pairs of hexadecimal characters separated by colors or hyphens. An example of a MAC address is

00:53:AD:B2:13:BA

or

00-53-AD-B2-13-BA

Unfortunately, because physical addresses have no structure to identify different networks, routing cannot be performed. To overcome this, a logical networking protocol is used, such as the IP, which allows network administrators to assign logical addresses and arrange them as needed as long as they follow the predefined set of rules.

The logical addresses used in a TCP/IP network are known as *IP addresses*. When data needs to be sent to a host in another network, it figures out the best way to get there by using a routing protocol or by using static routes, and sends the data to the next hop toward the remote host. Because all network traffic is really based on the physical MAC addresses, the *Address Resolution Protocol (ARP)* provides a mechanism so that can a host can learn a receiver's MAC address when knowing only the IP address.

When a host needs to send a data packet to another host on the same network, the sender application must know both the IP and MAC addresses of the intended receiver because the destination IP address is placed in the IP packet and the destination MAC address is placed in the LAN's protocol frame (such as Ethernet). If the destination host is on another network, the sender looks instead for the MAC address of the default gateway or router.

Anytime a computer needs to communicate with a local computer, it first looks in the ARP cache in memory to see whether it already knows the MAC address of a computer with the specified IP address. If it isn't in the ARP cache, it tries to discover the MAC address by broadcasting an ARP request packet. The station on the LAN recognizes its own IP address, and then sends an ARP response with its own MAC address. Then both the sender of the ARP reply and the original ARP requester record each other's IP address and media access control address as an entry in the ARP cache for future reference.

If a computer needs to communicate with another computer that is located on another network, it does the same except it sends the packet to the local router. Therefore, it searches for the MAC address of the local *port* of the router or it sends a broadcast looking for the address of the router's local port.

When you are communicating on a TCP/IP network, users do not typically use addresses, which tend to be difficult to remember. Instead, you use logical names such as domain names and hostnames. When you open up your browser and type `http://www.microsoft.com`, the computer uses *Domain Name System* (DNS) to find the IP address of www.microsoft.com. It then determines whether the address is a local address or a remote address. If it is a local address, the computer then resolves the MAC address of the destination host and sends the data to the destination host. If it is a remote address, the computer resolves the MAC address of the default gateway/router and forwards the data to the default gateway (see Figure 2.1).

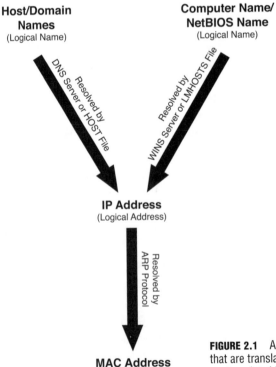

FIGURE 2.1 A representation of logical names that are translated into logical addresses, which are translated into physical addresses.

To view the arp table, use the following command:

```
arp -a
```

To add a static entry into the arp table (157.55.85.212 IPv4 address to the 00-aa-00-62-c6-09 MAC address), use the following command:

```
arp -s 157.55.85.212 00-aa-00-62-c6-09(c)IPv4 Addressing
```

Each connection on a TCP/IP address (logical address) is called a *host* (a computer or other network device that is connected to a TCP/IP network) and is assigned a unique IP address. A host is any network interface, including each network interface card or a network printer that connects directly onto the network. The format of the *IPv4* address is four 8-bit numbers (octet) divided by a period (.). Each number can be 0 to 255. For example, a TCP/IP address could be 131.107.3.1 or 2.0.0.1. Because the address is used to identify the computer, no two connections can use the same IP address. If they do, one or both of the computers cannot communicate.

Classful Addressing

When connecting to the Internet, network numbers are assigned to a corporation or business. The number system is divided into classes and therefore is known as a *classful* network. If the first number is between 1 and 126 (first bit is a 0), the network is a Class A. If the first number is between 128 and 191 (first two bits are 1 0), the network is a Class B. If the first number is between 192 and 223 (first three bits are 1 1 0), the network is a Class C. See Table 2.1.

TABLE 2.1   Standard IP Classes for the IP Address of w.x.y.z

Class Type	First Octet	Network Number	Host Number	Default Subnet Mask	Comments
A	1-126	W	x.y.z	255.0.0.0	Supports 16 million hosts on each of 126 networks.
B	128-191	w.x	y.z	255.255.0.0	Supports 65,000 hosts on each of 16,000 networks.
C	192-223	w.x.y	z	255.255.255.0	Supports 254 hosts on each of 2 million networks.

Two additional classes should be mentioned. These are used for special functions only and are not commonly assigned to individual hosts. Class D addresses may begin with a value between 224 and 239, and are used for IP multicasting. *Multicasting* is sending a single data packet to multiple hosts. Class E addresses begin with a value between 240 and 255, and are reserved for experimental use.

> **NOTE**
>
> Several address values are reserved and/or have special meaning. The network number 127 is used for loopback testing and the specific host address 127.0.0.1 refers to the local host or the actual host or computer that you are currently using.

The TCP/IP address is broken down into a network number (sometimes referred to as a network prefix) and a host number. The network number identifies the entire network, whereas the host number identifies the computer or connection on the specified network. If it is a Class A network, the first octet describes the network number and the last three octets describe the host address. If it is a Class B network, the first two octets describe the network number and the last two octets describe the host address. If it is a Class C, the first three octets describe the network number and the last octet describes the host number.

Example 1: Identifying the Network Address of a Classful Address

You have the following network address:

131.107.20.4

The 131 is between 128 and 191, identifying the address as a Class B network. Therefore, the 131.107 identifies the network and the 20.4 identifies the host or computer on the 131.107 network.

Example 2: Identifying the Network and Host Address of a Classful Address

You have the following network address:

208.234.23.4

The 208 is between 192 and 223, identifying the address as a Class C network. Therefore, the 208.234.23 identifies the network (network address is 208.234.23.0) and the 4 identifies the host or computer (host address is 0.0.0.4) on the 208.234.23.0 network.

Usually when you define TCP/IP for a network connection, you would also specify a subnet mask. The *subnet mask* is used to define which bits describe the network number and which bits describe the host address. The default subnet mask for a Class A network is 255.0.0.0. If you convert this to a binary equivalent, you would have 11111111.00000000.00000000.00000000, showing that the first 8 bits (first octet, marked with 1s), is used to define the network address, and the last 24 bits (marked with 0s) are used to define the host address. The default subnet mask for a Class B network is 255.255.0.0 (11111111.11111111.00000000.00000000), and the default subnet mask for a Class C network is 255.255.255.0 (11111111.11111111.11111111.00000000).

If an individual network is connected to another network and you must communicate with any computers on the other network, you must also define the *default gateway*, which specifies the local address of a router. If the default gateway is not specified, you cannot communicate with computers on other networks. Note: If the LAN is connected to more than one network, you specify one gateway. When a data packet is sent, it first determines whether the data packet needs to go to a local computer or a computer that is on another network. If it is meant to be sent to a computer on another network, it forwards the data packet to the router. The router then determines the best direction for the data packet to go to get to its destination. Occasionally, it has to go back through the network to get to another gateway.

Private Networks

Because TCP/IP addresses have become scarce for the Internet, a series of addresses have been reserved to be used by *private networks* (networks not connected to the Internet). They are:

- ▶ **Class A**: 10.x.x.x (1 Class A addresses)
- ▶ **Class B**: Between 172.16.x.x and 172.31.x.x (16 Class B addresses)
- ▶ **Class C**: 192.168.0.x and 192.168.255.x (256 Class C addresses)

If you are not connected to the Internet or are using a proxy server, it is recommended that you use private addresses to prevent a renumbering of your internetwork when you eventually connect to the Internet.

Subnetting the Network

The subnet mask can be changed to take a large network and break it into several small networks called *subnets*. This enables a corporation or organization to freely assign a distinct subnetwork number for each of its internal networks. This enables the organization to deploy additional subnets without needing to obtain a new network number from the ISP.

The subnet mask is used to define which bits represent the network address (including the subnet number) and which bits represent the host address. For a subnet, the network prefix, subnet number, and the subnet mask must be the same for all computers (see Figure 2.2).

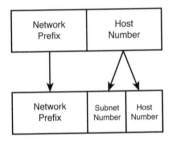

FIGURE 2.2   Classful address converting to a classless address.

Example 3: Subnetting a Classful Address

Your network is assigned a network number of 161.13.0.0. Because it is a Class B network, it already has default subnet mask of 255.255.0.0. Therefore, the TCP/IP address of any network interface card that belongs to this network must begin with 161.13. Because it is a Class B network, it uses 16 bits to define the host address, which allows the network to have up to 65,534 computers. I don't know of any single LAN that has 65,534 computers.

The network administrator could take this large network and divide it into several smaller subnets. For example, if 161.13 defines the entire corporation network (network prefix), the third octet could be used to define a site network or individual LAN (subnet number), whereas the last octet would be used to define the host address (host number).

Therefore, if you have three individual LANs, functioning in separate buildings, you can use the third octet to define these three LANs. The first building would have a network address of 161.13.1.0, the second building would have a network address of 161.13.2.0, and the third building would have a network address of 161.13.3.0. Because the last octet is used to define the host number and there are eight bits to define the host number, there can be 254 hosts for each local area networks. Of course, to let the network know that the 161.13.0.0 network is subnetted, the mask would have to be changed to 255.255.0.0 to 255.255.255.0 (11111111.11111111.11111111.00000000) to indicate that the first 24 bits indicate the network address.

To calculate the maximum number of subnets, you can use the following equation:

Number of subnets=$2^{number\ of\ masked\ bits}-2$

To calculate the maximum number of hosts, you can use the following equation:

Number of hosts=$2^{number\ unmasked\ bits}-2$

The –2 is used because you cannot use a network number, subnet number, or host number of all 0s and all 1s. For example, if you had an address of 131.107.3.4, 131.107 is the network address and 3.4 is the host address. If you send a packet to the 131.107.0.0 (host address is all zeros), you are sending the packet to the network itself, not to the individual computer on the network. If you send it to 131.107.255.255 (host address is all ones), you are doing a broadcast to all the computers on network 131.107. If you use the address of 0.0.3.4 (network number is all zeros), it assumes 3.4 is on the current or local network.

Example 4: Determining the Number of Subnets and Hosts

If you look at example 3, you have 8 bits used to define the subnet/site number and you have 8 bits used to define the host number. Therefore:

Number of subnets=$2^{number\ of\ masked\ bits}-2=2^8-2=254$ subnets or sites

Number of hosts=$2^{number\ unmasked\ bits}-2=2^8-2=254$ hosts for each subnet

Example 5: Determining the Number of Hosts Bits

Your network is assigned an address of 207.182.15. You choose to subnet your network into several smaller networks. The largest network that you have has 25 computers. Therefore, how many bits can you mask so that you can have the largest number of subnets or sites?

To start with, you only have the eight bits used for the host address to play with. The easiest way is to use the formula, which calculates the number of hosts. To determine how many unmasked bits that allows 25 or more computers, you would use the following calculations:

Number of hosts=$2^{number\ unmasked\ bits}-2=2^1-2=0$

Number of hosts=$2^{number\ unmasked\ bits}-2=2^2-2=2$

Number of hosts=$2^{number\ unmasked\ bits}-2=2^3-2=6$

Number of hosts=$2^{number\ unmasked\ bits}-2=2^4-2=14$

Number of hosts=$2^{number\ unmasked\ bits}-2=2^5-2=30$

Because you use 5 of the 8 bits for the host number, it leaves 3 bits that are masked, which gives:

Number of subnets=2number masked bits-2=2^3-2=6 subnets

Last, the subnet mask would be 11111111.11111111.11111111.11100000, which is equivalent to 255.255.255.224.

Example 6: Determining the Range of IP Addresses

Using the network discussed in Example 5, what is the range of TCP/IP addresses for the second subnet?

The network number is 207.182.15.0 with a subnet mask of 255.255.255.224, which declares that the first three bits of the forth octet are used for the subnet number. The possible subnet numbers (in binary) are

0 0 0
0 0 1
0 1 0
0 1 1
1 0 0
1 0 1
1 1 0
1 1 1

Of course, you cannot use 0 0 0 or 1 1 1, leaving six possible subnets.

Using binary counting, the second subnet is defined by 0 1 0. Because five bits are left, the five bits can range from 0 0 0 0 1 (remember, it can't be all 0s) to 1 1 1 1 0 (remember, it can't be all 1s). Therefore, the last octet is 0 1 0 0 0 0 0 1 to 0 1 0 1 1 1 1 0. If you translate these to decimal numbers, the last octet is 65 to 94. Therefore, the address range is 207.182.15.65 to 207.182.15.94, with a subnet mask of 255.255.255.224.

Example 7: Planning Your IP Network

You are the IT administrator for the Acme manufacturing company. Your main product is the design and production of widgets. It is your responsibility to plan out and implement the IP addresses for your company. You currently have 35 sites throughout the country with plans to add 5 more sites within the next three years. Currently, the largest site has 275 people but another 25 to 75 employees may be added at that site over the next two years, depending on the market. In addition, the corporate building has 10 web servers and 15 corporate servers that also need IP addresses. American Registry for Internet Numbers (ARIN) has assigned 182.24 prefix to your corporation. ARIN manages the distribution of Internet number for the United States, Canada, and many island nations in the Caribbean and North Atlantic Ocean:

- How would you subnet your network so that you can get the maximum number of people per site?

- What is the number of sites that your network can have with this configuration?

- What is the maximum number of people that your network can have with this configuration?

- What would the subnet mask be for your corporation?

- The primary site (which is also the largest site) is the corporate office. If you assign this site as your first subnet, what would the extended network prefix be for the corporate office site?

- What would the range of addresses be for this site?

- What is the broadcast address for this site?

Let's take the first question and determine how you would subnet your network to get the maximum number of people per site.

You know that you have a 182.24.0.0 (10110110.00011000) assigned by ARIN. Because it starts with 182, you know that it is a Class B network with a default subnet mask of 255.255.0.0 (11111111.11111111.00000000.00000000). This tells you that the first 16 bits are locked for you and the last 16 bits are yours to assign. You know that you will have 40 (35+5) sites to plan for with the maximum number of 375 (275+75+10+15) hosts. Because you want to maximize the number of hosts, you need to figure out how many bits it would take to assign the 40 sites:

Number of subnets=$2^{\text{number masked bits}}-2=2^1-2=0$

Number of subnets =$2^{\text{number masked bits}}-2=2^2-2=2$

Number of subnets =$2^{\text{number masked bits}}-2=2^3-2=6$

Number of subnets =$2^{\text{number masked bits}}-2=2^4-2=14$

Number of subnets =$2^{\text{number masked bits}}-2=2^5-2=30$

Number of subnets =$2^{\text{number masked bits}}-2=2^6-2=62$

Therefore, it would take 6 bits to define the subnets. As you can see, if you use 6 bits, you can actually grow to 62 sites (question 2). This leaves 10 bits (16-6) left to define the hosts. Using the following equation,

Number of hosts=$2^{\text{number masked bits}}$-2=$2^{10}$-2=1022

You can have up to 1022 hosts per site (question 3). Note: If this number was smaller than what you needed, you would have to come up with another solution so that you could get enough addresses for each site. Your options would be

▶ Assign multiple subnets per site

▶ Acquire a Class A network from ARIN (highly unlikely)

You would like to use a proxy server or a network address translation solution so that you can use one set of IP addresses for internal traffic (private network) and a second set of addresses for external traffic (IP addresses assigned by ARIN).

Because you are going to use 6 bits to define the subnets, the new subnet mask (question 4) would be

11111111.11111111.11111100.00000000

This is equivalent to

255.255.252.0

which would have to be assigned to every host on every subnet.

Looking at the 6 bits that define the subnets, you should number your subnets as shown in Table 2.2.

TABLE 2.2 Numbering of Subnets

Site Number (Decimal)	Site Number (Binary)	Extended Network Number (Binary)	Extended Network Number (Decimal)
1	000001	10110110.00011000.000001XX.XXXXXXXX	182.24.4.0
2	000010	10110110.00011000.000010XX.XXXXXXXX	182.24.8.0
3	000011	10110110.00011000.000011XX.XXXXXXXX	182.24.12.0
4	000100	10110110.00011000.000100XX.XXXXXXXX	182.24.16.0
5	000101	10110110.00011000.000101XX.XXXXXXXX	182.24.20.0
6	000110	10110110.00011000.000110XX.XXXXXXXX	182.24.24.0
7	000111	10110110.00011000.000111XX.XXXXXXXX	182.24.28.0

TABLE 2.2 *Continued*

Site Number (Decimal)	Site Number (Binary)	Extended Network Number (Binary)	Extended Network Number (Decimal)
8	001000	10110110.00011000.001000XX.XXXXXXXX	182.24.32.0
.	.	.	.
.	.	.	.
.	.	.	.
62	111110	10110110.00011000.111110XX.XXXXXXXX	182.24.248.0

NOTE

To calculate the extended network number in decimal, assign 0s to the hostbits.

Every host on the first site (the corporate site) starts with the following bits:

10110110.00011000.000001XX.XXXXXXXX

which gives an extended network number of 182.24.4.0.

The Xs define the hosts on that site. If you remember, you have 10 bits to assign to the host.

So the first host at this site would be

10110110.00011000.00000100.00000001

which is equivalent to

182.24.4.1

The last host at this site would be

10110110.00011000.00000111.11111110

which is equivalent to

182.24.7.254

As shown in Table 2.3, the range of address is for the first subnet is 182.24.4.1 to 182.24.7.254 (question 6).

TABLE 2.3: Numbering of Hosts Within a Subnet

Host Number (Binary)	Host Number (Decimal)	IP Address (Binary)	IP Address (Decimal)
00.00000001	0.1	10110110.00011000.00000100.00000001	182.24.4.1
00.00000010	0.2	10110110.00011000.00000100.00000010	182.24.4.2
00.00000011	0.3	10110110.00011000.00000100.00000011	182.24.4.3
00.00000100	0.4	10110110.00011000.00000100.00000100	182.24.4.4
00.00000101	0.5	10110110.00011000.00000100.00000101	182.24.4.5
00.00000110	0.6	10110110.00011000.00000100.00000110	182.24.4.6
00.00000111	0.7	10110110.00011000.00000100.00000111	182.24.4.7
00.00001000	0.8	10110110.00011000.00000100.00001000	182.24.4.8
00.00001001	0.9	10110110.00011000.00000100.00001001	182.24.4.9
.	.	.	.
.	.	.	.
.	.	.	.
11.11111110	3.254	10110110.00011000.00000111.11111110	182.24.7.254

The broadcast address (question 7) for the entire network would be

10110110.00011000.11111111.11111111

which is equivalent to 182.24.255.255.

The broadcast address for the corporate subnet (site 1) would be

10110110.00011000.00000111.11111111

which is equivalent to 182.24.7.255.

Classless Interdomain Routing (CIDR)

Becaues the Class B network IDs would be depleted and most organizations need something larger than a Class C network (does not contain enough host IDs to provide a flexible subnetting scheme with an organization), IP addresses are no longer given out under the Class A, B, or C designation. Instead a method called *Classless Internetwork Domain Routing* (CIDR)—pronounced "cider"—is used.

Routers that support CIDR do not make assumptions by looking at the first octet to determine the subnet mask, instead they rely on the prefix length information, /x, where x represents the number of network bits. Note: Allocation can also be specified with the traditional dotted-decimal mask notation.

Under IPv4 addressing, a Class C address (example 198.23.27.32) uses a subnet mask of 255.255.255.0 (which is equivalent to 11111111.11111111.11111111.00000000), which represents the first 24 bits as the network bits and the last 8 bits are the hostbits. In the CIDR addressing, the same address would be indicated as 198.23.27.32/24. The 24 represents that the first 24 bits indicate the network bits.

Because CIDR eliminates the traditional concept of Class A, Class B, and Class C network addresses, CIDR supports the deployment of arbitrarily sized networks rather than the standard 8-bit, 16-bit, or 24-bit network numbers associated with classful addressing. Therefore, with the CIDR, the addresses that were wasted for the Class A and Class B networks are reclaimed and redistributed.

Prefixes are viewed as bitwise contiguous blocks of IP address space. For example, all prefixes with a /20 prefix represent the same amount of address spaces (2^{12}-2, or 4,094 host addresses). Examples for the traditional Class A, Class B and Class C are

Traditional Class A	10.23.64.0/20	00001010.00010111.01000000.00000000
Traditional Class B	140.5.0.0/20	10001100.00000101.00000000.00000000
Traditional Class C	200.7.128.0/20	11001000.00000111.10000000.00000000

Table 2.4 provides information about the most commonly deployed CIDR address blocks.

TABLE 2.4 CIDR Address Blocks

CIDR Prefix Length	Dotted Decimal	# of Individual Addresses	# of Classful Networks
/13	255.248.0.0	512 K	8 Bs or 2048 Cs
/14	255.252.0.0	256 K	4 Bs or 1024 Cs
/15	255.254.0.0	128 K	2 Bs or 512 Cs
/16	255.255.0.0	64 K	1 B or 256 Cs
/17	255.255.128.0	32 K	128 Cs
/18	255.255.192.0	16 K	64 Cs
/19	255.255.224.0	8 K	32 Cs
/20	255.255.240.0	4 K	16 Cs
/21	255.255.248.0	2 K	8 Cs
/22	255.255.252.0	1 K	4 Cs

continues

TABLE 2.4 *Continued*

CIDR Prefix Length	Dotted Decimal	# of Individual Addresses	# of Classful Networks
/23	255.255.254.0	510	2 Cs
/24	255.255.255.0	254	1 C
/25	255.255.255.128	126	1/2 C
/26	255.255.255.192	62	1/4 C
/27	255.255.255.224	30	1/8 C

Much like VLSM, CIDR enables you to take a single network ID and subdivide its network into smaller segments, depending upon its requirements. Although VLSM divides the addresses on the private network, the CIDR divides the addresses by the Internet Registry, a high-level ISP, a mid-level ISP, a low-level ISP, or the private organization.

Like VLSM, another important benefit of CIDR is that it plans an important role in controlling the growth of the Internet's routing tables. The reduction of routing information requires that the Internet be divided into addressing domains. Within a domain, detailed information is available about all the networks that reside in the domain. Outside of an addressing domain, only the common network prefix is advertised. This allows a single routing table entry to specify a route to many individual network addresses.

Supernetting is the process of combining multiple IP address ranges into a single IP network such as combining several Class C networks to form a larger network. For example, rather than allocating a Class B network ID to an organization that has up to 2,000 hosts, the InterNIC allocates a range of eight Class C network IDs. Each Class C network ID accommodates 254 hosts, for a total of 2,032 host IDs.

Although this technique helps conserve Class B network IDs, it creates a new problem. Using conventional routing techniques, the routers on the Internet now must have eight Class C network ID entries in their routing tables to route IP packets to the company or organization (such as the Acme Corporation) that control the eight smaller network IDs. To prevent Internet routers from becoming overwhelmed with routes, CIDR is used to collapse multiple network ID entries into a single entry corresponding to all the Class C network IDs allocated to that company or organization.

Example 8: Supernetting with CIDR Blocks

For example, consider the following block of contiguous 32-bit addresses (192.32.0.0 through 192.32.7.0 in decimal notation). The supernet address (network address) for this block is 192.32.0.0 (11000000 00100000 00000000

00000000), the first 21 bits (/21) shared by all smaller networks. The next three bits would be used to number each of the smaller network IDs. The mask for the supernet address in this example is 255.255.248.0 (11111111 11111111 11111000 00000000).

192.32.0.0

192.32.1.0

192.32.2.0

192.32.3.0   /24   —————————————->   192.32.0.0   /21

192.32.4.0

192.32.5.0

192.32.6.0

192.32.7.0

Example 9: Using Supernetting

Before you combine the subnets, you need to look at how they can be grouped together based on their bit pattern. Therefore, you need to list the individual networks numbers defined by the CIDR block 198.35.64.0/20.

First, express the CIDR block in binary format:

198.35.64.0/20 11000110.00100011.01000000.00000000

The /20 mask is 4 bits shorter than the natural mask for a traditional /24. This means that the CIDR block identifies a block of 16 (or 2^4) consecutive /24 network numbers.

The range of /24 network numbers defined by the CIDR block 198.35.68.0/24 includes

Net #0: 11000110.00100011.01000000.xxxxxxxx 198.35.64.0/20
Net #1: 11001000.00111000.01000001.xxxxxxxx 198.35.65.0/20
Net #2: 11001000.00111000.01000010.xxxxxxxx 198.35.66.0/20
Net #3: 11001000.00111000.01000011.xxxxxxxx 198.35.67.0/20
Net #4: 11001000.00111000.01000100.xxxxxxxx 198.35.68.0/20
Net #5: 11001000.00111000.01000101.xxxxxxxx 198.35.69.0/20
Net #6: 11001000.00111000.01000110.xxxxxxxx 198.35.70.0/20
Net #7: 11001000.00111000.01000111.xxxxxxxx 198.35.71.0/20
Net #8: 11001000.00111000.01001000.xxxxxxxx 198.35.72.0/20

Net #9: 11001000.00111000.01001001.xxxxxxxx 198.35.73.0/20

Net #10: 11001000.00111000.01001010.xxxxxxxx 198.35.74.0/20

Net #11: 11001000.00111000.01001011.xxxxxxxx 198.35.75.0/20

Net #12: 11001000.00111000.01001100.xxxxxxxx 198.35.76.0/20

Net #13: 11001000.00111000.01001101.xxxxxxxx 198.35.77.0/20

Net #14: 11001000.00111000.01001110.xxxxxxxx 198.35.78.0/20

Net #15: 11001000.00111000.01001110.xxxxxxxx 198.35.79.0/20

Net #15: 11001000.00111000.01001111.xxxxxxxx 198.35.80.0/20

To aggregate or combine the 16 IP /24 network addresses to the highest degree would be 198.35.68.0.

Network Address Translation (NAT)

Because IP addresses are a scarce resource, most Internet Service Providers (ISPs) allocate only one address to a single customer. In a majority of cases, this address is assigned dynamically, so every time a client connects to the ISP a different address is provided. Big companies can buy more addresses, but for small businesses and home users, the cost of doing so is prohibitive. Because such users are given only one IP address, they can have only one computer connected to the Internet at one time. *Network address translation (NAT)* is a method of connecting multiple computers to the Internet (or any other IP network) but use only one IP address. With a NAT gateway running on this single computer, it is possible to share that single address between multiple local computers and connect them all at the same time. The outside world is unaware of this division and thinks that only one computer is connected.

To combat certain types of security problems, a number of firewall products are available that are placed between the user and the Internet to verify all traffic before allowing it to pass through. This means, for example, that no unauthorized user would be allowed to access the company's file or email server. The problem with firewall solutions is that they are expensive and difficult to set up and maintain, putting them out of reach for home and small business users.

NOTE

Recently, personal firewalls have become very popular and are available in Windows XP, Windows Vista, and Linux to protect individual computers that surf the Internet.

NAT automatically provides firewall-style protection without any special setup. The basic purpose of NAT is to multiplex traffic from the internal network (private network) and present it to the Internet (public network) as if it was coming from a single computer having only one IP address. The TCP/IP protocols include a multiplexing facility so that any computer can maintain multiple simultaneous connections with a remote computer. For example, an internal client can connect to an outside FTP server, but an outside client cannot connect to an internal FTP server because it would have to originate the connection, and NAT does not allow that. It is still possible to make some internal servers available to the outside world via inbound mapping, which maps certain well known TCP ports (for example, 21 for FTP) to specific internal addresses, thus making services such as FTP or web addresses available in a controlled way.

To multiplex several connections to a single destination, client computers label all packets with unique port numbers. Each IP packet starts with a header containing the source and destination addresses and port numbers. This combination of numbers completely defines a single TCP/IP connection. The addresses specify the two machines at each end, and the two port numbers ensure that each connection between this pair of machines can be uniquely identified.

Each separate connection is originated from a unique source port number in the client, and all reply packets from the remote server for this connection contain the same number as their destination port, so that the client can relate them back to its correct connection. In this way, for example, it is possible for a web browser to ask a web server for several images at once and to know how to put all the parts of all the responses back together.

A modern NAT gateway must change the source address on every outgoing packet to be its single public address. It therefore also renumbers the source ports to be unique, so that it can keep track of each client connection. The NAT gateway uses a port mapping table to remember how it renumbered the ports for each client's outgoing packets. The port mapping table relates the client's real local IP address and source port, plus its translated source port number, to a destination address and port. The NAT gateway can therefore reverse the process for returning packets and route them back to the correct clients.

When any remote server responds to a NAT client, incoming packets arriving at the NAT gateway all have the same destination address, but the destination port number is the unique source port number that was assigned by the NAT. The NAT gateway looks in its port mapping table to determine for which "real" client address and port number a packet is destined, and replaces these numbers before passing the packet on to the local client.

This process is completely dynamic. When a packet is received from an internal client, NAT looks for the matching source address and port in the port mapping table. If the entry is not found, a new one is created, and a new mapping port allocated to the client. Outgoing packets will go through the following translation process:

1. Incoming packet received on non-NAT port.

2. Look for source address and port in the mapping table.

3. If found, replace source port with previously allocated mapping port.

4. If not found, allocate a new mapping port.

5. Replace source address with NAT address, and source port with mapping port.

Packets received on the NAT port undergo a reverse translation process:

1. Incoming packet received on NAT port.

2. Look up destination port number in port mapping table.

3. If found, replace destination address and port with entries from the mapping table.

4. If not found, the packet is not for us and should be rejected.

Many higher-level TCP/IP protocols embed client addressing information in the packets. For example, during an "active" FTP transfer the client informs the server of its IP address & port number, and then waits for the server to open a connection to that address. NAT has to monitor these packets and modify them on the fly to replace the client's IP address (which is on the internal network) with the NAT address. Because this changes the length of the packet, the TCP sequence/acknowledge numbers must be modified as well.

Proxy Servers

A *proxy* is any device that acts on behalf of another. The term is most often used to denote web proxying. A web proxy acts as a "halfway" web server; network clients make requests to the proxy, which then makes requests on their behalf to the appropriate web server. Proxy technology is often seen as an alternative way to provide shared access to a single Internet connection.

The other purpose of proxy servers is to improve performance. This capability is usually called proxy server caching. In simplest terms, the *proxy server* analyzes user requests and determines which, if any, should have the content stored temporarily for immediate access. A typical corporate example would be a company's home page located on a remote server. Many employees may visit this page several times a day. Because this page is requested repeatedly, the proxy server would cache it for immediate delivery to the web browser. Cache management is a big part of many proxy servers, and it is important to consider how easily the cache can be tuned and for whom it provides the most benefit.

Unlike NAT, web proxying is not a transparent operation. It must be explicitly supported by its clients. Because of early adoption of web proxying, most browsers, including Internet Explorer and Netscape Communicator, have built-in support for proxies, but this must normally be configured on each client machine, and can be changed by the naive or malicious user.

A proxy server operates above the TCP level and uses the machine's built-in protocol stack. For each web request from a client, a TCP connection has to be established between the client and the proxy machine, and another between the proxy machine and the remote web server. This puts lot of strain on the proxy server machine; in fact, because web pages are becoming more and more complicated, the proxy itself may become a bottleneck on the network. Contrast this with a NAT, which operates on the packet level and requires much less processing for each connection.

IP Addressing

There are four forms of IP addressing, each with its own unique properties:

- ▶ Unicast
- ▶ Broadcast
- ▶ Multicast
- ▶ Anycast

Unicast

Unicast is the most commonly referred IP address. It refers to a single sender sending to a single receiver. Sending the same data to multiple *unicast* addresses requires the sender to send all the data many times over, once for each recipient.

Broadcast

Sending data to all possible destinations or broadcasting to all possible destinations permits the sender to send the data only once, and all receivers can copy it. In the IPv4 protocol, 255.255.255.255 represents a limited local *broadcast*. In addition, a directed (limited) broadcast can be made by combining the network prefix with a host suffix composed entirely of binary 1s (for example, to broadcast to all hosts within the 192.168.1.0, you would use 192.168.1.255, assuming the netmask is 255.255.255.0).

Multicast

A *multicast* address is associated with a group of interested receivers. According to RFC 3171, addresses 224.0.0.0 to 239.255.255.255 are designated as multicast addresses. This range was formerly called "Class D." The sender sends a single transmission (from the sender's unicast address) to the multicast address, and the routers take care of making copies and sending them to all receivers that have registered their interest in data from that sender.

Anycast

Like broadcast and multicast, *anycast* is a one-to-many routing topology. However, the data stream is not transmitted to all receivers, just the one which the router decides is the "closest" in the network. Anycast is useful for balancing data loads. It is used in DNS and UDP.

IPv6

As the TCP/IP protocol and the Internet become more and more popular, the Internet will eventually run out of network numbers. That has led to the advent of a new IP protocol, currently called *IPv6*.

IPv6 provides a number of benefits for TCP/IP-based networking connectivity, including:

- ▶ **Large address space**: The 128-bit address space for IPv6 potentially provides every device on the Internet with a globally unique address.

- ▶ **Efficient routing**: The IPv6 network packet supports hierarchical routing infrastructures, which enables more efficient routing than IPv4.

▶ **Straightforward configuration**: IPv6 can use both Dynamic Host Configuration Protocol for IPv6 (DHCPv6) and local routers for automatic IP configuration.

▶ **Enhanced security**: The IPv6 standard provides better protection against address and port scanning attacks and all IPv6 implementations support IPSec for protection of IPv6 traffic.

The IPv6 header includes a simplified header format that reduces the processing requirements and includes fields so that the packets can be identified for real-time traffic used in multimedia presentations. Those packets that need to be transported in real time, can be given a higher priority so that they are not delayed too long (Quality of Service). *Quality of Service (QOS)* is technology that gives certain packets guaranteed throughput. It does this by assigning those packets a higher priority on the network so those packets can be delivered in real-time (see Figure 2.3).

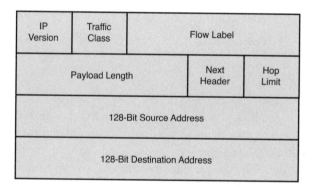

FIGURE 2.3 IPv6 IP header.

In addition, IPv6 introduces the Extension Header, which is described by a value in the IPv6 Next Header Field. Routers can view the Next Header value and then independently and quickly decide whether the Extension Header holds useful information. The Extension Headers carry much of the information that contributed to the large size of the IPv4 Header. This information supports authentication, data integrity, and confidentiality, which should eliminate a significant class of network attacks, including host masquerading attacks.

IPv6 has security built into it. Although it is not bulletproof security, it is enough to resist many of the common crippling problems that plagued IPv4. In IPv4, IPSec was optional; in IPv6, it is mandatory. *IPSec* (IP Security) is a set of protocols to support secure exchange of packets at the IP level. In an IPv6 packet's authentication header are fields specifying IPv6 parameters.

IPv6 Addressing

IPv4 is based on 32-bit-wide addresses which allow a little over 4 billion hosts. IPv6 uses 128 bits for its addresses, which can have up to 3.4×10^{38} hosts, which can handle all of today's IP-based machines without using NAT, to allow for future growth and to handle IP addresses for upcoming mobile devices, such as PDAs and cell phones.

EXAM ALERT

IPv4 uses 32-bit-wide addresses expressed in four octets ranging from 1–255 (decimal numbers). IPv6 uses 128 bits expressed in hexadecimal numbers.

Written IPv6 addresses are usually divided into groups of 16 bits written as four hex digits (one hexadecimal digit is equivalent to 4 bits), and the groups are separated by colons. An example is

FE80:0000:0000:0000:02A0:D2FF:FEA5:E9F5

Leading zeros within a group can be omitted. Therefore, the previous address can be abbreviated as

FE80:0:2A0:D2FF:FEA5:E9F5

You can also drop any single grouping of zero octets (as in the number above) between numbers as long as you replace them with a double colon (::) and they are complete octets. You cannot use the zero compression rule to drop more than one grouping of zero octets. For example, the previous address can be further abbreviated as

FE80::2A0:D2FF:FEA5:E9F5

Because there must always be a certain number of bytes in the address, IPv6 can intelligently determine where the zeros are through this scheme.

Addresses are split in two parts to make them manageable:

▶ The bits identifying the network on which a machine resides.

▶ The bits that identify a machine on a network or subnetwork.

The bits are known as *netbits* and *hostbits*, and in both IPv4 and IPv6, the netbits are the left, or most significant bits of an IP number; and the hostbits are the right, or least significant bits.

In IPv4, the border is drawn with the aid of the netmask, which can be used to mask all net/hostbits. In CIDR routing, the borders between net and hostbits stopped being 8-bit boundaries, and started to use the /x designation, such as /64, to indicate 64 bits as network bits. The same scheme is used in IPv6.

IPv6 addresses can come with prefixes, which replace the "subnet mask" convention from IPv4. Prefixes are shown with a slash:

2180:FC::/48

In this example, the /48 is a routing prefix. A /64 would be a subnet prefix.

Usually though, you would have an address such as

FE80:0000:0000:0000:02A0:D2FF:FEA5:E9F5/64

which reveals that the address used here has the first (left-most) 64 bits used as the network address, and the last (right-most) 64 bits to identify the machine on the network.

As with IPv4, several addresses are reserved for special uses. The IPv6 address ::/0 is the default address for a host (like 0.0.0.0 in IPv4). The address ::1/128 (0:0:0:0:0:0:0:1) is reserved for the local loopback (like 127.0.0.1 in IPv4).

Types of Unicast Addresses

In IPv6, each interface has at least one of the following:

▶ **Global unicast addresses**: Globally accessible, which is used to establish hierarchical boundaries for the operation of routing protocols.

▶ **Link local unicast addresses**: Provides addressing on a single link for the purpose of address auto-configuration, neighbor discovery, and internal routing. Link local unicast addresses are accessible only to other computers that share the link.

EXAM ALERT

If you need to connect the PC to the Internet, you have to have a global unicast address.

Global Unicast Addresses

In global unicast addresses, you take the 128-bit address and divide them into three parts. Providers usually assign /48 networks, which leaves 16 bits for subnetting and 64 hostbits. This means that for your corporation or organization, you can have up to 65,536 subnets and each subnet could have 18,446,744,073,709,551,616 hosts.

The idea behind having fixed-width (64-bit-wide host addresses) identities is so that it simplifies the network designs by having the same number of hostbits no matter which network you are on. In addition, if IPv6 host addresses follow the EUI64 addresses, you will not have to assign individual host addresses to each client because the EUI64 addresses are automatically derived from the MAC address of the network interface card. If the MAC address is

01:23:45:67:89:ab

an FF:FE is inserted in the middle of the MAC to become

01:23:45:ff:fe:67:89:ab

Therefore, the hostbits (64-bits) of the IPv6 address would be

:0123:45ff:fe67:89ab

These hostbits can now be used to automatically assign IPv6 addresses to hosts, which supports autoconfiguration of v6 hosts. All that is needed to get a complete v6 IP number is the net and subnet bits, which can be assigned automatically.

Link Local Unicast Addresses

For link local unicast addresses, the bits are distributed differently and the address uses a special site prefix. In a link local unicast address, a site prefix occupies the first 10 bits of the address rather than the first 48 bits, as is the case with a global unicast address. The site prefix used by a link local unicast address is fe80. In addition, the subnet ID has been extended from 16 bits to 64 bits, but they are not actually used and are therefore expressed as zeros. An example of a link local unicast address would be

fe80:0000:0000:0000:0000:0000:23a1:b152

which would normally be abbreviated as

fe80::23a1:b152

Link local unicast addresses are aimed at being a plug-and-play system, where you connect a host to the network, it is automatically assigned an address, and it is allowed to start communicating on the network with little user interaction. To make this possible, the Neighbor Discovery protocol discovers local nodes, routers, and link-layer addresses and maintains reachability information based on them.

By default, link local addresses are configured automatically for each interface on each IPv6 host or router. To communicate with non-neighboring nodes, a host also must be configured with unicast site-local or global addresses. A host obtains these additional addresses either from router advertisements or by manual assignment. Use commands in the `netsh interface ipv6` context to configure IPv6 addresses manually.

Unlike global addresses, you can reuse local-use addresses. Link local addresses are reused on each link. Site local addresses can be reused within each site of an organization. Of course, you need an additional identifier to specify the link on which an address is assigned or located, or within which site an address is assigned or located. This additional identifier is a zone identifier (ID), also known as a scope ID, which identifies a connected portion of a network that has a specified scope. The syntax specified in RFC 4007 for identifying the zone associated with a local-use address is as follows:

Address%zone_ID

Multicast Addresses

In an IPv6 multicast address, the first 8 bits consist of 1111 1111. When expressed in colon hexadecimal notation, a multicast address always begins with FF. The next 4 bits in a multicast address are known as flag bits. At the present time, the first 3 of these 4 bits are unused (and are therefore set to 0). The fourth flag bit is known as the transient bit. Its job is to express whether the address is a permanent or a temporary address. If the address is permanently assigned, this bit is set to 0; otherwise, it is set to 1 to indicate that the address is transient (temporary).

The next 4 bits in a multicast address are known as the scope ID bits. The amount of space reserved for the scope ID bits is 4 bits in length, which means that there are 16 different possible values. Although not all 16 available values are used at the present time, 7 of these values are used to determine the address' scope. For example, if an address has a global scope, then the address is valid across the entire Internet. The currently used scope ID bits are shown in Table 2.5. The remaining 112 bits make up the group ID. The group ID's size allows multicast addresses to consume 1/256th of the total IPv6 address space.

TABLE 2.5   Scope ID Bits Used in IPv6 Multicast Addresses

Decimal Value	Binary Value	Address Scope
0	0000	Reserved
1	0001	Node-local scope

continues

TABLE 2.5 *Continued*

Decimal Value	Binary Value	Address Scope
2	0010	Link local scope
5	0101	Site local scope
8	1000	Organization local scope
14	1110	Global scope
15	1111	Reserved

For example, to multicast to all nodes (node local scope):

FF01:0:0:0:0:0:1

Migration from IPv4 to IPv6

To aid in the migration from IPv4 to IPv6 and the coexistence of both types of hosts, the following addresses are defined:

▸ **IPv4-compatible address**: 0:0:0:0:0:0:w.x.y.z or ::w.x.y.z (where w.x.y.z is the dotted decimal representation of a public IPv4 address) is used by IPv6/IPv4 nodes that are communicating using IPv6. IPv6/IPv4 nodes support both IPv4 and IPv6 protocols. When an IPv4-compatible address is used as an IPv6 destination, the IPv6 is automatically encapsulated with an IPv5 header and sent to the destination within the IPv4 infrastructure.

▸ **IPv4-mapped address**: The IPv4-mapped IPv6 address has its first 80 bits set to zero, the next 16 set to one and the last 32 bits represents the IPv4 address. For example, ::FFFF:C000:280 is the mapped IPv6 address for 192.0.2.128. Remember, the 192.0.2.128 is written in decimal format, whereas the C000:280 is written in hexadecimal format. Note: The IPv4-mapped IPv6 addresses always identify IPv4-only nodes

▸ **6to4 address**: Used for communicating between two nodes running both IPv4 and IPv6 over an IPv4 routing infrastructure. The 6to4 address is formed by combining the prefix 2002::/16 with the 32 bits of a public IPv4 address of the node, forming a 48-bit prefix.

▸ **ISATAP address**: Used between two nodes running both IPv4 and IPv6 over an IPv4 routing infrastructure. ISATAP addresses use the locally administered interface ID ::0:5EFE:w.x.y.z, where w.x.y.z is any unicast IPv4 adress, which includes both public and private addresses. The ISA-TAP interface ID can be combined with any 64-bit prefix that is valid for IPv6 unicast addresses. This includes the link-local address prefix (FE80::/64), site-local prefixes, and global prefixes.

▶ *Teredo* **address**: Teredo tunneling enables you to tunnel across the IPv4 network when the clients are behind an IPv4 NAT. Teredo was created because many IPv4 routers use NAT to define a private address space for corporate networks. For two Windows-based Teredo clients, the most crucial Teredo processes are those that you use for initial configuration and communication with a different site's peer. Teredo addresses use the prefix 3FFE:831F::/32. Beyond the first 32 bits, Teredo addresses are used to encode the IPv4 address of a Teredo server, flags, and the encoded version of the external address and port of a Teredo client. An example of a Teredo address is 3FFE:831F:CE49:7601:8000:EFFF:62C3:FFFE.

TCP/IP Ports and Sockets

Every time a TCP/IP host communicates with another TCP/IP host, it uses the IP address and port number to identify the host and service/program running on the host. A TCP/IP port number is a logical connection place by client programs to specify a particular server program running on a computer on the network defined at the transport layer. The source port number identifies the application that sends the data, and the destination port number identifies the application that receives the data. Port numbers are from 0 to 65,536. Additionally, there are two types of ports, TCP and UDP, which are based on their respective protocols.

Today, the very existence of ports and their numbers is typically transparent to the users of the network, as many ports are standardized. Thus, a remote computer knows to which port it should connect for a specific service. IANA divides port numbers into three groups:

▶ **Well-known ports**: These are the most commonly used TCP/IP ports. These ports are in the range of 0 through 1,023. These ports can be used only by system processes or privileged programs. Well-known ports are TCP ports, but are usually registered to UDP as well.

▶ **Registered ports**: These are the ports in the range of 1,024 through 49,252. On most systems, user programs use registered ports to create and control logical connections between proprietary programs.

▶ **Dynamic (private) ports**: These are ports in the range of 49,152 through 65,535. These ports are unregistered and can be used dynamically for private connections. In a multi-user system, a program can define a port on the fly if more than one user requires access to the same service at the same time.

For example, when using your browser to view a web page, the default port to indicate the HTTP service is identified as port 80 and the FTP service is identified as port 21. Other application processes are given port numbers dynamically for each connection so that a single computer can run several services. When a packet is delivered and processed, the TCP protocol (connection-based services) or UDP protocol (connectionless-based services) reads the port number and forwards the request to the appropriate program. See Figure 2.4 and Table 2.6.

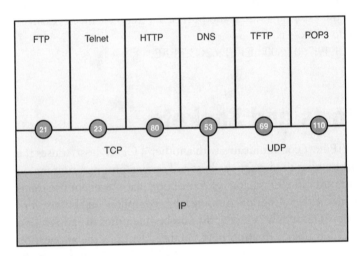

FIGURE 2.4 TCP/IP ports.

Table 2.6   Popular TCP/IP Services and Their Default Assigned Port Numbers

Network Program/Service	Default Assigned Port Number
FTP data transfer	TCP port 20
FTP control	TCP port 21
Telnet	TCP port 23
Simple Mail Transfer Protocol (SMTP)	TCP port 25
Domain Name Server (DNS)	TCP/UDP port 53
HTTP	TCP/UDP port 80
POP3	TCP port 110
Network News Transport Protocol (NNTP)	TCP port 119
NetBIOS Name Service	UDP port 137
NetBIOS Session Service	UDP port 139
Simple Network Management Protocol (SNMP)	UDP port 161

For a complete list of registered well-known port numbers, go to the following website: http://www.ietf.org/rfc/rfc1700.txt?number=1700

EXAM ALERT

For any Microsoft exam, it is always a good idea to know common protocols and the ports they use.

A socket identifies a single network process in terms of the entire Internet. An application creates a socket by specifying three items:

▶ The IP address of the host

▶ The type of service

▶ The port the application is using

NOTE

For Windows, it is the Windows socket (WinSock) that provides the interface between the network program or service and the Windows environment.

By default, when using a web page browser, port 80 is the default port. But if a website is using a different port, you can override that default by specifying the URL followed by a colon and the port number. For example, to specify port 2232, you would use

http://www.acme.com:2232

In addition to using domain names in URLs, you can also use IP addresses. For an IPv4 address, you could enter

http://24.235.10.4

When used in a browser, the browser will assume port 80 since no port was defined. If you want to specify the port, just specify the port number with a colon:

http://24.235.10.4:8080

Because most browsers expect the port number to follow the colon, entering an IPv6 address become a bit more tricky. Therefore, you have to use brackets:

http://[fa01:0f68:0000:0000:0000:0000:1986:69af]/

To specify the port number, add the colon and the port number:

http://[fa01:0f68:0000:0000:0000:0000:1986:69af]:8080/

Configuring IP Addresses in Windows Server 2008

To fully communicate properly on a TCP/IP network, the following needs to be configured on a Windows Server 2008 computer:

▶ IP address and its corresponding subnet mask

▶ Default gateway (nearest router that connects to the other networks or the Internet)

▶ One or more DNS servers to provide name resolution (domain/host-name to IP address)

In addition, depending on your network configuration, you may also need to configure one or more WINS servers that provide a less commonly used name resolution system. The IP address, subnet mask, default gateway, DNS servers, and WINS servers can be configured manually or automatically via a DHCP server. DNS, WINS, and DHCP services are explained more in the next chapter.

IP Configuration Using the GUI Interface

To configure the IP configuration in Windows Server 2008, follow these steps:

1. Open the Control Panel.

2. While in Category view, click Network and Internet, Network and Sharing Center, Manage Network Connection.

3. Right-click the connection that you want to change and click Properties.

4. Under the Networking tab, click either Internet Protocol version 4 (TCP/IPv4) or Internet Protocol version 6 (TCP/IPv6) and then click Properties.

To specify IPv4 IP address settings, you would do one of the following:

▶ To obtain IP settings automatically from a DHCP server, click Obtain an IP Address Automatically and then click OK.

▶ To specify an IP address, click Use the Following IP Address and then type the IP address settings in the IP address, Subnet mask, and Default gateway boxes (see Figure 2.5).

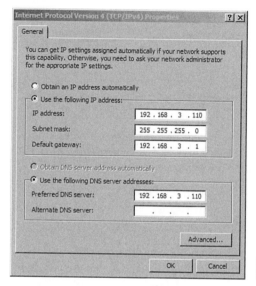

FIGURE 2.5 Configuring IPv4 settings in Windows Server 2008.

To specify IPv6 IP address settings, you would do one of the following:

▶ To obtain IP settings automatically, click Obtain an IPv6 Address Automatically and then click OK (see Figure 2.6).

▶ To specify an IP address, click Use the Following IPv6 Address. Then type the IP address settings in the IPv6 address, Subnet prefix length, and Default gateway boxes.

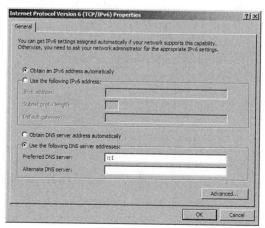

FIGURE 2.6 Configuring IPv6 configuration in Windows Server 2008.

Windows Server 2008 enables you to configure alternate IP address settings to support connecting to different networks. Although static IP addresses can be used with workstations, most workstations use dynamic or alternative IP addressing, or both. To configure dynamic and alternative addressing, follow these steps:

1. Click Start, Network. In Network Explorer, click Network and Sharing Center on the toolbar.

2. In Network and Sharing Center, click Manage Network Connections.

3. In Network Connections, right-click the connection you want to work with and then select Properties.

4. In the Local Area Connection Status dialog box, click Properties. This displays the Local Area Connection Properties dialog box.

5. Double-click Internet Protocol Version 6 (TCP/IPv6) or Internet Protocol Version 4 (TCP/IPv4) as appropriate for the type of IP address you are configuring.

6. Select Obtain an IPv6 Address Automatically or Obtain an IP Address Automatically, as appropriate for the type of IP address you are configuring. If desired, select Obtain DNS Server Address Automatically. Or select Use the Following DNS Server Addresses and then type a preferred and alternate DNS server address in the text boxes provided.

7. When you use dynamic IPv4 addressing with desktop computers, you should configure an automatic alternative address. To use this configuration, on the Alternate Configuration tab, select Automatic Private IP Address. Click OK twice, click Close, and then skip the remaining steps.

8. When you use dynamic IPv4 addressing with mobile computers, you'll usually want to configure the alternative address manually. To use this configuration, on the Alternate Configuration tab, select User Configured. Then in the IP Address text box, type the IP address you want to use. The IP address that you assign to the computer should be a private IP address and it must not be in use anywhere else when the settings are applied.

9. With dynamic IPv4 addressing, complete the alternate configuration by entering a subnet mask, default gateway, DNS, and WINS settings. When you're finished, click OK twice and then click Close.

EXAM ALERT

If you need to assign multiple addresses to the same interface, use the alternate configuration.

To specify DNS server address settings for IPv4 and IPv6:

▶ To obtain a DNS server address automatically, click Obtain DNS Server Address Automatically and then click OK.

▶ To specify a DNS server address, click Use the Following DNS Server Addresses. In the Preferred DNS Server and Alternate DNS Server boxes, type the addresses of the primary and secondary DNS servers.

Using the netsh Command

netsh.exe is a tool an administrator can use to configure and monitor various networking parameters from the command prompt, including the following:

▶ Configuring IP addresses, default gateway, and DNS servers

▶ Configuring interfaces

▶ Configuring routing protocols

▶ Configuring filters

▶ Configuring routes

▶ Configuring remote access behavior for Windows-based remote access routers that are running the Routing and Remote Access Server (RRAS) Service

▶ Displaying the configuration of a currently running router on any computer

▶ Using the scripting feature to run a collection of commands in batch mode against a specified router

Configuring IP configuration is a little bit more complicated because it is done entirely at the command prompt. To view the IP configuration, you can execute the following command:

```
ipconfig /all
```

To view your interfaces, execute the following command:

```
netsh interface ipv4 show interfaces
```

When you view the output of the netsh command, you need to note the name of the interfaces for your network adapter.

To set a static IP address and default gateway, use the following command:

```
netsh interface ipv4 set address name "<interface name>"
➥source=static address=<preferred IP address> mask=<SubnetMask>
➥gateway=<gateway address>
```

If you are configuring IPv6, specify ipv6 instead of ipv4. If the interface name includes spaces, surround the name with quotes (""). If you don't want to assign a gateway, specify gateway=none.

To set the static DNS address, use the following command:

```
netsh interface ipv4 add dnsserver name="<interface name>"
➥address=<IP address of the primary DNS server> index=1
```

For each DNS server that you want to set, increment the index= number each time. Therefore, the first DNS server's index would be 1. For the second DNS server, the index would be 2.

To change a server to the DHCP-provided IP address from a static IP address, use the following command:

```
netsh interface ipv4 set address name="<interface name>" source=DHCP
```

EXAM ALERT

Be sure you know how to use the netsh command to configure a network interface, including to configure the IP address, subnet mask, default gateway, and DNS server.

Troubleshooting IP Addressing

If Windows Network Diagnostics cannot resolve the problem, you should follow a logical troubleshooting process, using tools available in Windows Server 2008. Some of these tools are described in Table 2.7.

TABLE 2.7 IP Troubleshooting Command Descriptions

Command	Description
ipconfig	The `ipconfig` command displays current TCP/IP configuration. ▶ `ipconfig /all` command displays full TCP/IP configuration information. ▶ `ipconfig /release` releases the IPv4 address configured by a DHCP server. ▶ `ipconfig /release6` releases the IPv6 address configured by a DHCP server. ▶ `ipconfig /renew` renews the IPv4 address configured by a DHCP server. ▶ `ipconfig /renew6` renews the IPv6 address configured by a DHCP server. ▶ `ipconfig /flushdns` purges the DNS resolver cache. ▶ `ipconfig /registerdns` refreshes all DHCP leases and re-registers DNS names.
ping	Within the ICMP protocol, the `ping` command verifies connections to a remote computer by verifying configurations and testing IP connectivity.
tracert	The `tracert` command traces the route that a packet takes to a destination and displays the series of IP routers that are used in delivering packets to the destination. If the packets are unable to be delivered to the destination, the `tracert` command displays the last router that successfully forwarded the packet. The `tracert` command also uses the ICMP protocol.
nslookup	The `nslookup` command displays information that you can use to diagnose your DNS infrastructure. You can use `nslookup` to confirm connection to the DNS server and the existence of required records.

A typical troubleshooting process would look like this:

1. Check local IP configuration (`ipconfig`).

2. Use the `ping` command to gather more information on the extent of the problem:

   ▶ Ping the loopback address (127.0.0.1).

   ▶ Ping the local IP address.

   ▶ Ping the remote gateway.

   ▶ Ping the remote computer.

3. Identify each hop (router) between two systems, using the `tracert` command.

4. Verify DNS configuration, using the `nslookup` command.

Using `ipconfig` with the `/all` switch shows you the computer's IP configuration. If the IP address is invalid, communication may fail. If the subnet mask is incorrect, the computer has an incorrect network ID and therefore communication may fail, especially to remote subnets. If the computer can communicate with some hosts on the subnet but not *all*, check the subnet mask. If the default gateway is incorrect or missing, the computer can communicate with hosts within the same subnet but *cannot* communicate with remote subnets. If the DNS server is incorrect or missing, the computer may not be able to resolve names and communication may fail.

> **EXAM ALERT**
>
> Be sure you know the options available with the `ipconfig` command, including how to release and renew DHCP addresses and how to flush the DNS cache.

If the computer is set to accept a DHCP server and one does respond, the computer uses Automatic Private IP addressing, which generates an IP address in the form of 169.254.xxx.xxx and the subnet mask of 255.255.0.0. After the computer generates the address, it broadcasts this address until it can find a DHCP server. When you have an Automatic Private IP address, you can communicate only with computers on the same network/subnet that have an Automatic Private IP address.

> **EXAM ALERT**
>
> If a host is configured to receive a DHCP address and the host is assigned an address that begins with 169.255, the host cannot communicate with the DHCP server to get an address. Make sure the DHCP server is running and configured properly, the DHCP server and host is properly connected to the network and the host has the DHCP client running.

If you can successfully ping the IP address but not the name, name resolution is failing. If you successfully ping the computer name but the response does not resolve the FQDN name, resolution has not used DNS. This means a process such as broadcasts or WINS has been used to resolve the name, and applications that require DNS may fail. If you receive a `Request Timed Out` message, there is a known route to the destination computer but one or more computers or routers along the path, including the source and destination, are not configured correctly. A Destination Host Unreachable message indicates that the system cannot find a route to the destination system and therefore does not know where to send the packet on the next hop.

The ping Command

The ping command sends packets to a host computer and receives a report on their round trip time. For example, you can ping an IP address by typing the following command at a command prompt:

```
ping 127.0.0.1
ping 137.23.34.112
```

The ping command can also ping a host/computer by NetBIOS (computer) name or host/DNS name. Some examples would include the following:

```
ping FS1
ping WWW.MICROSOFT.COM
```

If you can ping a host by address but not by host or computer name, this tells you that the TCP/IP is running fine but the name resolution is not working properly. Therefore, you must check the LMHOSTS file and the WINS server to resolve computer names and HOSTS file and the DNS server to resolve domain names:

```
C:\>ping 132.233.150.4

Pinging 132.233.150.4 with 32 bytes of data:

Reply from 132.233.150.4: bytes=32 time<10ms TTL=128
Reply from 132.233.150.4: bytes=32 time<10ms TTL=128
Reply from 132.233.150.4: bytes=32 time<10ms TTL=128
Reply from 132.233.150.4: bytes=32 time<10ms TTL=128

Ping statistics for 132.233.150.4:
    Packets: Sent = 4, Received = 4, Lost = 0 (0% loss),
Approximate round trip times in milli-seconds:
    Minimum = 0ms, Maximum =  0ms, Average =  0ms
```

If the time takes up to 200 milliseconds, the time is considered very good. If the time is between 200 and 500 milliseconds, the time is considered marginal and can affect performance on some applications, especially those applications that are real-time. Time over 500 milliseconds is unacceptable. Of course, when looking at these numbers, you need to look at bandwidth, distance, and load on the network. Request timed out indicates total failure:

```
C:\>ping 132.233.150.2

Pinging 132.233.150.2 with 32 bytes of data:

Request timed out.
Request timed out.
Request timed out.
Request timed out.

Ping statistics for 132.233.150.2:
    Packets: Sent = 4, Received = 0, Lost = 4 (100% loss),
Approximate round trip times in milli-seconds:
    Minimum = 0ms, Maximum =  0ms, Average =  0ms
```

Viewing the current configuration, pinging the loopback address (ping 127.0.0.1), and pinging the IP address of your computer verifies that the TCP/IP protocol is functioning properly on your PC. By pinging the IP address of the default gateway or router, as well as other local IP computers, you determine whether the computer is communicating on the local network. If it cannot connect to the gateway or any other local computer, you are not connected properly or the IP protocol is misconfigured (IP address, IP subnet mask, or gateway address). If you cannot connect to the gateway but you can connect to other local computers, check your IP address, IP subnet mask, and gateway address. If the IP configuration is correct, then check to see whether the gateway is functioning by using the ping command at the gateway to your computer and other local computers on your network. You should also ping the other network connections on the gateway/router or ping computers on other networks to see the scope of the problem.

If you cannot ping another local computer, but you can ping the gateway, most likely the other computer is having problems and you need to restart this procedure at that computer. If you can ping the gateway, but you cannot ping the computer on another gateway, you need to check the routers and pathways between the two computers by using the ping or tracert commands.

NOTE

Some servers and/or firewalls will be configured to block ICMP packets. Therefore, when you try to ping these computers or use the tracert command on these computers, nothing is returned—although you can contact the server in other ways, such as by using your browser to access a mapped drive. One such example is if you ping Microsoft.com, you get a Request timed out message, yet you can communicate with Microsoft.com by using Internet Explorer and opening up a web page to Microsoft.com.

The `tracert` Command

Another useful command is the `tracert` command (Linux uses the `traceroute` command), which sends out a packet of information to each hop (gateway/router) individually. Therefore, the `tracert` command can help determine where the break is in a network:

```
C:\>tracert www.novell.com

Tracing route to www.novell.com [137.65.2.11]
over a maximum of 30 hops:

  1     97 ms      92 ms     107 ms   tnt3-e1.scrm01.pbi.net [206.171.130.74]
  2     96 ms      98 ms     118 ms   core1-e3-3.scrm01.pbi.net [206.171.130.77]
  3     96 ms      95 ms     120 ms   edge1-fa0-0-0.scrm01.pbi.net [206.13.31.8]
  4     96 ms     102 ms      96 ms   sfra1sr1-5-0.ca.us.ibm.net [165.87.225.10]
  5    105 ms     108 ms     114 ms   f1-0-0.sjc-bb1.cerf.net [134.24.88.55]
  6    107 ms     112 ms     106 ms   atm8-0-155M.sjc-bb3.cerf.net
➥[134.24.29.38]
  7    106 ms     110 ms     120 ms   pos1-1-155M.sfo-bb3.cerf.net
➥[134.24.32.89]
  8    109 ms     108 ms     110 ms   pos3-0-0-155M.sfo-bb1.cerf.net
➥ [134.24.29.202]
  9    122 ms     105 ms     115 ms   atm8-0.sac-bb1.cerf.net [134.24.29.86]
 10    121 ms     120 ms     117 ms   atm3-0.slc-bb1.cerf.net [134.24.29.90]
 11    123 ms     131 ms     130 ms   novell-gw.slc-bb1.cerf.net [134.24.116.54]
 12      *          *          *      Request timed out.
 13    133 ms     139 ms     855 ms   www.novell.com [137.65.2.11]

Trace complete.
```

Table 2.8 lists and describes the different options available with the `tracert` command.

TABLE 2.8 `tracert` Command Options

Command Option	Description
-d	In the event a name resolution method is not available for remote hosts, you can specify the –d option to prohibit the utility from trying to resolve hostnames as it runs. If you don't use this option, `tracert` still functions, but it runs very slow as it tries to resolve these names.
-h	By specifying the –h option, you can specify the maximum number of hops to trace a route to.

continues

TABLE 2.8 *Continued*

Command Option	Description
timeout_value	The *timeout_value* determines the amount of time in milliseconds the program waits for a response before moving on. If you raise this value and the remote devices are responding when they were not responding before, a bandwidth problem may be indicated.
-j	Known as lose source routing, tracert -j <router name> <local computer> allows tracert to follow the specified path to the router and return to your computer.

In addition to ping and tracert, newer versions of Microsoft offer a command called pathping. pathping is a command that combines ping and tracert into one command.

```
C:\>tracert 4.2.2.2

Tracing route to vnsc-bak.sys.gtei.net [4.2.2.2]
over a maximum of 30 hops:

  1    <1 ms    <1 ms     1 ms  192.168.3.1
  2     7 ms     6 ms    16 ms  c-24-10-16-1.hsd1.ca.comcast.net
➥[24.10.16.1]
  3    17 ms    28 ms     6 ms  ge-5-13-ur01.sacramento.ca.sacra.
➥comcast.net [68
.87.212.221]
  4    20 ms     7 ms     6 ms  te-9-4-ar01.sacramento.ca.sacra.
➥comcast.net [68.
87.212.9]
  5    16 ms    10 ms    11 ms  te0-7-0-1-ar01.oakland.ca.sfba.comcast.net
➥[68.8
6.90.142]
  6    21 ms    12 ms    11 ms  pos-0-2-0-0-cr01.sacramento.ca.ibone.
➥comcast.net
 [68.86.90.141]
  7    16 ms    12 ms    26 ms  pos-0-7-0-0-cr01.sacramento.ca.ibone.
➥comcast.net
 [68.86.85.181]
  8    17 ms    18 ms    28 ms  xe-10-3-0.edge1.SanJose1.Level3.net
➥[4.71.118.5]

  9    16 ms    19 ms    29 ms  vlan79.csw2.SanJose1.Level3.net
➥[4.68.18.126]
 10    14 ms    14 ms    13 ms  ge-11-0.core1.SanJose1.Level3.net
➥[4.68.123.38]

 11    16 ms    15 ms    14 ms  vnsc-bak.sys.gtei.net [4.2.2.2]

Trace complete.
```

The `netstat` Utility

The `netstat` command is a great way to see the TCP/IP connections, both inbound and outbound, on your machine. You can also use it to view the packet statistics, such as how many packets have been sent and received and the number of errors. Novell NetWare uses the `MONITOR.NLM` utility.

When `netstat` is used without any options, `netstat` produces output similar to that, which shows all the outbound TCP/IP connections. The `netstat` utility, used without any options, is particularly useful in determining the status of outbound web connections (see Figure 2.7).

> **NOTE**
>
> If you use `-N`, addresses and port numbers are converted to names.

FIGURE 2.7 The `netstat` command without any parameters.

The `netstat -a` command displays all connections, and `netstat -r` displays the routing table plus active connections. The `netstat -e` command displays Ethernet statistics, and `netstat -s` displays per-protocol statistics.

On occasion, you may need to have `netstat` occur every few seconds. Try placing a number after the `netstat -e` command, like so:

```
netstat -e 15
```

The command executes, waits the number of seconds specified by the number (in this example, 15), and then repeats until you press the Ctrl+C command.

Exam Prep Questions

1. What command would you use to renew the DHCP IPv4 addresses?

   ○ **A.** `ipconfig`

   ○ **B.** `ipconfig /renew`

   ○ **C.** `ipconfig /renew6`

   ○ **D.** `ipconfig /release_and_renew`

   ○ **E.** `ipconfig /registerdns`

2. What command would you use to flush the DNS cache stored on an individual Windows Vista machine?

   ○ **A.** `ipconfig`

   ○ **B.** `ipconfig /renew`

   ○ **C.** `ipconfig /renew6`

   ○ **D.** `ipconfig /registerdns`

   ○ **E.** `ipconfig /flushdns`

3. What command can be used to show network connectivity to a Windows computer?

   ○ **A.** `ipconfig`

   ○ **B.** `arp`

   ○ **C.** `ping`

   ○ **D.** `traceroute`

4. If you want to show IP addresses and their corresponding MAC addresses, what command would you use?

   ○ **A.** `ipconfig`

   ○ **B.** `ipconfig /all`

   ○ **C.** `arp`

   ○ **D.** `ping`

   ○ **E.** `tracert`

5. You work as the desktop support technician at Acme.com. You want to assign an address to a computer that will be available on the Internet, and it will have the same address for both IPv4 and IPv6. What kind of address is this?

   ○ **A.** A unique private address.

   ○ **B.** A multicast local address.

   ○ **C.** A site local address.

   ○ **D.** A global unicast address.

6. You work as the desktop support technician at Acme.com. You have a user that works between the Sacramento and New York offices. She currently has a static IP addresses assigned to her computer. When she is at the Sacramento office, her system has no problem connecting to the network. When travels to New York, her system cannot connect to the network. What is the problem?

   ○ **A.** You need to update the drivers for the network card.

   ○ **B.** You need to assign a public IPv4 address.

   ○ **C.** You need to run the troubleshooting wizard.

   ○ **D.** Within the TCP/IPv4 Properties dialog box, you need to select the Obtain an IP Address Automatically option.

7. You have a computer with Windows Server 2008 Server Core installed. You need to configure the server to point to 172.24.1.10 as the preferred DNS server. What should you do?

   ○ **A.** Open the Network and Sharing Center. Click Manage Network Connections. Double-click the network card and open the TCP/IP properties. Change the DNS to point to 172.24.1.10.

   ○ **B.** Execute the `netsh interface ipv4 add dnsserver "LAN" static 172.24.1.10 index=1` command.

   ○ **C.** Execute the `ipconfig /dnsserver:172.24.1.10 index=1` command.

   ○ **D.** Execute the `netsh interface ipv4 set address name "LAN" source=static address=172.24.1.10` command.

8. You have a computer with Windows Server 2008 Server Core installed. You need to configure the Local Area Connection interface to the IPv4 address 172.24.1.10 and a subnet mask of 255.255.255.0. In addition, you need to assign the default gateway of 172.24.1.1. What should you do?

   ○ A. Open the Network and Sharing Center. Click Manage Network Connections. Double-click the network card and open the TCP/IP properties. Change the DNS to point 172.24.1.10.

   ○ B. Execute the `netsh interface ipv4 Name="Local Area Connection" add 172.24.1.1 255.255.255.0 gate-way=172.24.1.1` command.

   ○ C. Execute the `ipconfig /dnsserver:172.24.1.10 index=1` command.

   ○ D. Execute the `netsh interface ipv4 set address name="Local Area Connection" source=static address=172.24.1.10 mask=255.255.255.0 gate-way=172.24.1.1` command.

9. Which of the following is not a private network range?

   ○ A. 10.24.5.2

   ○ B. 172.16.230.6

   ○ C. 192.168.130.130

   ○ D. 127.0.0.1

10. You have a Windows Vista computer that cannot connect to the network. When you use the `ipconfig` command, you find the following:

    IP address: 169.254.30.25

    Subnet mask: 255.255.0.0

    So what is the problem?

   ○ A. The 169.254.30.25 address is the incorrect assigned address.

   ○ B. The 255.255.0.0 mask should be 255.255.255.0.

   ○ C. The TCP/IP needs to be bound to the network interface.

   ○ D. The computer could not get an address from the DHCP server.

11. The Acme Corporation has been assigned the network ID 134.114.0.0. The corporation's eight departments require one subnet each. However, each department may grow to over 2,500 hosts. Which subnet mask should you apply?

○ **A.** 255.255.192.0

○ **B.** 255.255.240.0

○ **C.** 255.255.224.0

○ **D.** 255.255.248.0

12. You have successfully obtained a Class C subnet for your company. What is the default subnet mask?

○ **A.** 255.0.0.0

○ **B.** 255.255.0.0

○ **C.** 255.255.240.0

○ **D.** 255.255.255.0

13. How are the network ID and the host ID for an IP address determined?

○ **A.** Subnet mask

○ **B.** Range mask

○ **C.** Unicast mask

○ **D.** Multicast mask

14. IPv6 uses how many bits in its addressing scheme?

○ **A.** 26

○ **B.** 32

○ **C.** 64

○ **D.** 128

○ **E.** 256

15. If you have an IPv4 address of 20.34.120.5/24. What is the subnet mask?

○ **A.** 255.0.0.0

○ **B.** 255.255.0.0

○ **C.** 255.255.255.0

○ **D.** 255.255.255.240

16. Which of the following ports (by default) would be used by a web server? (Choose two answers.)

    ○ **A.** 80

    ○ **B.** 161

    ○ **C.** 137

    ○ **D.** 443

17. Your company is restructuring the network and creating 20 subnets, using a Class A IP address. It plans to add an additional 8 subnets within the next year. Which of the following subnet masks should you use?

    ○ **A.** 255.192.0.0

    ○ **B.** 255.224.0.0

    ○ **C.** 255.240.0.0

    ○ **D.** 255.248.0.0

Answers to Exam Prep Questions

1. Answer B is correct. To renew IPv4, you have to use the `ipconfig /renew` command. Answer A is incorrect because the `ipconfig` command without any options only displays basic IP configuration information. Answer C is incorrect because the `/renew6` option renewa IPv6 IP addresses. Answer D is incorrect because the `/release_and_renew` option does not exist. Answer E is incorrect because the `/registerdns` option is used to get the computer to register itself with the DNS server.

2. Answer E is correct. The way to flush local cached DNS information is to use the `ipconfig /flushdns` command. Answer A is incorrect because the `ipconfig` command without any options only displays basic IP configuration information. Answer B is incorrect because the `/renew` option renews the IPv4 IP addresses. Answer C is incorrect because the `/renew6` option renews IPv6 IP addresses. Answer D is incorrect because the `/registerdns` option is used to get the computer to register itself with the DNS server.

3. Answer C is correct. The two commands that show network connectivity to another computer are the `ping` command the `tracert` command. Answer A is incorrect because the `ipconfig` command without any options only displays basic IP configuration information. Answer B is incorrect because the `arp` command is used to view and manage IP address–to–MAC address mappings. Answer D is incorrect because the `traceroute` command would be found on UNIX and Linux machines. Windows machines use `tracert`.

4. Answer B is correct. To show all IP configuration information, you must use the `ipconfig /all` command. Answer A is incorrect because the `ipconfig` command without any options only displays basic IP configuration information. Answer C is incorrect because the `arp` command is used to view and manage IP address–to–MAC address mappings. Answers D and E are incorrect because `ping` and `tracert` are commands used to test network connectivity.

5. Answer D is correct. If you want an address to be available from the Internet and be the same address for both IPv4 and IPv6, it must be a global address that can be seen on the Internet. Answer A is incorrect because private addresses cannot be used on the public network, such as the Internet. Answer B is incorrect because it has to be a single address assigned to a single computer, not a multicast that is used to broadcast to multiple addresses at the same time. Answer C is incorrect because a local address cannot be seen on the outside.

6. Answer D is correct. Because this person travels between two sites, the user needs to have a local address on each site. Therefore, you should let the local DHCP server hand out the addresses when she connects to each network. It should be noted that you could use DHCP reservations so that the computer always gets the same IP address when connected to the individual's local IP address. DHCP reservations are discussed in Chapter 4. Answer A is incorrect because she can connect to one network. Therefore, the driver is working fine. Answer B is incorrect because assigning a public IPv4 address means that you are putting this computer directly on the Internet. Answer C is incorrect because running a troubleshooting wizard could be a lengthy process when the solution is simple.

7. Answer B is correct. You need to use the `netsh interface ipv4 add dnsserver` command. Because it specifies the preferred DNS server, you specify `index=1`. Answer A is incorrect because the Network and Sharing Center is not available on a Server Core. Answer C is incorrect because the `ipconfig.exe` command cannot be used to configure static addresses. Answer D is incorrect because the `netsh` command needs to use the `add dnsserver` option.

9. Answer D is correct. The 127.0.0.1 is the local host address. Answers A, B, and C are incorrect because they are within the private address ranges (10.x.x.x, 172.16.x.x to 172.31.x.x, and 192.168.0.x to 192.168.255.x).

10. Answer D is correct. If the computer is set to accept a DHCP server and one does respond, the computer uses Automatic Private IP addressing, which generates an IP address in the form of 169.254.xxx.xxx and the subnet mask of 255.255.0.0. Answers A and B are incorrect because the 169.255.30.25 is an address generated by Automatic Private IP addressing. Answer C is incorrect because TCP/IP is bound to the card because you would not be assigned an IP address.

11. Answer B is correct. The default subnet mask is 255.255.0.0. To accommodate eight subnets, you need to use 4 bits ($2^4-2=14$ subnets). That leaves 12 bits left, which can accommodate $2^{12}-2=4094$ hosts. Answer A is incorrect because the 192 means only 1 bit is used by subnets, which will not accommodate eight subnets. Answer C is

incorrect because the 224 means only 3 bits are used by subnets ($2^3-2=6$), which will not accommodate eight subnets. Answer D is incorrect because the 248 means that 11 bits are used for the host addresses, which means it would only accommodate $2^{11}-2=2046$ hosts.

12. Answer D is correct. The default subnet mask for Class C is 255.255.255.0. Answer A is incorrect because the 255.0.0.0 is the default subnet mask for a Class A network. Answer B is incorrect because the 255.255.0.0 is the default subnet mask for a Class B network. Answer C is incorrect because the 255.255.240.0 is not a default subnet mask for any network.

13. Answer A is correct. The subnet mask defines which bits are the network ID bits and which bits are the host ID bits. Answer B is incorrect because in TCP/IP, there is no range mask. Answers C and D are incorrect because there are no such things as uni-cast masks and multicast masks. The closest would be unicast addresses and multi-cast addresses.

14. Answer D is correct. The IPv6 address uses 128 bits for the addresses expressed in hexadecimal format. Answers A, C, and E are incorrect because none of these define the number of bits used by an address. Answer B is incorrect because 32 bits defines the number of bits for a IPv4 address.

15. Answer C is correct. The CIDR notation of /24 means 24 bits are used for the network bits, which translates to a 255.255.255.0 subnet mask. Answer A is incorrect because the CIDR notation for 255.0.0.0 is /8. Answer B is incorrect because the CIDR notation for 255.255.0.0 is /16. Answer D is incorrect because the CIDR notation for 255.255.255.240 is /28.

16. Answers A and D are correct. Port 80 is used for HTTP and port 443 is used for HTTPS. Answer B is incorrect because port 161 is used by SNMP. Answer C is incorrect because port 137 is used by the NetBIOS Name Service.

17. Answer D is correct. You should use the subnet mask of 255.248.0.0. This subnet mask will allow for a maximum of 30 subnets, which meets the company's new addressing requirements. Answers A, B, and C are incorrect. You should not select a subnet mask of 255.192.0.0 because it allows for only 2 subnets. However, the new infrastructure requires a maximum of 28. You should not select 255.224.0.0 because this subnet mask allows for a maximum of only 6 subnets, which does not meet the requirements. You should not select 255.240.0.0 because this subnet mask allows for a maximum of only 14 subnets, which does not meet the requirements.

Need to Know More?

For a thorough treatment of IP addressing, read the 3Com, "Understanding IP Addressing: Everything You Ever Wanted to Know" white paper located at

▸ http://www.3com.com/other/pdfs/infra/corpinfo/en_US/501302.pdf.

To find more information about the configuring Server Core, open the Server Core Installation Option of Windows Server 2008 Step-By-Step Guide, which can be found at

▸ http://technet2.microsoft.com/windowsserver2008/en/library/47a23a74-
  e13c-46de-8d30-ad0afb1eaffc1033.mspx?mfr=true

For more information about the `netsh` command, download the Windows Server 2008 Network Shell (Netsh) Technical Reference from the following website:

▸ http://www.microsoft.com/downloads/details.aspx?familyid=f41878de-
  2ee7-4718-8499-2ef336db3df5&displaylang=en

Patrick Regan. *Networking with Windows 2000 and 2003*. Upper Saddle River, New Jersey: Prentice Hall, 2004.

Patrick Regan. *Wide Area Networks*. Upper Saddle River, New Jersey: Prentice Hall, 2004.

CHAPTER THREE

Name Resolution

Terms you'll need to understand:

- ✓ Fully Qualified Domain Name (FQDN)
- ✓ HOSTS files
- ✓ Domain Name System (DNS)
- ✓ LMHOSTS file
- ✓ DNS zone
- ✓ Primary zone
- ✓ Secondary zone
- ✓ Active Directory integrated zone
- ✓ Stub zone
- ✓ Caching-only server
- ✓ Zone file
- ✓ Resource record (RR)
- ✓ DNS Manager

- ✓ Root hints
- ✓ Forwarder
- ✓ Round-robin
- ✓ Link-local multicast name resolution (LLMNR)
- ✓ Dynamic DNS
- ✓ Secured dynamic updates
- ✓ Zone transfers
- ✓ Universal name convention (UNC)
- ✓ Windows Internet Name Service (WINS)
- ✓ WINS proxy agent
- ✓ GlobalNames zone

Techniques/concepts you'll need to master:

- ✓ Install and configure DNS.
- ✓ Install and configure WINS.
- ✓ Create a DNS zone.
- ✓ Add and configure resource records.
- ✓ Create and configure a GlobalNames zone.
- ✓ Use common troubleshooting tools to troubleshoot name resolution problems.

Most users will find IPv4 and IPv6 addresses difficult to remember when communicating with other computers. That's why a user specifies a recognizable name and the name is translated into an address. For example, when a user opens Internet Explorer and specifies http://www.microsoft.com, the www.microsoft.com is translated into an IP address. The web page is then accessed from the server via the translated IP addresses.

Fully Qualified Domain Names (FQDNs), sometimes referred to as just *domain names*, are used to identify computers on a TCP/IP network. Examples would include

www.microsoft.com

www.intel.com

server1.acme.com

Early name resolution used to be done with *HOSTS files*, which would list hostnames and their IP address (IPv4 only). Unfortunately, every time you wanted to add a new hostname, you would have to modify the HOSTS file on every computer.

The most common way to translate the FQDN or hostname to the IP address is to use a *Domain Name System* (DNS) server. DNS is a distributed database (the database is contained in multiple servers) containing hostname and IP address information for all domains on the Internet. For every domain, there is a single authoritative name server that contains all DNS-related information about the domain. When you configure IP configuration, you need to specify the address of a DNS server so that you use the Internet or log in to a Windows Active Directory domain.

Another naming scheme on TCP/IP networks involves using the NetBIOS names (such as that used to identify share names for file and printers via the Universal Naming Convention or UNC, *computername**sharename*). To translate NetBIOS names to IP addresses, you use a WINS server or the LMHOSTS files.

> **NOTE**
>
> On Windows machines, the HOSTS and LMHOSTS files are located in the
> C:\Windows\System32\drivers\etc folder.

If you try to access a network resource by name instead of IP address and the device cannot be found, the problem is most likely with the DNS server/HOSTS file or the WINS server/LMHOSTS file. Either the servers cannot be contacted, or the servers or files have the wrong address associated with the name. The failure of these servers or files can also affect network applications that need to access various services or resources.

Domain Name System

Domain Name System (DNS) is a hierarchical client/server-based distributed database management system that translates Internet domain names such as microsoft.com to an IP address. As mentioned in previous chapters, it is used because domain names are easier to remember than IP addresses. The DNS clients are called resolvers and the DNS servers are called name servers.

The DNS system can be thought of as its own little network. If one DNS server doesn't know how to translate a particular domain name, the DNS server can be configured to ask another DNS server, and so on, until the correct IP address is returned. DNS is most commonly associated with the Internet, but private networks can also use DNS to resolve computer names and to locate computers within their local networks without being connected to the Internet.

The most popular implementation of the DNS protocol is the Berkeley Internet Name Domain (BIND), which was developed for the UC Berkeley's BSD UNIX operating system. The primary specifications for DNS are defined in Requests for Comments (RFC) 1034 and 1035. DNS uses either UDP port 53 or TCP port 53 as the underlying protocol.

Domain Name Space

The DNS name space describes the hierarchical structure of the DNS database as an inverted logical tree structure. Each node on the tree is a partition of the name space called a domain. Domains can be further partitioned at node points within the domain into subdomains. The names of the domain and subdomains can be up to 63 characters long.

The top of the tree is known as the root domain. It is sometimes shown as a period (.) or as empty quotation marks (""), indicating a null value. Immediately below the root domain, you can find the top-level domains. The top-level domains indicate a country, region, or type of organization. Three-letter codes indicate the type of organization. For example, com indicates Commercial (business) and edu stands for educational institution. They are listed in Table 3.1.

TABLE 3.1 Top-Level Domain Codes Indicating the Type of Organization

Traditional Top-Level Domains		New Top-Level Domains	
Code	**Meaning**	**Code**	**Meaning**
com	Commercial	Aero	Airline-related services
edu	Educational	Biz	Businesses
gov	Government	Coop	Cooperatives
int	International organization	Info	Websites providing information
mil	Military	Museum	Museums
net	Network related	Name	Personal websites and email addresses
org	Miscellaneous organization	Pro	Professionals, such as doctors and lawyers

Two-letter codes indicate countries, which follow the International Standard 3166. For example, CA stands for Canada, AU for Australia, FR for France, and UK for United Kingdom. For a list of two-letter codes, go to http://www.iso.org /iso/iso-3166-1_decoding_table.

The second-level domain names are variable-length names registered to an individual or organization for use on the Internet. These names are almost always based on the appropriate top-level domain, depending on the type of organization or geographic location where a name is used. Some examples are shown in Table 3.2.

TABLE 3.2 Second-Level Domain Names

Domain Name	Second-Level Domain Name
microsoft.com	Microsoft Corporation
cisco.com	Cisco Corporation
mti.edu	MTI University
ed.gov	United States Department of Education
army.mil	United States Army
w3.org	World Wide Web Consortium
nato.int	North Atlantic Treaty Organization
pm.gov.au	Prime Minister of Australia

The second-level domain names must be registered by the authorized party. For example, for years, Network Solutions, Inc. (www.networksolutions.com/) ran a government-sanctioned monopoly on registrations for .com, .net and .org domain names. But as the U.S. government handed the control of the Internet to an international body, several companies, including Network Solutions, Inc., now handle the registration of these three-letter codes. Note: Because most of the common top-level domains names are already taken, some countries such as Tonga (TO) and Tuvalu (TV) are selling their domain names. Therefore, some commercial and user sites may be using one of these two letter codes. This is especially true with the TV domain name because it is easily linked to television.

Subdomain names are additional names that an organization can create that are derived from the registered second-level domain name. The subdomain allows an organization to divide a domain into a department or geographical location, allowing the partitions of the domain name space to be more manageable. A subdomain must have a contiguous domain name space. This means that the domain name of a zone (child domain) is the name of that zone added to the name of the domain or parent domain. See Figure 3.1.

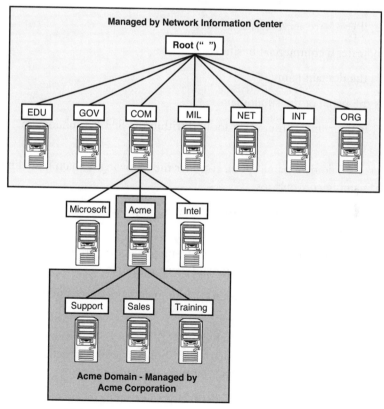

FIGURE 3.1 DNS name space.

A hostname is a name assigned to a specific computer within a domain or subdomain by an administrator to identify the TCP/IP host. Multiple hostnames can be associated with the same IP address, although only one hostname can be assigned to a computer using the Windows Control Panel/Network applet. If the DNS is seen as a tree, the host represents the leaf or object of the tree. Much like a subdomain, the hostname is the leftmost label of the DNS domain name. The hostname can then be used in place of an IP address, such as when using the ping command or other TCP/IP utilities. The total length of an FQDN cannot exceed 255 characters. Note: The hostname does not have to be the same as the NetBIOS (computer) name. By default, TCP/IP setup uses the NetBIOS name for the hostname, replacing illegal characters, such as the underscore, with a hyphen (-).

FQDN describes the exact position of a host (computer) within the domain hierarchy and it is considered to be complete. When used in a DNS domain name, it is stated by a trailing period (.) to designate that the name of the host is located off the root or highest level of the domain hierarchy.

For example, if you have server1.sales.acme.com,

- com indicates a commercial business.

- acme is the domain name.

- sales is the name of the subdomain.

- server1 is the name of the server located within the SALES subdomain.

When you create a domain name space, consider the following domain guidelines and standard naming conventions:

- To minimize the level of administrative tasks, limit the number of domain levels.

- If possible, each subdomain should have a unique name throughout the entire domain to ensure the subdomain name is unique.

- Use simple yet meaningful names so that domain names are easy to remember and navigate.

- Use standard DNS characters, including A-Z, a-z, 0-9, the hyphen, and Unicode characters, which include the additional characters needed for foreign languages, such as French, German, and Spanish.

- The names of the domain and subdomains can be up to 63 characters long.

- Total length of an FQDN cannot exceed 255 characters.

DNS Zones

A *DNS zone* is a portion of the DNS namespace whose database records exist and are managed in a particular DNS database file. Each zone is based on a specific domain node, which is also referred to as the zone's root domain. It is the authority source for that node. *Zone files* do not necessarily contain the complete DNS branch because subdomains may be their own zones. Note: If subdomains are added below the domain, the subdomains can be part of the same zone or belong to another zone.

The computer that maintains the master list for a zone is the primary name server for that zone and is considered the authority for that zone. A DNS server might be configured to manage one or more zones.

With Windows Server 2008, you can configure four types of zones. They are the standard *primary zone*, the standard *secondary zone*, the *Active Directory integrated zone*, and the *stub zone* (see Table 3.3).

TABLE 3.3 Zone Types

Zone Type	Description
Standard primary	The master copy of a new zone.
Standard secondary	A replica of an existing zone. Standard secondary zones are read only.
Active Directory integrated	A zone that is stored in Active Directory. Updates of the zone are performed during Active Directory replication.
Stub	A copy of a zone containing only those resource records necessary to identify the authoritative DNS servers for the master zone.

Primary and Secondary Zones

The primary name server is a name server that stores and maintains the zone file locally. Changes to a zone, such as adding domains or hosts, are made by changing files at the primary name server. A secondary name server gets the data from its zone from another name server, either a primary name server or another secondary name server, for that zone across the network. The process of obtaining this zone information across the network is referred to as a *zone transfer*. Zone transfers occur over TCP port 53. The Active Directory integrated zone is found only in Windows 2000 and above and has the zone defined within the Active Directory, not the zone files.

EXAM ALERT

The Windows Firewall is enabled by default in Windows Server 2008. For DNS to function, you need to configure the firewall to allow communication over TCP port 53.

The source of the zone information for a secondary name server is referred to as a master name server. A master name server can be either a primary or secondary name server for the requested zone. Because a secondary zone is merely a copy of a primary zone that is hosted on another server, it cannot be stored in AD DS.

There are three reasons to have a secondary name server. The first reason is for fault tolerance. You should have at least two DNS name servers serving each zone. In each client's configuration, both name servers would be listed. If the first server listed can't be contacted, the client then contacts the second name server. The second reason is to divide the load between different name servers to increase performance for name resolution. Last, the DNS servers can be used to service computers that are located in remote locations so that they do not have to use a slow WAN link.

Caching-Only Server

All DNS servers maintain a cache.dns file that contains a list of all Internet root servers. Any time a DNS server resolves a hostname to an IP address, the information is added to the cache file. The next time a DNS client needs to resolve that hostname, the information can be retrieved from the cache instead of the Internet.

Caching-only servers do not contain any zone information, which is the main difference between them and primary and secondary DNS servers. The main purpose of a caching-only server (other than providing name resolution) is to build the cache file as names are resolved. They resolve hostnames, cache the information, and return the results to the client. Because these servers hold no zone information, either hostnames are resolved from the cache or else another DNS server is required to resolve them.

Caching-only servers are useful when you need to reduce network traffic. Again, because there is no zone information, no zone transfer traffic is generated (meaning that no information is replicated between DNS servers). Hostname traffic is also reduced as the cache file is built up because names can be resolved locally using the contents of the local DNS server's cache.

EXAM ALERT

It's important to understand when caching-only servers should be implemented. Caching-only servers are useful when remote locations have slow WAN links. Configuring a caching-only server in these locations can reduce WAN traffic that would normally be generated between primary and secondary DNS servers, and can speed up hostname resolution after the cache file has been established. You should also note that the cache is flushed when the server is rebooted. So it takes a little longer to resolve addresses until the cache is rebuilt.

Active Directory Integrated Zones

Active Directory is a directory service that stores all information about the network resources and services such as user data, printers, servers, databases, groups, computers, and security policies. In addition, it identifies all resources on a network and makes them accessible to users and applications. Rather than maintaining two separate naming services (Active Directory and a DNS-based namespace), Active Directory integrated zones have the zone data stored as an Active Directory object and are replicated as part of domain replication. Of course, because Active Directory integrated zones are stored in the Active Directory, there is no zone database file on a primary server. When you store a zone in Active Directory, the zone database file is copied into the Active Directory and deleted on the primary server for the zone. One advantage of using the Active Directory integrated zone is that you can have more than one DNS server update a DNS zone.

EXAM ALERT

Active Directory integrated zones can be created only on servers that are configured as domain controllers and configured to run the DNS dynamic update protocol. In addition, if you want to use Active Directory, you must have a DNS server, not necessarily an Active Directory integrated zone.

Using Active Directory for storage and replication provides the following benefits:

- ▶ Increased fault tolerance
- ▶ Easier management
- ▶ Minimal traffic for zone replication
- ▶ Security

With primary and secondary servers, clients can be registered only at the primary server. With Active Directory DNS Servers, clients can register themselves dynamically on any of the servers. If you have several domain controllers with AD integrated zones, each of these domain controllers holds a writeable copy of the zone database. When the database on one DNS server gets modified, it is replicated to the other DNS servers, which eliminates a single point of failure because these zones automatically replicate to the other zones.

Dynamic DNS enables computers to register themselves automatically with the DNS server. Thus, management is easier because you do not have to input all the addresses for your clients.

To minimize zone replication traffic, AD integrated zones replicate on a per-property basis; they propagate only relevant changes, which is more efficient then full-zone transfers. Compression is also used.

Active Directory integrated zones enable you to implement secure dynamic updates. The DNS server accepts record registration only from clients with accounts in Active Directory, so an unknown computer cannot register with the DNS server. In addition, replications between standard and secondary DNS zones are unencrypted. When you create an AD integrated zone, DNS zone transfers are included in Active Directory replication, which has secure channels because of encryption.

Stub Zone

A stub zone lists information about the authoritative name servers of a zone so that the DNS server knows directly which server is the authority for a particular zone. It can then perform recursive queries using the stub zone's list of name servers without having to query the Internet or an internal root server for the DNS namespace. Stub zones contain the Start of Authority (SOA) *resource records* of the zone—the DNS resource records that list the zone's authoritative servers, and the glue A (address) resource records that are required for contacting the zone's authoritative servers.

By using stub zones throughout your DNS infrastructure, you can distribute a list of the authoritative DNS servers for a zone without using secondary zones. However, stub zones do not serve the same purpose as secondary zones, and they are not an alternative for enhancing redundancy and load sharing.

Zone Files and Resource Records

A zone file is a file that defines a zonekept on a DNS name server. Although editing these text files is the way to configure most DNS systems, such as UNIX, Microsoft DNS uses a user-friendly interface (*DNS Manager* console).

The zone database files are traditionally maintained on computers that are running the DNS Server service. Remember, in Windows, a zone can be stored in the Active Directory rather than in a zone database file.

The primary file, known as the zone database file (*%systemroot%*\SYSTEM32\DNS*domain_name*.DNS), contains the resource records (RR) for that part of the domain for which the zone is responsible. There are various resource record types that are defined for the DNS database. Table 3.4 lists some of the more common types of resource records.

EXAM ALERT

Be sure you know the various resource records for the exam.

TABLE 3.4   Common Resource Record Types

Resource Record	Purpose
SOA (Start of Authority)	Identifies the name server that is the authoritative source of information for data within a domain. An SOA record is created automatically when you create a new zone. A primary server for a given zone lists itself in the SOA record to show that it's the source for this zone. The first record in the zone database file must be the SOA Record.
NS (Name Server)	Provides a list of name servers (DNS servers) that are assigned to a domain.
A (Host Address)	Provides a hostname to an IPv4 (Internet Protocol version 4) 32-bit address.
AAA (Host Address)	Provides a hostname to an IPv6 (Internet Protocol version 6) 128-bit address.
PTR (Pointer)	Resolves an IP address to a hostname (reverse mappings).
CNAME (Canonical Name)—Alias	Creates an alias or alternate DNS domain name for a specified hostname. The most common or popular use of an alias is to provide a permanent DNS aliased domain name, for generic name resolution of a server-based name, such as www.acme.com and ftp.acme.com, to more than one computer or IP address used in a web server. This way, you can assign acme.com to one server, www.acme.com to a second server, and ftp.acme.com to a third server. If you do use the same server for all three entries and you decide to split the service to a separate service, you just have to change the CNAME resource record to point to the new server.

continues

TABLE 3.4 *Continued*

Resource Record	Purpose
SRV (Service)	Maps mapping a DNS domain name to a specified list of DNS host computers that offer a specific type of service, such as Active Directory domain controllers.
MX (Mail Exchanger)	Identifies which mail exchanger to contact for a specified domain and in what order to use each mail host.

The Start of Authority (SOA) record indicates the starting point or original point of authority for information stored in a zone. The value of the refresh interval in the SOA record, which has a default value of 15 minutes, decides how often the destination server should request to renew the zone. Increasing the value causes fewer zone transfers; however, the danger of increasing the refresh interval is inconsistencies in the network. Configuring the Notify List on the external DNS server to notify the secondary server forces changes to be transferred and thus avoids inconsistencies (see Figure 3.2). The retry interval determines how often other DNS servers that load and host the zone are to retry a request for update of the zones each time the refresh interval occurs.

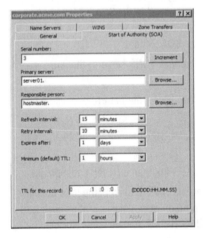

FIGURE 3.2 The SOA record in the DNS Manager Console.

The two most common record types are host (A) records and pointer (PTR) records. Host records are used to resolve hostnames to IP addresses, whereas pointer records are used to resolve IP addresses to hostnames.

When a Windows client needs to find a domain controller (for example, to log on to the domain), the client queries the DNS server to access the service (SRV) resource records to locate the logon server for accessing domain controller names. If you have a UNIX/Linux DNS server, the DNS must use BIND 8.2 or later to support SRV resource records and dynamic DNS (DDNS).

Name Resolution Process

When a client computer needs an IP address, the client computer sends a name query to the DNS client service (resolver) located on the client. The DNS client service then checks the locally cached information and local HOSTS file (if present). When previous queries are cached, the data is kept for a preset time period known as the *Time To Live (TTL)*. If the query does not match an entry in the cache, the resolution process continues with the client querying a DNS server to resolve the name.

Recursive and Iterative Queries

When the resolver queries a DNS server, it performs a recursive query. A recursive query asks the DNS server to respond with the requested data or with an error stating that the requested data doesn't exist or that the domain name specified doesn't exist. Note: The name server does not refer the query to another name server unless it is configured as a *forwarder*, in which it forwards the DNS request as a recursive query.

When the DNS server receives a request, it checks to see whether the hostname is located in its own zone database file, in which it is an authority. If it is not listed in the zone file, it then checks the cache area. From then on, the DNS server uses iterative queries to resolve the name. An iterative query gives the best answer it currently has back as a response. The best answer will be the address being sought or an address of a server that would have a better idea of its address.

A program needs to find the address of server.support.acme.com. The program sends the request to the resolver. The resolver looks in its cache area and its HOSTS file. If the address has not been found, the resolver forwards the query to its preferred DNS name server.

The DNS server checks to see whether it knows the address of server.support.acme.com. If it doesn't know it, the DNS server then asks the root server whether it knows the address of server.support.acme.com. Because it does not know the address of server.support.acme.com, it responds with the best answer by providing the address of the com root server. The DNS server then asks the com root server for the address of server.support.acme.com. The com root server responds back with its known best answer of the acme.com name server address. The DNS server queries theacme.com name server for the address of server.support.acme.com. The DNS server then responds back to the resolver with the address of support.acme.com. The DNS server queries the support.acme.com name server for the address of server.support.acme.com and responds back with the address.

The preferred server then responds back to the client with the correct address. The program then uses the IP address to communicate its needs.

As you can see by this example, the resolver queried its DNS server with a recursive query, whereas the DNS server queried other DNS servers with iterative queries (see Figure 3.3).

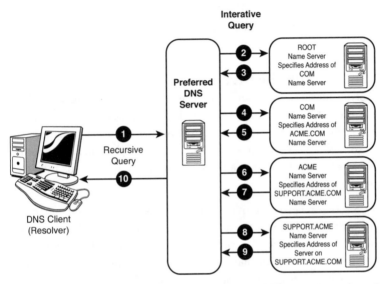

FIGURE 3.3 A DNS client accessing the local preferred DNS server to resolve a domain name.

Although the recursive query process can be resource intensive, it has some performance advantages for the DNS server. When the recursion process is complete, the server caches the information. The cache information will be used again to help speed the answering of subsequent queries. Over time, the cache information can grow to occupy a significant portion of the server memory resources.

Typically, the process of domain name resolution occurs very quickly. Occasionally, it may be delayed. If the delay is too long, the browser comes back and says that the domain does not exist even though you know that it does. It does so because your computer got tired of waiting and timed out. Yet, when you try again, there is a good chance it will work because the authoritative server has had enough time to reply and the name server has stored the information in its cache.

Root Hints

If the DNS server does not know the address of the requested site, then it forwards the request to another DNS server. The *root hints* file provides a list of IP addresses of DNS servers that are considered to be authoritative at the root level of the DNS hierarchy.

If your network is connected to the Internet, the root hints file should contain records for the root DNS servers on the Internet. In Windows, a root hints file with current Internet root DNS mappings is installed as the file Cache.dns file in the directory % SystemRoot %\System32\Dns.

If your network is not connected to the Internet, you must replace the NS and A records in the cache file with NS and A records for the DNS servers that are authoritative for the root of your private TCP/IP network. Of course, removing root hints or modifying the root hints helps you to control or restrict access to the Internet.

Forwarders and Conditional Forwarders

DNS servers can be configured to send all recursive queries to a selected list of servers (such as the DNS servers of your ISP), known as forwarders. Servers used in the list of forwarders provide recursive lookup for any queries that a DNS server receives that it cannot answer based on its own zone records. During the forwarding process, a DNS server configured to use forwarders essentially behaves as a DNS client to its forwarders. Typically, forwarders are used on remote DNS servers that use a slow link to access the Internet.

EXAM ALERT

Remember that you cannot configure a DNS server as a forwarder if a root zone exists. If you you need to use your DNS server as a forwarder, you must delete the root zone byopening the forward lookup zone in the DNS Manager console, right-clicking the root DNS zone and clicking Delete. The root zone entry is identified as ".".

A DNS server can be configured to send all queries that it cannot resolve locally to a forwarder, and you can also configure conditional forwarders. With conditional forwarders, DNS servers are configured to forward requests to different servers based on the DNS name within the query. When configuring conditional forwarding, you must specify the following information:

- ▶ The domain name for which queries are to be forwarded
- ▶ The IP address of the DNS server for which unresolved queries for a specified domain should be forwarded

Round-Robin

DNS servers use a mechanism called round-robin or load sharing to share and distribute loads for network resources. *Round-robin* rotates the order of resource records data returned in a query answer in which multiple resource records exist of the same resource record type for a queried DNS domain name. Because the client is required to try the first IP address listed, a DNS server configured to perform round-robin rotates the order of the resource records when answering client requests.

Reverse Queries

Occasionally, the resolver may perform a reverse query, in which a resolver knows an IP address and wants to know the hostname. To avoid searching all the domains for an inverse query, a special domain called *in-addr.arpa* was created. Nodes in the in-addr.arpa domain are named after the numbers in the IP address. Because IP addresses get more specific from left to right, the order of IP addresses is reversed when the in-addr.arpa domain is built. As soon as the in-addr.arpa domain is built, special resource records called pointer records (PTR) are added to associate the IP addresses to the corresponding hostnames. To find a hostname for an IP address, the resolver queries the DNS server for a PTR record for the address.in-addr.arpa. For example, to find the IP address of 1.2.3.4, the resolver would query the DNS server for a PTR record of 4.3.2.1.in-addr.arpa.

Link-Local Multicast Name Resolution

New to Windows Server 2008 is *Link-Local Multicast Name resolution* (LLMNR). LLMNR allows IPv4 and IPv6 hosts on a single subnet without a Domain Name System (DNS) server to resolve each other's names. This capability is useful for single-subnet home networks and ad hoc wireless networks. Rather than unicasting a DNS query to a DNS server, LLMNR nodes send their DNS queries to a multicast address on which all the LLMNR-capable nodes of the subnet are listening. The owner of the queried name sends a response. IPv4 nodes can also use LLMNR to perform local subnet name resolution without having to rely on NetBIOS over TCP/IP broadcasts.

Dynamic DNS

Because DNS has become the primary naming resolution tool, every computer that holds a network service such as file or print sharing has to be registered. A large network that has a lot of computers that use DHCP to obtain a new IP address needs to dynamically register and update the DNS resource records.

This reduces the need for manual administration of zone records, especially for clients that frequently move or change locations and use *Dynamic Host Configuration Protocol* (DHCP) to obtain an IP address.

By default, computers that are statically configured for TCP/IP attempt to dynamically register host (A) resource records and pointer (PTR) resource records for IP addresses that are configured and used by their installed network connections. By default, all computers register records based on their FQDN. The primary full computer name, an FQDN, is based on the primary DNS suffix of a computer, appended to its computer name.

When a client registers a resource record, that specific client becomes the owner of that entry in the zone database so only that client may update the record. This is true not only for the DHCP client that registers its own host (A) record, but for the DHCP server that registers the pointer (PTR) records for all the DHCP clients to which it leases IP addresses.

Dynamic updates can be sent for any of the following reasons or events:

▶ At start-up time, when the computer is turned on.

▶ When an IP address is added, removed, or modified in the TCP/IP properties configuration for any one of the installed network connections.

▶ When an IP address lease changes or renews with the DHCP server any one of the installed network connections. For example, when the computer is started or if the `ipconfig /renew` command is used.

▶ When the `ipconfig /registerdns` command is used, it manually forces the client to register or re-register itself in in DNS.

▶ A member server is promoted to a domain controller.

Dynamic updates are sent or refreshed periodically. By default, computers send a refresh once every seven days. If the update results in no changes to zone data, the zone remains at its current version and no changes are written. Updates result in actual zone changes or increased zone transfer only if names or addresses actually change.

When the DHCP client service registers host (A) and pointer (PTR) resource records for a computer, it uses a default caching Time to Live (TTL) of 15 minutes for host records. This determines how long other DNS servers and clients cache a computer's records when the records are included in a query response.

Secure Dynamic Updates

Windows Server 2008 supports *secure dynamic updates* for zones that store information within Active Directory. With secure updates, only those clients authorized within the domain are permitted to update resource records. This means that the DNS server accepts updates only from clients that have accounts within Active Directory. Any computers that do not have accounts are not permitted to register any records, thereby eliminating the chance that unknown computers will register with the DNS server. Secure updates for a zone can be configured by selecting the Secure Only option.

The benefit of selecting this option is, obviously, an increase in security. The resource records and zone files can be modified only by users who have been authorized to do so. This also provides administrators with a finer granularity of control because they can edit the access control list (ACL) for the zone and specify which users and groups can perform dynamic updates. You edit the ACL for a zone by right-clicking the zone, selecting Properties, and choosing the Security tab.

Zone Transfers

To distribute the load of the DNS database, improve name resolution, improve performance, and provide fault tolerance, additional servers are used to host a zone file. To replicate and synchronize all copies of the zone files, a zone transfer is required between the various DNS servers. When a new DNS server is added to the network and is configured as a new secondary server for an existing zone, it must perform a full initial transfer (AXFR) to obtain a full copy of the zone files.

After the Windows DNS servers are replicated and synchronized, they will keep the zone files synchronized by performing an incremental transfer (IXFR), in which the secondary server pulls only those zone changes it needs to synchronize its copy of the zone with its source. To keep track of the changes, each version of the zone file includes a serial number in the Start of Authority (SOA) resource record. If the serial number is the same between two zone files, no transfer is made. If the serial number at the source is greater than at the requesting secondary server, a transfer is made of only those changes to RRs for each incremental version of the zone.

For a zone transfer to occur, the secondary server sends a SAO query to the primary server when one of the following occur:

- ▶ The refresh interval expires for the zone as specified in the SOA resource record (default 900 seconds/15 minutes).

- ▶ A secondary server is notified of zone changes by its master server.

- ▶ A DNS server service is started at a secondary server for the zone.

- ▶ The DNS Manager console is used at a secondary server for the zone to manually initiate a transfer from its master server.

When the primary server receives the query, it will check the serial number within the SOA record to determine if the zone has changed.

Windows DNS permits a means of initiating notification to secondary servers when zone changes occur. DNS notification implements a push mechanism for notifying a select set of secondary servers for a zone when it is updated. Servers that are notified can then initiate a zone transfer. For secondary servers to be notified by the master DNS server, each secondary server must first have its IP address in the master server's notify list.

When a secondary name server starts up, it contacts the master name server and initiates a zone transfer for each zone for which it is acting as a secondary name server. If the data on the master name server has changed, zone transfers can occur periodically as set by the refresh parameters in the SOA record of the zone file.

Secure Zone Transfers

Because DNS has entries for just about every host and many devices, it is important that someone does not set up a fake DNS server to get a DNS zone transfer or to overwrite the DNS entries with bad data (known as DNS poisoning). A copy of a DNS zone can be used to gather information (reconnaissance), which is the first step in hacking a system. The DNS poisoning can lead to a denial of service attack or impersonation (to gather personal information including credit card numbers and passwords or to gather information about the network).

In addition to using Secure Dynamic DNS to help protect your DNS server, you need to secure zone replication. You can secure DNS zone replication by doing the following:

- ▶ Using Active Directory replication.

- ▶ Encrypting zone replication sent over public networks, such as the Internet, using IPSec or VPN tunnels.

- ▶ Restricting zone transfer to authorized servers.

Microsoft recommends that you use Active Directory integrated zones, which is more secure than file-based zone transfer. Replicating zones as part of Active Directory replication provides the following security benefits:

▶ Active Directory replication traffic is encrypted; therefore zone replication traffic is encrypted automatically.

▶ The Active Directory domain controllers that perform replication are mutually authenticated, and impersonation is not possible.

If you have secondary servers and you replicate your zone data by using zone transfer, configure your DNS servers to specify the secondary servers that are authorized to receive zone transfers. This prevents an attacker from using zone transfer to download zone data. If you are using Active Directory integrated zones instead, configure your servers to disallow zone transfer.

DNS Zone Replication in Active Directory Domain Services

Application partitions store information about applications in Active Directory. Each application determines how it stores, categorizes, and uses application specific information. To prevent unnecessary replication to specific application partitions, you can designate which domain controllers in a forest host specific application partitions. Unlike a domain partition, an application partition cannot store security principal objects, such as user accounts, computer accounts or groups. Security principal objects are Active Directory objects that are assigned security IDs (SIDs) and are unique within a domain. They can be used to log on to the network and can be assigned access to domain resources. In addition, the data in an application partition is not stored in the global catalog.

You have two application partitions if you use Active Directory integrated zones in DNS:

▶ **ForestDNSZones**: All domain controllers and DNS servers in a forest receive a replica of this partition. A forest-wide application partition stores the forest zone data.

▶ **DomainDNSZones**: All domain controllers that are DNS servers in a domain receive a replica of this partition. The application partitions store the domain DNS zone in the DomainDNSZones.

Each domain has a DomainDNSZones partition, but there is only one ForestDNSZones partition. No DNS data is replicated to the global catalog server.

DNS Services in Windows Server 2008

Windows Server 2008 does include DNS. Like many of the services and features that come with Windows Server 2008, it just needs to be installed and configured. Unlike UNIX and Linux operating systems, the configuring of DNS is quite easy with the DNS Manager console.

Installing DNS Services

Before installing a DNS server, you must make sure that the TCP/IP protocol is installed, a static IP address is assigned, and the appropriate DNS domain name is specified. Installing a Domain Name System (DNS) server involves adding the DNS server role to an existing Windows Server 2008 server. You can also install the DNS server role when you install the Active Directory Domain Services (AD DS) role. Of course, you need to be a member of the Administrators group or equivalent to accomplish this.

To install a DNS server, follow these steps:

1. Open Server Manager by clicking Start, Server Manager.
2. In the results pane, under Roles Summary, click Add roles.
3. In the Add Roles Wizard, if the Before You Begin page appears, click Next.
4. In the Roles list, click DNS Server, Next.
5. Read the information on the DNS Server page and click Next.
6. On the Confirm Installation Options page, verify that the DNS Server role will be installed and click Install.

Using the DNS Manager Console

The primary tool that you use to manage local and remote Windows 2008 DNS servers is the DNS Manager console (see Figure 3.4), which can be accessed from within the Administrative Tools folder or with the Microsoft Management Console (MMC) snap-in.

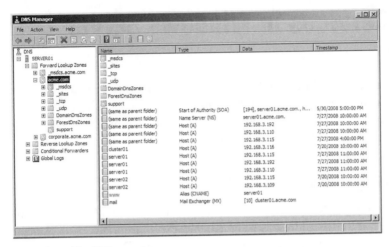

FIGURE 3.4 The DNS console.

Configuring a New DNS Server

To configure a new DNS server using the Windows interface, follow these steps:

1. Open DNS Manager.

2. If necessary, add the applicable server to the snap-in and then connect to it.

3. In the console tree, click the applicable DNS server.

4. On the Action menu, click Configure a DNS Server.

5. When the wizard starts, click Next.

6. Select to create a forward lookup zone, create forward and reverse lookup zones, or configure root hints.

7. Complete the wizard as needed.

Creating a Caching-Only DNS Server

By default, the DNS Server service acts as a caching-only server. Caching-only servers require little or no configuration. To install a caching-only DNS server, follow these steps:

1. Install the DNS server role on the server computer.

2. Do not configure the DNS server to load any zones.

3. Verify that server root hints are configured or updated correctly.

If you have created primary, secondary, Active Directory integrated zones and stub zones and you want to make the server into a caching-only DNS server, you need to uninstall and reinstall DNS.

Creating a New Forward or Reverse Lookup Zone

Follow these steps to add a forward lookup zone using the Windows interface:

1. Open DNS Manager.

2. In the console tree, right-click a DNS server and then click New Zone to open the New Zone Wizard.

3. Follow the instructions to create a new primary zone, secondary zone, or stub zone (see Figure 3.5).

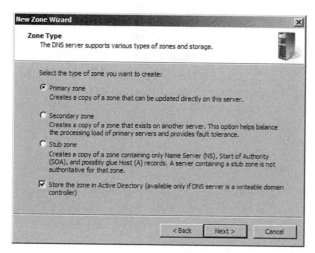

FIGURE 3.5 Creating a new DNS zone.

Take these steps to create a reverse lookup zone within the Windows interface:

1. Open DNS Manager.

2. In the console tree, right-click Reserve Lookup Zones and then click New Zone to open the New Zone Wizard.

3. Follow the instructions to create a new primary zone, secondary zone, or stub zone.

Creating Subdomains

To create a subdomain (from within the DNS Manager console), follow these steps:

1. Click to highlight the name of the zone in which you want to create the subdomain.

2. Right-click the zone name to bring up the shortcut menu and click on the New Domain option.

3. Type the name of the subdomain in the New Domain dialog box and click OK.

After you have created a subdomain, you can delegate authority of the subdomain to another DNS server/zone. This enables you to distribute the load of the DNS database and improve name resolution performance. Of course, when a query is being done on a zone, it refers to the NS (name server) resource records to find the name server for the target zone being queried.

To delegate authority for a subdomain, follow these steps:

1. Click to highlight the name of the domain to which you want to delegate authority (typically the domain, not the subdomain).

2. Right-click the domain name to bring up the shortcut menu and select the New Delegation option.

3. Follow the Add New Delegation wizard to guide you through the rest of the process, including specifying the name of the domain to which you are delegating authority and adding the names and IP address of the server or servers that are to host the delegated zone.

Configuring the SOA Record

To configure the SOA record,

1. Right-click the zone and select Properties.

2. Select the Start of Authority (SOA) tab.

You can then specify the primary server, zone administrator's email address, secondary zone expiration values, and minimum default TTL values for zone resource records.

Add Resource Records

To add a new host record to the forward lookup zone, take these steps:

1. Right-click the forward lookup zone and select New Host (A or AAAA).

2. Specify the name of the host (see Figure 3.6).

3. Specify the IP address.

4. If you want to also create an associated PTR record, keep the Create Associated Pointer (PTR) Record option selected.

5. Click the Add host button.

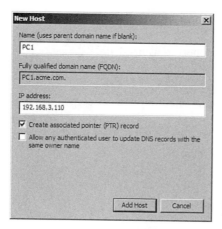

FIGURE 3.6 Creating a host record in the forward lookup zone.

To create MX record or alias, you would follow a similar process. SRV records for domain controllers are usually added automatically. However, if you need to create an SRV record, right-click the forward lookup zone and select Other New Records. Then select Service Location (SRV) and select Create Record.

To create a PTR record,

1. Right-click the reverse lookup zone and select create New Pointer (PTR).

2. Specify the IP address.

3. Specify the hostname.

4. Click OK.

Scavenging Resource Records

The DNS Server service supports aging and scavenging features. These features are provided as a mechanism for performing cleanup and removal of stale resource records, which can accumulate in zone data over time. You can use this procedure to change how a specific resource record is scavenged.

To set aging and scavenging properties for the DNS server, using the Windows interface,

1. Open DNS Manager.

2. In the console tree, right-click the applicable DNS server and click Set Aging/Scavenging for All Zones.

3. Select the Scavenge Stale Resource Records check box.

4. Modify other aging and scavenging properties as needed.

In addition to enabling scavenging for the server, you must also enable scavenging for each zone. To enable scavenging for a zone, follow these steps:

1. Open DNS Manager.

2. Right-click the zone and select Properties.

3. On the General tab, click Aging.

4. Select Scavenge State Resource Records.

5. Click OK to close the Zone Aging/Scavenging properties.

6. Click OK to close the zone properties.

EXAM ALERT

To scavenge old resource records, you must enable scavenging and aging at the DNS server and on the zone. By default, aging and scavenging of resource records is disabled.

Aging and scavenging properties that are configured by this procedure act as server defaults that apply only to Active Directory Domain Services (AD DS) integrated zones. For standard primary zones, you must set the appropriate properties at the applicable zone.

To reset aging and scavenging properties for a specified resource record, follow these steps:

1. Open DNS Manager.

2. In the console tree, click the applicable zone.

3. In the details pane, double-click the resource record for which you want to reset aging and scavenging properties.

4. Depending on the how the resource record was originally added to the zone, you'll need to do one of the following:

   ▶ If the record was added dynamically using dynamic update, clear the Delete this record when it becomes stale check box to prevent its aging or potential removal during the scavenging process. If dynamic updates to this record continue to occur, the Domain Name System (DNS) server will always reset this check box so that the dynamically updated record can be deleted.

   ▶ If you added the record statically, select the Delete this record when it becomes stale check box to permit its aging or potential removal during the scavenging process.

This procedure is necessary only for resource records that are dynamically registered. For records that you add to a zone manually, a time stamp value of zero always applies to the record, which excludes it from the scavenging process.

Configuring the Name Server List and Zone Transfers

If you right-click a zone and select Properties, you can configure the list of name servers and zone transfers:

1. Open DNS Manager.

2. Right-click a DNS zone and then click Properties.

3. On the Zone Transfers tab, choose one of the following:

   ▶ To disable zone transfers, clear the Allow Zone Transfers check box.

   ▶ To allow zone transfers, select the Allow Zone Transfers check box.

4. If you allowed zone transfers, choose one of the following:

   ▶ To allow zone transfers to any server, click To Any Server.

   ▶ To allow zone transfers only to the DNS servers that are listed on the Name Servers tab, click Only to Servers Listed on the Name Servers Tab.

   ▶ To allow zone transfers only to specific DNS servers, click Only to the Following Servers, and then add the IP address of one or more DNS servers.

To improve the security of your DNS infrastructure, allow zone transfers only for either the DNS servers in the name server (NS) resource records for a zone or for specified DNS servers. If you allow any DNS server to perform a zone transfer, you are allowing internal network information to be transferred to any host that can contact your DNS server.

Configuring Dynamic DNS Updates

To enable DNS dynamic updates for clients, open the DHCP console and right-click the applicable DHCP server. In the shortcut menu, pick the Properties option and click the DNS tab. Then put a check in the Automatically Update DHCP Client Information in DNS check box.

To allow only secure dynamic updates, right-click the applicable zone and select the Properties option. On the General tab, verify that the zone type is Active Directory-integrated and that the Allow Dynamic Update drop-down list is set to Only Secure Updates (see Figure 3.7).

DNS service also makes it possible to use WINS servers to look up names not found in the DNS domain namespace by checking the NetBIOS namespace managed by WINS. To use WINS lookup integration, two special resource record types are enabled and added to the zone, WINS and WINS-R. A good example of when to use WINS lookup is when you are using a mixed-mode client of Windows and UNIX clients, and the UNIX clients and some early version Microsoft clients can locate your WINS clients by extending DNS host-name resolution into the WINS-managed NetBIOS namespace. Note: If you use a mixture of Windows DNS servers and other DNS servers to host a zone, you should enable the Do Not Replicate This Record option for any primary zones when using the WINS lookup record. This prevents the WINS lookup record from being included in zone transfers to other DNS servers that do not support or recognize this record. If not, it would cause data errors and failed zone transfers.

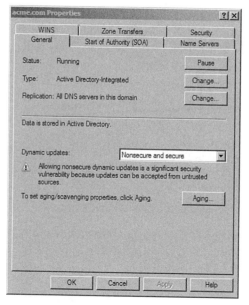

FIGURE 3.7 Configuring dynamic updates in DNS.

NOTE

WINS supports only IPv4 addresses; it doesn't support IPv6 addresses.

Configuring Forwarders and Root Hints

To update root hints on the DNS server, follow these steps:

1. Open DNS Manager.

2. In the console tree, click the applicable DNS server.

3. On the Action menu, click Properties.

4. Click the Root Hints tab.

5. Modify server root hints as follows:

   ▶ To add a root server to the list, click Add and then specify the name and IP address of the server to be added to the list.

   ▶ To modify a root server in the list, click Edit and then specify the name and IP address of the server to be modified in the list.

   ▶ To remove a root server from the list, select it in the list, and then click Remove.

▶ To copy root hints from a DNS server, click Copy from Server, and then specify the IP address of the DNS server from which you want to copy a list of root servers to use in resolving queries. These root hints do not overwrite any existing root hints.

To configure a DNS server to use forwarders using the Windows interface,

1. Open DNS Manager.

2. In the console tree, click the applicable DNS server.

3. On the Action menu, click Properties.

4. On the Forwarders tab, under DNS domain, click a domain name.

5. Under Selected Domain's Forwarder IP Address List, type the IP address of a forwarder and then click Add.

Zone Replication Scope

To change the zone replication scope (domain wide or forest wide), do the following:

1. Open DNS Manager.

2. In the console tree, right-click the applicable zone and then click Properties.

3. On the General tab, note the current zone replication type and then click Change.

4. Select a replication scope for the zone.

5. Click OK to close the Change Zone Replication Scope dialog box.

6. Click OK to close the Properties box.

Configuring Advanced DNS Server Options

Several options can be configured in the Advanced tab of the DNS server's properties window. Generally, the default settings should be acceptable and require no modifications. The advanced settings (see Figure 3.8) that can be configured are summarized in the following list:

▶ **Disable Recursion**: This determines whether the DNS server uses recursion. If recursion is disabled, the DNS server always uses referrals, regardless of the type of request from clients.

- **BIND Secondaries**: This determines whether fast transfers are used when transferring zone data to a BIND DNS server. Versions of DNS BIND earlier than 4.9.4 do not support fast zone transfers.

- **Fail on Load if Bad Zone Data**: This option determines whether the DNS server continues to load a zone if the zone data is determined to have errors. By default, the DNS server continues to load the zone.

- **Enable Round Robin**: This option determines whether the DNS server rotates and reorders a list of resource records when multiple resource records exist for a query answer.

- **Enable Netmask Ordering**: This determines whether the DNS server reorders host (A) records so that when a client is trying to resolve a hostname with multiple IP addresses, an address is chosen based on the client's IP address in an attempt to get the closest server to the host.

- **Secure Cache Against Pollution**: This determines whether the DNS server attempts to clean up responses to avoid cache pollution. This option is enabled by default.

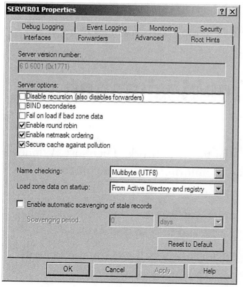

FIGURE 3.8 Advanced settings for a DNS server.

Configuring a DNS Suffix Search List

For DNS clients, you can configure a DNS domain suffix search list that extends or revises their DNS search capabilities. By adding additional suffixes to the list, you can search for short, unqualified computer names in more than one specified DNS domain. Then, if a DNS query fails, the DNS Client service can use this list to append other name suffix endings to your original name and repeat DNS queries to the DNS server for these alternate FQDNs.

To change the primary DNS suffix of a computer without setting a policy, follow these steps:

1. Open the System properties using the Control Panel.

2. Click the Network Identification tab.

3. Click Properties.

4. Click More.

5. Type a suffix in the Primary DNS suffix.

If you want to push the domain suffix search list to DNS clients, use group policies:

Computer Configuration/Administrative Templates/Network/DNS Client

Monitoring and Troubleshooting DNS Services

In Windows, DNS services are essential to the network. Therefore, Windows Server 2008 has several utilities for monitoring and troubleshooting DNS servers. These include

▸ The DNS administrative tool, which you can use to test DNS servers and monitor their capacity to process and resolve queries.

▸ Command-line utilities, such as NSLOOKUP, which you can use to verify resource records and troubleshoot DNS problems.

▸ Logging features, such as the DNS server log, which you can view with the Event Viewer.

You can configure the DNS Server service to perform queries on a scheduled basis to ensure that the service is operating correctly. In the DNS Manager console, right-click the server that you want to monitor, select the Properties option and click the Monitoring tab. From here, you can perform a simple query, a recursive query, or both. If the recursive query fails, the DNS server is unable to contact any of the servers listed in root hints. This can happen if the configuration of the root name server is invalid or the root name server cannot be contacted. See Figure 3.9.

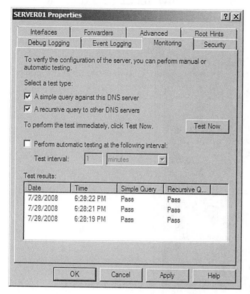

FIGURE 3.9   Testing DNS with the DNS console.

Using NSLookup

NSLookup is a diagnostic tool that displays information from the DNS servers. It is available only if the TCP/IP protocol has been installed. NSLookup has two modes:

> ▶ **Interactive**: Use interactive mode when you require more than one piece of data. To run interactive mode, at the command prompt, type **NSLookup**. To exit interactive mode, type **exit**.

> ▶ **Non-interactive**: Use non-interactive mode when you require a single piece of data. Type **NSLookup** at the command prompt with the proper parameters and the data is returned.

For example, you can type the following to find the address of server1.acme.com:

```
nslookup server1.acme.com
```

To find the hostname of the 192.168.3.110, type

```
nslookup 192.168.3.110
```

To find the SOA record information for acme.com, you need to enter interactive mode. Then set the type to SOA before doing the search. Figure 3.10 shows using NSLookup in non-interactive and interactive mode (showing the SOA and MX resource records for a domain).

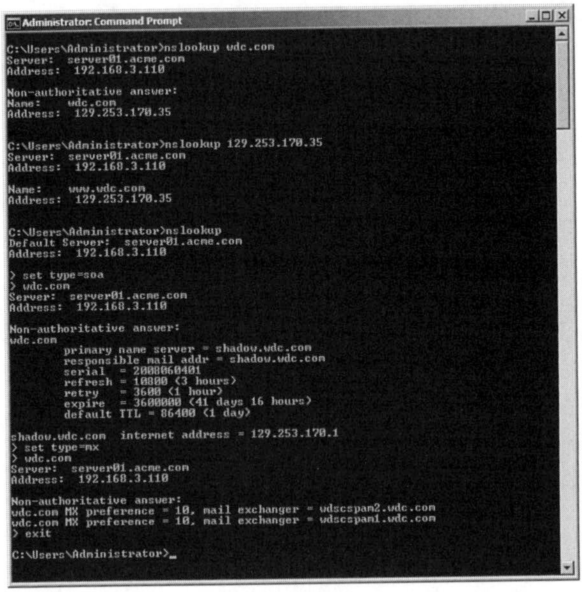

FIGURE 3.10
Using the NSLookup utility to troubleshoot name resolution problems.

Using DNSLint

A tool that is included with Windows Server 2008 but was introduced as a Windows Server 2003 support tool is DNSLint.exe. DNSLint has three functions that verify Domain Name System (DNS) records and generate an HTML report:

- ▶ dnslint /d: This diagnoses potentially causes "lame delegation" and other related DNS problems.

- ▶ dnslint /ql: This verifies a user-defined set of DNS records on multiple DNS servers.

- ▶ dnslint /ad: This verifies DNS records specifically used for Active Directory replication.

Name resolution problems can occur if a client computer is resolving names incorrectly or if the client computer name is not registered with the DNS servers on your network. If you determine that the client computer is resolving names incorrectly, you can use IPCONFIG /FLUSHDNS from the command prompt to flush and reset the cache on the client computer. If a client's name records are missing from the servers, use IPCONFIG /REGISTERDNS to force the client to renew its registration.

Using the Dnscmd Command

Dnscmd is another command-line utility used perform various DNS administrative tasks from the command prompt window. You can use the command to perform the following tasks:

▶ View and change the properties of a DNS server, zone, or resource record.

▶ Create and delete zones and resource records.

▶ Force replication events.

To view the complete syntax for this command, at a command prompt, type the following command and press Enter:

```
dnscmd /config /help
```

Table 3.5 shows the Dnscmd subcommands.

TABLE 3.5 Useful Dnscmd Subcommands

Subcommand	Description
Clearcache	Clears resource records from the DNS cache memory.
Config	Enables the user to modify a range of configuration values stored in the Registry and in individual zones.
Enumzones	Displays a complete list of zones configured for the server.
Info	Displays DNS server configuration information as stored in the server's Registry. You can specify which setting for which information will be returned.
Statistics	Displays or clears statistical data for the specified server. You can specify which statistics are to be displayed according to ID numbers.
Zoneadd zone_name	Adds a zone to the DNS server.

continues

TABLE 3.5 *Continued*

Subcommand	Description
Zonedelete *zone_name*	Deletes the specified zone from the DNS server.
Zoneexport *zone_name*	Exports all resource records in the specified DNS zone to a text file.
Zoneinfo *zone_name*	Displays Registry-based configuration information for the specified DNS zone.

To configure a new DNS server using a command line,

1. Open a command prompt.

2. Type the following command and press Enter:

   ```
   dnscmd <ServerName> /Config {<ZoneName>|..AllZones} <Property> {1|0}
   ```

   ▶ *<ServerName>*—Required. Specifies the DNS hostname of the DNS server. You can also type the IP address of the DNS server. To specify the DNS server on the local computer, you can also type a period (.).

   ▶ */Config*—Specifies that the command configures the specified zone.

   ▶ *{<ZoneName>|..AllZones}*—Specifies the name of the zone to be configured. To apply the configuration for all zones hosted by the specified DNS server, type **..AllZones.**

   ▶ *<Property>*—Specifies the server property or zone property to be configured. There are different properties available for servers and zones.

   ▶ *{1|0}*—Sets configuration options to either 1 (on) or 0 (off). Note that some server and zone properties must be reset as part of a more complex operation.

To add a zone to the DNS Server, use the following command:

```
dnscmd [ServerName] /zoneadd ZoneName ZoneType [/dp FQDN|

[ic:ccc]{/domain |/enterprise|/legacy}]
```

   ▶ *ServerName*: Specifies the DNS server the administrator plans to manage, represented by IP address, FQDN, or hostname. If omitted, the local server is used.

   ▶ *ZoneName*: Specifies the name of the zone.

▶ *ZoneType*: Specifies the type of zone to create. Each type has different required parameters:

▶ /dsprimary: Creates an Active Directory integrated zone.

▶ /primary /file *FileName*: Creates a standard primary zone and specifies the name of the file that is to store the zone information.

▶ /secondary *MasterIPAddress [MasterIPAddress...]*: Creates a standard secondary zone.

▶ /stub *Master IPAddress [MasterIPAddress...]* /file *FileName*: Creates a file-backed stub zone.

▶ /dsstub *Master IPAddress [MasterIPAddress...]*: Creates an Active Directory-integrated stub zone.

▶ /forwarder *Master IPAddress [MasterIPAddress]...* /file *FileName*: Specifies that the created zone forwards unresolved queries to another DNS server.

▶ /dsforwarder: Specifies that the created Active Directory integrated zone forwards unresolved queries to another DNS server.

▶ /dp *FQDN {/domain ¦ /enterprise ¦ /legacy}*: Specifies the directory partition on which to store the zone.

▶ *FQDN*: Specifies fully qualified domain name of the directory partition.

▶ /domain: Stores the zone on the domain directory partition.

▶ /enterprise: Stores the zone on the enterprise directory partition.

▶ /legacy: Stores the zone on a legacy directory partition.

To force a secondary DNS zone to update from the master, use the following the command:

dnscmd *ServerName* /zonerefresh *ZoneName*

▶ *ServerName*: Specifies the DNS server the administrator plans to manage, represented by IP address, FQDN, or hostname. If omitted, the local server is used.

▶ *ZoneName*: Specifies the name of the zone to be refreshed.

To update the specified Active Directory integrated zone from Active Directory, use this command:

```
dnscmd ServerName /zoneupdatefromds ZoneName
```

▶ *ServerName*: Specifies the DNS server the administrator plans to manage, represented by IP address, FQDN, or hostname. If omitted, the local server is used.

▶ *ZoneName*: Specifies the name of the zone to update.

To clear the DNS cache memory of resource records in the specified DNS server, use this command:

```
dnscmd [ServerName] /clearcache
```

▶ *ServerName*: Specifies the DNS server the administrator plans to manage, represented by IP address, FQDN, or hostname. If omitted, the local server is used.

To add a record to a specified zone in a DNS server, use the following command:

```
dnscmd [ServerName] /recordadd ZoneName NodeName RRType RRData
```

▶ *ServerName*: Specifies the DNS server the administrator is planning to manage, represented by local computer syntax, IP address, FQDN, or hostname. If omitted, the local server is used.

▶ *ZoneName*: Specifies the zone in which the record resides.

▶ *NodeName*: Specifies a specific node in the zone.

▶ *RRType*: Specifies the type of record to be added.

▶ *RRData*: Specifies the type of data that is expected when using a certain data type.

To delete a resource record from a specified zone, use this command:

```
dnscmd ServerName /recorddelete ZoneName NodeName RRType RRData[/f]
```

▶ *ServerName*: Specifies the DNS server the administrator plans to manage, represented by IP address, FQDN, or hostname. If omitted, the local server is used.

▶ *ZoneName*: Specifies the zone in which the record resides.

▶ *NodeName*: Specifies the name of the host.

- ▶ *RRType*: Specifies the type of record to be deleted.

- ▶ *RRData*: Specifies the type of data that is expected when using a certain data type.

- ▶ */f*: Executes the command without asking for confirmation. Because nodes can have more than one resource record, this command requires you to be very specific about the type of record that you want to delete. If you specify a data type and do not specify a type of resource record data, all records with that specific data type for the specified node are deleted.

Introduction to Windows Internet Name Service

Although DNS is the most commonly used name resolution method today, it is not the only one. Before hostnames, Windows computers were identified with NetBIOS name, most commonly known as the computer name. When connecting to a Microsoft Shared folder or printer, you would connect using the *Universal Name* Convention (\\servername\sharename).

Initially, much like HOSTS files, *LMHOSTS files* would be used to translate from NetBIOS name to IPv4 address. Unfortunately, every time you added a new hostname, you had to modify the LMHOST file on every computer.

Later, computers that needed to determine a NetBIOS would broadcast onto the network, asking for the computer's IP address. Unfortunately, the broadcast usually didn't go across routers, which meant that computers on other subnets didn't get resolved. In addition, if you had a lot of computers doing these types of broadcasts, the broadcasts slowed the network's performance.

To overcome this problem, *Windows Internet Name Service (WINS)* was created. WINS resolves NetBIOS names to IP addresses, which can reduce NetBIOS broadcast traffic and enable clients to resolve the NetBIOS names of computers that are on different network segments (subnets). A WINS server contains a database of IP addresses and NetBIOS (computer names) that update dynamically. For clients to access the WINS server, the clients must know the address of the WINS server. Therefore, the WINS server needs to have a static address that does not change. When the client accesses the WINS server, the client doesn't do a broadcast; the client sends a message directly to the WINS server. When the WINS server gets the requests, it knows which the computer sent the request and can reply directly to the originating IP address. The WINS database (located at *systemroot*\System32\WINS\Wins.mdb) stores the information and makes it available to the other WINS clients. The WINS registration generates little excessive network traffic because it doesn't use broadcast.

WINS is required because

▶ Older versions of Microsoft operating systems rely on WINS for name resolution.

▶ Some applications, typically older applications, rely on NetBIOS names.

▶ You may need dynamic registration of single-label names.

▶ Users may rely on the Network Neighborhood or My Network Places network browser features.

▶ You may not be using Windows Server 2008 as your DNS infrastructure.

WINS Registration

When a WINS client starts up, it registers its name, IP address, and type of services within the WINS server's database. The type of service is designated by a hexadecimal value, which is placed at the end of the name. For example, when a Windows computer called Server2 starts, it registers three mappings, including Server2[00h] (workstation), Server2[03h] (messenger), and Server2[20h] (File server).

> **NOTE**
>
> The NetBIOS can be only up to 15 characters, not counting the hexadecimal value, which represents the service.

See Table 3.6 for the list of NetBIOS network services.

TABLE 3.6 NetBIOS Network Services

NETBIOS NAME SUFFIX	NETWORK SERVICE/RESOURCE IDENTIFIER
\\computer_name[00h]	Workstation service
\\computer_name[03h]	Messenger service
\\computer_name[06h]	RAS
\\computer_name[20h]	Server service
\\computer_name[21h]	RAS client service (on a RAS client)
\\computer_name[BEh]	Network monitoring agent service

TABLE 3.6 *Continued*

NETBIOS NAME SUFFIX	NETWORK SERVICE/RESOURCE IDENTIFIER
\\domain_name[1Bh]	The PDC in its role as the domain master browser
\\domain_name[1Dh]	The master browser for each subnet
\\domain_name[1Ch]	The domain controllers (up to 25 IP addresses) within the domain

Because WINS was made only for Windows operating systems, traditional network devices and services (such as a network printer and UNIX machines) cannot register with a WINS service. Therefore, these addresses have to be added manually.

NOTE

Linux and other non-Windows operating systems can utilize a WINS server by using SAMBA.

Names that are held in the WINS database are given a TTL or Renewal interval during name registration. A name must be refreshed before this interval ends or the name is released from the database. The WINS client refreshes names by sending a Name Refresh Request to the WINS server. Windows clients attempt a refresh at half of the Renewal interval and keep trying to contact the WINS server until the time expires. NetBIOS names are explicitly released when the client performs proper shutdown or are silent when the name is not refreshed within the Renewal interval.

When a client node registers a name that already exists in the WINS database and the client node has a different IP address that what is in the database, the WINS server must determine whether the name with the old IP address still exists. Therefore, the WINS server sends a Name Query Request to the old IP address. If the old address responds with a Positive Name Query Response, the WINS server rejects the new registration with a Negative Name Registration Response. If the old address does not respond to the Name Query, the new registration is accepted.

Burst Handling

WINS servers can now support handling of high-volume (burst) server loads. Bursts occur when a large number of WINS clients actively and simultaneously try to register their local names in WINS, such as when a power failure occurs.

When power is later restored, many users start and register their names simultaneously on the network, which creates high levels of WINS traffic. With burst-mode support, a WINS server can respond positively to these client requests, even before it processes and physically enters those updates in the WINS server database.

Burst mode uses a burst-queue size as a threshold value that determines how many name registration and name refresh requests sent by WINS clients are processed normally before burst-mode handling is started. By default, the value is 500. A WINS server initiates burst handling whenever the number of WINS client registration requests exceeds the burst queue size.

In burst handling, additional client requests are immediately answered with a positive response by the WINS server. The response varies the TTL sent to clients so that client registration load is distributed more evenly over time.

Using the WINS console, you can choose to configure the level of burst handling used by the server, which modifies the size of the burst queue to accommodate either a low, medium, or large burst situation.

WINS Clients

A WINS client can be configured to use one of four NetBIOS name resolution methods. They include B (broadcast) node, P (point-to-point) node, M (mixed) node, and H (hybrid) node. See Table 3.7. In either case, when trying to resolve a computer name, it always checks its own local NetBIOS name cache. Just like the DNS name cache, it remembers names and addresses of computers with which it recently communicated. By default, when a system is configured to use WINS for its name resolution, it adheres to h-node for name registration. By using DHCP servers or by using the registry, you can force the client into one of these nodes.

TABLE 3.7   NetBIOS Resolution Modes

Node Types	Registry Value	Description
B- (broadcast) node	1	A computer doing B-node name resolution relies on broadcasts to convert names into IP addresses. B-node name resolution is not the best option on larger networks because the broadcast loads the network and usually does not go through routers. Note: Microsoft really uses B-node, which checks the LMHOSTS file after doing a broadcast.

TABLE 3.7 *Continued*

Node Types	Registry Value	Description
P- (point-to-point) node	2	A computer doing P-node name resolution uses a NetBIOS Name Server (NBNS)/WINS server to look up NetBIOS names to get IP addresses. All systems must know the IP address of the NBNS. The main drawback of P-node name resolution is that if the NBNS cannot be accessed, there is no way to resolve names and thus no way to access other systems on the network by using NetBIOS names.
M- (mixed) node	4	An M-node computer first tries a broadcast to resolve a name. It that attempt fails, the computer looks up the name in a NetBIOS name server. In other words, an M-node computer first acts as a B-node, and if that fails, tries to act as a P-node. M-Node has the advantage over P-node in that if the NBNS is unavailable, systems on the local subnet can still be accessed through B-node resolution. M-node is typically not the best choice for larger networks because it uses B-node and thus results in broadcasts. However, when you have a large network that consists of smaller subnetworks connected via slow Wide Area Network (WAN) links, M-node is a preferred method because it reduces the amount of communication across the slow links.
H- (hybrid) node (default)	8	An H-node computer first does a P-node lookup; if that fails, the computer does a broadcast. In either case, the NetBIOS name resolution tries the LMHOSTS file after trying a broadcast and/or WINS server.

If you are using H- (hybrid) node, it first checks to see whether the name is the local machine name. It then checks the NetBIOS cache area for remote names. Resolved Names remain in the cache area for 10 minutes. If the name hasn't been resolved yet, it tries the WINS server, then tries a broadcast. Last, it looks in the LMHOSTS file, if the system has one, and then uses the HOSTS file and DNS server if it was configured.

WINS Server Replication

To provide fault tolerance, it is recommended to have more than one WINS server with the same WINS database. By having more than one WINS server, a WINS client can go to the second WINS server when the first one is unavailable. To make sure that the WINS server has the same information, you must replicate the information from one WINS server to the other WINS server. These servers are known as replication partners.

> **NOTE**
>
> Windows Server 2008 supports up to 12 replication partners, whereas the first and second WINS servers are the primary and secondary servers, and any remaining servers are backup WINS servers.

A WINS replication partner can be added and configured as a pull partner, a push partner, or a push/pull partner:

- A *push/pull partner* is the default configuration and is the type recommended for use in most cases.

- A *pull partner* is a WINS server that requests new database entries from its partner. The pull occurs at configured time intervals or in response to an update notification from a push partner.

- A *push partner* is a WINS server that sends update notification messages. The update notification occurs after a configurable number of changes to the WINS database.

Because pull partners configure at certain time intervals, you should use a pull partner across slow links. For example, you could have it replicate every 24 hours, beginning at 12:00 at night. Therefore, the replication occurs when traffic is at a minimum. A push partner should be used with servers connected across fast links because push replication occurs when a particular number of updated WINS entries are reached.

> **NOTE**
>
> If you need certain changes to replicate immediately, you can use WINS console to force the WINS servers to replicate.

You can configure a WINS server to automatically configure other WINS server computers as its replication partners, using periodic multicasts to announce their presence. These announcements are sent as IGMP messages for the multicast group address of 224.0.1.24 (the well-known multicast IP address reserved for WINS server use). With this automatic partner configuration, other WINS servers are discovered when they join the network and are added as replication partners.

WINS Proxy Agent

A *WINS proxy agent* is a WINS-enabled computer configured to act on behalf of other host computer that cannot directly use WINS. WINS proxies help resolve NetBIOS name queries for computers located on a subnet where there is not a WINS server by hearing broadcasts on the subnet of the proxy agent and forwarding those responses directly to a WINS server. This keeps the broadcast local yet gets responses from a WINS server without using the P-node because most WINS proxies are useful or necessary only on networks that include NetBIOS broadcast-only (B-node) clients. Therefore, for most networks, WINS proxies are typically not needed.

Installing and Managing WINS Server

Before installing a WINS server, you must make sure that the TCP/IP protocol is installed and a static IP address is assigned. Then use the Server Manager console to install WINS as a feature.

WINS Console

The primary tool that you use to manage local and remote WINS servers is the *WINS console*, which can be accessed from within the Administrative Tools folder or by using the Microsoft Management Console (MMC) snap-in (see Figure 3.11).

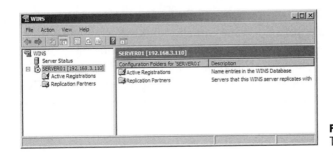

FIGURE 3.11
The WINS console.

Within the WINS console, right-click the WINS server and click Properties. You can configure several options from the Properties dialog box. Using the General tab, you can configure how often server statistics are updated (you can also disable this option) and specify a location in which to back up the WINS database. From the Intervals tab, the rate at which records are renewed, deleted, and verified can be configured as follows:

▶ **Renew Interval**: Specifies the number of days before a WINS client must renew its registered NetBIOS name.

▶ **Extinction Interval**: Specifies the amount of time before a record marked as released is marked as extinct.

▶ **Extinction Timeout**: Specifies the amount of time before a record marked as extinct is removed from the WINS database.

▶ **Verification Interval**: Specifies the amount of time before a WINS server must verify any records that have been replicated from a replication partner.

The Database Verification tab enables you to configure when and how often the WINS server should verify the records within its database.

The Advanced tab has several configurable options (see Figure 3.12). You can enable logging so WINS-related events are written to the system log. Burst handling can be enabled or disabled, which enables you to configure the number of requests to which a WINS server can successfully respond without actually registering the name within the database. You can also specify the location of the WINS database and configure the version number.

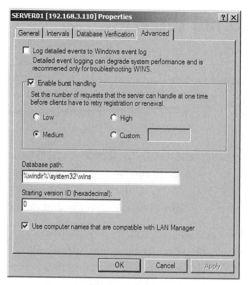

FIGURE 3.12   The WINS Advanced options.

Configuring Replication

WINS servers can be configured for replication The WINS management console can be used to configure WINS servers for replication. To configure replication, follow these steps:

1. Within the WINS management console, right-click Replication Partners and select New Replication Partner.

2. Enter the name or IP address of the WINS server you want to add as a replication partner. Click OK.

3. Right-click the WINS server that was added as a replication partner and click Properties.

4. From the Advanced tab within the WINS server's Properties window, use the drop-down list to select the replication partner type. Click OK.

If you do not want to manually set up WINS replication partners, you can configure WINS servers to automatically find one another and configure themselves for replication. They do so by multicasting to the IP address of 224.0.1.24. When WINS servers locate each other, they automatically configure themselves as push/pull replication partners. You can enable this automatic discovery option by right-clicking Replication Partners within the WINS management console and clicking Properties. From the Replication Partners Properties window, select the Advanced tab and choose the Enable Automatic Partner Configuration option.

Backing Up and Restoring the WINS Database

Through the WINS management console, you can configure a WINS server to periodically back up its local database. From the WINS Server properties window, you can specify a backup location. You can also right-click the WINS server and select the Backup Database option.

After you specify a backup location, the WINS server creates the Wins_bak\NewFolder within the location you specify and backs up the local database to this location every three hours. You also have the option of selecting whether the WINS server should perform a backup when the server is shut down.

If you have a backup of the WINS database, you can restore it by right-clicking the WINS server, choosing the Restore Database option, and specifying the location of folder to which the database was backed up. Keep in mind that before you perform a restore, the WINS service must be stopped. If the WINS service is running, the option to restore the database is not available.

Server Statistics

Viewing the statistics of a WINS server can provide an administrator with a general idea of what is happening. Within the WINS management console, you can right-click the WINS server and select the Display Server Statistics option. Some of the information provided includes when the server was last started, when replication last took place, and the number of name queries resolved.

Tombstoning

Records that are deleted or marked as extinct on one server can cause inconsistencies to the database of its replication partners. For example, a record that was deleted from the database on one server can easily still appear within the database of a replication partner.

Windows Server 2008 supports a feature known as *tombstoning*. After a record is marked as tombstoned it is no longer considered to be active on the local WINS server. The record remains within the local database for replication purposes. When a tombstoned record is replicated, all replication partners mark the record as being tombstoned and it becomes extinct, eventually being removed from the database.

You can manually delete or tombstone records within the WINS database by using the following process:

1. Within the WINS console, right-click the Active Registrations container and click either the Find by Name or Find by Owner option to locate the appropriate record.

2. If you select Find by Name, type the NetBIOS name for which you are searching. If you select Find by Owner, specify whether to have all entries in the local WINS database displayed or records from a specific WINS server. Click Find Now.

3. In the Details pane, right-click the appropriate record and click Delete.

4. Within the Delete Record dialog box, select one of the following options: Delete the Record Only from this Server or Replicate Deletion of the Record to Other Servers (Tombstone).

Verifying Database Consistency

With multiple WINS servers configured for replication, a WINS database can become inconsistent over a period of time. Using the Verify Database Consistency and Verify Version ID Consistency options, an administrator can periodically perform database consistency checks. Checking the WINS database for inconsistencies forces the local WINS server to check all names replicated from other WINS servers and compare them with the local versions on the servers that own the records. The WINS server then updates its local records.

Compacting the WINS Database

The WINS database uses the Extensible Storage Engine, a generic storage engine that serves Microsoft Exchange 5.5 servers. To recover the unused space, the WINS database is compacted. In Windows, WINS server database compaction occurs as an automatic background process during idle time after a database update. Because the database compaction is also dynamic, you do not need to stop the IWNS server to compact the database; this process is also known as online compaction. Although WINS performs regular online compaction, this reduces, but does not eliminate the need for offline compaction.

Microsoft recommends use of `jetpack.exe` to compact a jet database periodically whenever the database grows beyond 30MB in size. To compact a WINS database, you must first stop the WINS service and then use `jetpack.exe`:

```
jetpack database_name name_of_the_temporary_database
```

Troubleshooting NetBIOS Name Resolution

To troubleshoot NetBIOS name resolution over TCP/IP, you can use the NBTSTAT command. Its options are detailed in Table 3.8.

TABLE 3.8   NBTSTAT Options

Option	Description
nbtstat –n	Displays the names that were registered locally on the system by programs such as the server and redirector.
nbtstat –c	Shows the NetBIOS name cache, which contains name-to-address mappings for other computers.
nbtstat -R	Purges the name cache and reloads it from the LMHOSTS file.
nbtstat –RR	Releases NetBIOS names registered with a WINS server and then renews their registration.
nbtstat –a *name*	Performs a NetBIOS adapted status command against the computer specified by *name*. The adapter status command returns the local NetBIOS name table for that computer plus the adapter's media access control address.
nbtstat –S	Lists the current NetBIOS sessions and their status, including statistics.

Deploying a GlobalNames Zone

One advantage of WINS is its use of single-label names instead of the FQDNs that DNS uses. You can simplify the use of fully qualified domain nameby doing one of the following:

▶ Set a primary DNS suffix for each computer, which is placed after the computer or hostname to form the FQDN.

▶ Set a list of DNS servers for clients to use when resolving DNS names, such as a preferred DNS server, and any alternate DNS servers to use if the preferred server is not available.

▶ Set the DNS suffix search list or search method to be used by a client when it performs DNS query searches for short, unqualified domain names.

Unfortunately, this gets you only so far because the NetBIOS names/single-label names are not supported with IPv6.

To help network administrators migrate WINS to DNS for all name resolution, the DNS Server role in Windows Server 2008 supports a specially named zone called *GlobalNames*. By deploying a zone with this name, you can have the static, global records with single-label names without relying on WINS. These single-label names typically refer to records for important, well known, and widely used servers that typically have static addresses and are managed by the network administrators.

Keep in mind that the GlobalNames zone is not designed to completely replace WINS. It is not to be used for name resolution of records that are dynamically registered in WINS and records which typically are not managed by IT administrators.

To resolve names that are registered in the GlobalNames zone, all DNS servers that are authoritative for a zone and that serve client query requests must be running Windows Server 2008 and they must either be configured with a local copy of the GlobalNames zone or they must be able to contact remote DNS servers that host the GlobalNames zone. It is also recommend that the GlobalNames zone be integrated with Active Directory Domain Services (AD DS).

To deploy a GlobalNames zone, follow these steps:

1. Create the GlobalNames zone. The GlobalNames zone is not a special zone type; rather, it is simply an AD DS–integrated forward lookup zone that is called GlobalNames.

2. Enable GlobalNames zone support by using the following command on every authoritative DNS server in the forest:

   ```
   dnscmd <ServerName> /enableglobalnamessupport 1
   ```

   where ServerName is the DNS name or IP address of the DNS server that hosts the GlobalNames zone. To specify the local computer, replace ServerName with a period (.) For example,

   ```
   dnsmcd . /enableglobalnamesupport 1.
   ```

3. Replicate the GlobalNames zone to all domain controllers in the forest (that is, add the GlobalNames zone to the forest-wide DNS application partition).

4. Populate the GlobalNames zone for each server that you want to be able to provide single-label name resolution by adding the appropriate alias (CNAME) resource record to the GlobalNames zone.

5. Publish the location of the GlobalNames zone in other forests by adding service location (SRV) resource records to the forest-wide DNS application partition, using the service name _globalnames._msdcs and specifying the FQDN of the DNS server that hosts the GlobalNames zone.

6. You must run the `dnscmd ServerName /enableglobalnamessupport 1` command on every authoritative DNS server in the forests that does not host the GlobalNames zone.

7. Last, be sure to disable dynamic updates on the GlobalNames zone.

Exam Prep Questions

1. What is used to resolve hostnames to IP addresses? (Choose two answers.)

    ○ **A.** DNS

    ○ **B.** WINS

    ○ **C.** LMHOSTS files

    ○ **D.** HOSTS files

    ○ **E.** Active Directory

2. Which DNS resource record is used to translate from hostnames to IP addresses?

    ○ **A.** A and AAAA records

    ○ **B.** PTR records

    ○ **C.** SRV records

    ○ **D.** CNAME records

3. You have a Windows Server 2008 computer that hosts DNS. You have enabled DNS scavenging on Server1, but you later notice that the stale records are not being removed on your domain. What do you need to do to make sure that the records are being removed for your domain?

    ○ **A.** Restart the DNS service on the server.

    ○ **B.** Enable DNS scavenging on the zone.

    ○ **C.** Run the dnscmd *<name of server>* /scavengenow command.

    ○ **D.** Right-click the zone and authorize scavenging.

4. You have a Windows Server 2008 computer that hosts DNS for your domain. You need to ensure that public DNS zone records cannot be copied without impacting the public DNS name resolution.

    ○ **A.** Configure the Allow Zone Transfers Only to Servers Listed on the Name Servers option on the domain.

    ○ **B.** Disable the Allow-Read permission for the Everyone group on the DNS domain.

    ○ **C.** Modify the permissions for the SOA record.

    ○ **D.** Remove the public name servers from the Name Server list.

5. You have a Windows Server 2008 that hosts a DNS server with the DNS primary zone for the corporation. In addition, you have a DNS server that hosts a DNS secondary zone at each of the remote sites. You make a change on the corporate server to one of the key resource records and you need that change to be immediately recognized at a remote site. What should you do?

    ○ **A.** Restart the DNS service on the corporate DNS server.

    ○ **B.** Run the dnscmd command with the /zonerefresh option on the corporate server.

    ○ **C.** Run the dnscmd command with the /zonerefresh option on the server at the remote site.

    ○ **D.** Execute the ipconfig /flushdns command on the server at the remote site.

6. You have a Windows Server 2008 with a Active Directory integrated DNS zone. How does it keep track of the domain controllers that provide LDAP?

    ○. **A.** A records

    ○ **B.** SRV records

    ○ **C.** CNAME records

    ○ **D.** MX records

7. How do you configure the DNS suffix search list for your DNS clients?

    ○ **A.** Configure a DHCP option that defines the DNS suffix search list.

    ○ **B.** Configure the DNS suffix search list in the SOA record for the zone.

    ○ **C.** Create a search list record in DNS.

    ○ **D.** Configure a new GPO that configures the DNS suffix search list.

8. You have several DNS servers for your corporation. At one of the remote sites, you want to place a DNS server that can query any DNS server in the corporate office and you need to limit the number of DNS records that are transferred to the DNS server in the remote site. What should you do?

    ○ **A.** Configure a primary zone on the DNS server in the remote office.

    ○ **B.** Configure a secondary zone on the DNS server in the remote office.

    ○ **C.** Configure a stub zone on the DNS server in the remote office.

    ○ **D.** Configure a stub zone at the corporate office.

9. You have a Windows Server 2008 with DNS. You need to delete the pointer record for the IP address 10.24.1.30. What should you do?

- ○ **A.** Use the DNS manager to delete the 10.in-addr.arpa zone.

- ○ **B.** Run the dnscmd /RecordDelete 10.24.1.30 command at the command prompt.

- ○ **C.** Run the dnscmd /ZoneDelete 10.in-addr.arpa command at the command prompt.

- ○ **D.** Run the dnscmd /Record Delete 10.in-addr.arpa 30.1.24 PTR command at the command prompt.

10. You are the network administrator for the Acme Corporation. The corporation uses a single Active Directory forest with multiple domains. The Acme Corporation purchases Cat and Mouse University, which has its own Active Directory forest with a single domain. You need to configure the DNS system in the forest to provide name resolution for resources in both forests. What should you do?

- ○ **A.** Configure the client computers to use the DNS server in the other company as their secondary DNS server.

- ○ **B.** Create a conditional forwarder and store it in Active Directory. Replicate the new conditional forwarder to all DNS servers in the forest.

- ○ **C.** Create a host record that points to the new DNS servers in the other Active Directory forests.

- ○ **D.** Configure a trust relationship between the two forests.

11. What record is used to define where email is sent so that it can be processed by a company's mail server?

- ○ **A.** MX record
- ○ **B.** SRV record
- ○ **C.** PTR record
- ○ **D.** CNAME

12. You have an Active Directory domain. At the corporate office, you have two Windows Server 2008 servers. At the five remote sites, each remote site has a Windows Server 2008 server. What can you do to make sure that users in the remote offices are able to access network resources as quickly as possible?

   ○ **A.** Configure a primary DNS server at the corporate site and each of the remote sites. Configure the DNS servers at the remote site to forward to the primary server at the corporate office.

   ○ **B.** Configure an Active Directory integrated zone at the corporate office.

   ○ **C.** Configure an Active Directory integrated zone at the corporate office and a primary zone at each of the remote sites.

   ○ **D.** Configure one of the servers at the corporate office as the Primary DNS server and configure the other as a secondary DNS server. Configure each of the remote servers as a secondary server.

13. You have a single Active Directory forest with multiple domains. You need to ensure that all public DNS queries go through a single-caching only DNS server. What should you do?

   ○ **A.** Disable the root hints on your DNS servers and configure a forwarder to the caching DNS server.

   ○ **B.** Enable BIND secondaries.

   ○ **C.** Configure a GlobalNames host (A) record for the hostname of the caching DNS server.

   ○ **D.** Disable DNS and use WINS on those servers.

14. You have a Windows Server 2008 Core Installation with the DNS Server role. The server is called Server1 and it has an address of 172.24.1.20. You need to create a DNS zone named local.acme.com. What do you do?

   ○ **A.** Execute the `netsh interface ipv4 set dnsserver name=local.acme.com static 172.24.1.20` primary command.

   ○ **B.** Execute the `dnscmd Server1 /ZoneAdd local.acme.com /Primary /file local.acme.com.dns` command.

   ○ **C.** Execute the `dnscmd Server1 /ZoneAdd local.acme.com /DSPrimary` command.

   ○ **D.** Execute the `nslookup /registerdns:local.acme.com` command.

15. You have an Active Directory forest with DNS Active Directory integrated zones. You want to get rid of the WINS service but still keep forest-wide single name resolution for your key servers. What should you do?

    ○ **A.** Create SRV records for each server.

    ○ **B.** Create an Active Directory integrated zone named WINS. Create host (A) records for your servers.

    ○ **C.** Create an Active Directory integrated zone named GlobalNames. Create host (A) records for your servers.

    ○ **D.** Enable WINS-Emulation mode in DNS.

16. You currently have a primary and secondary DNS servers running on Windows Server 2008 domain controllers. You want to be able to perform updates to the zone data from any DNS server. What should you do?

    ○ **A.** In the Properties dialog box for the DNS server, select the General tab and click Change beside the zone type. Select the option to store the zone in Active Directory.

    ○ **B.** In the Properties dialog box for the zone, select the Zone Type tab and click Change. Select the Active Directory Integrated option.

    ○ **C.** In the Properties dialog box for the zone, select the General tab and click Change beside the zone type. Select the option to store the zone in Active Directory.

    ○ **D.** In the Properties dialog box for the DNS server, select the Zone Type tab and click Change. Select the Active Directory Integrated option.

17. You have a Windows Server 2008 computer that hosts your DNS server. You are trying to determine the hostname associated with the IP address of 192.168.0.20, using the NSLookup command from a workstation, but you are unsuccessful. What is most likely the cause of the problem?

    ○ **A.** There is no A record for the host that is assigned this address.

    ○ **B.** There is no PTR record for the host that is assigned this address.

    ○ **C.** There is no SRV record for the host that is assigned this address.

    ○ **D.** There is no entry in the LMHOSTS file for this host.

18. You have a primary DNS server at the corporate office and a secondary server at your remote offices. The WAN link between the remote offices and the corporate office is heavily used. You want to decrease the number of times that the secondary DNS server checks for zone updates. What should you do?

    ○ **A.** In the Properties dialog box for the DNS server, select the Zone Transfers tab and increase the refresh interval.

    ○ **B.** In the Properties dialog box for the zone, select the Start of Authority (SOA) tab and increase the refresh interval.

    ○ **C.** In the Properties dialog box for the zone, select the Start of Authority (SOA) tab and increase the retry interval.

    ○ **D.** In the Properties dialog box for the zone, select the General tab and increase the retry interval.

19. You have a Windows Server 2008 computer with WINS. All Windows clients are WINS-enabled and capable of updating their records dynamically. One of the subnets contains two UNIX servers. Hosts on the local subnet can communicate with the UNIX servers; however, hosts on other subnets are unsuccessful. Windows clients can resolve NetBIOS names for hosts on other subnets. Clients on all subnets need to be able to resolve the NetBIOS names of the UNIX servers. What should you do?

    ○ **A.** On each of the subnets, configure a secondary WINS server on each subnet.

    ○ **B.** Configure the WINS servers as replication partners.

    ○ **C.** Configure the WINS servers to back up their local databases.

    ○ **D.** Configure static mappings for the two UNIX servers.

20. You are a network administrator for your corporation that has multiple subnets. All Windows servers are running Microsoft Windows Server 2008. The network has a mixture of WINS and non-WINS clients. You have three WINS servers. You find out that the non-WINS clients are unable to browse hosts on other subnets. What should you do?

    ○ **A.** Configure static mappings for the non-WINS clients.

    ○ **B.** Install a WINS proxy on each subnet that does not have a local WINS server.

    ○ **C.** Configure replication between the three WINS servers.

    ○ **D.** Configure a DHCP relay agent on each subnet.

21. You have multiple WINS servers on different subnets on your corporate network. Which of the following describe push and pull partners? (Choose two answers.)

   O **A.** Pull partners replicated during configured time intervals.

   O **B.** Push partners replicate after a configured number of changes.

   O **C.** Pull partners replicate after a configured number of changes.

   O **D.** Push partners are replicated during configured time intervals.

22. When using WINS, which NetBIOS name resolution method first communicates with a WINS server and then uses a broadcast to resolve the name?

   O **A.** B-node

   O **B.** P-node

   O **C.** M-node

   O **D.** H-node

Answers to Exam Prep Questions

1. Answers A and D are correct. DNS is a service that resolves hostnames to IP addresses. HOSTS files can also be used to resolve hostnames. Answers B and C are incorrect because WINS and LMHOSTS files are used to translate NetBIOS/computer names to IP addresses. Answer E is incorrect because Active Directory is a directory service.

2. Answer A is correct. Host (A) records translate from hostnames to IPv4 32-bit IP addresses and Host (AAAA) records translate from hostnames to IPv6 128-bit IP addresses. Answer B is incorrect because Pointer (PTR) records are used to translate from IP address to hostname. Answer C is incorrect because service (SRV) records are used to locate services such as the LDAP services. Answer D is incorrect because the CNAME records are used define an alias that points to another name record.

3. Answer B is correct. To scavenge files, scavenging and aging must be enabled, both at the DNS server and on the zone. Answer A is incorrect because if you enable scavenging, you do not have to restart the DNS server to scavenge the resource records. Answer C is incorrect because there is no scavengnow option for the dnscmd command. Answer D is incorrect because there is no authorize scavenging option with the DNS Manager console.

4. Answer A is correct. To stop from other DNS servers to get zone transfers is to allow transfers only to servers listed on the name server. Answer B is incorrect because without the Allow-Read option, no one can access the domain for name resolution. Answer C is incorrect because if you modify the permissions on the SOA record, you affect everyone who tries to read the zone. Answer D is incorrect because the public name servers are not on the the the name server list.

5. Answer C is correct. You can force a secondary zone transfer by running the `dnscmd` command with the `/zonerefresh` option. Answer A is incorrect because restarting the DNS server on the corporate server does not force a zone transfer. Answer B is incorrect because executing the dnscmd command with the `/zonerefresh` option does not force a zone transfer. Answer D is incorrect because `ipconfig` `/flushdns` only clears out the local DNS cache on the server and does not execute a zone transfer.

6. Answer B is correct. SRV records define the location of LDAP servers. Answer A is incorrect because the host (A) record is used to translate from hostname to IP address. Answer C is incorrect because the CNAME records are used to define aliases. Answer D is incorrect because the MX defines the location of the mail servers.

7. Answer D is correct. To configure a DNS suffix search list, you need to create a group policy. Answer A is incorrect because there is no DHCP option that defines a suffix search list. Answer B is incorrect because there is no DNS suffix search list in the SOA record. Answer C is incorrect because there is no search list record in DNS.

8. Answer D is correct. The stub zones contain the Start of Authority (SOA) resource records of the zone—the DNS resource records that list the zone's authoritative server, and the glue A (address) resource records that are required for contacting the zone's authoritative servers. Answer A is incorrect because you would usually you're your primary zone at the corporate office and you can only have one primary zone. Answer B is incorrect because the secondary zone has a copy of every resource record sent to the remote site. Answer C Answer C is incorrect because the corporate office is your central point for DNS. Therefore, you should have the stub zone with your other zones.

9. Answer D is correct. You have to use the `dnscmd` `/Record Delete` command to delete the individual PTR record. Answers A and C are incorrect because these would delete the entire zone and all of the PTR records in the zone. Answer B is incorrect because you need to specify in which zone the record resides.

10. Answer B is correct. You should create a conditional forwarder that forwards requests to the other company's DNS server as necessary. Answer A is incorrect because a secondary DNS server is used only when the first one is not available. Answer C is incorrect because the host record provides name resolution for those hosts but would not help you locate any other resource records located on the other company's DNS servers. Answer D is incorrect because trust relationships are for Active Directory and not for name resolution.

11. Answer A is correct. The Mail Exchange (MX) record is used to resolve where to deliver emails. Answer B is incorrect because SRV records define the services available, such as the LDAP services. Answer C is incorrect because the PTR records are used for IP addresses to hostnames. Answer D is incorrect because CNAME records are for aliases.

12. Answer D is correct. You should configure the primary zone at the corporate office and secondary zones elsewhere. Clients perform DNS queries at the local site for quick name resolution. Answer A is incorrect because you can have only one primary DNS

zone. Answer B is incorrect because remote users have to perform DNS queries across a WAN link, which is slower than a local query. Answer C is incorrect because you can only have one primary zone. Those remote sites should have been secondary zones.

13. Answer A is correct. You need to disable root hints so that those servers do not go to the Internet for name resolution. Then configure a forwarder to the caching DNS server. Answer B is incorrect because Bind Secondaries determines whether fast transfers are used when transferring zone data to a BIND server. Versions of BIND earlier than 4.9.4 do not support fast zone transfers. Answer C is incorrect because the GlobalNames zone is used for resolving single label names, which has nothing to do with a caching DNS server.

14. Answer B is correct. You need to create the `dnscmd` with the `/ZoneAdd` command. You also need to specify where the file is located with the `/file` option. Answer A is not correct because the `netsh` command would be used to point to a DNS server, not to create a zone. Answer C is incorrect because this is not a domain controller and therefore cannot store an Active Directory integrated zone. Answer D is incorrect because `nslookup` is used to troubleshoot name resolution, not to create DNS zones.

15. Answer C is correct. You need to create a GlobalNames zone with the records for your servers. Answer A is incorrect because SRV records list certain services and where they can be located, such as LDAP. Answer B is incorrect because creating a WINS zone does not give you single name resolution. Answer D is incorrect because there is no WINS-Emulation mode in DNS.

16. Answer C is correct. You need to change the zones to Active Directory integrated zones. To change the zone type, right-click the zone within the DNS management console and click Properties. In the Properties dialog box, make sure the General tab is selected and click Change beside the zone type. Select the option to store the zone within Active Directory. Answer A is incorrect because the zone type is configured at the zone level. Answers B and D are incorrect because there is no Zone Type tab available in either the server's Properties dialog box or the zone's Properties dialog box. There is also no option known as Active Directory Integrated.

17. Answer B is correct. PTR records are used to resolve IP addresses to hostnames. Answer A is incorrect because A records are used to resolve hostnames to IP addresses. Answer C is incorrect because SRV records are used to locate key services such as LDAP. Answer D is incorrect because LMHOST files are used to resolve NetBIOS/computer names to IP addresses.

18. Answer B is correct. To increase the rate at which the secondary server polls for updates, select the Start of Authority (SOA) tab from the zone's Properties dialog box and increase the refresh interval. Answer A is incorrect because the interval at which a secondary server polls for updates is configured at the zone level. Answer C is incorrect because the retry interval defines how often the secondary server continues to poll if the server does not respond. Answer D is incorrect because you must configure the refresh interval, and it must be done from the Start of Authority (SOA) tab.

19. Answer D is correct. To allow hosts on other subnets to resolve the NetBIOS names of the UNIX servers, static mapping must be configured because the UNIX servers are unable to register their NetBIOS records dynamically. Answers A and C are incorrect because performing these tasks does not allow hosts to resolve the NetBIOS names of the UNIX servers. Answer B is incorrect because if the clients can already resolve the names of hosts on other subnets, replication is already configured between the WINS servers.

20. Answer B is correct. Since the non-WINS clients cannot use a WINS server for name resolution, they have to rely on broadcast for name resolution. To allow B-node broadcasts to be resolved across the network, a WINS proxy agent must be configured. The WINS proxy listens for B-node broadcasts and contacts the WINS servers on the other subnets to resolve the name resolution request on behalf of the non-WINS client. Therefore, answers A, C, and D are incorrect.

21. Answers A and B are correct. Pull partners replicate during time intervals and push partners replicate during configured time intervals. Therefore, answers C and D are incorrect.

22. Answer D is correct. A host using H-node (the default method), checks the cache first. The host then tries to communicate with a WINS server. If it cannot find the computer, it then tries a broadcast. Answer A is incorrect because B-node does a broadcast only. Answer B is incorrect because the P-node tries to communicate with only the WINS server. Answer C is incorrect because after M-node checks the cache, it does a broadcast first and then tries to communicate with a WINS server.

Need to Know More?

To learn more about DNS, visit the following websites:

▶ http://technet2.microsoft.com/windowsserver/en/library/6e45e81e-fb44-4a20-a752-ebe740e2acc61033.mspx?mfr=true

▶ http://technet.microsoft.com/en-us/network/bb629410.aspx

▶ http://www.howstuffworks.com/dns.htm

Regan, Patrick. *Networking with Windows 2000 and 2003*. Upper Saddle River, New Jersey: Prentice Hall, 2004.

Regan, Patrick. *Local Area Networks*. Upper Saddle River, New Jersey: Prentice Hall, 2004.

CHAPTER FOUR

DHCP Services

Terms you'll need to understand:

✓ Bootstrap Protocol (BOOTP)

✓ Preboot Execution Environment (PXE)

✓ Dynamic Host Configuration Protocol (DHCP)

✓ DHCP scope

✓ Multicast Address Dynamic Client Allocation Protocol (MADCAP)

✓ Client reservation

✓ Asynchronous backup

✓ Synchronous backup

✓ Conflict detection

✓ DHCP options

✓ DHCP relay agent

Techniques/concepts you'll need to master:

✓ Install and configure a DHCP server.

✓ Authorize the DHCP server in Active Directory.

✓ Create a scope with exclusions, reservations, and scope options.

✓ Monitor and troubleshoot DHCP problems.

You would need hours to complete IP configuration for hundreds of computers. DHCP empowers you to automatically configure the IP configuration of these computers and also lets you make any changes you might need to make later. As you learn about networks, you will quickly understand that the DHCP service is one of the most valuable tools, and most likely an essential tool, that you have in your arsenal.

Introduction to DHCP Services

Bootstrap Protocol (BOOTP), also known as *Preboot Execution Environment (PXE)*, is a UDP network protocol used by a network client to obtain its IP address automatically. This is usually done during the bootstrap process when a computer is starting up. The BOOTP servers assign the IP address from a pool of addresses to each client. BOOTP can then be used to load an advanced operating system over the network from a network disk. It can also be used by corporations to roll out a preconfigured client image such as Windows to newly installed computers.

Originally, BOOTP required a boot floppy disk to establish the initial network connection. Today, the protocol can often be found embedded in the BIOS of network cards themselves and in many modern motherboards, thus allowing direct network booting.

An extension to BOOTP is the *Dynamic Host Configuration Protocol (DHCP)*, which is used to automatically configure a host during boot-up on a TCP/IP network and to change settings while the host is attached. You can automatically set many parameters with the DHCP server. Some of the more common parameters include

- IP address
- Subnet mask
- Gateway (router) address
- Address of DNS servers
- Address of WINS servers
- WINS client mode

The DHCP database is stored in the *systemroot*\SYSTEM32\DHCF DHCP.MDB directory.

The DHCP role on Microsoft Windows Server 2008 supports several new feature

▶ DHCPv6 stateful and stateless configuration is supported for configurir clients in an IPv6 environment.

▶ Network Access Protection (NAP) with DHCP helps isolate potentially malware-infected computers from the corporate network.

▶ DHCP can be installed as a role on a Windows Server 2008 Server Cor installation.

The DHCP Requests

A DHCP server maintains a list of IP addresses called a *pool*. When a user nee an IP address, the server removes the address from the pool and issues it to th user for a limited time. Issuing an address is called leasing. Using a DHCP serve to issue addresses is more reliable and requires less labor than setting every con puter manually, and you can get by with fewer IP addresses because compute not on the network are not using IP addresses.

A host computer that is configured to get a DHCP address sends a DHCPDIS COVER message on the local IP subnet to find the DHCP server or server The client doesn't know the address or addresses of the DHCP server, so it use an IP broadcast address for the DHCPDISCOVER message. All availabl DHCP servers respond with a DHCPOFFER message. If more than one serve is available, the client usually selects the first server to respond, but no rule specifie which server the client has to use. No matter how many servers respond, th client broadcasts a DHCPREQUEST message that identifies which server th client will use and implicitly informs all other servers that the client won't us them. The selected server responds to the client with a DHCPPACK messag that contains the assigned IP address, any other network parameter assignments and the lease or amount of time for which the DHCP server assigns the clien the IP address. The client sends messages to UDP port 67 on the DHCP serve and the server sends messages to UDP port 68 on the DHCP client.

Installing DHCP

Before installing a DHCP server, you must make sure that the TCP/IP protocol is installed and a static IP address is assigned to the DHCP server. You then would install it as a server role:

1. Click Start, Administrative Tools, Server Manager, and then acknowledge User Account Control.

2. In Roles Summary, click Add Roles, Next, check DHCP server, and then click Next.

3. You then run a wizard to configure the network connection binding, IPv4 DNS, IPv4 WINS, DHCP scopes, DHCPv6 stateless mode, and IPv6 DNS settings.

DHCP Scope

Before your DHCP server can provide IP address leases to clients, you have to provide a range of IP addresses at the DHCP server. This range, known as a *scope*, defines a single physical subnet on your network to which DHCP services are offered. So, for example, if you have two subnets, your DHCP server must be connected to each subnet and you must define a scope for each subnet. Scopes also provide the primary way for the server to manage distribution and assignment of IP addresses and any related configuration parameters to clients on the network.

The available parameters are

- **Name (optional)**: The name of the scope.

- **Comment (optional)**: The optional comment for the scope, used primarily to describe it.

- **IP Address Range from Address**: The starting IP address of the scope or address pool.

- **IP Address Range to Address**: The ending IP address of the scope or address pool.

- **Mask**: The subnet mask assigned to DHCP clients.

- **Exclusion Range Start Address (optional)**: The starting IP address of the range to exclude within the scope or address pool.

- **Exclusion Range End Address (optional)**: The ending IP address of the range to exclude within the scope or address pool.

▸ **Lease Duration Unlimited**: A parameter that indicates that DHCP leases assigned to clients never expire.

▸ **Lease Duration Limited to**: The number of days, hours, and minutes that a DHCP client lease is available before it must be renewed. The default is eight days.

Traditionally, a DHCP server can have only one scope per subnet per DHCP server. If necessary, you can exclude addresses within the scope. For example, you decide that the scope that you will use is between 132.132.20.10 and 132.132.20.110. Let's say that you have a network printer assigned a static IP address of 132.132.20.50 and a UNIX server using a static IP address of 132.132.20.51, you would then have to exclude these two addresses. You cannot use the scopes of 132.132.20.10–132.132.20.49 and 132.132.20.52–132.132.20.110 because each subnet can only have one scope.

> **NOTE**
>
> When creating a scope, you also provide the scope's subnet mask and the duration of the lease (default is eight days).

When you use the DHCP console to create a scope, you use the New Scope Wizard. After inputting the scope with the wizard, you then specify the subnet mask and exclusion addresses. After you create a scope, you cannot change the IP address range or subnet mask that is assigned by the scope. Instead, you must delete the scope and create a new scope with the correct information.

After you create a scope, you must activate it to make it available for lease assignments. To activate a scope, in DHCP, right-click the entry for the scope, point to Task, and then click Activate.

> **NOTE**
>
> It is recommended that you finish configuring the scope before activating it so that clients receive complete configuration information.

When the DHCP lease has reached 50% of the lease time, the client attempts to renew the lease. This is an automatic process that occurs in the background. Computers may have the same IP address for a long period of time if they operate continually on a network without being shut down.

Superscopes

The Windows 2008 implementation of DHCP supports superscopes. A *superscope* enables you to group multiple scopes (child scopes) as a single administrative entity. Using a superscope, the DHCP server computer can activate and provide leases from more than one scope to clients on a single physical network.

Superscopes are useful when you are running out of addresses assigned to an address pool and more computers need to be added to the network. You can use a superscope to extend the address space for the same physical network segment by adding another range of addresses (scope).

To create a superscope, click the IPv4 under the name of the DHCP server, and click New Superscope from the Action menu. Note: The superscope option is available only if at least one scope, which is not currently part of a superscope, is available. You would then use the New Superscope wizard. A superscope can have scopes added to it during or after its creation.

Multicast Scopes

DHCP includes *Multicast Address Dynamic Client Allocation Protocol (MADCAP)*, which is used to perform multicast address assignment. When registered clients are dynamically assigned IP addresses through MADCAP, they can participate efficiently in the data stream process, such as for real-time video or audio network transmissions.

IP multicast enables a host to communicate with several hosts simultaneously by transmitting information with one data stream. Multicast can greatly reduce the network traffic that bandwidth-hungry applications such as videoconferencing, software distribution, and webcasting create.

You can create a multicast scope so that the DHCP server issues an IP address to an individual client and a shared multicast address to several clients.

> **NOTE**
>
> For multicasting to work correctly, all routers between the servers that are sending packets to the multicast address and the receiving client computers must be configured to recognize the multicast address.

To create a multicast scope,

1. Right-click the IPv4 under the name of the DHCP server and then click New Multicast Scope.

2. In the New Multicast Scope Wizard, specify the name and description of the multicast scope, the multicast IP address range, and the number of routers through which multicast traffic can pass.

3. Specify any excluded IP addresses and the lease duration.

4. Activate the multicast scope when prompted.

Client Reservation

If you have a client that must always use the same address, you can reserve an address by using *client reservation*. The DHCP server then assigns the reserved address to the computer with the specified MAC address. If multiple DHCP servers are configured with a scope that covers the range of the reserved IP address, the client reservation must be made and duplicated at each of these DHCP servers. Otherwise, the reserved client computer can receive a different IP address, depending on which DHCP responds.

Conflict Detection

Conflict detection can be used by either DHCP servers or clients to determine whether an IP address is already in use on the network before leasing or using the address. By default, the DHCP service does not perform any conflict detection. To enable conflict detection, increase the number of ping attempts that the DHCP service performs for each address before leasing that address to a client. Of course, if you enable conflict detection, the DHCP service performs more slowly as it verifies each lease address. This option can also be useful when replacing a failed DHCP server (and you cannot restore the DHCP database settings).

To enable address conflict detection, follow these steps:

1. Open the DHCP console.

2. In the console tree, click the applicable DHCP server.

3. On the Action menu, click Properties.

4. Click the Advanced tab.

5. For Conflict Detection Attempts, type a number greater than 0 (zero) and less than 6, and then click OK.

The number you type determines how many times the DHCP server tests an IP address before leasing it to a client. It is recommended to use 1 or 2. See Figure 4.1.

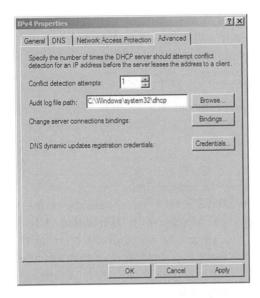

FIGURE 4.1 IPv4 Advanced options including conflict detection attempts.

> **EXAM ALERT**
>
> If you need to make sure that an address is not handed out that is already being used, you would use conflict detection.

DHCP Options

As you are running the Create Scope wizard, the wizard then asks to configure the DHCP options (Default gateway/router, Domain name, addresses of DNS server, addresses of WINS Server). If you decide to add DHCP options or change the current DHCP options, you can use the DHCP console. Table 4.1 shows the most common options used on today's networks and Figure 4.2 shows the DHCP options box.

TABLE 4.1   Common DHCP Options

DHCP Option	Description
003 Router	The IP address of a router or default gateway address.
006 DNS Server	The IP address of a DNS server.
015 DNS Domain Name	The DNS domain name for client resolution.
044 WINS/NBNS Servers	The IP address of a WINS server available to clients.

TABLE 4.1   *Continued*

DHCP Option	Description
046 WINS/NBT Node Type	The type of NetBIOS over TCP/IP name resolution to be used by the client. Options are 1 = B-node (broadcast) 2 = P-node (peer) 4 = M-node (mixed) 8 = H-node (hybrid)
047 NetBIOS Scope ID	The local NetBIOS scope ID.

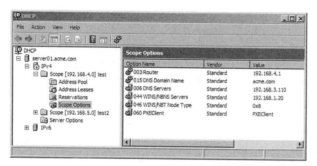

FIGURE 4.2   DHCP Scope Options in the DHCP console.

The optional parameters included with DHCP can be applied at four different levels, depending on to which DHCP clients you want the parameters applied:

▶ Server

▶ Scope

▶ Class

▶ Client

EXAM ALERT

Be sure to know the order in which DHCP clients are applied and understand that those applied later overwrite settings that were previously configured.

Options configured at the server level are applied to all DHCP clients, regardless of the subnet on which they reside. For example, if you want to configure the DNS and WINS server parameters where every computer is given dynamic addresses, you would most likely set them at the server level. To configure server-level options, right-click the Server Options container listed under the DHCP server and select Set Predefined Options from the menu.

If you want to configure DHCP options so that they apply only to DHCP clients on a specific subnet, configure the options at the scope level. For example, the IP address of the default gateway for a subnet should be configured at the scope level. Configuring scope-level options can be done by right-clicking the Scope Options container and selecting Configure Options from the menu.

Next, if you want to apply DHCP options to only a specific DHCP client, you can configure the options at the client level if the client has a client reservation. Client reservations, which are explained in more detail later in this chapter, are DHCP clients that are configured to always lease the same IP address. To configure a client-level option, right-click the client reservation and select Configure Options.

Traditionally, all DHCP clients are treated equally, and the server is unaware of the specific type of clients. This means that the configuration information issued by the DHCP server is the same for all DHCP clients. Starting with Windows 2000, you can use option classes to provide unique configurations to specific types of client computers.

There are two types of option classes, vendor-defined classes and user-defined classes. Vendor-defined classes identify a DHCP client's vendor type and configuration. For example, you can configure a vendor-defined class to provide a custom configuration for computers that are running a specific operating system. User-defined classes enable DHCP clients to differentiate themselves by specifying what type of client they are, such as a desktop or laptop. For example, because a notebook computer is constantly moved and reconnected to the network, you specify a shorter lease to the notebook computer compared to the desktop clients.

> **NOTE**
>
> A client computer needs to be configured with a user-defined class identifier before it sends this identifier to a DHCP server.

To create a new user or vendor class,

1. In the DHCP console, click the applicable DHCP server.

2. On the Action menu, choose either Define User Classes or Define Vendor Classes and click on the Add button.

3. In New Class, type the required information.

For Windows DHCP client computers, the `ipconfig /setclassid` *class* command (where *class* is the unique identify of the user class) can be used to set the specified DHCP class ID string, and the `ipconfig /showclassid` command can confirm that the user class was configured correctly.

Scope options are applied in the following order: server, scope, class, and client. Therefore, options set at the server option are overwritten by the scope options, which are overwritten by the class options, which are overwritten by the client options.

Bindings and DHCP Relay Agent

A *multihomed DHCP server* is a computer running a Windows Server 2008 operating system that uses the DHCP service for more than a single network connection. For a server computer to be multihomed, each network connection must attach the computer to more than a single physical network. This requires that additional hardware (in the form of multiple installed network adapters) be used on the computer.

A computer running a Windows Server 2008 operating system can perform as a multihomed DHCP server. For multihomed servers, the DHCP service binds to the first IP address statically configured for each network connection in use.

By default, the service bindings depend on whether the first network connection is configured dynamically or statically for TCP/IP. Based on the method of configuration it uses, reflected by its current settings in Internet Protocol (TCP/IP) properties, the DHCP Server service performs default service bindings as follows:

▶ If the first network connection uses a manually specified IP address, the connection is enabled in server bindings. For this to occur, a value for the IP address must be configured and the Use the Following IP Address option selected in Internet Protocol (TCP/IP) properties. In this mode, the DHCP server listens for and provides service to DHCP clients.

▶ If the first network connection uses an IP address configured dynamically, the connection is disabled in server bindings. This occurs when the Obtain an IP Address Automatically option is selected in Internet Protocol (TCP/IP) properties. For computers running Windows Server 2008 operating systems, this is the default setting. In this mode, the DHCP server does not listen for and provide service to DHCP clients until a static IP address is configured.

▶ The DHCP server binds to the first static IP address configured on each adapter.

By design, DHCP server bindings are enabled and disabled on a per-connection, not per-address basis. All bindings are based on the first configured IP address for each connection appearing in the Network Connections folder. If additional static IP addresses (for example, as set in Advanced TCP/IP properties) are configured for the applicable connection, these addresses are never used by DHCP servers running Windows Server 2008 and are inconsequential for server bindings.

DHCP servers running Windows Server 2008 never bind to any of the NDIS-WAN or DHCP-enabled interfaces used on the server. These interfaces are not displayed in the DHCP console under the current server bindings list because they are never used for DHCP service. Only additional network connections that have a primary static IP address configured can appear in the server bindings list (or be selectively enabled or disabled there).

A DHCP relay agent is a computer that relays DHCP and BOOTP messages between clients and servers on different subnets. This way, you can have a single DHCP server handle several subnets without the DHCP server being connected directly to those subnets.

EXAM ALERT

If you have the DHCP server located remotely that lies beyond a router, you need to install a DHCP relay agent on the remote site to forward those DHCP broadcasts to the DHCP server.

To add the DHCP Relay Agent, follow these steps:

1. Click Start, select the Programs option, select the Administrative Tools, and select the Routing and Remote Access option.

2. Right-click the general option and select the New Routing Protocol option. The General option can be found by opening the Servername option, followed by opening the IP routing option.

3. Select the DHCP Relay Agent routing protocol and click OK.

4. Right-click DHCP Relay Agent and select the New Interface option.

5. Click the interface you want to add and click OK.

6. If needed, in Hop-Count Threshold and Boot Threshold (Seconds), click the arrows to modify the thresholds. The hop-count threshold provides a space for you to type a value for the maximum number of DHCP relay agents that will handle DHCP relayed traffic. You can also click the arrows to select a new setting. The default value is 4 hops. The maximum value

is 16 hops. The Boot Threshold (Seconds) text box provides a space for you to type the number of seconds the relay agent waits before forwarding DHCP messages. You can also click the arrows to select a new setting. The default value is 4 seconds. This option is useful when you want a local DHCP server to respond first, but if the local DHCP server does not respond, you want to forward messages to a remote DHCP server. Click OK.

To specify the address where the DHCP Relay Agent is to forward the BOOTP/DHCP requests, right-click DHCP Relay Agent and select Properties. Then add the Server address of your DHCP server (see Figure 4.3).

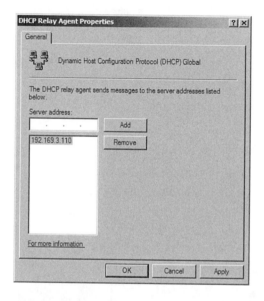

FIGURE 4.3 DHCP Relay Agent Properties.

NOTE

When using multiple DHCP servers, verify that you do not have scope overlaps. If you think there's a chance of scope overlap, consider using conflict detection.

Authorizing the DHCP Server

In Windows, you must authorize a DHCP server in Active Directory before the server can issue leases to DHCP clients (see Figure 4.4). If this is not done, the DHCP service on a Windows server in the forest does not initialize. This makes sure that somebody doesn't install another DHCP server (a rogue DHCP server), which can cause havoc on the network.

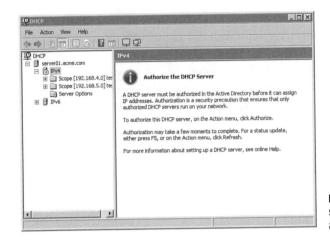

FIGURE 4.4 A DHCP
server that needs to be
authorized.

To authorize a DHCP server in Active Directory, follow these steps:

1. From the DHCP console, right-click DHCP and select the Browse Authorized Servers option.

2. In the Authorized Servers in the Directory dialog box, click Add.

3. In the Authorized DHCP Server dialog box, enter the name or IP address of the DHCP server to authorize and then click OK.

4. In the DHCP dialog box, click Yes to confirm the authorization.

EXAM ALERT

For you to use a DHCP server on an Active Directory domain, you must authorize the DHCP service.

A useful tool (part of the Resource Kit tools) that is available to locate DHCP servers, including locating unauthorized DHCP servers on your network, is the dhcploc.exe command. This is a great tool for eliminating rogue routers and access points that may be sourcing DCHP packets. The syntax for the dhcploc command is

```
dhcploc /p /a:"AlertNameList" /i:AlertInterval ComputerIPAddress
➥[ValidDHCPServerList]
```

▶ /p: Suppresses display of detected packets from any of the authorized DHCP servers specified in ValidDHCPServerList.

- ▶ /a:"*AlertNameList*": Sends alert messages to the names in *AlertNameList* if any unauthorized DHCP servers are found.

- ▶ /i:*AlertInterval*: Specifies the alert frequency in seconds.

- ▶ *ComputerIPAddress*: Specifies the IP address of the computer from which you are running dhcploc. If the computer has multiple adapters, you must specify the IP address of the adapter that is connected to the subnet you want to test.

- ▶ *ValidDHCPServerList*: Specifies the IP addresses of any number of authorized DHCP servers. The tool does not send alerts when it detects packets from the servers in this list; however, it displays those packets unless you use the /p parameter.

NOTE

If you run dhcploc.exe on a computer that is acting as a DHCP server, you may notice that the DHCP server no longer responds to all requests for IP addresses from DHCP clients. Therefore, you should run dhcploc.exe only from computers not acting as DHCP servers.

Fault Tolerance

There are two ways to provide fault tolerance. The first method is to split each scope between two servers (for example, using an 80/20 split). For two subnets, an example would be configuring each DHCP server with a superscope consisting of two scopes: one scope for subnet A (scope 1) and one scope for subnet B (scope 2). Make sure that the scopes for DHCP server A and DHCP server B do not overlap. Also make sure that the IP address ranges are split according to the 80/20 (or 75/25) rule, so that the local scope uses 80% (or similar) of the local IP address range, and the remote scope uses 20% (or similar) of the remote IP address range. Of course, for this to work, your router has to support DHCP relay.

The 80/20 rule holds true only if it takes longer than a few hours to get your failed DHCP server working again before you run out of IP addresses. Therefore, some administrators prefer a more conservative 50/50 rule, which actually works even better in a single-subnet environment anyway—provided both servers have enough addresses scoped to cover the needs of all the clients on the network. Then if one server goes down, the other one can take up the slack for as long as it takes to get the first one up and running again.

Another method to use for DHCP fault tolerance is to form an active-passive failover cluster. By using two servers, you can create an active-passive failover cluster. The active node services the DHCP clients while the passive node waits until the active node fails. When the active node fails, the passive node takes over the DHCP resources and becomes the active node.

Managing DHCP Databases

Windows Server 2008 stores the DHCP database in a Microsoft Jet Database located in the *systemroot*\SYSTEM32\DHCP directory. The Jet Database is a simple database used in several Microsoft products including DHCP and WINS that collects and stores information in a systematic way. By default, the database is automatically backed up every 15 minutes to the systemroot\ SYSTEM32\DHCP\BACKUP\JET\NEW directory. When the DHCP Server service starts, DHCP performs a consistency check of its database and attempts to fix any errors it encounters.

The DHCP Server service records service startup and shutdown events and critical errors in the Windows system log, which can be viewed with the Event Viewer. You can monitor the details of DHCP operations by enabling detailed event logging. If detailed event logging is enabled, it creates detailed log files of its activities in files called DHCPSRVLOG.*xxx* where *xxx* is the first three letters of the day of the week, which are placed in the DHCP database directory.

To enable logging in DHCP,

1. From the DHCP console, right-click the server you are configuring and select the Properties option.

2. In the DHCP Properties dialog box, on the General tab, click Enable DHCP Audit Logging.

If the event log contains Jet database messages that indicate a corruption of the DHCP database, you should first look for disk problems and back up the DHCP database. Then you can repair the database by using the JetPack program. Take these steps to run the JetPack program:

1. Stop DHCP server.

2. At a command prompt, change to the directory where the DHCP database is located (by default *systemroot*\system32\dhcp).

3. Type **JETPACK DHCP.MDB** *temp* (where *temp* is a file name for a temporary database location that is used during repair) and then press Enter.

4. Start the DHCP server.

Of course, if the JetPack program cannot correct the database, you then have to restore it from a backup.

> **NOTE**
>
> `JETPACK DHCP.MDB temp` also compacts the database.

Backing Up the DHCP Database

You can back up a DHCP database manually or you can configure it to back up automatically. An automatic backup is called a *synchronous backup*. A manual backup is called an *asynchronous backup*.

▶ **Automatic (synchronous) backup**: The DHCP database is backed up automatically every 60 minutes.

▶ **Manual (asynchronous) backup**: If you have an immediate need to create a backup, you can run the backup option in the DHCP console.

To manually back up the DHCP database, open the DHCP console, right-click the server, and select Backup.

In the event that you must move the DHCP Server role to another server, you should move the database to the new server as well. This ensures that client leases are retained and reduces the likelihood of client configuration issues.

You move the database initially by backing it up on the old DHCP server. Then shut down the DHCP service on the old DHCP server. The DHCP database then is copied to the new server, where you can restore it, using the normal database restore procedure.

Monitoring and Troubleshooting DHCP Services

DHCP is a core service in modern network environments. If the DHCP service is not working properly, or if a situation is causing problems with the DHCP server, it is important to know that an issue is occurring and how you can locate the problem. DHCP has three sources of information you can use for monitoring:

▶ DHCP statistics

▶ DHCP events in Event Viewer

▶ DHCP performance data

Some of the issues that you might see are included in Table 4.2.

TABLE 4.2   DHCP Issues

Issue	Description	Example
Address conflicts	The same IP address is offered to two different clients.	An administrator deletes a lease. However, the client who had the lease still believes the lease is valid. If the DHCP server does not verify the IP, it may release the IP to another machine, causing an address conflict. This also can occur if two DHCP servers have overlapping scopes.
Failure to obtain a DHCP address	The client does not receive a DHCP address and instead receives an Automatic Private IP Addressing (APIPA) self-assigned address.	If a client's network card drive is configured incorrectly, it may cause a failure to obtain a DHCP address.
Address obtained from incorrect scope	The client is obtaining an IP address from the wrong scope, causing it to experience communications problems.	This often occurs because the client is connected to the wrong network.
DHCP database suffers data corruption or loss	The DHCP database become unreadable or is lost due to a hardware failure.	A hardware failure can cause the database to become corrupted.
DHCP server exhausts its IP address pool	The DHCP server's IP scopes have been depleted. Any new client requesting an IP address is refused.	All the IPs assigned to a scope are leased.

DHCP statistics provide information about DHCP activity and usage. You can use this console to determine quickly whether there is a problem with the DHCP service or with the network's DHCP clients. To get the DHCP statistics, right-click the scope and select Display Statistics.

The audit log provides a traceable log of DHCP server activity. You can use this log to track lease requests, grants, and denials, and this information enables you to troubleshoot DHCP server performance. The DHCP audit logs are located by default at %windir%\System32\Dhcp.

DHCP performance counters become available after you install the DHCP Server role. You then can use Performance Monitor to load the performance counters. A DHCP server typically should not come under a heavy network load. However, if you notice the queue lengths are logging consistently high values, you should check the server for bottlenecks that could be slowing DHCP performance.

The performance counters should include

- ▶ **Packets received/second**: Monitor for sudden increases or decreases, which could reflect network problems.

- ▶ **Requests/second**: Monitor for sudden increases or decreases, which could reflect network problems.

- ▶ **Active queue length**: Monitor for both sudden and gradual increases, which could reflect increased load or decreased server capacity.

- ▶ **Duplicates dropped/second**: Monitor for any activity that could indicate that more than one request is being transmitted on behalf of clients.

Exam Prep Questions

1. You have a Windows Server 2008 computer that always receives the same IP address. In addition, the server must receive its DNS and IWNS settings from the DHCP server. What should you do?

   ○ **A.** Assign a static IP address to the server.

   ○ **B.** Create a DHCP reservation in the DHCP scope.

   ○ **C.** Use the Server Scope option that assigns the IP address to the same server.

   ○ **D.** Use the Registry editor to specify the static IP address.

2. You are the administrator at the Acme Corporation. The DHCP server is hosted on a Windows Server 2008 computer located at the corporate office. Users at a remote site have IP addresses in the range of 169.254.x.x. You need to ensure that computers can connect to shared resources in both the corporate office and the remote sites. What should you do?

   ○ **A.** Configure a DHCP relay agent on a member server in the corporate office.

   ○ **B.** Configure a DHCP relay agent on a member server in the remote sites.

   ○ **C.** Configure the Broadcast Address DHCP server option to include the corporate office's DHCP server address.

   ○ **D.** Configure the Resource Location Servers DHCP server option to include the IP addresses of the main office's server.

3. You have a DHCP server that has two network cards, each connected to a different LAN segment. You want the DHCP server to respond to DHCP clients on only the first LAN segment, not the second. What should you do?

   ○ **A.** Using the DHCP console, modify the bindings to associate only LAN1 with the DHCP service.

   ○ **B.** From the DHCP snap-in, create a new multicast scope.

   ○ **C.** From the properties of the LAN1 network connection, set the metric value to 1.

   ○ **D.** From the properties of the LAN2 network connection, set the metric value to 0.

4. You have a Windows Server 2008 computer that hosts your DHCP services. There is a grouping of 10 servers that have static IP addresses, and you must make sure that those addresses are not assigned to other servers. What should you do?

   ○ **A.** Create new scope for the 10 servers.

   ○ **B.** Create a reservation for the DHCP server.

     ○ **C.** When you create the scope, exclude those addresses of the 10 servers.

     ○ **D.** Create a superscope for the 10 servers.

5. You want to make sure that DHCP clients do not receive IP addresses that are currently in use on the network. What should you do?

     ○ **A.** Set the conflict detection value to 0.

     ○ **B.** Set the conflict detection value to 1 or 2.

     ○ **C.** Set the MAC detection to Enabled.

     ○ **D.** Run a utility that detects all addresses in use and input those addresses to the exclusion list.

6. You have an Active Directory domain with a Windows Server 2008 computer hosting the DHCP services. You try to start the DHCP server but it does not start. What do you need to do to overcome this problem?

     ○ **A.** Reboot the server.

     ○ **B.** Activate the scope on the server.

     ○ **C.** Change the logon account for the DHCP service.

     ○ **D.** Authorize the server in the Active Directory domain.

7. After a while, you discover that the DHCP database has grown quite large. How can you reduce its size?

     ○ **A.** From the DHCP console, scavenge the records.

     ○ **B.** Use `jetpack.exe` to compact the database.

     ○ **C.** Reduce the lease time of those IP addresses handed out.

     ○ **D.** Compress the folder where the DHCP database is.

8. Your network consists of two subnets: SubnetA and SubnetB. Each subnet has its own DHCP server. You configure a scope on DHCP1 for SubnetA. Users are leasing a valid IP address but report that they cannot access any resources outside their own subnet. How can you most easily solve the problem?

     ○ **A.** Activate the scope on DHCP1.

     ○ **B.** Configure the default gateway on each workstation.

     ○ **C.** Configure the 003 router option on DHCP1.

     ○ **D.** Configure the 006 DNS server option on DHCP1.

9. Your network consists of multiple subnets connected by routers. You have finished installing a Windows Server 2008 DHCP server. You create the necessary scopes and configure the 003 router option to assign all clients the IP address of their local router. All clients successfully lease an IP address. However, you soon discover that users on Subnet A are the only ones capable of communicating outside their local subnet. What could be causing the problem?

   ○ **A.** All the scopes have not yet been activated.

   ○ **B.** The DHCP option is configured at the server level.

   ○ **C.** The DHCP server has not yet been authorized.

   ○ **D.** The 003 router option must first be activated.

10. You are the network administrator for your company. All servers are running Microsoft Windows Server 2008. Client computers are running Microsoft XP Professional and Windows Vista. Several DHCP servers are being deployed in different domains throughout the forest. You want give another administrator the ability to authorize the DHCP servers. What should you do?

    ○ **A.** Add the user to the DNSUpdateProxy group.

    ○ **B.** Add the user to the Enterprise Admins group.

    ○ **C.** Add the user to the Domain Admins group.

    ○ **D.** Add the user to the local Administrators group on each DHCP server.

11. You are a junior network administrator. One of your tasks is to maintain a newly installed DHCP server. The scopes have not yet been created. The senior administrator documents all the required scopes and asks you to create them on the server. You notice that several DHCP options are to be configured, but it is not specified what type of scope options to configure. You are trying to recall how scope options are applied. Which of the following correctly lists the order in which they are applied to clients?

    ○ **A.** Server, scope, class, client

    ○ **B.** Server, class, scope, client

    ○ **C.** Server, scope, client, class

    ○ **D.** Scope, server, client, class

12. You are the network administrator for your company. All servers are running Microsoft Windows Server 2008. The company has opened a new branch office. You are in charge of implementing dynamic IP addressing in the new branch office. There is an existing DHCP server in the head office. Fault tolerance is a priority. Client computers in the branch office should be able to obtain an IP address if the WAN link to the head office becomes unavailable. What should you do? (Select three.)

○ **A.** Place a DHCP server in the branch office location.

○ **B.** Configure the local DHCP server with 80% of the available IP addresses. Configure the DHCP server within the head office with the remaining 20% of the IP addresses.

○ **C.** Enable the DHCP Relay Agent on a server within the branch office.

○ **D.** Configure all clients with the IP address of both DHCP servers.

13. What is the default lease time for the DHCP server?

○ **A.** 3 hours

○ **B.** 3 days

○ **C.** 8 hours

○ **D.** 8 days

Answers to Exam Prep Questions

1. Answer B is correct. You need to create a DHCP reservation in the DHCP scope where you specify the computer's MAC address. Answer A is incorrect because assigning a static IP address prevents it from receiving configuration from the DHCP server. Answer C is incorrect because there is no Server Scope option that assigns the IP address to the same server. Answer D is incorrect because you cannot use the Registry editor to specify a static IP address.

2. Answer B is correct. Because DHCP clients use a broadcast to request an IP address from a DHCP server, most broadcasts do not go over WAN links. Therefore, you need to configure a DHCP relay agent at the remote sites so that it can listen for these broadcasts and forward them to the remote DHCP server. Answer A is incorrect because you need a DHCP relay agent at the remote sites where the clients will be broadcasting their request. Answers C and D are incorrect because the Broadcast Address and Resource Location Server options do not assign IP addresses, and options do not apply until an IP address is assigned by a DHCP server.

3. Answer A is correct. You can specify which LANs the server will service by modifying the bindings. Answer B is incorrect because creating a multicast scope does not limit which LAN segments it services. Answers C and D are incorrect because metrics do not limit which LAN segments it services.

4. Answer C is correct. To make sure that the addresses used by the servers are not handed out, you need to do an exclusion. Answer A is incorrect because scopes service a LAN segment and you can have only one scope per LAN segment. Answer B is incorrect because although a reservation hands out addresses to only those computers

with the defined MAC addresses, the reservation makes sure that it does not hand out those addresses to any computer. Answer D is incorrect because a superscope combines subnets together to define a supernet, which would not help in this situation.

5. Answer B is correct. You need to set the conflict detection value to 1 or 2. It performs a ping to verify that the address is not in use. Answer A is incorrect because the conflict detection value of 0 performs 0 pings. Answer C is incorrect no MAC detection option is available. Answer D is incorrect because this would not accommodate addresses used in the future.

6. Answer D is correct. In Active Directory domains, you must authorize the server. Answer A is incorrect because rebooting the server or restarting the DHCP service does not fix the problem. Answer B is incorrect because activating the scope does not fix the problem. Answer C is incorrect because the default logon account of the service was automatically configured and is not the problem.

7. Answer B is correct. You can use the `jetpack.exe` to compact the database. Answer A is incorrect because you cannot scavenger records in the DHCP console. Answer C is incorrect because reducing the lease time of those IP addresses handed out will not shrink the database. Answer D is incorrect because compressing the folder you should not compress databases.

8. Answer C is correct. If clients have not been configured with the IP address of the default gateway, they cannot access resources outside their local subnet. Answer A is incorrect because the clients are already successfully leasing IP addresses from the server. Answer B would solve the problem but would not be the easiest solution; therefore, it is also incorrect. Answer D is incorrect because configuring the DNS Server option enables clients to resolve hostnames but doesn't give them access outside the local subnet.

9. Answer B is correct. Each subnet has its own gateway, so the 003 router option should be configured at the scope level instead of the server level. Answers A and C are incorrect because all clients are successfully leasing IP addresses. Answer D is incorrect because DHCP options do not have to be activated.

10. Answer B is correct. To authorize DHCP servers throughout the forest, the user account with which you log on must be a member of the Enterprise Admins group. Therefore, answers A, C, and D are incorrect.

11. Answer A is correct. The correct order in which DHCP options are applied is server, scope, class, and then client. Therefore, answers B, C, and D are incorrect.

12. Answers A, B, and C are correct. By placing a DHCP server within the branch office and configuring the server in the branch office with 20% of the IP addresses, you can eliminate DHCP and the WAN link as points of failure. The DHCP Relay Agent is required for DHCP clients to lease an IP address from a DHCP server on a remote subnet. Answer D is incorrect because clients are not configured with the IP address of DHCP servers.

13. Answer D is correct. The default lease time is 8 days. Therefore, Answers A, B, and C are incorrect.

Need to Know More?

For more information on DHCP Services, visit the following websites:

- ▶ http://technet.microsoft.com/en-us/network/bb643151.aspx
- ▶ http://technet2.microsoft.com/windowsserver2008/en/library/d952b747-aa30-4400-92c7-91b3124811191033.mspx?mfr=true

CHAPTER FIVE

Routing and Filtering Network Traffic

Terms you'll need to understand:

✓ Router

✓ Metric

✓ Hop

✓ Static routes

✓ Dynamic routes

✓ Router Information Protocol (RIP)

✓ Split-horizon

✓ Open Shortest Path First (OSPF)

✓ Firewall

✓ Stateful firewall

✓ Windows Firewall

✓ Windows Firewall with Advanced Security

✓ Usage profile

✓ Network address translation (NAT)

Techniques/concepts you'll need to master:

✓ Configure static routes using Router and Remote Access (RRAS) console and using the `Route.exe` command.

✓ Configure Router Information Protocol (RIP).

✓ Configure packet filtering, Windows Firewall, and Windows Firewall with Advanced Security.

✓ Configure dial-up routing.

✓ Configure Network address translation.

A *router* is a device that manages the flow of data between network segments, or subnets. As multiple LANs or segments are connected together, multiple routes are created to get data from one LAN or segment to another. A router directs incoming and outgoing packets based on the information it holds about the state of its own network interfaces and a list of possible destinations for network traffic.

By projecting network traffic and routing needs, you can decide whether you want to use a dedicated hardware router, such as a Cisco router, or a software-based router, such as those included with Windows Server 2008. If you have heavy routing demands, you would almost always use dedicated hardware routers. For smaller networks, a software-based routing solution could be used. For routing, Microsoft Windows Server 2008 includes the Routing and Remote Access service.

Routing and Routers

When you send a packet from one computer to another computer, it first determines whether the packet is sent locally to another computer on the same LAN or to router so that it can be routed to the destination LAN. If the packet is meant to go to a computer on another LAN, it is sent to the router (or gateway). The router then determines the best route to take and forwards the packets to that route. The packet then goes to the next router and the entire process repeats itself until it gets to the destination LAN. The destination router then forwards the packets to the destination computer.

To determine the best route, the routes use complex routing algorithms, which take into account a variety of factors, including the speed of each transmission media, the number of network segments, and the network segment that carries the least traffic. Routers then share status and routing information to other routers so that they can provide better traffic management and bypass slow connections. In addition, routers provide additional functionality, such as the capability to filter messages and forward them to different places based on various criteria. Most routers are multiprotocol routers because they can route data packets using many different protocols.

A *metric* is a standard of measurement, such as hop count, that is used by routing algorithms to determine the optimal path to a destination. A *hop* is the trip a data packet takes from one router to another router or from a router to another intermediate point to another in the network. On a large network, the number of hops a packet has taken toward its destination is called the hop count. When a computer communicates with another computer, and the computer has to go through four routers, it has a hop count of four. With no other factors taken into account, a metric of four would be assigned. If a router had a choice between a route with four metrics and a route with six metrics, it would choose the route with four metrics over the route with six metrics. Of course, if you want the router to choose the route with six metrics, you can overwrite the metric for the route with four hops in the routing table to a higher value.

To keep track of the various routes in a network, routers create and maintain routing tables. Routers communicate with one another to maintain their routing tables through a routing update message. The routing update message can consist of all or a portion of a routing table. By analyzing routing updates from all other routers, a router can build a detailed picture of network topology.

Static Versus Dynamic Routes

Static routing algorithms are hardly algorithms at all, but are table mappings established by the network administrator prior to the beginning of routing. These mappings do not change unless the network administrator alters them. Algorithms that use static routes are simple to design and work well in environments where network traffic is relatively predictable and where network design is relatively simple.

Because static routing systems cannot react to network changes, they generally are considered unsuitable for today's large, changing networks. Most of the dominant routing algorithms are *dynamic routing algorithms*, which adjust to changing network circumstances by analyzing incoming routing update messages. If the message indicates that a network change has occurred, the routing software recalculates routes and sends out new routing update messages. These messages flow through the network, stimulating routers to rerun their algorithms and change their routing tables accordingly.

> **NOTE**
>
> Dynamic routing algorithms can be supplemented with static routes where appropriate.

Distance-Vector Versus Link-State Algorithm

Routers use distance-vector–based routing protocols to periodically advertise or broadcast the routes in their routing tables, but they send it to only their neighboring routers. Routing information exchanged between typical distance-vector–based routers is unsynchronized and unacknowledged. Distance-vector–based routing protocols are simple and easy to understand and easy to configure. The disadvantage is that multiple routes to a given network can reflect multiple entries in the routing table, which leads to a large routing table. In addition, if you have a large routing table, network traffic increases as it periodically advertises the routing table to the other routers, even after the network has converged. Last, distance-vector protocol convergence of large internetworks can take several minutes.

Link-state algorithms are also known as shortest path first algorithms. Instead of using broadcast, link-state routers send updates directly (or by using multicast traffic) to all routers within the network. Each router, however, sends only the portion of the routing table that describes the state of its own links. In essence, link-state algorithms send small updates everywhere. Because they converge more quickly, link-state algorithms are somewhat less prone to routing loops than distance-vector algorithms. In addition, link-state algorithms do not exchange any routing information when the internetwork has converged. They have small routing tables because they store a single optimal route for each network ID. On the other hand, link-state algorithms require more CPU power and memory than distance-vector algorithms. Link-state algorithms, therefore, can be more expensive to implement and support and are considered harder to understand.

Routing Information Protocol

A popular routing protocol is the *Routing Information Protocol (RIP)*, which is a distance-vector protocol designed for exchanging routing information within a small- to medium-size network. The biggest advantage of RIP is that it is extremely simple to configure and deploy.

RIP uses a single routing metric of hop counts (number of routers) to measure the distance between the source and a destination network. Each hop in a path from source to destination is assigned a hop-count value, which is typically 1. When a router receives a routing update that contains a new or changed destination network entry, the router adds one to the metric value indicated in the update and enters the network in the routing table. The sender's IP address is used as the next hop.

Because RIP uses only hop count to determine the best path to an internetwork. If RIP finds more than one link to the same remote network with the same hop count, it automatically performs a round-robin load balance. RIP can perform load balancing for up to six equal-cost links.

However, a problem with using hops as the only metric is when two links to a remote network have different bandwidths. For example, if you have one link that is a 56KB switched link and a T1 running at 1.544Mbps, there would be some inefficiency when sending equal data through both pathways. This is known as pinhole congestion. To overcome pinhole congestion, you have to design a network with equal bandwidth links or use a routing protocol that takes bandwidth into account.

RIP prevents routing loops from continuing indefinitely by implementing a limit on the number of hops allowed in a path from the source to a destination. The maximum number of hops in a path is 15. If a router receives a routing update that contains a new or changed entry, and if increasing the metric value by one causes the metric to be infinity (in this case, 16), the network destination is considered unreachable. Of course, this makes it impossible for RIP to scale to large or very large internetworks. Note: The count-to-infinity problem is the reason why the maximum hop count of RIP for IP internetworks is set to 15 (16 for unreachable). Higher maximum hop count values would make the convergence time longer when count-to-infinity occurs.

Initially, the routing table for each router includes only the networks that are physically connected to it. A RIP router periodically (every 30 seconds) sends announcements that contain its routing table entries so that the other routers can update their routing tables. RIP version 1 uses IP broadcast packets for its announcements. RIP version 2 uses multicast or broadcast packets for its announcements. All RIP messages are sent over UDP port 520.

RIP routers can also communicate routing information through triggered updates, which are triggered when the network topology changes. Different from the scheduled announcements, the triggered updates are sent immediately rather than held for the next periodic announcement. For example, when a router detects a link or router failure, it updates its own routing table and sends the updated routes. Each router that receives the triggered update modifies its own routing table and propagates the change to the other routers.

You can configure each RIP router with a list of routers (by IP address) that accepts RIP announcements. By configuring a list of RIP peers, RIP announcements from unauthorized RIP routers are discarded. In addition, to prevent RIP traffic from being received by any node except neighboring RIP routers, you can set up some routers to use unicast RIP announcements to neighboring RIP routers.

Because the RIP is a distance-vector protocol, as internetworks grow larger in size, the periodic announcements by each RIP router can cause excessive traffic. Another disadvantage of RIP is its high convergence time. When the network topology changes, it may take several minutes before the RIP routers reconfigure themselves to the new network topology. As the network reconfigures itself, routing loops may form that result in lost or undeliverable data. To help prevent routing loops, RIP implements *split-horizon*.

To overcome some of RIP shortcomings, RIP Version 2 (RIP II) was introduced. RIP v2 provides the following features:

▶ You can use a password for authentication by specifying a key that is used to authenticate routing information to the router. Simple password authentication was defined in RFC 1723, but newer authentication mechanisms, such as Message Digest 5 (MD5), are available.

▶ RIP v2 includes the subnet mask in the routing information and supports variable-length subnets. Variable-length subnet masks can be associated with each destination, allowing an increase in the number of hosts or subnets that are possible on your network.

▶ The routing table can contain information about the IP address of the router that should be used to reach each destination. This helps prevent packets from being forwarded through extra routers on the system.

▶ Multicast packets speak only to RIP v2 routers and are used to reduce the load on hosts not listening to RIP v2 packets. The IP multicast address for RIP v2 packets is 224.0.0.9. Note: Silent RIP nodes must also be listening for multicast traffic sent to 224.0.0.9. If you are using Silent RIP, verify that your Silent RIP nodes can listen for multicasted RIP v2 announcements before deploying multicasted RIP v2.

EXAM ALERT

RIPv2 supports multicasting for updating the routing tables. RIPv1 does not support this feature. RIPv1 routers cannot communicate with RIPv2 routers that use multicasting for updates.

Open Shortest Path First (OSPF)

For small or medium networks, distributing data throughout the network and maintaining a route table at each router is not a problem. When the network grows to a size that includes hundreds of routers, the routing table can be quite large (several megabytes) and calculating routes requires significant time as the number of router interfaces goes up or down.

Some protocols, such as *Open Shortest Path First (OSPF)*, allow areas (grouping of contiguous networks) to be grouped together into an autonomous system (AS). Areas that make up the autonomous areas usually correspond to an administrative domain, such as a department, a building, or a geographic site. An AS can be a single network or a group of networks, which is owned and administered by a common network administrator or group of administrators.

OSPF is a link-state routing protocol used in medium-sized and large networks that calculates routing table entries by constructing a shortest-path tree. OSPF is designed for large internetworks (especially those spanning more than 15 router hops). The disadvantage of OSPF is that it's generally more complex to set up and requires a certain amount of planning.

> **EXAM ALERT**
>
> The Open Shortest Path First (OSPF) routing protocol component in Routing and Remote Access has been removed from Windows Server 2008.

Routing and Remote Access Service (RRAS)

With *Routing and Remote Access (RRAS)*, a computer running Windows Server 2008 can function as a network router, which routes IP packets between networks. This router service allows LANs and WANs to be interconnected easily. The routing technology is built into the operating system, providing small and large businesses with a cost-effective and secure way of interconnecting their networks.

You install the Routing and Remote Access service by using the Add Roles Wizard. To install the Routing and Remote Access service, follow these steps:

1. In the Server Manager main window, under Roles Summary, click Add roles. Or if you use the Initial Configuration Tasks window, under Customize This Server, click Add roles.

2. In the Add Roles Wizard, click Next.

3. In the list of server roles, select Network Policy and Access Services. Click Next twice.

4. In the list of role services, select Routing and Remote Access Services to select all the role services. You can also select individual server roles. Click Next.

5. Proceed through the steps in the Add Roles Wizard to complete the installation.

After you complete the installation, the Routing and Remote Access service is installed in a disabled state. To enable the Routing and Remote Access service, follow these steps:

1. Open Routing and Remote Access.

2. By default, the local computer is listed as a server.

3. To add another server, in the console tree, right-click Server Status, and then click Add Server.

4. In the Add Server dialog box, click the applicable option, and then click OK.

5. In the console tree, right-click the server you want to enable, and then click Configure and Enable Routing and Remote Access. Click Next.

6. Click Custom Configuration and click Next.

7. To enable LAN routing, select LAN routing and click Next.

8. Click the Finish button.

To enable LAN and WAN routing after Routing and Remote Access service has been enabled:

1. Open Routing and Remote Access.

2. Right-click the server name for which you want to enable routing and then click Properties.

3. On the General tab, select the appropriate IPv4 and IPv6 Router check boxes and select either Local Area Network (LAN) Routing Only or LAN and Demand-Dial Routing.

4. Click OK.

Creating Static Routes

In some instances you need to add a static route to your Windows Server 2008 router. This, of course, has its advantages and disadvantages. Creating a static route is simple; however, the routes you configure are not shared between routers. Static routes specify the network address and subnet mask that tell the router how to reach a certain destination. The router uses the information to determine to which gateway to forward the packet so that the packet can reach the destination host.

Static routes can be configured in one of two ways:

▶ Using the route command.

▶ Using the RRAS management console.

Using the Route Command

The route command is used to view and modify the network routing tables of an IP network. The route print command displays a list of current routes that the host knows (see Figure 5.1).

```
Administrator: Command Prompt                                            _|□|×|
C:\Users\Administrator>route print
===========================================================================
Interface List
 10 ...00 11 d8 ae 36 ab ...... SiS 900 PCI Fast Ethernet Adapter
  1 ........................... Software Loopback Interface 1
 12 ...00 00 00 00 00 00 00 e0  isatap.{057A0E5D-0032-4319-870B-50C26B128862}
 11 ...02 00 54 55 4e 01 ...... Teredo Tunneling Pseudo-Interface
===========================================================================

IPv4 Route Table
===========================================================================
Active Routes:
Network Destination        Netmask          Gateway       Interface  Metric
          0.0.0.0          0.0.0.0      192.168.3.1   192.168.3.110    276
        127.0.0.0        255.0.0.0          On-link       127.0.0.1    306
        127.0.0.1  255.255.255.255          On-link       127.0.0.1    306
  127.255.255.255  255.255.255.255          On-link       127.0.0.1    306
      192.168.3.0    255.255.255.0          On-link   192.168.3.110    276
      192.168.3.1  255.255.255.255          On-link       127.0.0.1     51
    192.168.3.110  255.255.255.255          On-link   192.168.3.110    276
    192.168.3.115  255.255.255.255          On-link   192.168.3.110    276
    192.168.3.192  255.255.255.255          On-link   192.168.3.110    276
    192.168.3.255  255.255.255.255          On-link   192.168.3.110    276
        224.0.0.0        240.0.0.0          On-link       127.0.0.1    306
        224.0.0.0        240.0.0.0          On-link   192.168.3.110    276
  255.255.255.255  255.255.255.255          On-link       127.0.0.1    306
  255.255.255.255  255.255.255.255          On-link   192.168.3.110    276
===========================================================================
Persistent Routes:
Network Address          Netmask  Gateway Address  Metric
        0.0.0.0          0.0.0.0      192.168.3.1  Default
===========================================================================

IPv6 Route Table
===========================================================================
Active Routes:
 If Metric Network Destination      Gateway
  1    306 ::1/128                   On-link
  1    306 ff00::/8                  On-link
===========================================================================
Persistent Routes:
  None

C:\Users\Administrator>
```

FIGURE 5.1 *Route Print* command output.

Routes added to a routing table are not made persistent unless the -p switch is specified. Non-persistent routes last only until the computer is restarted or until the interface is deactivated. The interface can be deactivated when the plug-and-play interface is unplugged (such as for laptops and hot-swap PCs), when the wire is removed from the media card (if the adapter supports media fault sensing), or when the interface is manually disconnected from the adapter in the Network and Dial-up Connections folder.

The usage for the route command is

```
ROUTE [-f] [-p] [command [destination]] [MASK netmask] [gateway]
➥ [METRIC metric]
```

▶ -f—Clears the routing tables of all gateway entries. If this is used in conjunction with one of the commands, the tables are cleared before the command is run.

▶ -p—When used with the add command, makes a route persistent across boots of the system. By default, routes are not preserved when the system is restarted. When used with the print command, displays the list of registered persistent routes. Ignored for all other commands, which always affects the appropriate persistent routes.

▶ Destination—Specifies the network or host to which packets are being sent to.

▶ MASK *netmask*—Specifies a subnet mask to be associated with this route entry. If a netmask value is not specified, it defaults to 255.255.255.255.

▶ *gateway*—Specifies gateway or router.

▶ METRIC *metric*—Assigns an integer cost metric (ranging from 1 to 9,999) to be used in calculating the fastest, most reliable, and/or least expensive routes.

The commands usable in the preceding syntax are PRINT, ADD, DELETE, and CHANGE:

▶ PRINT—Displays a route

▶ ADD—Adds a route

▶ DELETE—Deletes a route

▶ CHANGE—Modifies an existing route

EXAM ALERT

Persistent routes are stored in the following Registry location:
HKEY_LOCAL_MACHINE\SYSTEM\CurrentControlSet\Services\Tcpip\Parameters\
PersistentRoutes

For example, to create a static route, you could type

```
route ADD 132.133.200.0 MASK 255.255.255.0  63.197.142.1 METRIC 2
```

After this command is executed, any packet that is sent to the 132.133.200.0 network or host with an IP address ranging between 132.133.200.1 and 132.133.200.254 will be forwarded to the router with a local host address of 63.197.142.1. If multiply entries specify these destination addresses, this route has a metric of two hops.

Using Routing and Remote Access

To add a static route to a Windows Server 2008 multihomed computer, you would use the Routing and Remote Access program located under Administrative Tools or use the appropriate MMC snap-in. Next, right-click Static Routes under IPv4 or IPv6 and select New Static Route for IP Networks (see Figure 5.2).

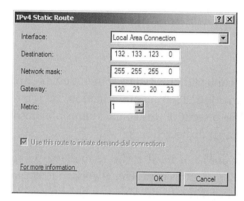

IPv4 Static Route

Interface: Local Area Connection

Destination: 132 . 133 . 123 . 0

Network mask: 255 . 255 . 255 . 0

Gateway: 120 . 23 . 20 . 23

Metric: 1

☑ Use this route to initiate demand-dial connections

For more information

OK   Cancel

FIGURE 5.2 Using the Routing and Remote Access console to create a static route.

For a static IP route, in Interface, Destination, Network Mask, Gateway, and Metric, enter the interface, destination, network mask, gateway, and metric. If this is a demand-dial interface, Gateway is unavailable. You can also select the Use This Route to Initiate Demand-Dial Connections check box to initiate a demand-dial connection for traffic that matches the route.

For IP static addresses, the destination provides a space for you to type a destination for the route. The destination can be a host address, subnet address, network address, or the destination for the default route (0.0.0.0). The subnet mask provides a space for you to type the network mask for the static route. The network mask number is used in conjunction with the destination to determine when the route is used.

The mask of 255.255.255.255 means that only an exact match of the destination number can use this route. The mask of 0.0.0.0 means that any destination can use this route. The gateway provides a space for you to type the forwarding IP address for this route. For LAN interfaces, the gateway address must be configured and must be a directly reachable IP address for the network segment of the selected interface. Again, for demand-dial interfaces, the gateway address is not configured or used. The metric provides a space to type the cost associated with this route to reach the destination. The metric is commonly used to indicate the number of routers (hops) to the destination. When deciding between multiple routes to the same destination, the route with the lowest metric is selected as the best route.

Demand-Dial Routing

Two types of demand-dial connections can be created for routing:

▸ On-demand connections

▸ Persistent connections

With demand-dial connections, a connection with the remote router is established only when necessary. A connection is established to route information and is terminated when the link is not in use. The benefit of this connection is obviously the cost savings associated with not using a dedicated link.

With persistent connections, the link does not need to be terminated. Even when it is not in use, it remains open. Connections between network routers can be one-way or two-way initiated, meaning that a connection can be initiated by only one router or by both the routers. With one-way–initiated connections, one router is designated as the answering router and the other is designated as the calling router, which is responsible for initiating any connections.

One-Way Demand-Dial Routing

Demand-dial connections can be created within the Routing and Remote Access snap-in. How you configure the connection depends on whether you are configuring a one-way– or two-way–initiated connection. To create a demand-dial interface on the calling router follow these steps:

1. Right-click Network Interfaces within the RRAS console and click New Demand-Dial Interface. This launches the Demand-Dial Interface Wizard. Click Next.

2. Type a name for the interface. Click Next.

3. Select the connection type. Click Next. Select the device that is used for making the connection. Click Next.

4. Type in the phone number of the remote server you are dialing. Click Next.

5. From the Protocols and Security window, select the necessary options:

▶ Route IP Packets on This Interface

▶ Add a User Account So a Remote User Can Dial In

▶ Send a Plain-Text Password If That Is the Only Way to Connect

▶ Use Scripting to Complete the Connection with the Remote Router

6. Configure a static route to the remote network. Click Next.

7. From the Dial Out Credentials window, specify the username and password that the dial-out router will use to connect to the remote router. Click Next.

8. Click Finish.

NOTE

Before you attempt to create a new demand-dial interface, make sure the router is enabled for LAN and demand-dial routing rather than just LAN routing. You can enable this option by right-clicking the RRAS server and choosing Properties. From the General tab, select LAN and Demand-Dial Routing.

The answering router also needs to be configured for one-way demand-dial connections. A user account must be created on the answering router with dial-in permissions and the appropriate policy permissions. The user account is used to authenticate connections from the calling routers. A static route can then be configured on the user account. Also make sure when creating a user account that the Password Never Expires option is selected and the User Must Change Password at Next Logon option is not selected.

EXAM ALERT

When configuring the calling router, make sure that the dial-out credentials match the user account name configured on the answering router.

Two-Way Demand-Dial Routing

Creating a two-way demand-dial connection is similar to configuring a one-way connection, but there are a few distinct differences. A demand-dial interface is created on each RRAS server by the process outlined previously to create a one-way demand-dial connection. You must assign a name to the interface and specify the phone number to dial, the device to be used, the protocol and security settings, and the dial-out credentials. You must also configure a user account, with the appropriate remote access permissions, on each RRAS server. Keep in mind that the user account name must be identical to the name assigned to the demand-dial interface of the calling router. Finally, you must configure a static route using the demand-dial interface.

> **EXAM ALERT**
>
> Remember when you are configuring two-way demand dialing that the user account names on the answering router must be identical to the demand-dial interface names on the calling routers.

Configuring Demand-Dial Routing

When a demand-dial connection has been created, you can configure it further using the Properties window for the connection. From the Options tab, configure the connection type: either demand-dial or persistent. You can also set the dialing policy by specifying the number of times that the calling router should redial if there is no answer and by specifying the interval between redial attempts.

The Security tab enables you to configure the security options for the dial-out connection. This configuration includes whether unsecured passwords are permitted, whether the connection requires data encryption, and whether a script will be run after dialing.

You can make several other configurations to a demand-dial interface. Demand-dial filtering enables you to control the type of IP traffic that can initiate a connection. You can allow or deny a connection based on the type of IP traffic. For example, you might want only web and FTP traffic to initiate the demand-dial connection. Dial-out hours determine the times of day that a connection can be initiated. This enables an administrator to control when the demand-dial connection is used.

Managing RIP

After the demand-dial or LAN interfaces have been created, configuring the appropriate routing protocol interfaces is the last step in configuring the RRAS server as a network router. You must first add the routing protocol by right-clicking the General node and choosing New Routing Protocol. The window that appears lists the protocols from which you can choose. Select RIPv2 and click OK.

After the routing protocol has been added, you must add the interfaces. To do so, right-click the appropriate routing protocol and select New Interface. After you select an interface and click OK, the Properties window for the interface appears, enabling you to configure it.

Every RIP interface has it own Properties window from which you can configure a number of options. Within the RRAS console, expand IP Routing, RIP; and then right-click one of the available interfaces and click Properties.

The General tab enables you to configure the operation mode. You can select either Autostatic Update Mode or Periodic Update Mode. With autostatic update, RIP announcements are sent when other routers request updates. Any routes learned while in autostatic update mode are marked as static and remain in the routing table until the administrator manually deletes them. In periodic update mode, announcements are sent out periodically. (The Periodic Announcement Interval determines how often.) These routes are automatically deleted when the router is stopped and restarted. The outgoing and incoming packet protocol enables you to configure the type of packets, such as RIPv1 or RIPv2, the router sends and accepts.

The Activate Authentication and Password options enable you to maintain an added level of security. If authentication is enabled, all outgoing and incoming packets must contain the password specified in the password field. When using authentication, make sure that all neighboring routers are configured with an identical password.

From the Security tab, an administrator can configure RIP route filters. The router can be configured to send and accept all routes, send and accept only routes from the ranges specified, or accept and send all routes except for those specified.

The Neighbors tab is used to configure how the router interacts with other RIP routers. The Advanced tab has several configurable options:

- ▶ **Periodic Announcement Interval**: Controls the interval at which periodic update announcements are made.

- ▶ **Time Before Route Expires**: Determines how long a route remains in the routing table before it expires.

- ▶ **Time Before Route Is Removed**: Determines how long an expired route remains in the routing table before being removed.

- ▶ **Enable Split Horizon Processing**: Ensures that routing loops do not occur because the routes learned from a router are not rebroadcast to that network.

▶ **Enable Triggered Updates**: Controls whether changes in the routing table are sent out immediately.

▶ **Send Clean-Up Updates when Stopped**: Controls whether the router sends an announcement when it is stopped to notify other routers that the routes for which it was responsible are no longer available.

▶ **Process Host Routes in Received Announcements**: Controls whether host routes received in RIP announcements are accepted or denied.

▶ **Include Host Routes in Send Announcements**: Controls whether host routes are included in RIP announcements.

▶ **Process Default Routes in Received Announcements**: Controls whether default routes received in RIP announcements are accepted or denied.

▶ **Process Default Routes in Send Announcements**: Controls whether default routes are included in RIP announcements.

▶ **Disable Subnet Summarization**: This option is available only for RIPv2. It controls whether subnets are advertised to routers on different subnets.

EXAM ALERT

When a routing loop occurs, packets bounce back and forth between routers. When split-horizon processing is enabled, routes are not advertised back to the router from which they are learned. For example, if RouterB receives advertised routes from RouterA, RouterB does not advertise these routes back to RouterA. When Split Horizon with Poison Reverse is enabled, routes are advertised back to the router from which they were learned with a hop count of infinity.

Packet Filters

Packet filtering enables an administrator to specify the type of inbound and outbound traffic that is allowed to pass through a Windows Server 2008 router. When configuring packet filters, you can allow all traffic except traffic prohibited by filters. Or you can deny all traffic except traffic that is allowed by filters.

To add a packet filter, follow these steps:

1. Open Routing and Remote Access.

2. In the console tree, click General under Routing and Remote Access/Server Name/[IPv4 or IPv6].

3. In the details pane, right-click the interface on which you want to add a filter, and then click Properties.

4. On the General tab, click either Inbound Filters or Outbound Filters.

5. In the Inbound Filters or Outbound Filters dialog box, click New.

6. In the Add IP Filter dialog box, type the settings for the filter, and then click OK.

7. In Filter action, select the appropriate filter action, and then click OK.

After a packet filter is created, you can edit it at any time by selecting the filter from the list and clicking Edit.

Windows Firewall

Windows Firewall is a packet filter and stateful host-based *firewall* that allows or blocks network traffic according to the configuration. A packet filter protects the computer by using an access control list (ACL), which specifies which packets are allowed through the firewall based on IP address and protocol (specifically the port number). A *stateful firewall* monitors the state of active connections and uses the information gained to determine which network packets are allowed through the firewall. Typically, if the user starts communicating with an outside computer, it remembers the conversation and allows the appropriate packets back in. If an outside computer tries to start communicating with a computer protected by a stateful firewall, those packets are dropped automatically unless access was granted by the ACL.

EXAM ALERT

Windows Firewall is on by default. Any program or service that needs to communicate on a network must be opened in a firewall, including sharing files, pinging the server, or providing basic services, such as DNS and DHCP.

Compared to Windows Firewall introduced with Windows XP SP2, the Windows Firewall used with Windows Server 2008 has some major improvements, including the following:

▶ Windows Firewall supports IPv6 connection filtering.

▶ By using outbound packet filtering, you can help protect the computer againt spyware and viruses that attempt to contact outside computers.

- ▸ With the advanced packet filter, rules can also be specified for source and destination IP addresses and port ranges.

- ▸ Rules can be configured for services by the service name chosen from a list, without needing to specify the full path filename.

- ▸ IPSec is fully integrated with Windows Firewall, allowing connections to be allowed or denied based on security certificates, Kerberos authentication, and so on. Encryption can also be required for any kind of connection.

- ▸ A new management console snap-in named Windows Firewall with Advanced Security provides access to many advanced options and enables remote administration.

- ▸ You can use separate firewall profiles for when computers are domain-joined or connected to a private or public network.

Basic Configuration

Windows Firewall is on by default. When Windows Firewall is on, most programs are blocked from communicating through the firewall. If you want to unblock a program, you can add it to the Exceptions list (on the Exceptions tab). For example, you might not be able to send photos in an instant message until you add the instant messaging program to the Exceptions list. To add a program to the Exceptions list, click the Add program button and select it from the available list or browse for it by clicking the Browse button.

To turn on or off Windows Firewall, follow these steps:

1. Open Windows Firewall by clicking the Start button, clicking Control Panel, clicking Security, and then clicking Windows Firewall.

2. Click Turn Windows Firewall On or Off (see Figure 5.3). If you are prompted for an administrator password or confirmation, type the password or provide confirmation.

3. Click On (recommended) or Off (not recommended) and then click OK.

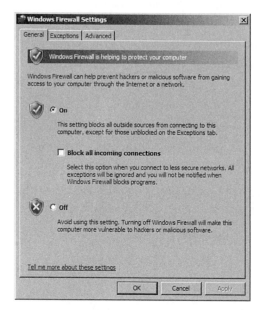

FIGURE 5.3 Windows Firewall options in the Control Panel.

If you want the firewall to block everything, including the programs selected on the Exceptions tab, select the Block All Incoming Connections check box. Block All Incoming Connections blocks all unsolicited attempts to connect to your computer. Use this setting when you need maximum protection for your computer, such as when you connect to a public network in a hotel or airport, or when a computer worm is spreading over the Internet. With this setting, you are not notified when Windows Firewall blocks programs, and programs on the Exceptions list are ignored.

The Windows Firewall Settings interface has three tabs:

- ▶ **General**: Enables you to turn Windows Firewall on and off, as well as to block all incoming connections, no matter how you have configured the exceptions.

- ▶ **Exceptions**: Enables you to configure programs and ports for which you want to allow communication into and out from your Windows Vista computer. Only create an exception that is specifically required, and remove exceptions that you no longer need. Never create an exception for a program when you are unsure of the functionality of that program.

- ▶ **Advanced**: Enables you to select the network interfaces that you want Windows Firewall to protect.

To configure programs as exceptions,

1. Open Windows Firewall by clicking Start > Control Panel > Security > Windows Firewall.

2. Click Allow a program through Windows Firewall. If you are prompted for an administrator password or confirmation, type the password or provide confirmation.

3. In the Windows Firewall dialog box, select the Exceptions tab and then click Add Program.

4. In the Add A Program dialog box, select the program in the Programs list or click Browse to use the Browse dialog box to find the program.

5. By default, any computer, including those on the Internet, can access this program remotely. To restrict access further, click Change Scope.

6. Click OK three times to close all open dialog boxes.

To open a port in Windows Firewall,

1. Open Windows Firewall by clicking the Start button, clicking Control Panel, clicking Security, and then clicking Windows Firewall.

2. Click Allow a program through Windows Firewall. If you are prompted for an administrator password or confirmation, type the password or provide confirmation.

3. Click Add port.

4. In the Name box, type a name that will help you remember what the port is used for.

5. In the Port number box, type the port number.

6. Click TCP or UDP, depending on the protocol.

7. By default, any computer, including those on the Internet, can access this program remotely. To change scope for the port, click Change scope, and then click the option that you want to use. ("Scope" refers to the set of computers that can use this port opening.)

8. Click OK two times to close all open dialog boxes.

Windows Firewall with Advanced Security

Similar to the Windows Firewall with Advanced Security introduced in Windows Vista, the *Windows Firewall with Advanced Security* in Windows Server 2008 is a Microsoft Management Console (MMC) snap-in that allows you to set up and view detailed inbound and outbound rules and integrate with Internet Protocol security (IPSec).

The Windows Firewall with Advanced Security management console enables you to configure:

- ▶ **Inbound rules**: Windows Firewall will block all incoming traffic unless solicited or allowed by a rule.

- ▶ **Outbound rules**: Windows Firewall will allow all outbound traffic unless blocked by a rule.

- ▶ **Connection security rules**: Windows Firewall uses a connection security rule to force two peer computers to authenticate before they can establish a connection and to secure information transmitted between the two computers. Connection security rules use IPsec to enforce security requirements. Connection security rules will be explained more in the next chapter.

- ▶ **Monitoring**: Windows Firewall uses the monitoring interface to display information about current firewall rules, connection security rules, and security associations.

Windows Firewall is on by default. When Windows Firewall is on, most programs are blocked from communicating through the firewall. If you want to unblock a program, you can add it to the Exceptions list (on the Exceptions tab). For example, you might not be able to send photos in an instant message until you add the instant messaging program to the Exceptions list. To add a program to the Exceptions list, see Allow a program to communicate through Windows Firewall.

To turn on or off Windows Firewall:

1. Open Windows Firewall with Advanced Security located in Administrative Tools.

2. Click the Windows Firewall Properties.

3. Under Firewall state, Select either On (recommended) or Off (not recommended) and click the OK button. See Figure 5.4.

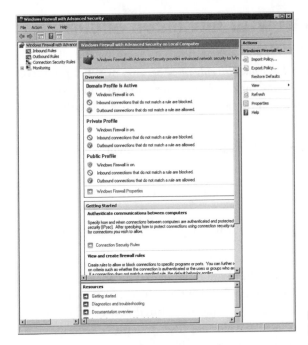

FIGURE 5.4 Windows Firewall properties.

Creating Inbound and Outbound Rules

You create inbound rules to control access to your computer from the network. Inbound rules can prevent

▶ Unwanted software being copied to your computer

▶ Unknown or unsolicited access to data on your computer

▶ Unwanted configuration of your computer from remote locations

To configure advanced properties for a rule using the Windows Firewall with Advanced Security, follow these steps:

1. Right-click the name of the inbound rule and click Properties.

2. From the properties dialog box for an inbound rule, configure settings on the following tabs:

   ▶ **General**: The rule's name, the program to which the rule applies, and the rule's action (allow all connections, allow only secure connections, or block).

- **Programs and Services**: The programs or services to which the rule applies.

- **Users and Computers**: If the rule's action is to allow only secure connections, the computer accounts that are authorized to make protected connections.

- **Protocols and Ports**: The rule's IP protocol, source and destination TCP or UDP ports, and ICMP or ICMPv6 settings.

- **Scope**: The rule's source and destination addresses.

- **Advanced**: The profiles or types of interfaces to which the rule applies.

You can also use the Windows Firewall with Advanced Security to create outbound rules to control access to network resources from your computer. Outbound rules can prevent:

- Utilities on your computer accessing network resources without your knowledge.

- Utilities on your computer downloading software without your knowledge.

- Users of your computer downloading software without your knowledge.

Determining a Firewall Profile

A firewall profile is a way of grouping settings, such as firewall rules and connection security rules that are applied to the computer, depending on where the computer is connected. On computers running this version of Windows, there are three profiles for Windows Firewall with Advanced Security. Only one profile is applied at a time.

The available profiles are

- **Domain**: Applied when a computer is connected to a network in which the computer's domain account resides.

- **Private**: Applied when a computer is connected to a network in which the computer's domain account does not reside, such as a home network. The private settings should be more restrictive than the domain profile settings.

▶ **Public**: Applied when a computer is connected to a domain through a public network, such as those available in airports and coffee shops. The public profile settings should be the most restrictive because the computer is connected to a public network where the security cannot be as tightly controlled as within an IT environment.

Using `netsh` Command to Configure the Windows Firewall

To view the current firewall configuration, including ports that have been opened, use the following command:

```
netsh firewall show state
```

> **NOTE**
>
> If the Firewall status shows that the Operational mode is set to Enable, this means that the Windows Firewall is enabled but no specific ports have been opened.

To open ports at the firewall for DNS (port 53), use the following command:

```
netsh firewall add portopening ALL 53 DNS-server
```

To view the firewall configuration, use the following command:

```
netsh firewall show config
```

To enter the `netsh advfirewall` context, at the command prompt, type

```
netsh
```

When you enter the `netsh` context, the command prompt displays the `>netsh` prompt. At the `>netsh` prompt, enter the `advfirewall` context type:

```
advfirewall
```

After you are in the `advfirewall` context, you can type commands in that context.

Commands include the following:

▶ `Export`: Exports the current firewall policy to a file.

▶ `Help`: Displays a list of available commands.

▶ `Import`: Imports a policy from the specified file.

- ► Reset: Restores Windows Firewall with Advanced Security to the default policy.

- ► Set: Supports the following commands:

  - ► set file: Copies the console output to a file.

  - ► set machine: Sets the current machine on which to operate.

  - ► show: Shows the properties for a particular profile. Examples include show allprofiles, show domainprofile, show privateprofile and show publicprofile.

In addition to the commands available for the advfirewall context, advfirewall also supports several subcontexts. To enter a subcontext, type the name of the subcontext at the netsh advfirewall> prompt. The available subcontexts are

- ► consec: Enables you to view and configure computer security connection rules

- ► Firewall: Enables you to view and configure firewall rules

- ► Monitor: Enables you to view and set monitoring configuration

Managing Windows Firewall with Advanced Security via Group Policy

To centralize the configuration of large numbers of computers in an organization network that uses the Active Directory directory service, you can deploy settings for Windows Firewall with Advanced Security through Group Policy. Group Policy provides access to the full feature set of Windows Firewall with Advanced Security, including profile settings, rules, and computer connection security rules.

Network Address Translation

Because IPv4 addresses are a scare resource, most ISPs provide only one address to a single customer. In majority of cases, this address is assigned dynamically, so every time a client connects to the ISP, a different address is provided. Big companies can buy more addresses, but for small businesses and home users, the cost of doing so is prohibitive. Because such users are given only one IP address, they can have only one computer connected to the Internet at one time.

NAT Overview

Network address translation (NAT) technology was developed to provide a temporary solution to the IPv4 address-depletion problem. NAT is a method of connecting multiple computers to the Internet (or any other IP network) using just one IP address. With a NAT gateway running on this single computer, it is possible to share that single address between multiple local computers and connect them all at the same time. The outside world is unaware of this division and thinks that only one computer is connected.

To combat certain types of security problems, a number of firewall products are available. These are placed between the user and the Internet to verify all traffic before allowing it to pass through. This means, for example, that no unauthorized user is allowed to access the company's file or email server.

NAT automatically provides firewall-style protection without any special setup. The basic purpose of NAT is to multiplex traffic from the internal network and present it to the Internet as if it was coming from a single computer having only one IP address. The TCP/IP protocols include a multiplexing facility so that any computer can maintain multiple simultaneous connections with a remote computer. For example, an internal client can connect to an outside FTP server, but an outside client cannot connect to an internal FTP server because it would have to originate the connection and NAT does not allow that. It is still possible to make some internal servers available to the outside world via inbound mappings, which map certain well known TCP ports (for example, 21 for FTP) to specific internal addresses, thus making services such as FTP or web available in a controlled way.

A modern NAT gateway must change the source address on every outgoing packet to be its single public address. It therefore also renumbers the source ports to be unique, so that it can keep track of each client connection. The NAT gateway uses a port mapping table to remember how it renumbered the ports for each client's outgoing packets. The port mapping table relates the client's real local IP address and source port plus its translated source port number to a destination address and port. The NAT gateway can therefore reverse the process for returning packets and route them back to the correct clients.

Enabling NAT

To enable NAT addressing, follow these steps:

1. Open Routing and Remote Access.

2. To add NAT, right-click General under IPv4 and select New Routing Protocol. Select NAT and click OK.

3. In the console tree, click NAT under IPv4.

4. Right-click NAT and then click Properties.

5. On the Address Assignment tab, select Automatically Assign IP Addresses by Using the DHCP Allocator check box.

6. (Optional) To allocate to DHCP clients on the private network, in IP address and Mask, configure the range of IP addresses.

7. (Optional) To exclude addresses from allocation to DHCP clients on the private network, click Exclude, click Add, and then configure the addresses.

To specify the internal and external interfaces, right-click NAT under IPv4 and select New Interface. Select the physical interface and click OK. Specify either Private Interface Connected to the Private Network or Public Interface Connected to the Internet. If you select Public Interface Connected to the Internet, you would then select Enable NAT on This Interface. Click OK.

To forward a protocol to a specific internal server through the NAT server, follow these steps:

1. Right-click the public interface and select Properties.

2. Select the Services and Ports tab.

3. Select the protocol that you want to forward.

4. When the Edit Services dialog box appears, specify the private address and click OK to close the Edit Services dialog box.

5. Click OK to close the Properties dialog box.

NAT and Teredo

IPv6 traffic that is tunneled with Teredo is not subject to the IPv4 packet filtering function of typical NATs. Although this might sound like Teredo is bypassing the NAT and allowing potentially malicious IPv6 traffic on private networks, consider the following:

- Teredo does not change the behavior of NATs. Teredo clients create dynamic NAT translation table entries for their own Teredo traffic. The NAT forwards incoming Teredo traffic to the host that created the matching NAT translation table entry. The NAT does not forward Teredo traffic to computers on the private network that are not Teredo clients.

- Teredo clients that use a host-based, stateful firewall that supports IPv6 traffic (such as Windows Firewall) are protected from unsolicited, unwanted, incoming IPv6 traffic. Windows Firewall is enabled by default for Windows XP with SP2, Windows Vista, and Windows Server 2008.

If you wish for Teredo to communicate through a Windows Server 2008 computer with the firewall enabled, you have to configure the firewall to allow the use of Teredo.

Exam Prep Questions

1. You have a Windows Server 2008 computer at the corporate office and a Windows Server 2008 computer at a remote site. You want to configure the routing on the server at the branch office. What should you do?

   - ○ **A.** Install the Routing and Remote Access role and enable the IPv4 LAN routing.

   - ○ **B.** Run the `netsh interface ipv4 enable` command.

   - ○ **C.** Enable NAT by executing the `netsh NAT enable` command.

   - ○ **D.** Install the NPS role on the server.

2. You have a Windows Server 2008 server. You need to add a new static route to the routing table on the server. The new route is to the network ID 192.168.126.0 with a subnet mask of 255.255.255.0, using the default gateway of 192.168.125.1. What command do you need to execute?

   - ○ **A.** `route -p 192.168.126.0 mask 255.255.255.0 192.168.125.1 metric 2`

   - ○ **B.** `route add 192.168.126.0 mask 255.255.255.0 192.168.125.1 metric 2`

   - ○ **C.** `route add 192.168.126.0 255.255.255.0 192.168.125.1 metric 2`

   - ○ **D.** `route add 192.168.126.0 mask 255.255.255.0 gateway 192.168.125.1 metric 2`

3. You have a network with several subnets. Windows Server 2008 routers are used to connect the subnets. You need to configure a static route. The static router must not be deleted from the routing table if the computer is restarted. Which of the following parameters should you use with the `route` command?

   - ○ **A.** /f
   - ○ **B.** /s
   - ○ **C.** /r
   - ○ **D.** /p

4. You have a server that runs Windows Server 2008. You need to prevent the server from establishing communication sessions to other computers by using TCP port 21. What should you do?

   - ○ **A.** From Windows Firewall, add an exception.

   - ○ **B.** From Windows Firewall, enable the Block All Incoming Connections option.

○ **C.** From the Windows Firewall with Advanced Security snap-in, create an inbound rule.

○ **D.** From the Windows Firewall with Advanced Security snap-in, create an out-bound rule.

5. You have a Windows Server 2008 computer. You want to disable all incoming connections to the server. What should you do?

○ **A.** From the Services snap-in, disable the Server service.

○ **B.** From the Services snap-in, disable the Net Logon service.

○ **C.** Disable the Windows Firewall with Advanced Security.

○ **D.** From the Windows Firewall, enable the Block All Connections option on the Domain Profile.

6. Your internetwork consists of seven subnets. All subnets are connected by Windows Server 2008 computers with RRAS. Nonpersistent demand-dial connections have been configured. You do not want to be burdened with updating the routing tables, and you want any changes to the network topology to be propagated immediately. Which of the following routing options should you implement?

○ **A.** Static routes

○ **B.** ICMP

○ **C.** OSPF

○ **D.** RIPv2

7. The network consists of three different subnets. Dynamic routing is being implemented on three multihomed computers running Windows Server 2008 on which Routing and Remote Access has been enabled. You open the Routing and Remote Access console on the first server and configure the computer for LAN routing. You select New Routing Protocol from the General node of the IP Routing node, and you choose RIP version 2 for Internet Protocol from the New Routing Protocol dialog box. What should you do next?

○ **A.** Add the IP address of the DHCP server to the properties dialog box for the DHCP Relay Agent.

○ **B.** Add the interface that RIP will run, using the RIP node.

○ **C.** Use the `route` command to configure the routes to the remote subnets.

○ **D.** Use the `route` command to delete all static routers from the routing tables.

8. You are the network administrator for your company. All servers are running Microsoft Windows Server 2008. Several of the servers are configured as routers with RIP enabled. You want to eliminate any routing loops from occurring. You open the properties window for the interface assigned to the RIP protocol and select the Advanced tab. Which of the following options meets these requirements?

   ○ **A.** Enable split-horizon processing.

   ○ **B.** Enable triggered updates.

   ○ **C.** Process host routes in received announcements.

   ○ **D.** Disable subnet summarization.

9. You have a network with several Windows Server 2008 computers. Your company has opened a new remote office. You are in charge of configuring a two-way demand-dial connection between your corporate office and the new remote office. You configure the demand-dial routers with the following settings:

   Corporate Office Router Settings:

   > Interface: SRV02_Public

   > User Account: SRV02

   > Calling Number: 555-3434

   Site Router Settings:

   > Interface: SRV01_Public

   > User Account: SRV01

   > Calling Number: 555-1212

   When you go to test your configuration, neither of the routers can establish a connection. What should you do?

   ○ **A.** Change the interface name on the router in the head office to SRV01_Public.

   ○ **B.** Change the demand-dial interface name on each router to match the name of the user account on the remote answering router.

   ○ **C.** Change the interface name on the router in the branch office to SRV02_Public.

   ○ **D.** Change the names assigned to the user accounts on each router so they are identical.

10. You have a Windows Server 2008 configured as a NAT server. You need to ensure that administrators can access a server named FS1 by using FTP. What should you do?

    ○ **A.** Configure NAT1 to forward ports 20 and 21 to FS1.

    ○ **B.** Configure NAT1 to forward ports 80 and 443 to FS1.

    ○ **C.** Configure NAT1 to forward port 25 to FS1.

    ○ **D.** Configure NAT1 to forward port 3389 to FS1.

11. You have a Windows Server 2008 computer with IPv4 and IPv6 and NAT at the corporate office and each of your site offices. What do you need to allow IPv6 computers from the corporate office and the various sites to use Teredo to communicate with each other?

    ○ **A.** Configure dynamic NAT on the firewall.

    ○ **B.** Configure the firewall to allow the use of Teredo.

    ○ **C.** Enable a static route between the two networks.

    ○ **D.** Load the Teredo emulator.

Answers to Exam Prep Questions

1. Answer A is correct. You need to install the Routing and Remote Access role and you then need to enable IPV4 LAN routing. Answer B is incorrect because the netsh command is not used to enable routing; instead, it could be used to configure a network interface. Answer C is incorrect because NAT would not enable routing and you do not use the netsh command to enable NAT. Answer D is incorrect because NPS does not enable routing. NPS is used as a RADIUS server and for implementing RAS policies.

2. Answer B is correct. The correct syntax when adding new static routes using the route command is route add mask metric. Answers A, C, and D are incorrect because they do not use the proper syntax.

3. Answer D is correct. You use the /p parameter to add a persistent route to the routing table. The route is not removed from the routing table when the router is restarted. Therefore, answers A, B, and C are incorrect.

4. Answer D is correct. You need create an outbound rule using the Windows Firewall with Advanced Security snap-in to block port 21. Answers A and B are incorrect because you should be using the Windows Firewall with Advanced Security snap-in with Windows Server 2008 computers for the fine control that it offers over standard Windows Firewall. In addition, an exception would be used to allow traffic, and if you block all incoming connections, other protocols would also be blocked and no traffic

would be able to go through the server. Answer C is incorrect because you want an outbound rule, not an inbound rule because the traffic from this server to the other servers would be outbound.

5. Answer D is correct. You could quickly open the Windows Firewall, and enable Block All Connections to disable all incoming connections. The Domain profile is applied when a computer is connected to a network in which the computer's domain account resides. Answer A is incorrect because the Server service stops file and print sharing. The Net Logon service prevents logins but not necessarily all connections. Answer C is incorrect because disabling a firewall allows all traffic to flow.

6. Answer D is correct. To have changes propagated throughout the network when changes occur and to reduce the administrative overhead associated with updating the routing tables, a routing protocol is required. Because OSPF cannot be used with non-persistent connections and OSPF is not available in Windows Server 2008, RIPv2 must be used. Therefore, answers A and C are incorrect. Answer B is incorrect because ICMP is not a routing protocol.

7. Answer B is correct. You should use the context menu of the Routing Interface Protocol (RIP) node to add at least one interface to RIP. When you add a routing protocol, the protocol is not configured by default to use an interface, so you must identify one or more interfaces, such as a LAN connection, that the protocol can use. Answer A is incorrect because the scenario does not indicate that there is a DHCP sever on the network. Answer C is incorrect because the routing tables are built automatically. Answer D is incorrect because there is no need to remove all static routes from the routing table.

8. Answer A is correct. The correct answer is enable split-horizon processing. You must select this option to ensure that any routes learned from a network are not sent as RIP announcements on the network. With this option enabled, a router cannot advertise a route on the same connection from which it was learned. Answers B, C, and D do not help eliminate routing loops.

9. Answer B is correct. You must change the user account name on each router to match that of the name assigned to the demand-dial interface name on the answering routing. For a two-way demand-dial connection to work, the user account names used for authentication must be identical to the name assigned to the demand-dial interface. The name of the demand-dial interface on the branch office router must be changed to SRV02. The name of the demand-dial interface on the head office routing must be changed to SRV01. Answer D is incorrect because the user accounts used for remote authentication between the demand-dial routers do not need to be identical. Answers A and C are incorrect because the demand-dial interface name on the calling router must be identical to the user account name on the calling router.

10. Answer A is correct. You need to forward the port 20 and 21 to FS1. Ports 20 and 21 are the ports used by FTP. Answer B is incorrect because port 80 and 443 are used by web servers. Answer C is incorrect because port 25 is used for SMTP. Answer D is incorrect because port 3389 is used by Remote Desktop Protocol.

11. Answer B is correct. By default, the firewall is started and Teredo is blocked. Answer A is incorrect because you already have NAT. Answer C is incorrect because there are already routes between the sites. Answer D is incorrect because there is no such thing as a Teredo emulator.

Need to Know More?

For more information about Routing and Remote Access, including Routing and Remote Access Deployment Guides, Routing and Remote Access Operations Guide, Routing and Remote Access Technical Reference and Routing, and Remote Access Troubleshooting Reference, visit the following website:

▶ http://technet2.microsoft.com/windowsserver2008/en/library/82b70b7a-b336-4604-9a43-0ed8f55c7d471033.mspx?mfr=true

For more information about Windows Firewall with Advanced Security and IPSec, visit the following website:

▶ http://technet2.microsoft.com/windowsserver2008/en/library/c042b3c5-dee1-4a31-ac35-e90e846290441033.mspx?mfr=true

For more information on Teredo, view the following website:

▶ https://www.microsoft.com/technet/network/ipv6/teredo.mspx

Regan, Patrick. *Wide Area Networks*. Upper Saddle River, New Jersey: Prentice Hall, 2004.

CHAPTER SIX

Controlling Network Access

Terms you'll need to understand:

- ✓ Dial-up networking
- ✓ Point-to-Point Protocol (PPP)
- ✓ Authentication
- ✓ Password Authentication Protocol (PAP)
- ✓ Challenge Handshake Authentication Protocol (CHAP)
- ✓ Microsoft Challenge Handshake Authentication Protocol Version
- ✓ Extensible Authentication Protocol (EAP)
- ✓ Smart card
- ✓ Protected Extensible Authentication Protocol (PEAP)
- ✓ Remote Authentication Dial-In User Service (RADIUS)
- ✓ Network Policy Server (NPS)
- ✓ IP Security (IPSec)

- ✓ Virtual private networking (VPN)
- ✓ Point-to-Point Tunneling Protocol (PPTP)
- ✓ Layer 2 Forwarding (L2F)
- ✓ Secure Socket Tunneling Protocol (SSTP)
- ✓ Remote access server (RAS)
- ✓ Connection Manager Administration Kit (CMAK)
- ✓ Network Access Protection (NAP)
- ✓ Statement of Health (SoH)
- ✓ System Health Validators (SHVs)
- ✓ Wireless Equivalency Protection (WEP)
- ✓ WiFi Protected Access (WPA)
- ✓ Wi-Fi Protected Access Version 2 (WPA2)
- ✓ 802.1X authentication

Techniques/concepts you'll need to master:

- ✓ Install and configure a remote access server.
- ✓ Configure VPN connections with a remote access server.
- ✓ Install and configure a wireless access point to use RADIUS.
- ✓ Create a Network Access Protection policy to limit access to a network.
- ✓ Use the Connection Manager Administration Kit to create an installable VPN client.
- ✓ Enable IPSec communication between servers.
- ✓ Monitor IPSec.

Today, modern networks offer *remote access server (RAS)*, which enables users to connect remotely using various protocols and connection types. A remote access server is the computer and associated software that is set up to handle users seeking access to network remotely. Sometimes called a communication server, a remote access server usually includes or is associated with a firewall server to ensure security and a router that can forward the remote access request to another part of the corporate network.

Dial-Up Networking

Dial-up networking refers to the arrangement in which a remote access client makes a nonpermanent, dial-up connection to a physical port on a remote access server by using the service of a telecommunications provider such as analog phone or ISDN. The best example of dial-up networking is that of a dial-up networking client who dials the phone number of one of the ports/modem of a remote access server.

Dial-Up Remote Access Clients

The two main communication protocols used by dial-up remote access clients are the *Point-to-Point Protocol (PPP)* and the *Serial Line Internet Protocol (SLIP)*. PPP has become an industry-standard communications protocol because of its popularity.

Point-to-Point Protocol (PPP) has become the predominant protocol for modem-based access to the Internet, and provides full-duplex, bi-directional operations between the host and the private network. Furthermore, a multilink version of PPP is also used to access ISDN lines, inverse multiplexing analog phone lines, and high-speed optical lines.

There are four distinct phases of negotiation with a PPP connection. Each phase must complete successfully before the PPP connection is ready to transfer user data:

1. PPP configuration

2. Authentication

3. Callback (optional)

4. Protocol configuration

PPP configures PPP protocol parameters using the LCP (Link Control Protocol). During the initial LCP phase, each device on both ends of a connection negotiates communication options that are used to send data and to include PPP parameters (compression, authentication protocols, and multilink options). Note: An authentication protocol is selected but not implemented until the authentication phase.

After the PPP configuration is determined, the authentication protocol agreed upon by the remote access server and the remote access client is implemented. The nature of this traffic is specific to the PPP authentication protocol.

The Microsoft implementation of PPP includes an optional callback phase that uses the *Callback Control Protocol (CBCP)* immediately after authentication. For a remote access client user to get called back, the dial-in properties of the user account must be enabled for callback and either the remote access client can specify the callback number or the remote access server must specify the call-back number. If a connection implements callback, both PPP peers hang up and the remote access server calls the remote access client at the negotiated number (the same number that initially made the call or a predefined number).

After the PPP is configured and callback is complete, network layer protocols can be configured. With remote access on Windows 32-bit operating systems, the remote access server sends the remote access client Configuration-Request messages for all the LAN protocols enabled for remote access on the remote access server. The remote access client either continues the negotiation of the LAN protocols enabled at the remote access client or sends an LCP Protocol-Reject message containing the Configuration-Request message.

Authentication Protocols

Authentication, which is an essential part of network security, is the process by which the system validates the user's logon information. Authentication is crucial to secure communications. Users must be able to prove their identity to those with whom they communicate and must be able to verify the identity of others. Typically, after logging on, the user is authenticated for all network resources that the user has permissions to use. The user has to log on only once even though the network resources may be located throughout several computers.

There are a number of PPP authentication protocols, some of which are supported by the RADIUS protocol. Each protocol has advantages and disadvantages in terms of security, usability, and breadth of support:

- ▶ Password Authentication Protocol (PAP)

- ▶ Challenge Handshake Authentication Protocol (CHAP)

> ▸ Microsoft Challenge Handshake Authentication Protocol Version 2
>   (MS-CHAPv2)
>
> ▸ Extensible Authentication Protocol (EAP)

Table 6.1 shows PPP authentication protocols, descriptions, and security levels.

EXAM ALERT

Be sure to know the different PPP authentication protocols and when to use them.

Table 6.1 PPP Authentication Protocols

Protocol	Description	Security Level
PAP	Uses plain text (unencrypted) passwords.	The least secure authentication.
	Typically used if the remote access client and remote access server can not negotiate a more secure form of validation.	Does not protect against replay attacks, remote client impersonation, or remote server impersonation.
CHAP	A challenge-response authentication protocol that uses the industry standard MD5 hashing scheme to encrypt the response.	An improvement over PAP in that the password is not sent over the PPP link.
		Requires a plain text version of the password to validate the challenge response.
		Does not protect against remote server impersonation.
MS-CHAPv2	An upgrade of MS-CHAP. Two-way authentication, also known as mutual authentication, is provided.	Provides stronger security than CHAP.
	The remote access client receives verification that the remote access server into which it is dialing has access to the user's password.	
EAP	Allows for arbitrary authentication of a remote access connection through the use of authentication schemes, known as EAP types.	Offers the strongest security by providing the most flexibility in authentication variations.

Password Authentication Protocol (PAP)

Password Authentication Protocol (PAP) is the least secure authentication protocol because it uses clear text/plain text (unencrypted) passwords. The steps when using PAP are as follows:

1. The remote access client sends a PAP Authenticate-Request message to the remote access server containing the remote access client's username and clear text password. Clear text, also referred to as plain text, is textual data in ASCII format.

2. The remote access server checks the username and password and sends back either a PAP Authenticate-Acknowledgment message when the user's credentials are correct, or a PAP Authenticate-No Acknowledgment message when the user's credentials are not correct.

Therefore, the password can easily be read with a protocol analyzer. In addition, PAP offers no protection against replay attacks, remote client impersonation, or remote server impersonation. Therefore, to make your remote access server more secure, ensure that PAP is disabled. Another disadvantage of using PAP is that if your password expires, PAP doesn't have the capability to change your password during authentication.

Challenge Handshake Authentication Protocol (CHAP)

Historically, *Challenge Handshake Authentication Protocol (CHAP)* is the most common dial-up authentication protocol used. It uses an industry Message Digest 5 (MD5) hashing scheme to encrypt authentication. A hashing scheme scrambles information in such a way that it's unique and can't be reversed back to the original format.

CHAP doesn't send the actual password over the wire; instead, it uses a three-way challenge-response mechanism with one-way MD5 hashing to provide encrypted authentication without sending the password over the link:

1. The remote access server sends a CHAP Challenge message containing a session ID and an arbitrary challenge string.

2. The remote access client returns a CHAP Response message containing the username in clear text and a hash of the challenge string, session ID, and the client's password, using the MD5 one-way hashing algorithm.

3. The remote access server duplicates the hash and compares it to the hash in the CHAP Response. If the hashes are the same, the remote access server sends back a CHAP Success message. If the hashes are different, a CHAP Failure message is sent.

Because standard CHAP clients use the plain text version of the password to create the CHAP challenge response, passwords must be stored on the server to calculate an equivalent response.

Because CHAP uses an arbitrary challenge string per authentication attempt, it protects against replay attacks. However, CHAP does not protect against remote server impersonation. In addition, because the algorithm for calculating CHAP responses is well known, it is very important that passwords be carefully chosen and sufficiently long. CHAP passwords that are common words or names are vulnerable to dictionary attacks if they can be discovered by comparing responses to the CHAP challenge with every entry in a dictionary. Passwords that are not sufficiently long can be discovered by brute force by comparing the CHAP response to sequential trials until a match to the user's response is found. In addition, CHAP does not protect against remote server impersonation.

Microsoft Challenge Handshake Authentication Protocol Version 2 (MS-CHAPv2)

Microsoft Challenge Handshake Authentication Protocol Version 2 (MS-CHAPv2) provides stronger security for remote access connections (including stronger initial data encryption keys and different encryption keys for sending and receiving) and allows for mutual authentication where the client authenticates the server.

Extensible Authentication Protocol (EAP) and Protected Extensible Authentication Protocol (PEAP)

Another form of authentication is EAP. Because security and authentication is a constantly changing field, embedding authentication schemes into an operating system is impractical at times. To solve this problem, Microsoft has included support for *Extensible Authentication Protocol (EAP)*, which allows new authentication schemes to be plugged in as needed. Therefore, EAP allows third-party vendors to develop custom authentication schemes such as retinal scans, voice recognition, finger print identification, *smart card*, Kerberos, and digital certificates. In addition, EAP offers mutual authentication.

A new member of the EAP family is the *Protected Extensible Authentication Protocol (PEAP)*. PEAP uses Transport Layer Security (TLS) to create an encrypted channel between an authenticating EAP client, such as a wireless computer, and an EAP authenticator, such as the RADIUS server. PEAP does not specify an authentication method but provides a secure "wrapper" for other EAP authentication protocols that operate within the TLS-encrypted channel provided by PEAP. PEAP is used as an authentication method for 802.11 wireless client computers, but it does not support VPNs or other remote access clients.

EXAM ALERT

Knowing the features and differences among the preceding authentication protocols is important for achieving success on the exam. For example, if your remote access clients use smart card authentication, you need to enable EAP on the remote access server. Or, if smart cards are not deployed, and all remote access clients are running Windows XP or Windows Vista, you should enable only MS-CHAPv2 or EAP because they provide the most security.

Configuring Dial-Up Remote Access Server

After RRAS has been loaded, you must first enable IPv4 Remote Access Server and/or IPv6 Remote Access Server by right-clicking the server and enabling the appropriate option in the General tab see Figure 6.1).

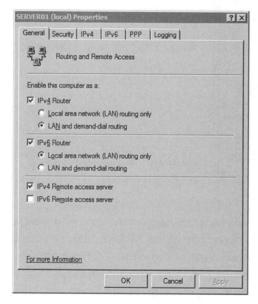

FIGURE 6.1 Enabling routing and demand-dial routing with Routing and Remote Access.

Next, configure PPP by using the PPP tab, including enabling or disabling LCP and software compression (see Figure 6.2). You can also enable the Multilink Connections option to allow remote access clients to aggregate multiple phone lines into a single logical connection, which increases bandwidth. For example, you can combine two B channels from an ISDN BRI connection. Although multilink enables multiple connections to act as a single logical connection, on its own it does not provide a way of dynamically adding and dropping links based on bandwidth requirements.

The *Bandwidth Allocation Protocol (BAP)* provides this feature. BAP enables multilink connections to be added and dropped as bandwidth requirements change. For example, if the bandwidth utilization for a link goes beyond a configured level, the client who is requesting an additional link can send a BAP request message. The Bandwidth Allocation Control Protocol (BACP) works in conjunction with the Link Control Protocol (LCP) to elect a favored "peer" so that a favored peer can be identified if multiple BAP requests are received simultaneously.

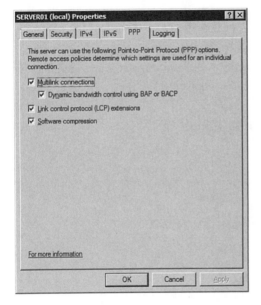

FIGURE 6.2 PPP options in Routing and Remote Access.

Configuring inbound connections allows a remote access server to accept incoming connections from remote access clients. After RRAS has been enabled, a number of ports are created. Additional ports can be created, if necessary. You can configure the ports by right-clicking the Ports icon under the RAS and selecting Properties. Select the ports that you want to configure and click Configure. Keep in mind that the configuration changes made apply to all ports (see Figure 6.3).

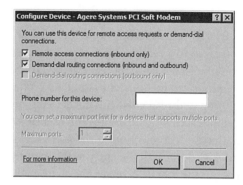

FIGURE 6.3 Configuring ports within Routing and Remote Access.

Lastly, if you select the Security tab and click Authentication Methods, you can then configure the authentication methods used by the remote access server (see Figure 6.4).

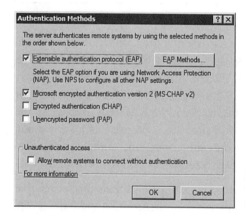

FIGURE 6.4 Configuring authentication methods within Routing and Remote Access.

Authentication with RADIUS

Remote Authentication Dial-In User Service (RADIUS is the industry standard client/server protocol and software for enabling remote access servers to communicate with a central server and database to authenticate dial-in users and authorize their access to the requested system or service for authenticating remote users. It provides better security, enabling a company to set up a policy that can be applied at a single administered network point. And because RADIUS has a central server, it also means that it is easier to perform accounting of network usage for billing and for keeping network statistics.

Users can connect to your network as a RADIUS client through a network access server, wireless access points, 802.1X authenticating switches, dial-up servers, and VPN servers. When a user dials in to a remote access device/server, the remote access device or service communicates with the central RADIUS server to determine whether the user is authorized to connect to the LAN. The RADIUS server performs the authentication and responds with an "accept" or a "reject." If the user is accepted, the remote access server routes the user onto the network; if not, the RAS terminates the user's connection. If the user's login information, username, and/or password does not match the entry in the remote access server, or if the RAS isn't able to contact the RADIUS server, the connection is denied.

NOTE

Besides being deployed in remote access servers, RADIUS can also be deployed on routers and firewalls.

A *RADIUS proxy* is a device that forwards or routes RADIUS connection requests and accounting messages between RADIUS clients (and RADIUS proxies) and RADIUS servers (or RADIUS proxies). The RADIUS proxy uses information within the RADIUS message, such as the User-Name or Called-Station-ID RADIUS attributes, to route the RADIUS message to the appropriate RADIUS server. A RADIUS proxy can be used as a forwarding point for RADIUS messages when the authentication, authorization, and accounting must occur at multiple RADIUS servers in different organizations.

The user account database is the list of user accounts and their properties that can be checked by a RADIUS server to verify authentication credentials and user account properties containing authorization and connection parameter information. The user account databases that RADIUS can use are the local Security Accounts Manager (SAM), or an Active Directory directory service.

EXAM ALERT

In Windows Server 2003, the RADIUS server is the Internet Authentication Service (IAS). In Windows Server 2008, IAS has been replaced by the *Network Policy Server (NPS)*.

Enabling RADIUS in the Routing and Remote Access Console

If you have not loaded Network Policy Server, you can configure your Windows Server 2008 to use a RADIUS server for authentication by following these steps:

1. Open the Routing and Remote Access console.

2. Right-click the server and select Properties.

3. In the Security tab, select RADIUS Authentication for the Authentication Provider.

4. Click Configure.

5. To specify one or more RADIUS servers, use the Add button.

6. Click OK to exit the Radius Authentication dialog box.

7. Click OK to exit the server properties.

If you load NPS on a Windows Server 2008 computer, the Authentication Provider is not available in the Routing and Remote Access console.

NPS as a RADIUS Client

NPS acts as a RADIUS client when you configure it as a RADIUS proxy to forward Access-Request messages to other RADIUS servers for processing. When you use NPS as a RADIUS proxy, follow these general configuration steps:

1. Network access servers, such as wireless access points and VPN servers, are configured with the IP address of the NPS proxy as the designated RADIUS server or authenticating server. This enables the network access servers, which create Access-Request messages based on information they receive from access clients, to forward messages to the NPS proxy.

2. You configure the NPS proxy by adding each network access server as a RADIUS client. This configuration step enables the NPS proxy to receive messages from the network access servers and to communicate with them throughout authentication. In addition, connection request policies on the NPS proxy are configured to specify which Access-Request messages to forward to one or more RADIUS servers. These policies are also configured with a remote RADIUS server group, which tells NPS where to send the messages it receives from the network access servers.

3. The NPS or other RADIUS servers that are members of the remote RADIUS server group on the NPS proxy are configured to receive messages from the NPS proxy. You do so by configuring the NPS proxy as a RADIUS client.

When you add a RADIUS client to the NPS configuration through the NPS snap-in or through the use of the `netsh` commands for NPS, you are configuring NPS to receive RADIUS Access-Request messages from either a network access server or a RADIUS proxy.

To configure a Windows Server 2008 computer with NPS loaded to use a RADIUS server (which includes pointing to itself), follow these steps:

1. Open the Network Policy Server console.

2. Right-click RADIUS client and select New RADIUS Client.

3. Configure the following options in the Properties dialog box:

   ▶ **Friendly Name**: A friendly name for the RADIUS client, which makes it easier to identify when using the NPS snap-in or `netsh` commands for NPS.

   ▶ **Address**: The Internet Protocol version 4 (IPv4) address or the Domain Name System (DNS) name of the RADIUS client.

   ▶ **Vendor Name**: The vendor of the RADIUS client. Otherwise, you can use the RADIUS standard value for Client-Vendor.

   ▶ **Shared Secret**: A text string that is used as a password between RADIUS clients, RADIUS servers, and RADIUS proxies. When the Message Authenticator attribute is used, the shared secret is also used as the key to encrypt RADIUS messages. This string must be configured on the RADIUS client and in the NPS snap-in.

   ▶ **Message Authenticator attribute**: A Message Digest 5 (MD5) hash of the entire RADIUS message. If the RADIUS Message Authenticator attribute is present, it is verified. If it fails verification, the RADIUS message is discarded. If the client settings require the Message Authenticator attribute and it is not present, the RADIUS message is discarded. Use of the Message Authenticator attribute is recommended.

NOTE

The Message Authenticator attribute is required and enabled by default when you use EAP authentication.

▶ **RADIUS Client Is NAP-Capable**: A designation that the RADIUS client is compatible with *Network Access Protection (NAP)*, and NPS sends NAP attributes to the RADIUS client in the Access-Accept message.

See Figure 6.5.

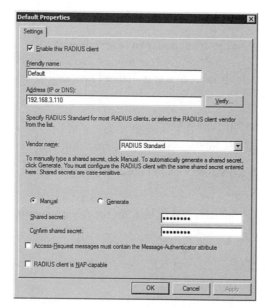

FIGURE 6.5 Configuring RADIUS clients.

Registering the NPS Server in Active Directory Domain Services (AD DS)

When Network Policy Server is a member of an Active Directory domain, NPS performs authentication by comparing user credentials that it receives from network access servers with the credentials that are stored for the user account in Active Directory Domain Services (AD DS). In addition, NPS authorizes connection requests by using network policies and by checking user account dial-in properties in AD DS.

For NPS to have permission to access user account credentials and dial-in properties in AD DS, the NPS server must be registered in AD DS. To register the NPS server in the default domain using Network Policy Server,

1. Open Network Policy Server.

2. Right-click NPS (Local) and then click Register Server in Active Directory. When the Register Network Policy Server in Active Directory dialog box appears, click OK.

To register the NPS server in the default domain with the `netsh` command,

1. Open the command prompt.

2. At the command prompt, type **`netsh ras add registeredserver`**.

To register the NPS server in the default domain using Active Directory Users and Computers,

1. Open Active Directory Users and Computers.

2. In the console tree, click the Users folder in the appropriate domain.

3. In the details pane, right-click RAS and NPS Servers, and then click Properties.

4. In the RAS and NPS Servers Properties dialog box, on the Members tab, add each of the NPS servers.

You can also add the NPS server to the RAS and NPS Servers group with the `Dsmod` tool.

Logging and RADIUS Accounting

To configure remote-access logging, open the Routing and Remote Access Service console, right-click *servername* and then click Properties. Click the Logging tab to view the available options for, and the location of, the tracing log.

The four levels of event logging that Windows Server 2008 Routing and Remote Access Service makes available are

- Log Errors Only

- Log Errors and Warnings

- Log All Events

- Do Not Log Any Events

You can configure Network Policy Server (NPS) to perform RADIUS accounting for user authentication requests, Access-Accept messages, Access-Reject messages, accounting requests and responses, and periodic status updates. You can use this procedure to configure the log files where you want to store the accounting data.

To prevent the log files from filling the hard drive, it is strongly recommended that you keep them on a partition that is separate from the system partition. NPS makes it possible to log on to a Microsoft SQL Server database in addition to, or instead of, logging to a local file.

If you do not supply a full path statement in Log File Directory, the default path is used, which is c:\windows\system32\NPSLogFile. Follow these steps to configure log file properties within the Windows interface:

1. Open the Network Policy Server MMC snap-in.

2. In the console tree, click Accounting.

3. In the details pane, in Local File Logging, click Configure Local File Logging. The Local File Logging dialog box opens.

4. On the Log File tab, in Directory, type the location where you want to store NPS log files. The default location is the systemroot\System32\LogFiles folder.

5. In Format, click Database-compatible. Or, to keep your log files in IAS format, click IAS.

To configure NPS to start new log files at specified intervals, click the interval that you want to use:

▶ For heavy transaction volume and logging activity, click Daily.

▶ For lesser transaction volumes and logging activity, click Weekly or Monthly.

▶ To store all transactions in one log file, click Never (unlimited file size).

▶ To limit the size of each log file, click When Log File Reaches This Size, and then type a file size, after which a new log is created. The default size is 10 megabytes (MB).

To configure NPS to automatically delete log files when the disk is full, click When Disk Is Full Delete Older Log Files. If the oldest log file is the current log file, it is not deleted.

The Routing and Remote Access service in Windows Server 2008 has an extensive tracing capability that you can use to troubleshoot complex network problems.

You can enable the components in Windows Server 2008 to log tracing information to files, either by using the `netsh` command or through the Registry.

To enable tracing with the `netsh` command, use the following command:

```
netsh ras diagnostics set rastracing * enabled.
```

You can also configure the tracing function by changing settings in the registry under `HKEY_LOCAL_MACHINE\SOFTWARE\Microsoft\Tracing`.

Tracing consumes system resources and should be used sparingly to help identify network problems. After the trace is captured or the problem is identified, you should immediately disable tracing. Most of the time this information is useful only to Microsoft support professionals or to network administrators who are very experienced with the Routing and Remote Access service. Tracing information can be saved as files and sent to Microsoft support for analysis.

IPSec

Internet Protocol (IP) Security, more commonly known as *IPSec*, is not a single protocol but a suite of protocols that provide a mechanism for data integrity, authentication, and privacy for the IP. IPSec can provide either message authentication and/or encryption. The IPSec protocol suite is used to protect data that is sent between hosts on a network by creating secure electronic tunnels between two machines or devices. IPSec can be used for remote access, VPN, server connections, LAN connections, or WAN connections.

IPSec ensures that data cannot be viewed or modified by unauthorized users while being sent to its destination. Before data is sent between two hosts, the source computer encrypts the information by encapsulating each data packet in a new packet that contains the information necessary to set up, maintain, and tear down the tunnel when it is no longer needed. The data is then decrypted at the destination computer.

IPSec Modes

A couple of modes and a couple of protocols are available in IPSec, depending on whether they are implemented in the end hosts—such as the server or the routers—and the level of security. IPSec can be used in one of two modes:

▶ **Transport mode**: Used to secure end-to-end communications, such as between a client and a server.

▶ **Tunnel mode**: Used for server-to-server or server-to-gateway configurations. The tunnel is the path a packet takes from the source computer to the destination computer. This way, any IP packets sent between the two hosts or between the two subnets, depending on the configuration, are secured.

EXAM ALERT

IPSec/L2TP or PPTP (Point-to-Point Tunneling Protocol) is used for VPN connections. Tunnel mode is not used for remote access VPNs. Tunnel mode is used for systems that cannot use IPSec/L2TP or PPTP VPNs.

The IPSec protocols are

▶ **Encapsulating Security Payload (ESP)**: Provides confidentiality, authentication, integrity, and anti-replay for the IP payload only, not the entire packet. ESP operates directly on top of IP, using IP protocol number 50.

▶ **Authentication Header (AH)**: Provides authentication, integrity, and anti-replay for the entire packet (both the IP header and the data payload carried in the packet). It does not provide confidentiality, which means that it does not encrypt the payload. The data is readable, but protected from modification. Some fields that are allowed to change in transit are excluded because they need to be modified as they are relayed from router to router. AH operates directly on top of IP, using IP protocol number 51.

ESP and AH can be combined to provide authentication, integrity, and anti-replay for the entire packet (both the IP header and the data payload carried in the packet) and confidentiality for the payload.

EXAM ALERT

The AH protocol is not compatible with network address translation (NAT) because NAT devices need to change information in the packet headers. To allow IPSec-based traffic to pass through a NAT device, you must ensure that IPSec NAT-T is supported on your IPSec peer computers.

Although AH and ESP provide the means to protect data from tampering, preventing eavesdropping and verifying the origin of the data, it is the Internet Key Exchange (IKE) that defines the method for the secure exchange of the initial encryption keys between the two endpoints. IKE allows nodes to agree on authentication methods, encryption methods, the keys to use, and the lifespan of the keys.

The information negotiated by IKE is stored in a Security Association (SA). A SA is like a contract laying out the rules of the VPN connection for the duration of the SA. An SA is assigned a 32-bit number that, when used in conjunction with the destination IP address, uniquely identifies the SA. This number is called Security Parameters Index (SPI).

Implementing IPSec

IPSec can be used with Windows in various ways. To enable IPSec communications for a Windows Server 2008 computer, you create group policies and assign them to individual computers or groups of computers. The policies determine the level of security that is to be used.

IPSec consists of three components that work together to provide secure communications between hosts:

- ▶ **IPSec Policy Agent**: Responsible for retrieving policy information from the local computer or Active Directory.

- ▶ **ISAKMP/Oakley Key Management Service**: Responsible for establishing a secure channel between hosts and creating the shared key that is used to encrypt the data. It also establishes a security association between hosts before data is transferred. The security association determines the mechanisms that are used to secure data.

- ▶ **IPSec Driver**: Monitors IP packets on the sending computer. Packets matching a configured filter are secured using the security association and shared key. The IPSec driver on the receiving computer decrypts the data.

The following steps outline how the different components work together to provide secure communications:

1. When Computer1 starts, the IPSec policy agent retrieves policy information from the local computer or Active Directory.

2. When Computer1 attempts to send data to Computer2, the IPSec driver examines the IP packets to determine whether they match the configured

filters. If a match is determined, the IPSec driver notifies the ISAKMP/Oakley.

3. The ISAKMP/Oakley service on the two computers is used to establish a security association and a shared key.

4. The IPSec driver on Computer1 uses the key and security association to encrypt the data.

5. The IPSec driver on Computer2 decrypts the information and passes it to the requesting application.

You can enable IPSec by using the Local Security Policy snap-in. The following list describes the three default policies. You can enable any policy for the local computer by right-clicking the policy and choosing the Assign option:

► **Client (Respond Only):** This is used for computers that should not secure communications most of the time, but if requested to set up a secure communication, they can respond.

► **Server Secure (Require Security):** When this option is selected, the server requires all communications to be secure. If a client is not IPSec-aware, the session is not allowed.

► **Server (Request Security):** This is used for computers that should secure communications most of the time. In this policy, the computer accepts unsecured traffic but always attempts to secure additional communications by requesting security from the original sender.

To assign an IPSec policy to Group Policy, right-click the policy and click the Assign option.

To create a new IPSec policy, follow these steps:

1. Click Start and click the Run command. Type **mmc** and click OK.

2. Click File and select Add/Remove Snap-In. Click Add.

3. From the list of available snap-ins, select IP Security Policy Management. Click Add. Click Finish. Click Close.

4. Click OK.

5. To create a new policy, right-click IP Security Policies on Local Computer and select Create IP Security Policy. Click Next.

6. Type a name for the new policy. Click Next.

7. From the Requests for Secure Communications window, leave the default option of Activate the Default Response Rule selected to have the computer respond to those that request security. Click Next.

8. Select the authentication method. You can choose Kerberos, certificates, or a preshared key. You can edit the policy afterward to add multiple authentication methods. Click Next.

9. Click Finish.

To configure an IPSec tunnel, follow these steps:

1. From the Properties window of the IPSec policy that you want to manage, select the rule you want to edit and click Edit.

2. Select the Tunnel Setting tab.

3. Select the tunnel endpoint that is specified by this IP address option and type the IP address of the tunnel endpoint.

4. After the tunnel endpoint has been specified, you can configure the tunneling mode by using the Filter Actions tab. For ESP tunnel mode, select High. For AH tunnel mode, select Medium.

Customizing IPSec Policies and Rules

An IPSec policy tells a server what actions to perform on network traffic when using IPSec. The components of an IPSec policy define what type of IP traffic is covered by the policy, the type of authentication mechanism should be used, and what happens to the traffic when it does or does not meet the criteria of a policy.

You can edit each policy by using the policy's Properties window. IPSec policies consist of several components, including the following:

- ▶ **Rules**: Determine how and when communication is secured.

- ▶ **Filter lists**: Determine what type of IP packets trigger security negotiations.

- ▶ **IPSec security methods**: Determine the security requirements of the rule.

- ▶ **IPSec authentication methods**: Determine the ways in which hosts can identify themselves.

- ▶ **IPSec connection types**: Determine the types of connections, such as remote access or local area connections, to which the rule applies.

Let's take a look at an example. You can create an IPSec policy that blocks all ping traffic to and from a computer:

1. Configure an IP Filter List that includes ICMP traffic.

2. Create a Filter Action that blocks the designated traffic.

3. Create a new IPSec policy.

4. Add the IP Filter List and Filter Action you created to the IPSec policy.

5. Assign the IPSec policy.

To begin configuring an IPSec policy, right-click the policy and click Properties. From the General tab of an IPSec policy's Properties window, you can change the name and description for the policy and configure the interval at which the computer is to check for policy updates. Using the Advanced button, you can configure the Key Exchange Settings.

NOTE

When configuring the Key Exchange Settings, you can select the Master Key Perfect Forward Secrecy option. This ensures that no previously used keying material is used to generate new master keys. You can also specify the interval at which authentication and key generation must take place.

The Rules tab lists all the rules that are configured for the policy. You can add other rules by clicking Add; you can edit the existing rules by using Edit. Clicking Edit opens the Edit Rule Properties window.

The IP Filter List tab defines the type of traffic to which the rule is to apply. The Filter Action tab defines whether the rule negotiates for secure traffic and how the traffic is to be secured. Configuring the filter actions enables you to define the different security methods that can be negotiated. The security algorithms supported by IPSec include MD5 and SHA1. The encryption algorithms supported include DES and 3DES.

The Authentication Methods tab enables you to configure the method used to establish trust between the two computers. If multiple authentication methods are configured for a rule, you can change the order in which they are used. The authentication methods available include

- **Kerberos**: Kerberos 5 is the default authentication method in a Windows Server 2008 domain. Users running the Kerberos protocol within a trusted domain can authenticate using this method.

▶ **Certificates**: If a trusted certification authority is available, certificates can be used for authentication.

▶ **Preshared key**: For non-Windows Server 2008 computers or those not running Kerberos, a preshared key can be used for authentication.

The Connection Type tab enables you to define the types of connections to which the rule applies. This enables you to define different rules for different types of connections. Rules can be applied to local area connections, remote access connections, or all network connections.

The Tunnel Setting tab enables you to specify a tunnel endpoint where communication will take place between two specific computers.

You can edit the existing policies, or you can create and assign a new policy through the Group Policy snap-in. To create a new policy, right-click IP Security Policies on Active Directory within a Group Policy Object and select Create IP Security Policy. A wizard walks you through the process of creating the initial policy, which you can configure further in the Properties window for the new policy.

EXAM ALERT

Windows Server 2008 uses the `gpupdate` command to refresh policy settings. When the command is used on its own, both the computer and user settings are applied. If you use the command with the `/target` switch, you can specify that only the computer or user settings are applied. The `/force` switch causes all policy settings to be reapplied, regardless of whether they have changed.

One of the first steps to try when a client and server cannot communicate is to disable the IPSec policy. Matching policies must exist on both computers before communication can take place.

Configuring IPSec Using the Windows Firewall with Advanced Security

In Windows XP and Windows Server 2003, the Windows Firewall and IP are configured separately. Unfortunately, because both can block or allow incoming traffic, it is possible that the firewall and IPSec rules can conflict with each other. In Windows Vista and Windows Server 2008, Windows Firewall with Advanced Security provides a single, simplified interface for managing both firewall filters and IPSec rules.

Windows Firewall with Advanced Security uses authentication rules to define IPSec policies. No authentication rules are defined by default. To create a new authentication rule, follow these steps:

1. In Windows Firewall with Advanced Security, select the Computer Connection Security node.

2. Right-click the Computer Connection Security node in the console tree and then click New Rule to start the New Connection Security Rule Wizard.

3. From the Rule Type page of the New Authentication Rule wizard, you can select the following:

   ▶ **Isolation**: Used to specify that computers are isolated from other computers based on membership in a common Active Directory domain or current health status. You must specify when you want authentication to occur (for example, for incoming or outgoing traffic and whether you want to require or only request protection), the authentication method for protected traffic, and a name for the rule.

   ▶ **Authentication Exemption**: Used to specify computers that do not have to authenticate or protect traffic by their IP addresses.

   ▶ **Server to Server**: Used to specify traffic protection between specific computers, typically servers. You must specify the set of endpoints are to exchange protected traffic by IP address, when you want authentication to occur, the authentication method for protected traffic, and a name for the rule.

   ▶ **Tunnel**: Used to specify traffic protection that is tunneled, typically used when sending packets across the Internet between two security gateway computers. You must specify the tunnel endpoints by IP address, the authentication method, and a name for the rule.

   ▶ **Custom**: Used to create a rule that does not specify a protection behavior. You would select this option when you want to manually configure a rule, perhaps based on advanced properties that cannot be configured through the pages of the New Authentication Rule wizard. You must specify a name for the rule.

The Connection Security Rule wizard has a page where you can configure the Authentication Method to configure the credential used for authentication. If the rule already exists, you can use the Authentication tab of the Connection Security Properties dialog box of the rule you want to edit:

▸ **Default**: Use the authentication method configured on the IPSec Settings tab.

▸ **Computer and User (Kerberos V5)**: Request or require that both the user and computer authenticate before communications can continue; domain membership required.

▸ **Computer (Kerberos V5)**: Request or require the computer to authenticate using Kerberos V5; domain membership required.

▸ **User (Kerberos V5)**: Request or require the user to authenticate using Kerberos V5; domain membership required.

▸ **Computer Certificate**: Request or require a valid computer certificate; requires at least one Certification Authority (CA). This method accepts only health certificates. It also requests or requires a valid health certificate to authenticate and it requires IPSec NAP.

▸ **Advanced**: Configure any available method, including specifying First and Second Authentication.

Follow these steps to configure advanced properties for the security rule:

1. Right-click the name of the rule and then click Properties.

2. From the properties dialog box for a rule, you can configure settings on the following tabs:

   ▸ **General**: The rule's name and description and whether the rule is enabled.

   ▸ **Computers**: The set of computers, by IP address, for which traffic is protected.

   ▸ **Authentication**: When you want authentication for traffic protection to occur (for example, for incoming or outgoing traffic and whether you want to require or only request protection) and the authentication method for protected traffic.

   ▸ **Advanced**: The profiles and types of interfaces to which the rule applies and IPSec tunneling behavior.

On the Windows Firewall with Advanced Security Properties dialog box, you can configure the following IPSec settings within the IPSec tab:

▶ **IPSec Defaults**: These are the default IPSec settings that are applied when you create Connection Security rules (the new name for IPSec policies). When you create Connection Security Rules, you have the option to change the settings on each rule from the defaults.

▶ **IPSec Exemptions**: By default, IPSec exemptions are disabled. However, you might find network troubleshooting with `ping`, `tracert`, and other ICMP-dependent tools a lot easier if you change it from No (default) to Yes.

If you click the Customize button in the IPSec defaults frame, you can configure the following without going through the Connection Security Rule wizard:

▶ Key Exchange Security

▶ Data Protection (encryption algorithms)

▶ Authentication Method

See Figure 6.6.

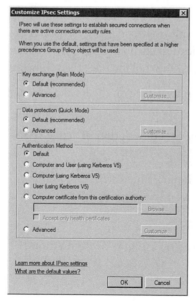

FIGURE 6.6 Configuring RADIUS clients.

EXAM ALERT

If you configure Windows Server 2008 as VPN server and you have the Windows Firewall enabled, you need to open up the appropriate ports for the VPN to function. This includes the following ports:

PPTP—TCP port 1723

SSTP—TCP port 443

L2TP—TCP port 1701

IPSec—UDP port 500

Monitoring Network Protocol Security

Organizations want to ensure that communications remain secure. Therefore, it's important for network administrators to monitor network communications to ensure that communications are indeed trustworthy. A number of tools included with Windows Server 2008 can be used to monitor network protocol security.

As part of managing and maintaining network security, administrators can use the IP Security Monitor tool (found within the Windows Firewall with Advanced Security or a stand-alone MMC) to validate that communications between hosts are indeed secure. It provides information such as which IPSec policy is active and whether a secure communication channel is being established between computers. Some of the functionality of the tool includes the following:

▶ Administrators have the capability to monitor IPSec on the local computer or on a remote system.

▶ It provides information such as the name and description of active IPSec policies.

▶ Administrators can view main mode and quick mode statistics. Main mode and quick mode are the two phases of IKE negotiations.

▶ The refresh rates can be customized.

▶ Administrators can search for filters based on a source or destination IP address.

Take these steps to open the IP Security Monitor snap-in:

1. Click Start and click Run.

2. Type **mmc** and click OK.

3. In the Microsoft Management Console, click File and then click Add/Remove Snap-in.

4. From the Add/Remove Snap-in window, click Add.

5. From the list of available snap-ins, select IP Security Monitor and click Add. Click Close.

6. Click OK.

You can use the IP Security Monitor console to view IPSec information locally or on a remote computer. To add another computer to the console, right-click the IP Security Monitor container within the console and click Add Computer. Type the name of the computer to which you want to connect, or click Browse to search for it.

Expanding the IP Security Monitor container displays the name of the local computer or any remote computer to which you are connected. If you expand the container, you see three containers:

▶ Active Policy

▶ Main Mode

▶ Quick Mode

As noted previously, IP Security Monitor can be used to view the active IPSec policies on a computer. Clicking the Active Policy container within the console displays the following information:

▶ **Policy Name**: Lists the name of the active IPSec policy.

▶ **Policy Description**: Lists an optional description of the policy, which should describe the policy's purpose.

▶ **Policy Last Modified**: Indicates when the policy was last modified. This option is applicable only to policies applied to a local computer.

▶ **Policy Store**: Specifies the storage location for the active IPSec policy.

▶ **Policy Path**: Specifies the Lightweight Directory Access Protocol path to the IPSec policy.

▶ **Organizational Unit**: Specifies the Organizational Unit to which the group policy is applied.

▶ **Group Policy Object Name**: Specifies the name of the group policy object to which the IPSec policy is applied.

You'll notice two other containers listed under your server within the IP Security Monitor console: Main Mode and Quick Mode. Clicking either container displays a number of other containers. In any case, you can use these different options to monitor communications between hosts. A multitude of statistics can be used to monitor IPSec.

VPN Overview

Virtual private networking (VPN) involves the creation of secured, point-to-point connections across a private network or a public network, such as the Internet. A VPN client uses special TCP/IP-based protocols called tunneling protocols to make a virtual call to a virtual port on a virtual private networking server. The best example of virtual private networking is that of a VPN client who makes a VPN connection to a remote access server that is connected to the Internet. The remote access server answers the virtual call, authenticates the caller, and transfers data between the VPN client and the corporate network.

VPN uses one network to connect the components of another. The basic technology that defines a VPN is tunneling. Tunneling is the method of transferring data over the Internet or other public network, providing security and features formerly available only on private networks. A tunneling protocol encapsulates the data packet in a header that provides routing information to enable the encapsulated payload to securely traverse the network. The entire process of encapsulation and transmission of packets is tunneling, and the logical connection through which the packets travel is the tunnel.

As a comparison, tunneling is similar to sending a letter from one company's building in Los Angles to the same company's building in Chicago. The letter is initially sent through the corporation's mail service. When the letter gets to the mail root, it is then be sent to Chicago via the U.S. mail. The U.S mail carrier then delivers it to the second building. The letter is then sent through the corporate mail server to the correct office.

Types of VPN Connections

There are two types of VPN connections:

- ▶ Remote access VPN
- ▶ Site-to-site VPN

Remote Access VPN

Remote access VPN connections enables users who are working at home or on the road to connect to a remote access server on the corporate private network, which can then be used to access the rest of the corporate network. In other words, the users become part of the corporate network through a VPN tunnel.

Site-to-Site VPN

Site-to-site VPN connections (also known as router-to-router VPN connections) enable organizations to have routed connections between separate offices or with other organizations over a public network while helping to maintain secure communications. A routed VPN connection across the Internet logically operates as a dedicated wide area network (WAN) link. When networks are connected over the Internet, a router forwards packets to another router across a VPN connection. To the routers, the VPN connection operates as a data-link layer link.

A site-to-site VPN connection connects two portions of a private network. The VPN server provides a routed connection to the network to which the VPN server is attached. The calling router (the VPN client) authenticates itself to the answering router (the VPN server), and, for mutual authentication, the answering router authenticates itself to the calling router. In a site-to site VPN connection, the packets sent from either router across the VPN connection typically do not originate at the routers.

VPN Protocols

Two types of tunneling protocols can be used to connect to a VPN server:

- ▶ Point-to-Point Tunneling Protocol (PPTP)
- ▶ Layer 2 Tunneling Protocol (L2TP)

Both protocols are automatically installed by default.

Point-to-Point Tunneling Protocol (PPTP)

Point-to-Point Tunneling Protocol (PPTP) was developed by Microsoft and Ascend Communications. PPTP wraps various protocols inside an IP datagram. This process lets the protocols travel through an IP network tunnel, without user intervention. In addition, PPTP saves companies the work of building proprietary and dedicated network connections for their remote users and instead lets them use the Internet as their conduit.

PPTP is based on the point-to-point protocol. The difference between PPP and PPTP is that PPTP allows Internet access as the connection medium, rather than requiring a direct connection between the user and the network. In other words, instead of having to dial up the corporate network directly, a remote user could log in to a local Internet Service Provider, and PPTP makes the connection from that provider to the corporate network's Internet connection. From there, it continues into the corporate network the same as if the users had dialed in directly.

PPTP is used over PPP connections on an IP-based network and supports the encryption and encapsulation of IP, IPX, and NetBEUI packets. PPTP has built-in encryption technologies and uses MPPE 40-bit to 128-bit encryption.

PPTP has certain drawbacks. PPTP has weak encryption technology, so it is not a good choice for highly secure transmission over the Internet. Its authentication features (the same used by PPP) are also weak. Therefore, big corporations tend to prefer IPSec.

Layer 2 Tunneling Protocol (L2TP)

To compete against the PPTP-protocol, Cisco developed the *Layer 2 Forwarding (L2F)* protocol, which enables a server to frame dial-up traffic using PPP and transmit over WAN links to an L2F server or router, which then unwraps the packets before releasing them to the network.

The *Layer 2 Tunneling Protocol (L2TP)* is a combination of the L2F and PPTP, and enables remote users to access networks in a secure fashion. Therefore, L2TP represents the next generation of tunneling protocols. L2TP provides tunneling and supports header compression, but it does not provide encryption. Instead, it provides a secure tunnel by cooperating with other encryption, such as IPSec. IPSec does not require L2TP, but its encryption functions complement L2TP to create a secure VPN solution. IPSec uses the Data Encryption Standard (DES) to encrypt data with supported key lengths between 56-bit (DES) and 168-bit (3DES). Because the L2TP-based VPN connections are a combination of L2TP and IPSec, both L2TP and IPSec must be supported by both routers. L2TP is installed with the Routing and Remote Access service and, by default, is configured for five L2TP ports.

Secure Socket Tunneling Protocol (SSTP)

A new technology added to Windows Server 2008 is *Secure Socket Tunneling Protocol (SSTP)*, which uses the HTTPS protocol over TCP port 443 to pass traffic through firewalls and web proxies that might block PPTP and

L2TP/IPsec traffic. SSTP provides a mechanism to encapsulate PPP traffic over the Secure Sockets Layer (SSL) channel of the HTTPS protocol. The use of PPP allows support for strong authentication methods, such as EAP-TLS. SSL provides transport-level security with enhanced key negotiation, encryption, and integrity checking. When a client tries to establish a SSTP-based VPN connection, SSTP first establishes a bidirectional HTTPS layer with the SSTP server. Over this HTTPS layer, the protocol packets flow as the data payload. SSTP can be used only with client computers running Windows Vista Service Pack 1 (SP1) or Windows Server 2008.

A common deployment option is to use network address translation (NAT) on one or both sides of a connection that links offices in different geographical locations. The Routing and Remote Access service in Windows Server 2008 provides three types of VPN site-to-site connections. PPTP and SSTP can work with NAT. L2TP with IPSec can work with NAT if you use the IPSec NAT Traversal (NAT-T) feature.

Configuring a VPN

After configuring the server as a remote access server, you must first configure the TCP/IP settings for the Internet or perimeter network interface and for the intranet interface. Because of routing issues related to configuring TCP/IP automatically, it is recommended that you not configure a VPN server as a DHCP client. Therefore, you should manually configure the Internet or perimeter network interface of the VPN server with a static IP address and a default gateway. Configure the TCP/IP settings with a public IP address, a subnet mask, and the default gateway of either the firewall (if the VPN server is connected to a perimeter network) or an ISP router (if the VPN server is connected directly to the Internet).

The IP address must be a public IP address assigned by an ISP. As an option, you can configure the VPN server with a private IP address but assign it a published static IP address by which it is known on the Internet. When packets are sent to and from the VPN server, a network address translation (NAT) device that is positioned between the Internet and the VPN server translates the published IP address to the private IP address. In addition to configuring the IP address, you should give your VPN servers names that can be resolved to IP addresses using DNS.

To enable remote access, open RRAS and open the server properties. In the general tab, you can enable IPv4 and IPv6.

By default, there are five L2TP and five PPTP ports active. If you need to change the number of ports available, you can right-click Ports in RRAS and select Properties. You would then select the port that you want to configure and click Configure.

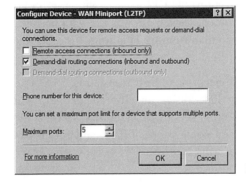

FIGURE 6.7   Configuring PPTP.

Using a Network Connection to Connect to a VPN

To create the VPN connection in Windows Vista or a Windows Server 2008 computer, follow these steps:

1. Open the Network and Sharing Center.

2. Under Tasks, click Set Up a Connection or Network.

3. When the Set Up a Connection or Network box appears, select Connect to a Workplace and click Next.

4. Click Use My Internet Connection (VPN).

5. Specify the hostname or IP address in the Internet address for the external address for the VPN connection.

6. Specify a name to call the VPN connection in the Destination Name text box.

7. Select the Don't Connect Now, Just Set It Up So I Can Connect Later option.

8. Specify the username and password and the domain name (optional).

9. After the connection is created, you can configure the VPN connection by selecting Manage Network Connections under Tasks.

10. Right-click the VPN connection you just created and select Properties.

11. If you want to use the Windows username and password, click the Security tab and select the Automatically Use My Windows Logon Name and Password option.

12. To modify the data encryption settings or authentication method, click the Advanced (Custom Settings) option and then click Settings.

13. To specify PPTP VPN, L2TP IPSec VPN, or Secure Socket Tunneling Protocol (SSTP), select the Networking tab and select the appropriate option under the type of VPN.

14. By default, the network connections use the default gateway on the remote VPN connection. If you want to use your local default gateway, select the Networking tab, select the Internet Protocol Version 4 or Internet Protocol Version 6 and click Properties.

15. Click the Advanced button. Deselect the Use Default Gateway on Remote Network check box.

By default, Windows XP with SP2, Windows Vista, and the Windows Server 2008 operating system do not support IPSec network address translation traversal (NAT-T) security associations to servers that are located behind a NAT device. Therefore, if the VPN server is behind a NAT device, a Windows-based VPN client computer cannot make a Layer 2 Tunneling Protocol (L2TP)/IPsec connection to the VPN server. To overcome this problem, you need to modify the Registry as explained in the following Microsoft support articles:

http://support.microsoft.com/kb/885407

http://support.microsoft.com/kb/926179

Connection Manager Administration Kit

Connection Manager is a versatile client dialer and connection software that you can customize by using the *Connection Manager Administration Kit (CMAK)* wizard. It enables you to create an executable program that can be installed and then creates a preconfigured network connection for a VPN. Doing so differs from manually creating a connection using the Network and Sharing Center in that you can customize the network connection in ways that you cannot configure the manual connection, including specifying a proxy server that web users have to use when connected through the VPN and running scripts and other programs before and after the connection is made. The CMAK wizard creates an executable file, which you can distribute in many ways, including using group policies or SMS or as part of an operating-system image.

To install CMAK, follow these steps:

1. Click Start, Administrative Tools, Server Manager.

2. If the User Account Control dialog box appears, confirm that the action it displays is what you want and then click Continue.

3. In Server Manager, in the left-hand pane, double-click Manage Roles to expand it.

4. Check to see whether the Network Access Services role is already present. If it is not present, proceed to step 5 to install the server role. If it is present, in the left pane right-click Network Access Services and then click Add Role Services. Skip steps 5–8 and proceed to step 9 to install the role service.

5. Right-click Manage Roles and then click Add Roles.

6. If the Before You Begin page appears, click Next.

7. On the Select Server Roles page, select Network Access Services and then click Next.

8. On the Introduction to Network Access Services page, click Next.

9. On the Select Role Services page, select Connection Manager Administration Kit (CMAK) and then click Next.

10. On the Confirm Installation Options page, click Install.

11. When the installation is complete, confirm that the installation was successful and then click Close.

Network Access Protection (NAP)

Network Access Protection (NAP) is a Microsoft technology for controlling a computer host's network access based on the host's system health. With Network Access Protection, system administrators of an organization's computer network can define policies for system health requirements. Examples of system health requirements are whether the computer has the most recent operating system updates installed, whether the computer has the latest version of the anti-virus software signature, or whether the computer has a host-based firewall installed and enabled. Connecting or communicating computers have their health status evaluated. Computers that comply with system health requirements can communicate with other compliant computers and have normal access to the network. Computers that do not comply with system health requirements are unable to communicate with compliant computers and may have restricted access to the network.

The NAP system consists of NAP clients, which are computers that request access to a NAP-enforcing network. NAP policies are enforced at NAP Enforcement Points, which lie at the edge of a protected network. NAP Enforcement Points are systems through which an unprotected network can connect to the internal network; these may be NAP-capable routers, VPN servers, DHCP servers, proxy servers, or specialized computers called Health Registration Authorities (HRA), which run Windows Server 2008.

For clients to be ready for core NAP functionality, you need the built-in NAP client called the *Network Access Protection Agent*, which is included in Windows XP with SP3, Windows Vista, and Windows Server 2008. However, the Network Access Protection Agent does not start automatically by default. The NAP client consists of five Enforcement Agents, which need to be enabled separately through the use of `napclcfg.msc` on the client or centrally for the whole network through the use of Group Policy (Computer Configuration\Windows Settings\Security Settings\Network Access Protection).

Network Policy Server (NPS)

When processing connection requests as a RADIUS server, Network Policy Server (NPS) performs both authentication and authorization for the connection request. NPS verifies the identify of the user or computer that is connecting to the network during the authentication process. NPS determines whether the user or computer is allowed to access the network during the authorization process.

To make this determination, NPS uses network policies that you configure in the NPS Microsoft Management Console (MMC) snap-in. To perform authorization, NPS also examines the user account's dial-in properties in Active Directory.

NOTE

In Internet Authentication Service (IAS) in the Windows Server 2003 family of operating systems, network policies were called remote access policies.

Network policies are sets of conditions, constraints, and settings that enable you to designate who is authorized to connect to the network and the circumstances under which they can, or cannot, connect. They limit network access of computers based on predefined health requirements. If a computer doesn't comply with those requirements, it gets no or limited access to the internal network. They can also be used to remedy a client automatically. So-called remediation servers make sure that a client fulfills the requirements before it gets full network access. For example, Windows Update Services is an example of a remediation server that is NAP-aware, which can be used to install Windows updates to make a computer compliant.

NPS uses network policies (formerly named remote access policies) and the dial-in properties of user accounts to determine whether to authorize a connection request to the network. You can configure a new network policy in either the NPS MMC snap-in or the Routing and Remote Access Service MMC snap-in (see Figure 6.8).

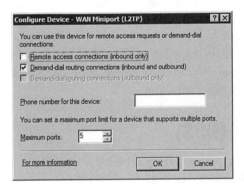

FIGURE 6.8 Configuring network policies.

Follow these steps to add a network policy using the Windows interface:

1. Open the NPS console and double-click Policies.

2. In the console tree, right-click Network Policies and then click New. The New Network Policy wizard opens.

3. Specify the Policy Name in the appropriate text box and specify the type of network access server. Click Next.

4. When the Specify Conditions box appears, click Add to specify the condition you want to impose for connecting to the server. Some of these conditions include which users, groups, computers can access the remote server; day and time restrictions; authentication type; and IP address. Click Next.

5. When the Specify Access Permissions dialog box appears, specify whether access is to be granted or denied if the conditions are met. Click Next.

6. When the Configure Authentication Methods window box appears, specify the authentication method (such as MS-CHAPv2, CHAP or EAP). Click Next.

7. When the Configure the Constraints box appears, you can configure option parameters, including how long a server has to be idle before being disconnected, how long a connection is active, and so on. Click Next.

8. When the Configure Settings box appears, you can specify the connection settings for if a connection was granted. These settings include IP filters, encryption settings, and IP address settings. Click Next.

9. When the wizard is completed, click Finish.

Windows Security Health Validators (SHVs)

Health policies consist of one or more *System Health Validators (SHVs)* and other settings that enable you to define client computer configuration requirements for the NAP-capable computers that attempt to connect to your network. When NAP-capable clients attempt to connect to the network, the client computer sends a *Statement of Health (SoH)* to the Network Policy Server (NPS). The SoH is a report of the client configuration state, and NPS compares the SoH to the requirements defined in the health policy. If the client configuration state does not match the requirements defined in the health policy, NPS takes one of the following actions, depending on how NAP is configured:

▶ The connection request by the NAP client is rejected.

▶ The NAP client is placed on a restricted network (quarantined) where it can receive updates from remediation servers that bring the client into compliance with health policy. After the client is compliant with health policy, it is allowed to connect.

▶ The NAP client is allowed to connect to the network despite being non-compliant with health policy.

You can define client health policies in NPS by adding one or more SHVs to the health policy, including the following health requirements: desktop firewall is enabled, virus protection is on and up to date, antispyware application is on and up to date, automatic updating is enabled, clients received all/low/moderate/important/critical security updates.

After a health policy is configured with one or more SHVs, you can add the health policy to the Health Policies condition of a network policy that you want to use to enforce NAP when client computers connect to your network.

You can create health policies in NPS by naming the policy, setting the type of client health validator check, and adding one or more SHVs to the new health policy.

To create a health policy, follow these steps:

1. Open the NPS console.

2. In the console tree, double-click Policies, right-click Health Policies, and then click New. The Create New Health Policy dialog box opens.

3. In the Create New Health Policy dialog box, on the Settings tab, in Policy Name, type a name for the health policy.

4. On the Settings tab, in Client SHV checks, select one of the following:

   ▸ **Client passes all SHV checks**: If this option is selected, NAP-capable client computer configuration must not match any SHVs that are configured in the policy.

   ▸ **Client fails all SHV checks**: If this option is selected, NAP-capable client computer configuration must match any SHVs that are configured in the policy.

   ▸ **Client passes one or more SHV checks**: If this option is selected, NAP-capable client computer configuration must match at least one SHV configured in the policy.

   ▸ **Client fails one or more SHV checks**: If this option is selected, NAP-capable client computer configuration must not match at least one SHV configured in the policy.

   In SHVs used in this health policy, check the SHVs that you want to include in the health policy. One or more SHVs must be selected.

5. Click OK.

To configure the Security Health Validators, select System Health Validators under Network Access Protection. Then double-click the System Health Validators and click Configure (see Figure 6.9).

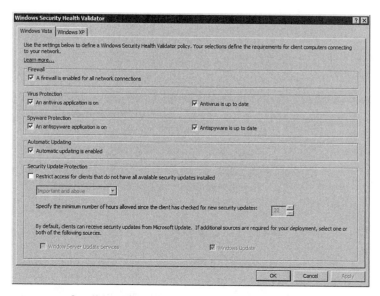

FIGURE 6.9 Specifying the Windows Security Health Validators for RADIUS clients.

Depending on which SHVs are used in the health policies, the client SHAs may need different operating system components. For example, if you use the Microsoft-provided Windows Security Health Validator, you must configure the client to always run Security Center (manually or through group policies) so the client-side SHA can get the necessary information on Windows Firewall, Automatic Updates, malware protection, and other security settings.

NAP Enforcement Methods

Network Policy Server enforces NAP health policies for the following technology:

- ▶ **DHCP enforcement**: DHCP enforcement enables you to specify special scope options for noncompliant machines that don't fulfill your SHV policy. For example, you can configure DHCP enforcement so that the IP settings for noncompliant computers don't specify a router address. This prevents those computers from accessing the Internet. Furthermore, they can access only the remediation servers.

- ▶ **VPN enforcement**: Noncompliant clients connecting to the network using the Windows VPN client can be quarantined to a restricted network if you apply packed filters. Clients can contact remediation servers in this restricted network to download updates, for example.

▶ **802.1X enforcement**: If your network switches support *802.1X authentication* and allow VLAN assignment according to RADIUS attributes, then you can use this method to quarantine noncompliant clients to a certain VLAN.

▶ **IPSec enforcement**: Compliant NAP clients receive a health certificate from a certification authority (CA). This CA can also be installed on Windows Server 2003 or Windows Server 2008. Basically, IPSec enforcement defines an IPSec policy that assures that only clients with a certain health certificate can establish connections to other computers on the network. If you are using this method, you have to configure IPSec for all your computers.

▶ **TS Gateway enforcement**: TS Gateway is a new feature of Windows Server 2008 Terminal Services that allows RDP over HTTPS to establish an encrypted connection to a TS Server. TS Gateway enforcement denies access to a TS server if the SHV policy is unmet. It is the only enforcement method that doesn't support auto-remediation.

For most of these, you can use automatic remediation. For example, NAP can automatically turn on Windows Firewall if you configured this as a health requirement.

NAP supports three different enforcement levels for noncompliant clients: access to a restricted network, full network access for a limited time, and full network access. The latter option can be used to test NAP for some time if you run it in report mode.

Wireless Connection

A quickly advancing field in networking is wireless technology. Today's computers can have a wireless network adapter to connect to other computers or to a wireless access point, which in turn enables the users to connect to the Internet or the rest of the internal network. Today's wireless adapters include PC cards for notebooks, Peripheral Component Interconnect (PCI) cards for desktops, and Universal Serial Bus (USB) devices (which can be used with notebooks or desktops).

Wireless Overview

Wireless adapters can run in one of two operating modes:

- **Ad hoc**: Wireless adapter to connect directly to other computers with wireless adapters.

- **Infrastructure**: Wireless adapter connect to an access point. All communication with other hosts go through the access point.

The most widely used wireless network adapters and access points are based on the Institute of Electrical and Electronics Engineers (IEEE) 802.11 specification (as shown in Table 6.2). Most wireless networks used by companies are 802.11b, 802.11g, or 802.11n networks. Wireless devices that are based on this specification can be Wi-Fi Certified to show they have been thoroughly tested for performance and compatibility.

NOTE

Because these devices use common public low-powered wireless frequencies, other wireless devices, such as wireless phones or handsets, may interfere with wireless adapters if they use the same frequency when they are used at the same time.

Table 6.2   Popular Wireless Standards

Wireless Standard	802.11a	802.11b	802.11g	802.11n
Speed	Up to 54Mbps	Up to 11Mbps	Up to 54Mbps	Up to 240Mbps
Transmission frequency	5GHz	2.4GHz	2.4GHz	2.4GHz
Effective indoor range	Approximately 25 to 75 feet	Approximately 100 to 150 feet	Approximately 100 to 150 feet	Approximately 300 feet–450 feet.
Compatibility	Incompatible with 802.11b and 802.11g	802.11b wireless devices can interoperate with 802.11g devices (at 11Mbps); 802.11g wireless adapters can operate with 802.11b access points (at 11Mbps)	802.11g wireless devices can operate with 802.11b devices (at 11Mbps)	80.2.11g can interoperate with 802.11b and 802.11g devices.

Of course, because a wireless network signal can be captured by anyone within the range of the antennas it is easy for someone to intercept the wireless signals that are being broadcast. Therefore, it is always recommended that you use some form of encryption.

The most basic wireless encryption scheme is *Wireless Equivalency Protection (WEP)*. With WEP, you encrypt data by using 40-bit, 128-bit, 256-bit, or higher private key encryption. With WEP, all data is encrypted with a symmetric key derived from the WEP key or password before it is transmitted, and any computer that wants to read the data must be able to decrypt it with the key. However, it is easy for someone with a little knowledge or experience to break the shared key because it doesn't change automatically over time. Therefore, it is recommended to use a higher form of wireless encryption then WEP.

Today, it is recommended to use *WiFi Protected Access (WPA)* and *Wi-Fi Protected Access Version 2 (WPA2)*. WPA was adopted by the Wi-Fi Alliance as an interim standard prior to the ratification of 802.11i. WPA2 is based on the official 802.11i standard and is fully backwards compatible with WPA.

WPA provides strong data encryption via Temporal Key Integrity Protocol (TKIP), while WPA2 provides enhanced data encryption via Advanced Encryption Standard (AES), which meets the Federal Information Standard (FIPS) 140-2 requirement of some government agencies. To help prevent someone from hacking the key, WPA and WPA2 rotate the keys and change the way keys are derived.

WPA-compatible and WPA2-compatible devices can operate in personal or enterprise mode:

- ▶ Personal mode provides authentication via a preshared key or password.
- ▶ Enterprise mode provides authentication using IEEE 802.1X and EAP.

In personal mode, WPA or WPA2 uses a preshared encryption key rather than a changing encryption key. The preshared encryption key is programmed into the access point and all wireless devices, and is used as a starting point to mathematically generate session keys. The session keys are then changed regularly so that the same session key is never used twice. Because the key rotation is automatic, key management is handled in the background.

In enterprise mode, wireless devices have two sets of keys:

▶ Session keys are unique to each association between an access point and a wireless client. They are used to create a private virtual port between the access point and the client.

▶ Group keys are shared among all clients connected to the same access point.

Both sets of keys are generated dynamically and are rotated to help safeguard the integrity of keys over time. The encryption key could be supplied through a certificate or smart card.

Configuring the Wireless Adapter

If you haven't previously connected to a wireless network, you can create a connection for the network by completing the following steps:

1. Click Start, Network. In Network Explorer, click Network and Sharing Center on the toolbar.

2. In Network and Sharing Center, click Set Up a Connection or Network. This starts the Set Up a Connection or Network Wizard.

3. Select Manually Connect to a Wireless Network and then click Next.

4. Enter information about the wireless network to which you want to connect. Your network administrator should have this information.

5. In the Network Name box, enter the network name, also referred to as the network's Service Set Identifier (SSID).

6. Use the Security Type selection list to select the type of security being used. The encryption type is then filled in automatically for you.

7. With WEP and WPA-Personal, you must enter the required security key or password phrase in the Security Key/Passphrase box.

8. By default, the connection is started automatically whenever the user logs on. If you also want the computer to connect to the network regardless of whether it can be reached, such as when the computer is out of range of the wireless base, select Connect Even if the Network Is Not Broadcasting.

9. Click Next to connect to the wireless network, using the settings you've entered.

If you have multiple computers that need to be configured to connect to a wireless network, you can use a USB flash drive to carry the configuration from computer to computer. To save the USB information to a USB drive, follow these steps:

1. Click Start, Control Panel.

2. Click Network and Internet, Network and Sharing Center, Add a Wireless Device.

3. Follow the steps in the wizard to save your wireless network settings to the USB flash drive.

To add a wireless computer running Windows Server 2008 using a USB flash drive, follow these steps:

1. Log on to the computer.

2. Plug the USB flash drive into a USB port on the computer.

3. For a computer running Windows Vista, in the AutoPlay dialog box, click Wireless Network Setup Wizard.

You might be prompted to restart the computer.

If you're previously connected to a wireless network, you can use these steps to easily connect to it or disconnect from it:

1. Click Start, Network. In Network Explorer, click Network and Sharing Center on the toolbar.

2. In Network and Sharing Center, click Connect to a Network. By default, all available networks are listed by name, status, and signal strength. If a network that should be available isn't listed, try clicking the Refresh button (the small two arrows at the top of the screen; see Figure 6.10) or pressing the F5 key on the keyboard.

3. Moving the pointer over a wireless network entry displays a message box that provides the network name, signal strength, security type, radio type (the wireless standard supported), and the link's security ID.

4. You can now connect to or disconnect from wireless networks. To connect to a wireless network, click the network and then click Connect. To disconnect from a wireless network, click the network and then click Disconnect. Confirm the action by clicking Disconnect again.

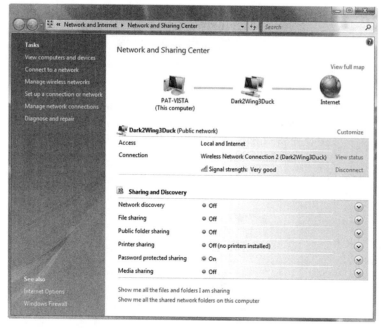

FIGURE 6.10 Using the Network and Sharing Center.

You can manage wireless networks with Manage Wireless Networks. To access Manage Wireless Networks,

1. Click Start, Network. In Network Explorer, click Network and Sharing Center on the toolbar.

2. In Network and Sharing Center, click Manage Wireless Networks.

Manage Wireless Networks lists wireless networks in the order in which the computer should try to use the available networks. The network listed at the top of the list is tried before any others. If the computer fails to establish a connection over this network, the next network in the list is tried, and so on.

To change the preference order of a network, click it and then use the Move Up or Move Down buttons to set the order in which the computer should try to use the network. As necessary, click Add to create a new wireless network that will be added to the wireless networks list, or select an existing network and click Remove to delete a listed wireless network.

Any wireless access point broadcasting within range should be available to a computer with a wireless adapter. By default, Windows Server 2008 is set to allow you to configure the network settings that should be used. This enables you to configure different authentication, encryption, and communication options as necessary.

If you click View Status for the wireless connection, you see a status dialog box. You can use the Wireless Network Connection Status dialog box to check the connection's status and to maintain the connection, in much the same way as you can for other types of connections. You can also see the duration and speed of the connection (see Figure 6.11).

FIGURE 6.11 The status of a wireless connection.

Requiring Certificates for Authentication and Encryption

Wireless networks make it possible for network users to access data and resources from multiple locations without relying on a physical connection to the network. The large number and variety of wireless clients and the potential security risks that they pose make it important for administrators to enhance data protection and to prevent unwanted clients from accessing the network. Certificates issued and supported by a Microsoft certification authority (CA) can enhance the security of a wireless network with strong certificate-based authentication and encrypted communication between clients and network servers.

To accomplish this, follow these steps:

1. Install a public key infrastructure (PKI), including a Subordinate Certification Authority.

2. Install and configure certificate templates, including the RAS and IAS Server, Workstation Authentication, and User Certificate templates.

3. Configure Automatic Certificate Enrollment.

4. Deploy RAS and IAS Server certificates.

5. Configure 802.1X wireless clients by using Group Policy.

6. Configure 802.1X wireless access points as (RADIUS) clients in NPS.

7. If you want to perform authorization by group, create a user group in Active Directory Domain Services (AD DS) that contains the users who are allowed to access the network through the wireless access points.

8. In NPS, configure one or more network policies for 802.1X wireless access.

Configuring a RADIUS Server for 802.1X Wireless or Wired Connections

Client computers, such as wireless laptop computers and other computers running client operating systems, are not RADIUS clients. RADIUS clients are network access servers—such as wireless access points, 802.1X authenticating switches, VPN servers, and dial-up servers—because they use the RADIUS protocol to communicate with RADIUS servers such as NPS servers.

In both cases, these network access servers must meet the following requirements:

▶ Support for IEEE standard 802.1X authentication

▶ Support for RADIUS authentication and RADIUS accounting

When you deploy 802.1X wired or wireless access with NPS as a RADIUS server, you must take the following steps:

1. Install and configure network access servers (RADIUS clients).

2. Deploy components for authentication methods.

3. Configure NPS as a RADIUS server.

For 802.1X wireless and wired, you can use the following authentication methods:

▸ Extensible Authentication Protocol (EAP) with Transport Layer Security (TLS), also called EAP-TLS.

▸ Protected EAP (PEAP) with Microsoft Challenge Handshake Authentication Protocol version 2 (MS-CHAPv2), also called PEAP-MS-CHAPv2.

▸ PEAP with EAP-TLS, also called PEAP-TLS.

For EAP-TLS and PEAP-TLS, you must deploy a Public Key Infrastructure (PKI) by installing and configuring Active Directory Certificate Services (AD CS) to issue certificates to domain member client computers and NPS servers. These certificates are used during the authentication process as proof-of-identity by both clients and NPS servers. If preferred, you can deploy smart cards rather than use client computer certificates. In this case, you must issue smart cards and smart card readers to organization employees.

For PEAP-MS-CHAPv2, you can deploy your own certification authority (CA) with AD CS to issue certificates to NPS servers or you can purchase server certificates from a public trusted root CA that clients trust, such as Verisign.

When you configure NPS as a RADIUS server, you must configure RADIUS clients, network policy, and RADIUS accounting. There are two stages to configuring RADIUS clients:

▸ Configure the physical RADIUS client, such as the wireless access point or authenticating switch, with information that allows the network access server to communicate with NPS servers. This information includes configuring the IP address of your NPS server and the shared secret in the access point or switch user interface.

▸ In NPS, add a new RADIUS client. On the NPS server, add each access point or authenticating switch as a RADIUS client. NPS allows you to provide a friendly name for each RADIUS client, as well as the IP address of the RADIUS client and the shared secret.

Using Group Policies to Configure Wireless Network (IEEE 802.11) Policies

The New Vista Wireless Network (IEEE 802.11) Policies enable you to configure, prioritize, and manage multiple wireless profiles that each use different profile names and different wireless settings, while using the same Service Set Identifier (SSID). For example, you can use the same SSID to configure two (or more) profiles; one profile to use Smart Cards and one profile to use Protected Extensible Authentication Protocol Microsoft Challenge Handshake Authentication Protocol version 2 (PEAP-MS-CHAPv2), or one using Wi-Fi Protected Access version 2 (WPA2)-Enterprise and one using WPA-Enterprise. The ability to configure mixed-mode deployments using a common SSID is one of the enhancements in the Wireless Network (IEEE 802.11) Policies for Windows Vista. You can also use these features to configure security and authentication settings, manage wireless profiles, and specify permissions for wireless networks that are not configured as preferred networks.

> **NOTE**
>
> The Windows Vista Wireless Network (IEEE 802.11) Policies to configure wireless computers can be used to configure only Windows Vista and Windows Server 2008 computers. You cannot use this policy to configure computers running Windows XP.

Take these steps to open the Wireless Network (IEEE 802.11) Policies properties:

1. Open the Group Policy Management Console (GPMC).

2. In Default Domain Policy, open Computer Configuration, open Windows Settings, open Security Settings, and then select Wireless Network (IEEE 802.11) Policies. If there is a Wireless Network Policy shown in the details pane, with the Type listed as Vista, right-click that policy and then click Properties to access the properties of the wireless policy.

From here, you can then configure network permissions, set the preference order for wireless networks, require authentication and encryption, and more.

Exam Prep Questions

1. You decided to implement tighter remote access security by using smart cards on all remote access client computers. You have installed the smart cards and need to configure the remote access server to support the new authentication mechanism. Which of the following protocols should be enabled?

    ○ **A.** PAP

    ○ **B.** EAP

    ○ **C.** MS-CHAP

    ○ **D.** SPAP

2. You are the network administrator for your organization. Company servers have been upgraded to Microsoft Windows Server 2008. You have enabled RRAS on SERVER01. All remote access clients are running Microsoft Windows XP Professional and Windows Vista. You want to configure the most secure authentication protocol. Which of the following should you enable?

    ○ **A.** PAP

    ○ **B.** CHAP

    ○ **C.** MS-CHAP version 1

    ○ **D.** MS-CHAP version 2

3. You have a Windows Server 2008 computer with the Routing and Remote Access role service installed. You implemented Network Access Protection (NAP) for the domain. Which authentication method should you choose?

    ○ **A.** Password Authentication Protocol (PAP)

    ○ **B.** Challenge Handshake Authentication Protocol (CHAP)

    ○ **C.** Extensible Authentication Protocol (EAP)

    ○ **D.** Microsoft Challenge Handshake Authentication Protocol version 2 (MS-CHAPv2)

4. What provides RADIUS in Windows Server 2008?

    ○ **A.** RRAS

    ○ **B.** NPS

    ○ **C.** IAS

    ○ **D.** NAP

5. You have deployed Network Access Protection (NAP) on a Windows Server 2008 computer. You also configured your access points to use 802.1x authentication. What do you need to ensure that all computers that connect through an access point are evaluated by NAP?

   ○ **A.** Configure all user systems as RADIUS clients to the Network Policy Server (NPS).

   ○ **B.** Configure all access points as RADIUS clients to the Network Policy Server (NPS).

   ○ **C.** Create a network policy that defines Remote Access Server as a required network connection method.

   ○ **D.** Create a network policy that species EAP-TLS as the only available authentication method.

6. You have enabled Routing and Remote Access on a computer running Microsoft Windows Server 2008. You need to configure the RRAS to support up to 20 clients that use PPTP. What do you need to do?

   ○ **A.** From the RRAS, open the Server Properties window for the server and select the Ports tab.

   ○ **B.** From the RRAS, open the Server Properties window and click the Edit Profile button. Then select the Ports tab.

   ○ **C.** From RRAS, right-click Ports to open Ports Properties.

   ○ **D.** Use the PPTP tab from the Ports Properties window.

7. You have a network with several servers running Windows Server 2008. You are planning a VPN solution for the company network. The branch office will connect to the head office via a VPN connection. You need to enable the correct protocols on the remote access server. Which of the following protocols should you use to establish a VPN tunnel with a Windows Server 2003 VPN server?

   ○ **A.** PPP

   ○ **B.** PPTP

   ○ **C.** SLIP

   ○ **D.** L2TP

8. You are the network administrator for your company. Servers are running Microsoft Windows Server 2008. Client computers are running Microsoft Windows XP Professional and Windows Vista. You have been advised that all communication between clients and the web server on the intranet should be secured. However, you need to ensure that non-IPSec-aware clients can authenticate to the web server. Which of the following policies should you assign to the web server?

   ○ **A.** Client (Respond Only)

   ○ **B.** Server (Request Security)

   ○ **C.** Secure Server (Require Security)

   ○ **D.** Secure Client (Respond Only)

9. You are the network administrator for your company. All domain controllers and member servers are running Microsoft Windows Server 2008. You have configured multiple IPSec policies throughout the Active Directory hierarchy. You discover that the correct IPSec policy settings are not configured on SRV01. You need to determine which IPSec policy is being used on SRV01. What should you do?

   ○ **A.** Launch Network Monitor and capture all IPSec traffic coming to and from SRV01.

   ○ **B.** Open the IP Security Monitor on SRV01.

   ○ **C.** Launch the Resultant Set of Policy on SRV01.

   ○ **D.** Open the IP Security Policy Management on SRV01.

10. You are the network administrator for a large insurance agency. All servers are running Microsoft Windows Server 2008. You have implemented an IPSec policy on several company servers. You want to specify default traffic exemptions on these servers. You need to accomplish this with as little administrative effort as possible. What should you do?

   ○ **A.** Execute the `netdiag` command to make the necessary IPSec configuration changes.

   ○ **B.** Execute the `ipsecmon` command with the required parameters then make the change.

   ○ **C.** Use the IPSec Policy Management tool to configure IPSec.

   ○ **D.** Create a script that uses the `netsh` command to configure IPSec.

11. You are the network administrator for a large insurance company. The network consists of 50 servers running Microsoft Windows Server 2008. There are 700 client computers running Microsoft Windows XP Professional and Windows Vista. The company has updated its security policy and requires all network traffic to be encrypted. You are deploying IPSec in a test environment that has a single server and 10 client computers.

You have assigned the required IPSec policies. You need to verify that traffic between the server and the client computers is being secured. What should you do?

- ○ **A.** Launch IP Security Monitor and open the Security Associations folder and then open Main Mode.
- ○ **B.** Launch the Event Viewer and examine the contents of the security log.
- ○ **C.** Run the Resultant Set of Policy in logging mode.
- ○ **D.** Execute the `ipsecmon.exe` command.

12. You are the network administrator for your company. Servers have been upgraded to Microsoft Windows Server 2008. You have just updated the IPSec policy settings and want to apply changes immediately. What should you do?

- ○ **A.** Execute the `secedit /target:machine` command.
- ○ **B.** Execute the `gpupdate /target:machine` command.
- ○ **C.** Execute the `secedit /target:user` command.
- ○ **D.** Execute the `gpupdate /target:user` command.

13. You have a corporate office with multiple remote sites. The company has a single Active Directory domain. You need to ensure that the VPN connections between the corporate office the remote sites are encrypted from end to end and that the VPN connections use computer-level authentication instead of usernames and passwords. What should you?

- ○ **A.** Configure a PPTP connection to use digital certificates.
- ○ **B.** Configure a L2TP/IPsec connection to use the EAP-TLS authentication.
- ○ **C.** Configure a L2TP/IPsec connection to use version 2 of the MS-CHAPv2 authentication.
- ○ **D.** Configure a GPO to require IPSec on the server.

14. You have a Windows Server 2008 computer with Network Access Protection (NAP) configured. You want to ensure that all data is encrypted when a user connects using portal computers. You need to ensure that only users that have computers that comply with this requirement are allowed access while others are blocked. What should you do?

- ○ **A.** Create an IPsec enforcement network policy.
- ○ **B.** Create an 802.1X enforcement network policy.
- ○ **C.** Create a VPN enforcement network policy.
- ○ **D.** Create a TS Gateway enforcement policy.

15. You have a Windows Server 2008 VPN server behind a firewall. The firewall is configured to allow only secured web communications. How would you allow the users to connect to the VPN server through the firewall?

    ○ **A.** Create an SSTP VPN connection.

    ○ **B.** Create a PPTP VPN connection.

    ○ **C.** Create a L2TP VPN connection.

    ○ **D.** Use a TS Gateway.

16. You have a server that runs Windows Server 2008. How would you enable the server to act as a VPN server?

    ○ **A.** Install the Windows Deployment Services role.

    ○ **B.** Install the Network Policy Server role and Routing and Remote Access Services role.

    ○ **C.** Install the Routing and Remote Access Services role and the IAS role.

    ○ **D.** Install the IPSec role and the Routing and Remote Access Services role.

17. You have a group of users who should not be able to access the VPN server remotely from 10:00 pm to 6:00 am. What should you do?

    ○ **A.** Modify the logon hours for the default domain policy.

    ○ **B.** Use Active Directory User and Computers to specify the day and time restrictions.

    ○ **C.** Use the Registry Editor to configure the day and time restrictions.

    ○ **D.** Create a network policy for VPN connections and modify the day and time restrictions.

Answers to Exam Prep Questions

1. **Answer B is correct.** The Extensible Authentication Protocol (EAP) is required to support smart card authentication. Answers A, C, and D are incorrect because they do not support smart card authentication.

2. **Answer D is correct.** Because all the remote access users are running Windows XP Professional and Windows Vista, the authentication protocol should be MS-CHAP version 2. Answers B and C are incorrect because they are not as secure as MS-CHAP version 2. Answer A is incorrect because PAP sends credentials in clear text and should be used only for non-Windows clients.

3. Answer C is correct. Of the protocols listed, EAP offers the strongest and most flexible authentication method available. It also offers mutual authentication. Therefore, answers A, B, and D are incorrect.

4. Answer B is correct. NPS provides RADIUS. Answer A is incorrect because RRAS is used to provide routing and remote access, such as dial-up and VPNs. Answer C is incorrect because IAS was the RADIUS server used in Windows Server 2003. Answer D is incorrect because NAP is used to control network access.

5. Answer B is correct. You need to configure the access points as RADIUS clients. As users connect to the network, they connect to the access point, which then authenticates each user through the RADIUS server. Answer A is incorrect because the access points should be the RADIUS client. Answer C is incorrect because all users are going through the access points, not RAS. Answer D is incorrect because EAP-TLS is needed for smart cards, but not necessarily for wireless connections. In addition, it would force connections to be evaluated by NAP.

6. Answer C is correct. To increase the number of available PPTP ports, open the Ports Properties window within the Routing and Remote Access management console. Select PPTP and click Configure. Therefore, answers A, B, and D are incorrect.

7. Answer D is correct. The two tunneling protocols supported by Windows Server 2008 that are listed are the Point-to-Point Tunneling Protocol (PPTP) and the Layer 2 Tunneling Protocol (L2TP). However, when all systems are running Windows Server 2008, PPTP should not be used. PPTP should be used only for backward compatibility. Therefore answer B is incorrect. PPP and SLIP establish dial-up connections. Therefore, answers A and C are incorrect.

8. Answer B is correct. If you assign the Server (Request Security) policy, the server attempts secure communications with clients. If the client is not IPSec-aware, it is still able to authenticate. Answer A is incorrect because the server responds only to client requests for secure communications. Answer C is incorrect because the server requires secure communications and does not allow sessions for non-IPSec aware clients. Answer D is incorrect because there is no such default policy.

9. Answer B is correct. IP Security Monitor can be used to gather and monitor IPSec statistics. The Active Policy container tells you which IPSec policy is currently being used. Answer A is incorrect because Network Monitor is used to capture and analyze IP packets. The results do not indicate which policy is in effect. Answer C is incorrect because Resultant Set of Policy does not tell you which IPSec policy is currently being used. This tool can be used to identify existing policy settings. Answer D is incorrect because IP Security Policy Management is used only to create and manage IP Security policies.

10. Answer D is correct. The `netsh` command-line utility can be used to configure IPSec. It can be used with scripting, making it easier to deploy changes to multiple servers. Answer A is incorrect because this command-line utility is no longer used to configure IPSec. Answer B is incorrect because this command is used to launch the IP Security

Monitor in Windows 2000. Answer C is incorrect because it would be easier to deploy the changes by using a script rather than by making the configuration change on each server. In addition, you can not use the IPSec Policy Management console to specify default traffic exemptions.

11. Answer A is correct. You should open the Main Mode Security Associations on the server. The Main Mode Security Associations area displays the persistent security association for the computer on which the MMC snap-in is focused. Security associations are established between computers after the key exchange and mutual authentication. Answer B is incorrect because the security log contains only entries that relate to auditing. Answer C is incorrect because RSoP is used to determine the IPSec policies that are assigned to a computer. Answer D is incorrect because this command was available in Windows 2000 but has been replaced by the IP Security Monitor snap-in in Windows Server 2003.

12. Answer B is correct. To refresh policy settings, you can use the `gpupdate` command. Because the IPSec policy is configured under the computer policy, you must refresh the computer policy settings. This is done by using the `/target:machine` option. Answers A and C are incorrect because this was the command used in Windows 2000. Answer D is incorrect because you need to refresh the computer policy settings, not the user policy settings.

13. Answer B is correct. To provide the end-to-end encryption, you would use L2TP with IPSec. IPSec actually provides the encryption. To use computer-level authentication instead of usernames and passwords, you would use EAP-TLS, which uses digital certificates. Answer A is incorrect because PPTP cannot be configured to use digital certificates. Answer C is incorrect because MS-CHAPv2 uses usernames and passwords. Answer D is incorrect because using a GPO would mean that all traffic including internal network traffic would have to be encrypted with IPSec. In addition, IPSec is not a VPN protocol.

14. Answer A is correct. IPSec enforcement defines an IPSec policy that assures that only clients with a certain health certificate can establish connections to other computers on the network. Answer B is incorrect because 802.1X is used for authentication, not for encryption. Answer C is incorrect because VPN enforcement is used to restrict VPN, not wireless connections. Answer D is incorrect because TS Gateway is used to allow access to a terminal server through an encrypted connection.

15. Answer A is correct. To create a VPN tunnel over SSL, you would use SSTP VPN. Answers B and C are incorrect because they do not operate over SSL. Answer D is incorrect because the TS Gateway is used to allow access to a terminal server through an encrypted connection. It does not allow VPN traffic through the firewall.

16. Answer B is correct. Install the Routing and Remote Access Services role and the Network Policy Server role to provide VPN access. Answer A is incorrect because Windows Deployment Services is used to deploy Windows. Answer C is incorrect because IAS is the RADIUS server for Windows Server 2003. Answer D is incorrect because there is no such thing as an IPSec role.

17. Answer D is correct. You need to create a network access policy to limit when a VPN can be accessed. Answer A is incorrect because logon hours configured with a group policy affect local logins also. Answer B is incorrect because using Active Directory Users and Computers would also affect local logins. Answer C is incorrect because you cannot configure the day and time restrictions in the Registry Editor.

Need to Know More?

For more information about Routing and Remote Access, including Routing and Remote Access Deployment Guides, Routing and Remote Access Operations Guide, Routing and Remote Access Technical Reference, and Routing and Remote Access Troubleshooting Reference, visit the following website:

▶ http://technet2.microsoft.com/windowsserver2008/en/library/ 82b70b7a-b336-4604-9a43-0ed8f55c7d471033.mspx?mfr=true

For more information about Routing and Remote Access, visit the following website:

▶ http://technet.microsoft.com/en-us/network/bb545655.aspx

For more information about IPSec, visit the following website:

▶ http://technet.microsoft.com/en-us/network/bb531150.aspx

For more information about VPNs, visit the following website:

▶ http://technet.microsoft.com/en-us/network/bb545442.aspx

For more information about Windows Firewall with Advanced Security and IPSec, visit the following website:

▶ http://technet2.microsoft.com/windowsserver2008/en/library/ c042b3c5-dee1-4a31-ac35-e90e846290441033.mspx?mfr=true

Regan, Patrick. *Wide Area Networks*. Upper Saddle River, New Jersey: Prentice Hall, 2004.

7

File Services

Terms you'll need to understand:

- ✓ NTFS
- ✓ Access control list (ACL)
- ✓ Explicit permission
- ✓ Inherited permission
- ✓ Shared folder
- ✓ Server Message Block (SMB)
- ✓ Public folder
- ✓ Administrative shares
- ✓ Offline folder
- ✓ Encrypting File System (EFS)
- ✓ BitLocker Drive Encryption
- ✓ Trusted Platform Module (TPM)

- ✓ Distributed File System (DFS)
- ✓ DFS namespace
- ✓ DFS replication
- ✓ Shadow copies
- ✓ Differential backup
- ✓ Incremental backup
- ✓ wbadmin.exe
- ✓ System state
- ✓ Backup catalog
- ✓ Disk quota
- ✓ Network File System (NFS)

Techniques/concepts you'll need to master:

- ✓ Configure NTFS permissions.
- ✓ Create and configure a shared folder and configure shared permissions.
- ✓ Use DFS to create a replicated folder and DFS namespace.

- ✓ Using the Windows backup and wbadmin, back up a drive and system state.
- ✓ Re-create a backup catalog.
- ✓ Configure disk quota on a disk.
- ✓ Enable and configure NFS on Windows Server 2008.

The disk structure does not describe how a hard drive or floppy disk physically works, but how it stores files on the disk. In other words, it describes the formatting of the disk (file system, partitions, the root directory, and the directories). A file system is the overall structure in which files are named, stored, and organized. Files systems used in Windows Vista include FAT, FAT32, and NTFS. Although FAT and FAT32 were primarily used in older operating systems, NTFS is the preferred file system.

An older file system used by DOS was the *File Allocation Table (FAT)*. FAT is a simple file system that uses minimum memory. Although it is based on filenames of 11 characters, which include the 8 characters for the file name and 3 characters for the file extension, it has been expanded to support long filenames. Early DOS used FAT12, which used a 12-bit number for each cluster, but was later expanded to FAT16, which would recognize volumes up to 2GB.

FAT32, which was introduced in the second major release of Windows 95, is an enhancement to the FAT file system. It uses 32-bit FAT entries, which support hard drives of up to 2TB, although Windows 2000, Windows XP, Windows Vista, Windows Server 2003, and Windows Server 2008 support volumes up to 32GB. FAT32 does not have the security that NTFS provides, so if you have a FAT32 partition or volume on your computer, any user who has access to your computer can read any file on it. The main reason to use FAT32 is because you have a computer that will sometimes run Windows 95, Windows 98, or Windows Millennium edition and at other times run newer versions of Windows. This is known as a multi-boot configuration.

NTFS is the preferred file system for this version of Windows. It has many benefits over the earlier FAT32 file system, including

- ▶ Improved support for much larger hard disks.

- ▶ Automatic recovery from some disk-related errors, which is possible because NTFS is a journaling file system that keeps track of its transactions to make sure that an entire transaction is completed before it is recognized.

- ▶ Better security because you can use permissions and encryption to restrict access to specific files to approved users.

Rights and Permissions

A right authorizes a user to perform certain actions on a computer, such as logging on to a system interactively/logging on locally to a computer, backing up files and directories, performing a system shutdown, or adding/removing a device driver. Administrators can assign specific rights to individual user accounts or group accounts. Rights are managed with the User Rights policy. For Windows Server 2008, user rights can be found via Group Policy, Computer Configuration, Windows Settings, Security Settings, Local Policies, User Rights Assignment.

Permission defines the type of access granted to an object or object attribute. The permissions available for an object depend on the type of object. For example, a user has different permissions than a printer. When a user or service tries to access an object, its access is granted or denied by an Object Manager. File and Folder permissions as well as Shared permissions are handled by Windows Explorer.

NTFS Permissions

A primary advantage of NTFS over FAT and FAT32 is that NTFS volumes can apply NTFS permissions to secure folders and files. By setting the permissions, you specify the level of access for groups and users for accessing files or directories. For example, to one user or group of users, you can specify permission to only read the file; another user or group of users can read and write to the file; and others have no access. No matter whether you are logged on locally at the computer or accessing a computer through a network, NTFS permissions always apply.

Assigning NTFS Permissions

The NTFS permissions that are granted are stored in an *access control list (ACL)* with every file or folder on an NTFS volume. The ACL contains an access control entry (ACE) for each user account and group that has been granted access for the file or folder, as well as the permissions granted to each user and group. To simplify the task of administration, the NTFS permissions have been logically grouped into the standard folder and file NTFS permissions as shown in Table 7.1. If you need finer control, you need to use special permissions. Table 7.2 shows the special permissions.

NOTE

Remember that to manage your folders and files and when you open up a drive or folder, you are using Windows Explorer.

EXAM ALERT

Be sure that you understand the various NTFS permissions and how they are explicating assigned and how those permission flow down (are inherited).

Table 7.1   Standard NTFS Folder and File Permissions

Permission Level	Description
Full control	Users can read files and folders; execute files; write, modify, and delete files; change attributes of files and folders; change permissions; and take ownership of files.
Modify	Users can read files and folders, execute files, write and modify files, delete files and folders, and change attributes of files and folders.
List folder contents	Users can view the names of folders and subfolders in the folder. This permission is available only at the folder level and is not available at the file level.
Read & execute	Users can see the contents of existing files and folders and can run programs in a folder.
Read	Users can see the contents of a folder and open files and folders.
Write	Users can create new files and folders and make changes to existing files and folders. Users cannot create new files or folders and cannot delete files and folders.

TABLE 7.2   NTFS Folder Permissions

Special Permissions	Full Control	Modify	Read & Execute	List Folder Contents	Read	Write
Traverse Folder/Execute File	X	X	x	X		
List Folder/Read Data	X	X	x	X		
Read Attributes	X	X	x	X	x	
Read Extended Attributes	X	X	x	X	x	
Create Files/Write Data	X	X				x
Create Folders/Append Data	X	X				x
Write Attributes	X	X				x
Write Extended Attributes	X	X				x
Delete Subfolders and Files	X					
Delete	X	X				
Read Permissions	X	X	x	X	x	x

TABLE 7.2 *Continued*

Special Permissions	Full Control	Modify	Read & Execute	List Folder Contents	Read	Write
Change Permissions	X					
Take Ownership	X					
Synchronize	X	X	x	X	x	x

> **NOTE**
>
> Although list folder contents and Read & Execute appear to have the same permissions, these permissions are inherited differently. List Folder Contents is inherited by folders but not files, and it should appear only when you view folder permissions. Read & Execute is inherited by both files and folders and is always present when you view file or folder permissions.

To set, view, change, or remove permissions on files and folders, follow these steps:

1. Right-click the file or folder for which you want to set permissions and click Properties.

2. Click the Security tab. See Figure 7.1.

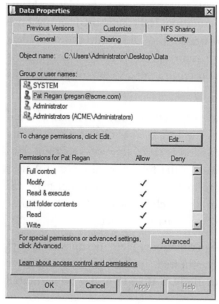

FIGURE 7.1 The Data Properties dialog box can be used to configure NTFS permissions.

3. Click Edit to open the Permissions for the Name of File or Folder dialog box.

4. Do one of the following:

   ▶ To set permissions for a group or user that does not appear in the Group or User Names box, click Add. Type the name of the group or user for which you want to set permissions and then click OK.

   ▶ To change or remove permissions from an existing group or user, click the name of the group or user. To allow or deny a permission, in the Permissions for User or Group box, select the Allow or Deny check box. To remove the group or user from the Group or User Names box, click Remove.

5. To view the special permissions, click Advanced.

6. To change the special permissions, click Edit.

Explicit and Inherited Permissions

Permissions are giving to a folder or file as either *explicit permissions* or *inherited permissions*. Explicit permissions are those granted directly to the folder or file. Some of these permissions are granted automatically, such as when a file or folder is created, whereas others have to be assigned manually.

When you set permissions to a folder (explicit permissions), the files and subfolders that exist in the folder inherit these permissions (called inherited permissions). In other words, the permissions flow down from the folder into the subfolders and files, indirectly giving permissions to a user or group. Inherited permissions ease the task of managing permissions and ensure consistency of permissions among the subfolders and files within the folder.

When you view the permissions, the permissions are checked, cleared (unchecked), or shaded. If the permission is checked, the permission was explicitly assigned to the folder or file. If the permission is clear, the user or group does not have that permission explicitly granted to the folder or file. Note: A user may still obtain permission through a group permission or a group may still obtain permission through another group. If the check box is shaded, the permission was granted through inheritance from a parent folder.

Windows enables you to deny individual permissions. Deny permission always overrides the permissions that have been granted, including when a user or group has been giving full control. For example, if the group has been granted

Read and Write, yet a person has been denied the Write permission, the user's effective rights would be the Read permission.

When you set permissions to a folder (explicit permission), the files and subfolders in the folder inherit these permissions (inherited permissions). In other words, the permissions flow down from the folder into the subfolders and files, indirectly giving permissions to a user or group. Inherited permissions ease the task of managing permissions and ensure consistency of permissions among the subfolders and files within the folder.

Similar to permissions granted at a lower level, NTFS file permissions override folder permissions. Therefore, if a user has access to a file, the user can still gain access to a file even if he or she does not have access to the folder containing the file. Of course, because the user doesn't have access to the folder, the user cannot navigate or browse through the folder to get to the file. Therefore, the user has to use either the universal naming convention (UNC) or local path to open the file.

When assigning permissions to a folder, by default, the permissions apply to the folder being assigned and the subfolders and files of the folder. If you show the permission entries, you can specify how the permissions are applied to the folder, subfolder, and files.

To stop permissions from being inherited, you can select Replace All Existing Inheritable Permissions on All Descendants with Inheritable Permissions from This Object in the Advanced Security Settings dialog box. It then asks you whether you are sure. You can also clear the Allow Inheritable Permissions from Parent to Propagate to This Object check box. When the check box is clear, Windows responds with a Security dialog box. When you click Copy, the explicit permission is copied from the parent folder to the subfolder or file. You can then change the explicit permissions of the subfolder or file. If you click Remove, the inherited permission is removed altogether.

Because users can be members of several groups, it is possible for them to have several sets of explicit permissions to a folder or file. When this occurs, the permissions are combined to form the effective permissions, which are the actual permissions for logging in and accessing a file or folder. They consist of explicit permissions plus any inherited permissions.

Copying and Moving Files

When you copy and move files and folders from one location to another, you need to understand how the NTFS folder and file permissions are affected. If you copy a file or folder, the new folder and file automatically acquire the permissions of the drive or folder to which the folder and file is being copied.

If the folder or file is moved within the same volume, the folder or file retains the same permissions that were already assigned. When the folder or file is moved from one volume to another volume, the folder or file automatically acquires the permissions of the drive or folder to which it is being copied. An easy way to remember the difference is when you move a folder or file from within the same volume, the folder and file is not physically moved but the Master File Table is adjusted to indicate a different folder. When you move a folder or file from one volume to another, the folder or file is copied to the new location and deleted from the old location. Therefore, the moved folder and files are new to the volume and acquire the new permissions.

EXAM ALERT

When you copy a file or folder or move a file or folder to a new volume, it automatically acquires the permission and attributes (compressions and encryption) of the drive or folder to which the it is being copied. If you move the file or folder to the same volume, it keeps the same permissions and attributes that it already has.

When you are managing NTFS permissions, remember the following:

▶ You can set file and folder permissions only on drives formatted to use NTFS.

▶ Performing this procedure might require you to elevate permissions through User Account Control.

▶ To change permissions, you must be the owner or have been granted permission to do so by the owner.

▶ Groups or users that are granted Full Control for a folder can delete files and subfolders within that folder, regardless of the permissions that protect the files and subfolders.

▶ If the check boxes under Permissions for User or Group are shaded or if the Remove button is unavailable, the file or folder has inherited permissions from the parent folder.

▶ When a new user or group is added, by default this user or group has Read & Execute, List Folder Contents, and Read permissions.

Folder and File Owners

Every folder and file has an owner, a person who controls how permissions are set on a folder or file and who grants permissions to others. When a folder or file is created, The person who created the folder or file automatically becomes the owner. To be able to take ownership of a folder or file, the user has to be granted Take Ownership permission or be the administrator. After logging in, the user can take ownership by taking the following steps:

1. Right-click the folder or file and select Properties.

2. Click the Security tab and then click Advanced.

3. Click the Owner tab.

4. Click Edit.

5. Click the user or group who will take ownership. If the user to which you want to give ownership is not listed, you can click Other Users or Groups. When the user is selected, click OK.

6. When the Windows Security dialog box appears, click OK.

7. Click OK to close the Advanced Properties dialog box.

8. Click OK to close the Properties dialog box.

Sharing Files and Folders

A *shared folder* on a computer makes the folder available for others to use on the network. A shared drive on a computer makes the entire drive available for others to use on the network. Shared drives and folders can be used on FAT/FAT32 and NTFS volumes. If used on an NTFS volume, the user still needs NTFS permissions before accessing the share.

When you share a folder with Microsoft Windows, file sharing is based on the network basic input/output system (NetBIOS) protocol and *server message block (SMB)*. NetBIOS, which runs on top of TCP/IP, was created for IBM for its early PC networks, but it was adopted by Microsoft and has since become a de facto industry standard. It is responsible for establishing logical names (computer names) on the network, establishing a logical connection between the two computers, and supporting reliable data transfer between computers that established a session.

As soon as a logical connection is established, computers can exchange data in the form of NetBIOS requests or in the form of a server message block. The SMB protocol, which was jointly developed by Microsoft, Intel, and IBM, allows shared access to files, printers, serial ports, and miscellaneous communications between nodes on a network.

SMB 2.0 was introduced with Windows Vista and is used in Windows Server 2008. It makes it possible to compound multiple actions into a single request, which significantly reduces the number of round trips the client needs to make to the server, improving performance as a result. Larger buffer sizes are supported, also increasing performance with large file transfers. In addition, durable file handles were introduced, which allow a connection to an SMB server to survive brief network outages, such as with a wireless network, without requiring that a new session be constructed.

When using the SMB protocol to share a directory or drive, you access these resources by using the Uniform Naming Convention (UNC):

*servername**sharedname*

The *servername* could be a NetBIOS name (computer name) or an IP address.

Network Discovery and Browsing

With earlier versions of Windows, you could use Network Neighborhood to browse network resources such as shared folders and printers. However, this system was inefficient because it relied on network broadcast to gather such information.

To fix this problem, Windows Vista (which is included in Windows Server 2008) introduced Link Layer Topology Discovery (LLDT), which queries each device that supports Plug and Play Extensions (PnP-X) or web services for devices to determine the capabilities of the device and to determine the topology of the network. It also uses version control to keep the information current. It also describes the Quality of Service (QoS) Extensions that enable stream prioritization and quality media streaming experiences, even on networks with limited bandwidth.

The information that is gathered to create the network map and to determine which information the computer gives out to other Windows Vista and Windows Server 2008 computers varies depending on which network services you have enabled or configured in the Network and Sharing Center. See Table 7.3 and Figure 7.2.

Sharing Files and Folders

TABLE 7.3   Network Services Managed with the Network and Sharing Center

Feature	Settings	Result
Network Discovery—Allows this computer to see other network computers and devices and is visible to other network computers.	On Off	Turns on Network Discovery. Turns off Network Discovery.
File sharing—Files and printers that you have shared from this computer can be accessed by people on the network.	On Off	Shares created on this computer can be accessed from the network. Shares created on this computer can not be accessed from the network.
Public folder sharing—People on the network can access files in the public folder.	Off On (Read) On (Change)	Only local users can access the Public folder. Local and network users can read the contents of the Public folder, but cannot change them. Local and network users can change the contents of the Public folder.
Printer sharing—Allows users to access shared printers.	On Off	Printers directly connected to this computer can be shared. Printers directly connected to this computer cannot be shared.

FIGURE 7.2   Managing Network Services with the Network and Sharing Center.

To view the topology or to view the network resources, open a network folder or the Network and Sharing Center. However, a Windows Server 2008 computer is not visible on the network map, and it cannot map other hardware devices on the network until you enable Network Discovery service. To see the full map, click the View Full Map link in the Network and Sharing Center (see Figure 7.3).

> **NOTE**
>
> LLTD is installed by default, but functions only if you enable Network Discovery.

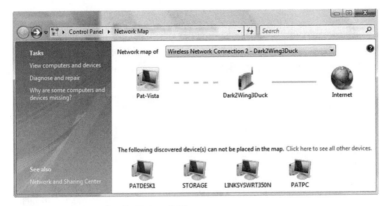

FIGURE 7.3   A sample of a Network Map.

Public Folder

Windows Server 2008 supports two ways to share folders: public file sharing and standard file sharing. Of these two models, standard file sharing is preferred because it is more secure than public file sharing. However, Public folder sharing is designed to enable users to share files and folders from a single location quickly and easily.

Windows Server 2008 supports the use of only one *Public folder* for each computer. Any files that you want to make available publicly can be copied or moved to an appropriate folder inside the Public folder. The Public folder is located at C:\Users\Public and contains the following sub-folders:

▶ Public Documents

▶ Public Downloads

▶ Public Music

- ▶ Public Pictures

- ▶ Public Videos

- ▶ Recorded TV

Another folder worth mentioning is the Public Desktop folder, which is used for shared desktop items. Any files and program shortcuts placed in the Public Desktop folder appear on the desktop of all users who log on to the computer (and to all network users if network access has been granted to the Public folder).

To access Public folders with Windows Explorer, follow these steps:

1. Clicking Start, Computer.

2. In Windows Explorer, click the leftmost option button in the address list and then click Public.

Public folder sharing settings are set on a per-computer basis. If you want to share a file, you just need to copy or move the file into the C:\Users\Public folder. When the file is copied or moved to the Public folder, access permissions are changed to match that of the Public folder so that all users who log on to the computer and all network users, if network access has been granted to the Public folder, can access the file.

Because Windows Server 2008 is designed to act as a fully fledged file server, Public folder sharing is disabled by default. By default, files stored in the Public folder hierarchy are available to all users who have an account on this computer and can log on to it locally. You cannot access the Public folder from the network. To enable and configure public folder sharing, follow these steps:

1. Click Start, Computer. In Windows Explorer, click the leftmost option button in the address list and then click Public.

2. On the Windows Explorer toolbar, click Sharing Settings.

3. Open the Network and Sharing Center.

4. Expand the Public Folder Sharing Panel by clicking Expand.

5. Under Public Folder Sharing, select the public folder sharing option you want to use. The options available are

   - ▶ Turn On Sharing So Anyone with Network Access Can Open Files

   - ▶ Turn On Sharing So Anyone with Network Access Can Open, Change, and Create Files

   - ▶ Turn Off Sharing

Permissions are shown in Table 7.4.

6. Click Apply to save the changes.

NOTE

Windows Firewall settings might prevent external access.

TABLE 7.4 Share and NTFS Permissions for the Public Folder

Access Type	Share Permission	NTFS File System Permissions
Open files	Read	Read & Execute, List Folder Contents, Read
Open, change, and create files	Full Control	All (Full Control, Modify, Read & Execute, List Folder Contents, Read/Write)

Standard Sharing

Creating and managing a shared folder is a little bit more of a manual process then the public sharing model, but enables you to share any folder on the Windows Server 2008 computer and it gives you more fine-tuned control over sharing the folders.

Standard file sharing enables you to use a standard set of permissions to allow or deny initial access to files and folders over the network. Standard file sharing settings are enabled or disabled on a per-computer basis. Take these steps to enable File Sharing:

1. Click Start, Network.

2. On the Explorer toolbar, click Network and Sharing Center.

3. Expand the File Sharing Panel by clicking the related Expand button.

4. To enable file sharing, select Turn On File Sharing. To disable file sharing, select Turn Off File Sharing.

5. Click Apply.

When a user accesses a file or folder in a share over the network, two levels of permissions are used, share permissions and NTFS permissions (if it is on an NTFS volume). The three share permissions are:

▶ **Owner/Co-owner**: Users allowed this permission have Read and Change permissions, as well as the additional capabilities to change file and folder permissions and take ownership of files and folders. If you have Owner/Co-owner permissions on a shared resource, you have full access to the shared resource.

▶ **Contributor**: Users allowed this permission have Read permissions and the additional capability to create files and subfolders, modify files, change attributes on files and subfolders, and delete files and subfolders. If you have Contributor permissions on a shared resource, the most you can do is perform read operations and change operations.

▶ **Reader**: Users with this permission can view file and subfolder names, access the subfolders of the share, read file data and attributes, and run program files. If you have Reader permissions on a shared resource, the most you can do is perform read operations.

EXAM ALERT

If the user accesses the computer directly where the share folder is located and accesses the folder directly without going through the share, share permissions do not apply.

Because a user can be member of several groups, it is possible for the user to have several sets of permissions to a shared drive or folder. The effective permissions are the combination of all user and group permissions. For example, if a user has Contributor permissions to the user and Reader permission to the group of which the user is a member, the effective permission would be the Contributor permission. Like NTFS permissions, Deny permissions override the granted permission.

Creating a shared folder, using the shared folder model, is a multipart process:

1. Share the folder so that it can be accessed.

2. Set the share permissions.

3. Check and modify the NTFS file system permissions.

You can use one of two methods to set permissions on a shared resource, depending on the resource type:

▶ Use the File Sharing Wizard to set permissions of a file or folder. You can start the File Sharing wizard by right-clicking the file or folder and then clicking Share. The wizard enables you to select the user and group that can share the file or folder, and enables you to set permissions on the file or folder for each user or group.

▶ Use Windows Explorer to set permissions on a resource. You can use Windows Explorer to set permissions through the Share option or through the Properties page on a resource. When you right-click the object, selecting the Share or Properties option displays the Properties dialog box. You can set or modify permissions by using the Advanced Sharing button on the Sharing tab.

When a folder is shared, a symbol of two users is added at the bottom left of the folder icon (see Figure 7.4).

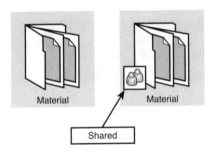

Material   Material

Shared

FIGURE 7.4 A non-shared and shared folder.

If you click the Show Me All the Files and Folders I Am Sharing option in Network and Sharing Center, you can view all shared folders on the system (see Figure 7.5).

When accessing a shared folder on an NTFS volume, the effective permissions that a person can have in the shared folder are calculated by combining the shared folder permissions with the NTFS permissions. When combining the two, first determine the cumulative NTFS permissions and the cumulative shared permissions and apply the more restrictive permissions—that is, the one that gives the least permission.

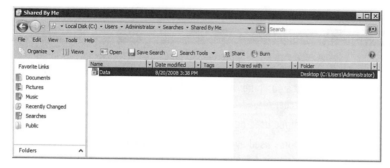

FIGURE 7.5 Using the Show Me All the Files and Folders I am Sharing option in the Network and Sharing Center.

EXAM ALERT

When figuring out the overall access a person has, combine the NTFS permissions and determine the cumulative NTFS permissions. Then determine the cumulative shared permissions. Then apply the more restrictive permissions between the NTFS and shared permission. Don't forget that deny permissions always win out.

Special and Administrative Shares

In Windows Server 2008, several special shared folders are automatically created by Windows for administrative and system use (see Table 7.5). Different from regular shares, these shares do not show when a user browses the computer resources with Network Neighborhood, My Network Place, or similar software. In most cases, special shared folders should not be deleted or modified. For Windows Server 2008 computers, only members of the Administrators, Backup Operators, and Server Operators group can connect to these shares.

TABLE 7.5 Special Shares

Special Share	Description
Drive letter$	A shared folder that allows administrative personnel to connect to the root directory of a drive, also known as an administrative share. It is shown as A$, B$, C$, D$, and so on. For example, C$ is a shared folder name by which drive C might be accessed by an administrator over the network.
ADMIN$	A resource used by the system during remote administration of a computer. The path of this resource is always the path to the Windows 2008 system root (the directory in which Windows 2008 is installed: for example, C:\Windows).

continues

TABLE 7.5 *Continued*

Special Share	Description
IPC$	A resource sharing the named pipes that are essential for communication between programs. It is used during remote administration of a computer and when viewing a computer's shared resources.
PRINT$	A resource used during remote administration of printers.
NETLOGON	A resource used by the Net Logon service of a Windows 2008 Server computer while processing domain logon requests.
FAX$	A shared folder on a server used by fax clients in the process of sending a fax. The shared folder is used to temporarily cache files and access cover pages stored on the server.

An administrative share is a shared folder typically used for administrative purposes. To make a shared folder or drive into an administrative share, the share name must have a $ at the end of it. Because the share folder or drive cannot be seen during browsing, you have to use a UNC name, which includes the share name (including the $) to access it. By default, all volumes with drive letters automatically have *administrative shares* (C$, D$, E$ and so on). Other administrative shares can be created as needed for individual folders.

Accessing a Shared Folder

After you share a file or folder, users can connect to it as a network resource or map to it by using a drive letter on their machines. After a network drive is mapped, users can access it just as they would a local drive on their computer.

You can map a network drive to a shared file or folder by completing the following steps:

1. Click Start, Computer.

2. In Windows Explorer, click the Map Network Drive button on the toolbar. This displays the Map Network Drive dialog box.

3. Use the Drive field to select a free drive letter to use and then click Browse to the right of the Folder field.

4. In the Browse for Folder dialog box, expand the Network folders until you can select the name of the workgroup or the domain with which you want to work. When you expand the name of a computer in a workgroup or a domain, you'll see a list of shared folders. Select the shared folder you want to use and then click OK.

5. Select Reconnect at Logon if you want Windows Server 2008 to connect to the shared folder automatically at the start of each session.

6. If your current logon doesn't have appropriate access permissions for the share, click the Different User Name link. You can then enter the user-name and password of the account with which you want to connect to the shared folder. Typically, this feature is used by administrators who log on to their computers with a limited account and also have an administrator account for managing the network.

7. Click Finish.

If you later decide you don't want to map the network drive, click Start, Computer. In Windows Explorer, under Network Location, right-click the network drive icon and choose Disconnect.

You can also type in a UNC in the Run box or the address bar in Windows Explorer. To display the Run box quickly, press and hold the Windows Key logo and the R key. If you don't have a Windows logo key or if you prefer to use the mouse, you can add the Run option to the Start menu in Windows Vista:

1. Right-click Start and choose Properties.

2. On the Start Menu tab, click the Customize button to the right of the Start Menu option.

3. In the Customize Start Menu dialog box, scroll down and place a check mark next to the Run option.

4. Click OK to save your changes.

Managing Shares

By using the Shared Folders snap-in (included in the Computer Management console), you can manage the server's shared folders. With the Shared Folder snap-in, you can do the following:

▶ Create, view, and set permissions for shares, including shares on Windows 2000, Windows XP, Windows Vista, Windows Server 2003, and Windows Server 2008.

▶ View a list of all users who are connected to the computer over a network and disconnect one or all of them.

▶ View a list of files opened by remote users and close one or all of the open files.

Working with Shared Folder Offline Settings

Offline folder access to files by network users is enabled by default for each share that you create under Windows Server 2008. However, you can specify the offline-files setting for each share from its properties sheet. To configure offline settings, take these steps:

1. Right-click a folder that is already shared in the Shared Folders snap-in and select Properties.

2. Click the Offline Settings button from the General tab.

3. Select one of the available options for offline files (see Figure 7.6):

   ▶ **Only the Files and Programs That Users Specify Will Be Available Offline**: This default setting is also known as manual caching.

   ▶ **All Files and Programs That Users Open from the Share Will Be Automatically Available Offline**: This setting is known as automatic caching. This feature automatically caches offline all data files that users open. When you enable this setting, you can mark the Optimized for Performance check box to automatically cache program files on each local computer to reduce network traffic for network-based applications.

   ▶ **Files or Programs from the Share Will Not Be Available Offline**: This setting disables offline files for the share.

4. In the Offline Settings box, click OK.

5. Click OK for the share's properties sheet to save the settings.

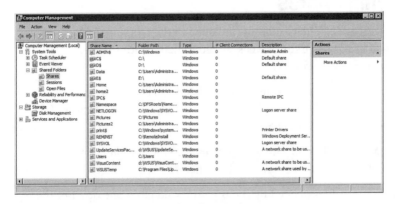

FIGURE 7.6 Configuring shared folder offline settings.

Restricting Offline Files Usage with Group Policy

Many settings are available from the GPMC or from the GPO Editor under Computer Configuration\Administrative Templates\Network\Offline Files. For example, to enable or disable offline files, double-click the Allow or Disallow Use of the Offline Files Feature policy to specify a setting in the GPO Editor. Several other GPO settings are available under User Configuration\Administrative Templates\Network\Offline Files. Just remember that any conflicting GPO settings are always overridden by the GPO setting in the Computer Configuration container.

File Encryption

If someone has administrative privilege on a Windows Vista computer or has unauthorized physical access to the device, including if the computer and/or hard drive was stolen, he or she can take ownership of files and folders, change permissions of a file, and access the file. You can secure data against these risks by using encryption.

Encryption is the process of converting data into a format that cannot be read by another user. After a user has encrypted a file, it automatically remains encrypted when the file is stored on disk. Decryption is the process of converting data from encrypted format back to its original format. After a user has decrypted a file, the file remains decrypted when stored on disk.

Windows Vista offers two file encrypting technologies, *Encrypting File System (EFS)* and *BitLocker Drive Encryption*. EFS is used to help protect individual files on any drive on a per-user basis. BitLocker is designed to help protect all the personal and systems files on the drive on which Windows is installed if your computer is stolen, or if unauthorized users try to access the computer. You can use BitLocker Drive Encryption and the Encrypting File System together to get the protection offered by both features. Table 7.6 shows compares EFS and BitLocker Drive Encryption.

TABLE 7.6 Comparison Between Encrypting File System (EFS) and BitLocker Drive Encryption

Encrypting File System (EFS)	BitLocker Drive Encryption
EFS encrypts individual files on any drive.	BitLocker encrypts all personal and system files on the drive where Windows is installed.

continues

TABLE 7.6 *Continued*

Encrypting File System (EFS)	BitLocker Drive Encryption
EFS encrypts individual files on any drive. files based on the user account associated with it. If a computer has multiple users or groups, each can encrypt their own files independently.	BitLocker encrypts all personal and system files on the drive where Windows is installed.EFS encrypts BitLocker does not depend on the individual user accounts associated with files. BitLocker is either on or off, for all users or groups.
EFS does not require or use any special hardware.	BitLocker uses the *Trusted Platform Module (TPM)*, a special microchip in some newer computers that supports advanced security features.
You do not have to be an administrator to use EFS.	You must be an administrator to turn BitLocker encryption on or off after it's enabled.

Encrypting File System

Windows Vista includes the encrypting file system (EFS), which allows a user to encrypt and decrypt files that are stored on an NTFS volume. If you use EFS, folders and files are still kept secure against those intruders who might gain unauthorized physical access to the device, for example, by stealing a notebook computer or a removable drive.

EFS is used to encrypt data in files and folders with a key. This key is stored in protected storage as part of your user profile, and it provides transparent access to the encrypted data.

Several improvements have been made to EFS in Windows Vista. Smart Cards are now supported for storing user EFS keys in addition to administrative recovery keys. If you use smart cards for logon, EFS can operate as a single sign-on service that gives transparent access to your encrypted files. The System Page file can also be protected by EFS when you configure it by using group policy.

When you are using encrypted files on a network, client-side cached copies of network files can also be encrypted, providing security for these files even if the portable computer is lost or stolen. When you use Windows Vista in conjunction with a supported server platform, encrypted files can be transmitted over the network, and the receiving Windows Vista client decrypts them.

To encrypt a folder or file:

1. Right-click the folder or file you want to encrypt and then click Properties.

2. Click the General tab and then click Advanced.

3. Select the Encrypt Contents to Secure Data check box and then click OK.

After you encrypt the file, encrypted files are colored green in Windows Explorer.

To decrypt a folder or file,

1. Right-click the folder or file you want to decrypt and then click Properties.

2. Click the General tab and then click Advanced.

3. Clear the Encrypt Contents to Secure Data check box and then click OK.

The first time you encrypt a folder or file, you should back up your encryption certificate. If your certificate and key are lost or damaged and you do not have a backup, you won't be able to use the files that you have encrypted. Take these steps to back up your EFS certificate:

1. Open Certificate Manager by clicking Start, typing `certmgr.msc` into the Search box, and then pressing Enter.

2. Click the arrow next to the Personal folder to expand it.

3. Click Certificates.

4. Click the certificate that lists Encrypting File System under Intended Purposes. (You might need to scroll to the right to see this.) If there is more than one EFS certificate, you should back up all of them.

5. Click the Action menu, point to All Tasks and then click Export.

6. In the Export wizard, click Next, click Yes, export the private key, and then click Next.

7. Click Personal Information Exchange and then click Next.

8. Type the password you want to use, confirm it, and then click Next. The export process creates a file to store the certificate.

9. Enter a name for the file and the location (include the whole path), or click Browse and navigate to the location and then enter the filename.

10. Click Finish.

11. Store the backup copy of your EFS certificate in a safe place.

If the encrypted file needs to be shared with another user on the same computer, you then need to do the following:

1. Export the EFS certificate.

2. Import the EFS certificate.

3. Add the EFS certificate to the shared file.

The person with whom you want to share files needs to export his or her EFS certificate and give it to you by doing the following:

1. Open Certificate Manager by clicking Start, typing `certmgr.msc` into the Search box, and then pressing Enter.

2. Click the arrow next to the Personal folder to expand it and then click the EFS certificate that you want to export.

3. Click the Action menu, point to All Tasks, and then click Export.

4. In the Certificate Export Wizard, click Next.

5. Click No, Do Not Export the Private Key. Click Next.

6. On the Export File Format page, click Next to accept the default format.

7. The export process creates a file in which to store the certificate. Type a name for the file and the location (include the whole path). Or click Browse, navigate to the location, and then type the filename.

8. Click Finish.

After you get the EFS certificate from the person with whom you want to share the file, you need to import the certificate:

1. Open Certificate Manager by clicking Start, typing `certmgr.msc` into the Search box, and then pressing Enter.

2. Select the Personal folder.

3. Click the Action menu, point to All Tasks, and click Import.

4. In the Certificate Import wizard, click Next.

5. Type the location of the file that contains the certificate. Or click Browse, navigate to the file's location, and then click Next.

6. Click Place All Certificates in the Following Store, click Browse, click Trusted People, and then click Next.

7. Click Finish.

To add the EFS certificate to the shared file,

1. Right-click the file you want to share and then click Properties.

2. Click the General tab and then click Advanced.

3. In the Advanced Attributes dialog box, click Details.

4. In the dialog box that appears, click Add.

5. In the Select User dialog box, click the certificate and then click OK.

BitLocker Drive Encryption

A new feature that was added to Windows Vista and is included with Windows Server 2008 was BitLocker Drive Encryption, which is designed to protect computers from attackers who have physical access to a computer. Without BitLocker Drive Encryption, an attacker could start the computer with a boot disk and then reset the administrator password to gain full control of the computer. Or the attacker could access the computer's hard disk directly by using a different operating system to bypass file permissions.

BitLocker Drive Encryption is the feature in Windows Vista that makes use of a computer's TPM. A *Trusted Platform Module (TPM)* is a microchip that is built into a computer. It is used to store cryptographic information, such as encryption keys. Information stored on the TPM can be more secure from external software attacks and physical theft. BitLocker Drive Encryption can use a TPM to validate the integrity of a computer's boot manager and boot files at startup, and to guarantee that a computer's hard disk has not been tampered with while the operating system was offline. BitLocker Drive Encryption also stores measurements of core operating system files in the TPM.

If the computer is equipped with a compatible TPM, BitLocker uses the TPM to lock the encryption keys that protect the data. As a result, the keys cannot be accessed until the TPM has verified the computer's state. Encrypting the entire volume protects all the data, including the operating system itself, the Windows Registry, temporary files, and the hibernation file. Because the keys needed to decrypt data remain locked by the TPM, an attacker cannot read the data just by removing your hard disk and installing it in another computer.

During the startup process, the TPM releases the key that unlocks the encrypted partition only after comparing a hash of important operating system configuration values with a snapshot taken earlier. This verifies the integrity of the Windows startup process. During computer startup, if BitLocker detects a system condition that could represent a security risk (for example, disk errors, a change to the BIOS, or changes to any startup files), it locks the drive, goes into Recovery mode, and requires a special BitLocker recovery password (a 48-decimal-digit key entered with the function keys in six groups of six digits) to unlock it. Make sure that you create this recovery password when you turn on BitLocker for the first time; otherwise, you could permanently lose access to your files. Recovery mode is also used if a disk drive is transferred to another system.

On computers with a compatible TPM, BitLocker can be used in three ways:

▶ **TPM-only**: This is transparent to the user, and the user logon experience is unchanged. If the TPM is missing or changed, or if the TPM detects changes to critical operating system startup files, BitLocker enters its recovery mode, and you need a recovery password to regain access to the data.

▶ **TPM with startup key**: In addition to the protection provided by the TPM, a part of the encryption key is stored on a USB flash drive. This is referred to as a startup key. Data on the encrypted volume cannot be accessed without the startup key.

▶ **TPM with PIN**: In addition to the protection provided by the TPM, BitLocker requires a PIN to be entered by the user. Data on the encrypted volume cannot be accessed without entering the PIN.

By default, the BitLocker setup wizard is configured to work seamlessly with the TPM. An administrator can use Group Policy or a script to enable additional features and options.

On computers without a compatible TPM, BitLocker can provide encryption, but not the added security of locking keys with the TPM. In this case, the user is required to create a startup key that is stored on a USB flash drive.

On computers with a compatible TPM, BitLocker Drive Encryption can use one of two TPM modes:

▶ **TPM-only**: In this mode, only the TPM is used for validation. When the computer starts up, the TPM is used to validate the boot files, the operating system files, and any encrypted volumes. Because the user doesn't need to provide an additional startup key, this mode is transparent to the user and the user logon experience is unchanged. However, if the TPM is missing or the integrity of files or volumes has changed, BitLocker enters recovery mode and requires a recovery key or password to regain access to the boot volume.

▶ **Startup key**: In this mode, both the TPM and a startup key are used for validation. When the computer starts up, the TPM is used to validate the boot files, the operating system files, and any encrypted volumes. The user must have a startup key to log on to the computer. A startup key can be either physical, such as a USB flash drive with a machine-readable key written to it, or personal, such as a personal identification number (PIN) set by the user. If the user doesn't have the startup key or is unable to provide the correct startup key, BitLocker enters recovery mode. As before, BitLocker also enters recovery mode if the TPM is missing or the integrity of boot files or encrypted volumes has changed.

BitLocker has the following system requirements:

▶ Because BitLocker stores its own encryption and decryption key in a hardware device that is separate from your hard disk, you must have one of the following:

  ▶ A computer with Trusted Platform Module (TPM). If your computer was manufactured with TPM version 1.2 or higher, BitLocker stores its key in the TPM.

  ▶ A removable USB memory device, such as a USB flash drive. If your computer doesn't have TPM version 1.2 or higher, BitLocker stores its key on the flash drive.

▶ Your computer must have at least two partitions. One partition must include the drive on which Windows is installed. This is the drive that BitLocker encrypts. The other partition is the active partition, which must remain unencrypted so that the computer can be started. Partitions must be formatted with the NTFS file system.

▶ Your computer must have a BIOS that is compatible with TPM and supports USB devices during computer startup. If this is not the case, you need to update the BIOS before using BitLocker.

To find out whether your computer has Trusted Platform Module (TPM) security hardware,

1. Open Bitlocker Drive Encryption by clicking Start, Control Panel, Security, Bitlocker Drive Encryption. If you are prompted for an administrator password or confirmation, type the password or provide confirmation.

2. If the TPM administration link appears in the left pane, your computer has the TPM security hardware. If this link is not present, you need a removable USB memory device to turn on BitLocker and store the BitLocker startup key that you'll need whenever you restart your computer.

To turn on BitLocker,

1. Open Bitlocker Drive Encryption by clicking Start, Control Panel, Security, Bitlocker Drive Encryption. If you are prompted for an administrator password or confirmation, type the password or provide confirmation.

2. Click Turn On BitLocker. This opens the BitLocker setup wizard. Follow the instructions in the wizard.

To turn off or temporarily disable BitLocker,

1. Open Bitlocker Drive Encryption by clicking Start, Control Panel, Security, Bitlocker Drive Encryption. If you are prompted for an administrator password or confirmation, type the password or provide confirmation.

2. Click Turn Off BitLocker. This opens the BitLocker Drive Encryption dialog box.

3. To decrypt the drive, click Decrypt the Volume. To temporarily disable BitLocker, click Disable BitLocker Drive Encryption.

The BitLocker control panel applet enables you to recover the encryption key and recovery password at will. You should consider carefully how to store this information, because it grants access to the encrypted data. It is also possible to escrow or store this information into Active Directory.

To escrow BitLocker recovery information in Active Directory, follow these steps:

1. Open the Group Policy Editor by executing the gpedit.msc command.

2. Expand Computer Configuration, expand Administrative Templates, and expand Windows Components. Click BitLocker Drive Encryption.

3. Double-click Turn on BitLocker backup to Active Directory Domain Services.

4. Select Enabled. Select Require BitLocker backup to AD DS. Select Recovery Passwords and key packages.

5. Click Apply and then OK.

Compression

Windows Server 2008 supports two types of data compression:

▶ Compressed (Zipped) Folders

▶ NTFS compression

Compressed (Zipped) Folders

Files and folders compressed with the Compressed (Zipped) Folders feature remain compressed under all three supported file systems: NTFS, FAT, and FAT32. Compressing any system folders, such as the \Windows folder or the \Program Files folder, is not recommended and should be avoided. Compressed (Zipped) Folders are identified by a zipper symbol that is part of the folder's icon.

To create a Compressed (Zipped) Folder, right-click a folder, point to Send To, and click Compressed (Zipped) Folder. This action actually creates a Zip file that Windows Server 2008 recognizes as a Compressed (Zipped) Folder that contains the folder you selected to be compressed along with all of that folder's contents. You can also use any popular third-party utility, such as WinZip or PKZip, to read, write, add to, or remove files from any Compressed (Zipped) Folder. Unless you install such a third-party zip utility, Windows Server 2003 displays standard zip files as Compressed (Zipped) Folders.

NTFS Compression

NTFS compression selectively compresses the contents of individual files, entire directories, or entire drives on an NTFS volume. NTFS compression uses file compression that works by substitution. It starts by locating repetitive data with another pattern, which is shorter. Windows track which files and folders are compressed via a file attribute. As far as the user is concerned, the compressed drive, folder, or file is simply another drive, folder, or file that works like any other. Although you expand the amount of space for volume, the performance of the PC is slower because it has to process the compression and decompression of files. Therefore, do not use compression unless you are compressing files that are rarely used or when disk space is critical. If disk space is critical, use this as a temporary solution until you can delete or move files from the drive or can extend the volume.

To compress a file or folder on an NTFS drive,

1. Open Windows Explorer.

2. Right-click the file or folder that you want to compress and select Properties.

3. Click Advanced.

4. Select the Compress contents to save disk space check box.

5. Click OK or Apply.

6. If you select to compress a drive or folder, select Apply Changes to This Folder Only or Apply Changes to the Folder, Subfolder and Files and click OK.

To compress an NTFS drive,

1. Click Start, Computer.

2. Right-click the drive that you want to compress.

3. Select the Compress Drive to Save Disk Space check box.

4. Click OK or Apply.

To uncompress a drive, folder, or file, uncheck the Compress Contents to Save Disk Space or Compress Drive to Save Disk Space box.

> **NOTE**
>
> You cannot use NTFS compression to compress files or folders that are encrypted with EFS.

Distributed File System

Distributed File System (DFS) is a set of client and server services that allows a large enterprise to organize many distributed SMB file shares into a distributed file system. DFS provides location transparency and redundancy to improve data availability in the face of failure or heavy load by allowing shares in multiple different locations to be logically grouped under one folder, or DFS root.

Distributed File System in Windows Server 2008 is implemented as a role service of the File Services role. Distributed File System consists of two role services:

- ▶ DFS Namespaces
- ▶ DFS Replication

Installing DFS Management

To manage *DFS Namespaces* and DFS Replication, you must install the DFS Management snap-in. Use one of the following methods to install the DFS Management snap-in on a computer running Windows Server 2008:

- ▶ From Server Manager, use the Add Roles Wizard to select the File Services role and then select the Distributed File System role service. This configures the server to be a file server, installs the DFS Management snap-in, and installs and starts the DFS Namespaces and DFS Replication services.

- ▶ From Server Manager, use the Add Features Wizard to install the Remote Server Administration Tools feature and select the File Services feature with the DFS Management option. The DFS Management option installs the DFS Management snap-in, but it does not install any DFS services on the server.

To manage Distributed File System from a command prompt, use the DfsUtil, DfsCmd, DfsrAdmin, and DfsrDiag commands or write scripts that use Windows Management Instrumentation (WMI).

DFS Namespaces

DFS Namespaces enables you to group shared folders that are located on different servers into one or more logically structured namespaces. Each namespace appears to users as a single shared folder with a series of subfolders. However, the underlying structure of the namespace can consist of numerous shared folders that are located on different servers and in multiple sites. In other words, a namespace is a virtual view of shared folders in an organization.

The path to a namespace is similar to a Universal Naming Convention (UNC) path to a shared folder, such as \\servername\sharename. The components that make up a DFS namespace include the following:

- **Namespace server**: A namespace server hosts a namespace. The namespace server can be a member server or a domain controller.

- **Namespace root**: The namespace root is the starting point of the namespace.

- **Folder**: Folders without folder targets add structure and hierarchy to the namespace, and folders with folder targets provide users with actual content. When users browse a folder that has folder targets in the namespace, the client computer receives a referral that transparently redirects the client computer to one of the folder targets.

- **Folder targets**: A folder target is the UNC path of a shared folder or another namespace that is associated with a folder in a namespace. The folder target is where data and content is stored.

You can create a new namespace when you install the DFS Namespaces role service by using the Add Roles Wizard or Add Role Service Wizard of Server Manager. If DFS is already installed, you can use the following procedures to create a namespace:

1. Click Start, Administrative Tools, DFS Management. See Figure 7.7.

2. In the console tree, right-click the Namespaces node and then click New Namespace.

3. Specify the server name and click Next.

4. Specify a name for the namespace and click Next.

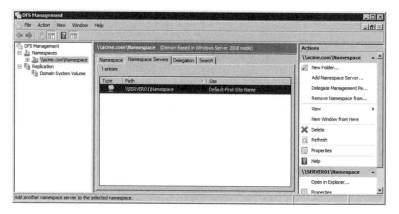

FIGURE 7.7 The DFS Management console.

You can select one of the following:

▶ **Domain-based namespace**: Stored on one or more namespace servers in Active Directory Domain Services that increase the availability of a domain-based namespace. You can also enable Windows Server 2008 mode for increased scalability and access-based enumeration.

▶ **Standalone namespace**: Stored on a single namespace server.

5. Click Next.

6. When the Review Settings and Create Namespace window appears, click Create.

7. When the Confirmation screen appears, click Close.

You can increase the availability of a domain-based namespace by specifying additional namespace servers to host the namespace.

To add a namespace server to a domain-based namespace,

1. Click Start, Administrative Tools, DFS Management.

2. In the console tree, under the Namespaces node, right-click a domain-based namespace and then click Add Namespace Server.

3. Enter the path to another server (or click Browse to locate a server).

You can use folders to create additional levels of hierarchy in a namespace. You can also create folders with folder targets to add shared folders to the namespace. DFS folders with folder targets cannot contain other DFS folders, so if you want to add a level of hierarchy to the namespace, do not add folder targets to the folder.

To create a folder in a namespace, follow these steps:

1. Click Start, Administrative Tools, DFS Management.

2. In the console tree, under the Namespaces node, right-click a namespace or a folder within a namespace and then click New Folder.

3. In the Name text box, type the name of the new folder.

4. To add one or more folder targets to the folder, click Add and specify the Universal Naming Convention (UNC) path of the folder target.

5. Click OK.

A folder target is the Universal Naming Convention (UNC) path of a shared folder or another namespace that is associated with a folder in a namespace. Adding multiple folder targets increases the availability of the folder in the namespace. Take these steps to add a folder target:

1. Click Start, Administrative Tools, DFS Management.

2. In the console tree, under the Namespaces node, right-click a folder and then click Add Folder Target.

3. Type the path to the folder target (or click Browse to locate the folder target).

4. If the folder is replicated through the use of DFS Replication, you can specify whether to add the new folder target to the replication group.

If you access the namespace properties, you can optimize polling (surveying) of the domain controller. The two selections include

▶ **Optimize for consistency (default option)**: The Distributed File System service attempts to keep the domain-based namespace highly consistent on all namespace servers by polling the primary domain controller (PDC) emulator every hour by default. This process can cause an increase load on the PDC emulator in namespaces that have more than 16 namespace servers and in namespaces that change frequently.

▶ **Optimize for scalability**: Allows organizations to use more than the recommended 16 namespace servers for hosting a domain-based namespace in consistency mode. When root scalability mode is enabled, namespace servers do not send change notification messages to other namespaces servers when the namespace changes, nor do they poll the PDC emulator every hour. Instead, they poll their closest domain controller every hour to discover updates to the namespace.

In addition to the polling, you can also configure referral. A referral is an ordered list of targets that a client computer receives from a domain controller or namespace server when the user accesses a namespace root or folder with targets. After the client receives the referral, the client attempts to access the first target in the list. If the target is not available, the client attempts to access the next target. Targets on the client's site are always listed first in a referral. Targets outside of the client's site are listed according to the ordering method.

The three ordering methods are

▸ **Random order**: Targets in the same AD DS site as the client are listed in random order at the top of the referral. Targets outside the client's site are listed in random order. If no same-site target servers are available, the client computer is referred to a random target server regardless of how expensive the connection is or how distant the target is.

▸ **Lowest cost**: Targets in the same site as the client are listed in random order at the top of the referral. Targets outside the client's site are listed in order of lowest cost to highest cost. Referrals with the same cost are grouped together, and the targets are listed in random order within each group.

▸ **Exclude targets outside of the client's site**: The referral contains only the targets that are in the same site as the client. These same-site targets are listed in random order. If no same-site targets exist, the client does not receive a referral and cannot access that portion of the namespace.

DFS Replication

You can use *DFS Replication* to keep the contents of folder targets in sync so that users see the same files no matter to which folder target the client computer is referred. DFS Replication is an efficient, multiple-master replication engine you can use to keep folders synchronized between servers across limited-bandwidth network connections. It replaces the File Replication Service (FRS) as the replication engine for DFS Namespaces, as well as replicating the Active Directory Domain Services (AD DS) SYSVOL folder in domains that use the Windows Server 2008 domain functional level.

DFS Replication uses a compression algorithm known as remote differential compression (RDC). RDC detects changes to the data in a file and enables DFS Replication to replicate only the changed file blocks instead of the entire file.

To use DFS Replication, you must create replication groups and add replicated folders to the groups. Replication groups, replicated folders, and members are illustrated in the following figure.

Creating multiple replicated folders in a single replication group simplifies the process of deploying replicated folders because the topology, schedule, and bandwidth throttling for the replication group are applied to each replicated folder. To deploy additional replicated folders, you can use `Dfsradmin.exe` or follow the instructions in a DFS Replication Wizard to define the local path and permissions for the new replicated folder.

Each replicated folder has unique settings, such as file and subfolder filters, so that you can filter out different files and subfolders for each replicated folder.

The replicated folders stored on each member can be located on different volumes in the member, and the replicated folders do not need to be shared folders or part of a namespace. However, the DFS Management snap-in makes it easy to share replicated folders and optionally publish them in an existing namespace.

To use DFS Replication replicate folder targets,

1. Click Start, Administrative Tools, DFS Management.

2. In the console tree, under the Namespaces node, right-click a folder that has two or more folder targets and then click Replicate Folder.

To create a replication group and two replicated folders,

1. Click Start, Administrative Tools, DFS Management.

2. In the console tree, right-click the Replication node and then click New Replication Group.

3. Select the type of replication. You can use a Multipurpose replication group in cases in which data is changed at all members of the replica set, users share information, and so on. Or you can choose the Replication group for data collection. This type of replication is typically used only for branch server content replication to a hub server for centralized backup.

4. Enter a name, description, and domain for the replica group. Click Next.

5. The next screen prompts for the members of the replica set. As you add each member, the system performs a check for its suitability as a member of the set.

6. Select the type of replication topology. If more than three servers are part of the replica set, you can choose a "hub-and-spoke topology." Otherwise, the options are "full mesh," in which every node replicates to every other node (which really scales up to only 10 nodes), or no replication at all, in which case you need to create a custom topology.

7. Select the amount of bandwidth to use for replication. By default, you have the full bandwidth available for use. You can also specify a schedule that allows an amount of bandwidth to be specified for each hour of each day of the week. Using this feature, you can limit bandwidth during the day and catch up at night (making sure that users are aware that there might be differences in replica sets at locations).

8. Select the authoritative server from the list of servers in the replica set. During the initial replication, the selected primary server governs the content of the replicas. If data exists on a non-primary server in the replication folder that isn't in the primary server's replication folder, it is deleted.

9. Select the folder to replicate on the primary server. You can select multiple folders, if necessary.

10. On the next screen, select the folder to use for the other members of the replica set by selecting the member from the dialog box and editing the folder property.

11. A summary of the actions and configuration appears. Click Create to begin creating the DFSR set.

12. When the set is complete, click Close. A notification message appears, informing you that replication won't begin until all members have contacted Active Directory Domain Controllers for the configuration information. This process requires AD replication to have occurred and the replica to poll the DC.

When you first set up replication, you must choose a primary member. Choose the member that has the most up-to-date files that you want to replicate to all other members of the replication group, because the primary member's content is considered "authoritative." This means that during initial replication, the primary member's files always win the conflict resolution that occurs when the receiving members have files that are older or newer than the associated files on the primary member.

Initial replication always occurs between the primary member and the receiving replication partners of the primary member. After a member has received all files from the primary member, that member replicates files to its receiving partners as well. In this way, replication for a new replicated folder starts from the primary member and then progresses to the other members of the replication group.

Initial replication does not begin immediately. The topology and DFS Replication settings must be replicated to all domain controllers, and each member in the replication group must poll its closest domain controller to obtain these settings. The amount of time this takes depends on AD DS replication latency and the long polling interval (60 minutes) on each member.

When receiving files from the primary member during initial replication, if a receiving member contains files that are not present on the primary member, those files are moved to their respective DfsrPrivate\PreExisting folder. If a file is identical to a file on the primary member, the file is not replicated. If the version of a file on the receiving member is different from the primary member's version, the receiving member's version is moved to the Conflict and Deleted folder and remote differential compression (RDC) can be used to download only the changed blocks.

To determine whether files are identical on the primary member and receiving member, DFS Replication compares the files by using a hash algorithm. If the files are identical, only minimal metadata is transferred.

After the initialization of the replicated folder, when all existing files in the replicated folder are added to the DFS Replication database, the primary member designation is removed. That member is then treated like any other member and its files are no longer considered authoritative over other members that have completed initial replication. Any member that has completed initial replication is considered authoritative over members that have not completed initial replication.

To add a member to a replication group, follow these steps:

1. Click Start, Administrative Tools, click DFS Management.

2. In the console tree, under the Replication node, right-click a replication group and then click New Member.

3. Enter the name of the server to add to the replication group. The server must have the DFS Replication Service installed. Click Next.

4. Select the Antivirus Signatures replicated folder, click Edit, Enabled, and then enter the local path of the replicated folder to be created on the new member. When you close the Edit Local Path dialog box, notice that the LOB Data replicated folder shows <Disabled>, which means that this replicated folder will not be replicated to the new member. Because you want only the Antivirus Signatures folder to be replicated to the new member, you can ignore the warning message that appears. Click Next.

5. Under Available Members, click a member and then click Add. Repeat this step to add the second member. The new member replicates directly with both existing members. Click Next.

6. Select Custom Connection Schedule and then click Edit Schedule. In the Edit Schedule dialog box, click Details to expand the schedule and then select the entry that begins Sunday 12:00 a.m. and then click Edit. In the Edit Schedule dialog box, under Bandwidth usage, click 128Mbps. Click Next.

7. Click Create to add the new member to the Data Distribution replication group.

8. When the confirmation screen appears, click Close to close the wizard.

9. Click OK to close the dialog box that warns you about the delay in initial replication.

10. Follow the instructions in the New Member Wizard.

To create a connection, follow these steps:

1. Click Start, point to Administrative Tools, and then click DFS Management.

2. In the console tree, under the Replication node, right-click the replication group in which you want to create a new connection and then click New Connection.

3. Specify the sending and receiving members, and specify the schedule to use for the connection. At this point, replication is one-way.

4. Select Create a Second Connection in the opposite direction to create a second connection for two-way replication between the sending and receiving members.

Although it is technically possible to create a one-way replication connection, doing so can cause numerous issues including health check topology errors, staging issues, and issues with the DFS Replication database. A better solution is to simulate a one-way connection by doing one of the following:

▶ Train administrators to make changes on only the server(s) that you want to designate as primary servers.

▶ Configure the share permissions on the destination servers so that end-users do not have Write permissions.

To edit the replication schedule for a replication group or to force replication with a specific member of a replication group,

1. Click Start, Administrative Tools, DFS Management.

2. In the console tree, under the Replication node, right-click the replication group with the schedule that you want to edit and then click Edit Replication Group Schedule.

To force replication immediately,

1. In the console tree, under the Replication node, select the appropriate replication group.

2. Click the Connections tab.

3. Right-click the member you want to use to replicate and then click Replicate Now.

To enable or disable replication for a specific connection,

1. Click Start, Administrative Tools, DFS Management.

2. In the console tree, under the Replication node, click the replication group that contains the connection you want to edit.

3. In the details pane, click the Connections tab.

4. To disable a connection, right-click the connection and then click Disable. To enable a connection, right-click the connection and then click Enable.

To share a replicated folder without publishing the folder to a DFS namespace,

1. Click Start, Administrative Tools, DFS Management.

2. In the console tree, under the Replication node, click the replication group that contains the replicated folder you want to share.

3. In the details pane, on the Replicated Folders tab, right-click the replicated folder that you want to share and then click Share and Publish in Namespace.

4. In the Share and Publish Replicated Folder Wizard, click Share the Replicated Folder and then follow the steps in the wizard.

To share a replicated folder and publish it to a DFS namespace,

1. Click Start, Administrative Tools, DFS Management.

2. In the console tree, under the Replication node, click the replication group that contains the replicated folder you want to share.

3. In the details pane, on the Replicated Folders tab, right-click the replicated folder that you want to share and then click Share and Publish in Namespace.

4. In the Share and Publish Replicated Folder Wizard, click Share and publish the replicated folder in a namespace and then follow the steps in the wizard.

The replication topology consists of the logical connections that DFS Replication uses to replicate files among servers. When choosing a topology, keep in mind that two one-way connections are created between the members you choose. These two connections allow data to flow in both directions.

To create a replication topology,

1. Click Start, Administrative Tools, DFS Management.

2. In the console tree, under the Replication node, right-click the replication group to create a new topology and then click New Topology.

3. Follow the instructions in the New Topology Wizard to choose one of the following topologies:

   ▶ **Hub and spoke**: This topology requires three or more members. For each spoke member, choose a required hub member and an optional second hub member for redundancy. This optional hub ensures that a spoke member can still replicate if one of the hub members is unavailable. If you specify two hub members, the hub members have a full-mesh topology between them (see Figure 7.8).

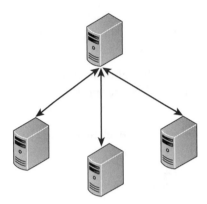

FIGURE 7.8 The hub and spoke topology in DFS.

▶ **Full mesh**: In this topology, every member replicates with all other members of the replication group. This topology works well when the replication group has ten or fewer members (see Figure 7.9).

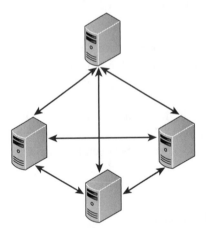

FIGURE 7.9 The full mesh topology in DFS.

DFS Management in Windows Server 2008 includes the capability to run a propagation test and generate two types of diagnostic reports:

▶ **Propagation test**: Tests replication progress by creating a test file in a replicated folder.

▶ **Propagation report**: Generates a report that tracks the replication progress for the test file created during a propagation test.

▶ **Health report**: Generates a report that shows the health of replication and replication efficiency.

Take these steps to create a diagnostic report for DFS replication:

1. Click Start, Administrative Tools, DFS Management.

2. In the console tree, under the Replication node, right-click the replication group for which you want to create a diagnostic report and then click Create Diagnostic Report.

3. Follow the instructions in the Diagnostic Report Wizard.

Shadow Copies of Shared Folders

Windows Server 2003 introduces a new feature called *shadow copies* of shared folders, which his also used in Windows Server 2008. Shadow copies, when configured, automatically create backup copies of the data stored in shared folders on specific drive volumes at scheduled times. The drive volumes must be formatted as NTFS. Shadow copies are set up per individual drive volume, and the copies are created at scheduled times by the new Volume Shadow Copy service (VSS) in conjunction with the Task Scheduler service.

By default, shadow copies are stored on the same drive letter as the one where the shared folders are located. Shadow copies enable users to retrieve previous versions of files and folders on their own, without requiring IT personnel to restore files or folders from backup media. This feature reduces IT staffing overhead and enables users to almost instantly restore deleted or damaged data files by themselves.

Enabling Shadow Copies

Best practice dictates that you should place the shadow copies on a separate physical disk, if possible, as an extra fault-tolerant measure. At least 100MB of free space must be available on a drive volume or partition where shadow copies are to be stored. Obviously, you might need more disk space depending on the size of the data in the shared folders that are being shadowed. To set up shadow copies for a drive letter, follow these steps on a Windows Server 2008 computer:

1. From My Computer or Windows Explorer, right-click an NTFS drive volume, select Properties, and click the Shadow Copies tab. Alternatively, from the Computer Management console, right-click the Shared Folders node and select All Tasks, Configure Shadow Copies.

2. From the Shadow Copies tab, select the drive volume that you want to shadow and then click Settings.

3. From the Settings dialog box, click the Located on This Volume drop-down list box to select the drive letter where the shadow copies for this drive volume will be stored (see Figure 7.10). You can select the same volume or a different NTFS drive volume.

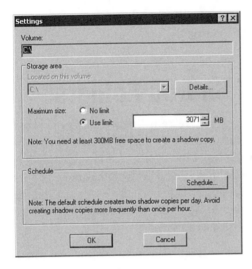

FIGURE 7.10 Configuring shadow copies.

4. Select a maximum size by clicking either the No Limit option or by clicking the Use Limit option and typing the storage restriction in the spinner box.

5. Click the Schedule button to specify how often you want to create shadow copies for this drive volume.

6. From the Schedule tab, you have two daily scheduled shadow copies set up by default: 7:00 a.m. and 12:00 noon, Monday through Friday of each week.

   ▶ To accept the defaults, make no changes.

   ▶ To set up an additional scheduled shadow copy, click New.

   ▶ To remove an existing scheduled shadow copy, select the schedule from the drop-down list box and click Delete.

   ▶ To modify an existing scheduled shadow copy, select the schedule from the drop-down list box and make the appropriate changes to the Scheduled Task drop-down list box, the Start Time spinner box, and the Schedule Task section.

7. Click OK to save your settings for shadow copy scheduling.

8. Click OK to save your settings for the Settings dialog box and return to the Shadow Copies tab. Shadow copies for the drive volume are now enabled.

> ► You can manually create additional shadow copies by clicking Create Now.

> ► You can delete previous shadow copies by selecting one of the date and time stamps in the Shadow Copies of Selected Volume list box and clicking Delete Now.

> ► To disable shadow copies for a volume, select the volume and click Disable.

9. Click OK to close the properties window for the Shadow Copies tab.

EXAM ALERT

Windows Server 2008 stores up to a maximum of 64 shadow copy snapshots per shadow-copy–enabled partition or volume. Keep this in mind when setting up a daily schedule for shadow copies to be created. After 64 shadow copy snapshots are created, each subsequent snapshot overwrites the oldest snapshot.

Accessing Previous Versions of Files from Shadow Copies

For users to be able to access shadow copies of shared folders from older operating systems including Windows XP and Windows Server 2003, you must install client software on those computers. This software can be found at http://technet.microsoft.com/en-us/windowsserver/bb405951.aspx.

You do not need to install the client software on Windows Vista or Windows Server 2008.

If you have the Previous Versions software, when a user selects a data file that has one or more shadow copies available, the View Previous Versions option appears in the File and Folder task pane in Windows Explorer and My Computer. A Previous Versions tab is also available when a user views the properties sheet for a data file that has one or more shadow copies, as shown in Figure 7.11. The Previous Versions tab gives you the option to Open, Copy, or Restore a previous version of a file or folder. You can use the Copy option to store a copy of a previous version to a different drive letter or folder than its original location. You can copy a previous version to a FAT, FAT32, or NTFS drive letter.

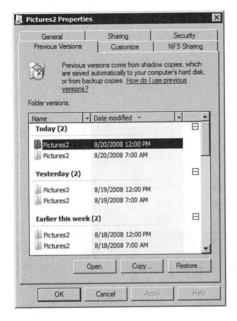

FIGURE 7.11   Accessing previous versions.

EXAM ALERT

To use the Shadow Copies of Shared Folders feature to access previous versions of files, you must navigate to the folder where the file(s) you want to restore is (are) stored, using a Uniform Naming Convention (UNC) path or via a mapped network drive letter! If you are accessing the file(s) over the network, this is not a problem, of course. But if you are working with the file(s) locally on a Windows Server 2008 computer, you must navigate to the files through a UNC path. The Previous Versions link does not appear, and the Previous Versions tab does not exist on a file's properties sheet when you view the file from a local drive letter window.

Using the VSSAdmin.exe Tool

The Windows Server 2008 Volume Shadow Copy Service can also be administered from the command line with the VSSAdmin tool that is included with Windows Server 2008. This tool replicates the features of the Shadow Copies tab of the volume Properties screen and can be called from batch files and scripts.

VSSAdmin options include

- **List Providers**: Lists Volume Shadow Copy providers configured on the system.

- **List Shadows**: Lists volume shadow copies that are stored on a system.

- **List ShadowStorage**: Lists Volume Shadow Copy storage areas.

- **List Writers**: Lists Volume Shadow Copy writers known to the system.

- **List Volumes**: Lists system volumes that are eligible for shadow copies.

- **Query Reverts**: Queries the status of in-progress revert operations.

- **Create Shadow**: Creates a shadow copy of a configured volume.

- **Revert Shadow**: Reverts a volume to a shadow copy.

- **Delete Shadows**: Deletes one or more volume shadow copies.

- **Add ShadowStorage**: Used to configure additional shadow storage areas.

- **Delete ShadowStorage**: Deletes Volume Shadow Copy storage areas.

- **Resize ShadowStorage**: Resizes a Volume Shadow Copy storage area.

Backup and Restore

Data is the raw facts, numbers, letters or symbols that the computer processes into meaningful information. Examples of data include a letter to a company or a client, a report for your boss, a budget proposal of a large project, or an address book of your friends and business associates. Whatever the data is, it can be saved (or written to disk) so that it can be retrieved at any time, it can be printed on paper or it can be sent to someone else over the telephone lines.

Data stored on a computer or stored on the network is vital to the users and probably the organization. The data represents hours of work and is sometimes irreplaceable. Data loss can be caused by many things including hardware failure, viruses, user error, and malicious users. When disaster occurs, the best way to make sure you can recover data is to back up, back up, back up. When disaster has occurred and the system does not have a backup of its important files, it is often too late to recover the files.

A backup of a system is an extra copy of data and/or programs. As a technician, consultant, or support person, you need to emphasize at every moment to back up on servers and client systems. In addition, it is recommended that the clients save their data files to a server so that you have a single, central location to back up. You may go as far as selecting and installing the equipment, doing the backup, or training other people in doing the backup. When doing all this, be sure to select the equipment and method that assures that the backup will be completed on a regular basis. Remember that if you have the best equipment and software but no one completes the backup, the equipment and software is wasted.

> **NOTE**
>
> The best method for data protection and recovery is back up, back up, back up!

When developing for a backup,

1. Develop a backup plan.

2. Stick to the backup plan.

3. Test the backup plan.

When developing a backup plan, you must consider the following:

▶ What equipment will be used?

▶ How much data needs to be backed up?

▶ How long will it take to do the backup?

▶ How often must the data be backed up?

▶ When will the backup take place?

▶ Who will do that backup?

Whatever equipment, person, or method is chosen, you must make sure that the backup will be done. If you choose the best equipment, the best software and the brightest person, and the backup is not done for whatever reason, you have wasted your resources and put your data at risk.

How often the backup is done depends on the importance of the data. If you have many customers loaded into a database that is constantly changed or you have files that represent the livelihood of your business, you should back them up every day. If there are a few letters that get sent throughout the week with nothing vitally important, you can back up once a week.

Types of Backups

All types of backups can be broken into the following categories:

- ▶ **Normal/Full**: The full backup backs up all files selected and shuts off/clears the Archive File attribute, indicating the file has been backed up.

- ▶ **Incremental**: An *incremental backup* backs up the files selected if the Archive File attribute is on (files since the last full or incremental backup). After the file has been backed up, it shuts off/clears the File attribute, indicating that the file has been backed up. Note: You should not mix incremental and differential backups.

- ▶ **Differential**: A *differential backup* backs up the files selected if the Archive File attribute is on (files since the last full backup). Different from the incremental backup, it does not shut off or clear the Archive attribute. Note: You should not mix incremental and differential backups.

- ▶ **Copy backup**: A normal backup, but it does not shut off the Archive attribute. This is typically used to back up the system before you make a major change to the system. The Archive attribute is not shut off or cleared so that your normal backup procedures are not affected.

For example, you decide to back up the entire hard drive once a week on Friday and you decide to use the full backup method. Therefore, you perform a full backup every Friday. If the hard drive goes bad, you use the last backup to restore the hard drive.

Another example is if you decide to back up the entire hard drive once a week on Friday and you want to use the incremental method. You would thenperform a full backup on week 1. This shuts off all the Archive attributes, indicating that all of the files have been backed up. On week 2, week 3, and week 4, you perform incremental backups using different tape or disk. Because the incremental backup turns off the Archive attribute, it backs up only new files and changed files. Therefore, all four backups make up the entire backup. It is much quicker to back up a drive using an incremental backup than a full backup. Of course, if the hard drive fails, you must restore backup #1, backup #2, backup #3, and backup # 4 to restore the entire hard drive.

After the backups are complete, you should check to see whether the backups actually worked. This can be done by picking a nonessential file and restoring it to the hard drive. This helps discover whether the backups are empty or a backup/restore device is faulty.

You should keep more than one backup. Tapes and disks do fail. One technique is to rotate through three sets of backups. If you perform a full backup once a week, use three sets of backup tapes or disks. During week 1, use tape/disk #1. During week 2, use tape/disk #2 and during week 3, use tape/disk #3. On week 4, start over and use tape/disk #1. If you have to restore a hard drive and the tape or disk fails, you can always go to the tape or disk from the week before. You should also perform monthly backups and store them elsewhere. You would be surprised how many times a person loses a file and may not know for several weeks. If the data is important enough, you may consider keeping a backup set in a fireproof safe off-site. Finally, when a system is initially installed and when you make any major changes to the system's configuration, make two backups before proceeding. This way, if anything goes wrong, you can restore everything back to the way it was before the changes. Two backups are necessary because tapes have been known to go bad on occasion.

Some places use the Grandfather, Father, Son (GFS) backup rotation, which requires 21 tapes based on a 5-day rotation. Each month, create a grandfather backup, which is stored permanently offsite and never to be reused. Each week, create a full weekly backup (Father); each day, create a differential or incremental backup (Son).

After completing a backup, properly label the tape or disk before removing the tape or disk and then store the tape and disk in a secure, safe place. In addition, you should keep a log of what backups have been completed, especially if you need to rebuild the server. The log keeps a record of what was backed up and when it was backed up. It also helps you track those who might be forgetting to perform backups.

Windows Server Backup

Windows Server 2008 has Windows Server Backup to protect your operating system, volumes, files, and application data. Backups can be saved to single or multiple disks, DVDs, removable media, or remote shared folders. They can be scheduled to run automatically or manually.

You can create a backup using the Backup Schedule Wizard to enable backups to be run on a regular schedule or using the Backup Once Wizard to run a one-time backup. You can access both these wizards from the Windows Server Backup Microsoft Management Console (MMC) snap-in. You can also create regular or one-time backups by using the wbadminwbadmin command.

Installing Windows Server Backup Tools

To access backup and recovery tools for Windows Server 2008, you must install the Windows Server Backup, Command-line Tools, and Windows PowerShell items that are available in the Add Features Wizard in Server Manager. To install or run Windows Server Backup, you must be a member of the Backup Operators or Administrators group, or you must have been delegated the appropriate authority. This installs the following tools:

- Windows Server Backup Microsoft Management Console (MMC) snap-in.

- wbadmin command-line tool.

- Windows Server Backup cmdlets (Windows PowerShell commands)

The wbadmin command replaces the ntbackup command that was released with previous versions of Windows. You cannot recover backups that you created with ntbackup by using wbadmin. However, a version of ntbackup is available as a download for Windows Server 2008 and Windows Vista users who want to recover backups that they created using ntbackup. This downloadable version of ntbackup enables you to perform recoveries only of legacy backups, and it cannot be used on computers running Windows Server 2008 or Windows Vista to create new backups. To download this version of ntbackup, see http://go.microsoft.com/fwlink/?LinkId=82917.

To access the Windows Server Backup snap-in, click Start, Administrative Tools, Windows Server Backup. To access and view the syntax for wbadmin, click Start, right-click Command Prompt and then click Run as Administrator. At the prompt, type **wbadmin /?**.

The Windows Backup MMC snap-in is not available on Windows Server 2008 Standard Edition and all core installations. To manage backups for a computer with Windows Server 2008 Standard Edition installed, you must use the snap-in on another computer to manage the backups remotely or use command-line tools on the local computer.

Backing Up Your Server

You can use Windows Server Backup to protect your operating system, volumes, files, and application data. Backups can be saved to single or multiple disks, DVDs, removable media, or remote shared folders. They can be scheduled to run automatically or manually.

Besides the volumes, backups can also back up the System State of a server. The *System State* is a collection of system-specific data, including the following:

▶ Registry.

▶ COM+ Class Registration database.

▶ Boot files, including the system files.

▶ Certificate Services database, if the server has the Certificate Services server.

▶ Active Directory directory service, if it is a domain controller.

▶ SYSVOL directory, if it is a domain controller.

▶ Cluster service information, if it is a cluster.

▶ IIS Metadirectory, if IIS is installed.

▶ System files that are under Windows File Protection.

You can create a backup, using the Backup Schedule Wizard to enable backups to be run on a regular schedule or using the Backup Once Wizard to run a one-time backup. You can access both these wizards from the Windows Server Backup Microsoft Management Console (MMC) snap-in. You can also create regular or one-time backups by using the wbadmin command.

As part of creating a backup, you need to specify the volumes that you want to include. The volumes you select impact what you can recover. You have the following options:

▶ **Full server (all volumes)**: Back up all volumes if you want to be able to recover the full server (all the files, data, applications, and the system state).

▶ **Critical volumes**: Back up just critical volumes (volumes containing operating system files) if you want to be able to recover only the operating system or system state.

▶ **Noncritical volumes**: Back up just individual volumes if you want to be able to recover only files, applications, or data from that volume.

You also need to specify a location to store the backups that you create. Depending on the type of storage you specify, you should be aware of the following issues:

- **Shared folder**: If you store your backup in a remote shared folder, your backup will be overwritten each time you create a new backup. Do not choose this option if you want to store a series of backups. Also, if you create a backup to a shared folder that already contains a backup and the backup process fails, you might be left without any backups. To work around this, you can create subfolders in the shared folder to store your backups.

- **DVD, other optical media, or removable media**: If you store your backup on optical or removable media, you can recover only entire volumes, not applications or individual files. In addition, backing up to media that has less than 1GB of free space is not supported.

- **Local hard disk**: If you store your backup on an internal hard disk, you can recover files, folders, applications, and volumes, and perform system state and operating system recoveries if the backup used contains all the critical volumes. However, you cannot perform an operating system recovery if the backup is on the same physical disk as one or more critical volumes. Also, the local disk you choose is dedicated for storing your scheduled backups and is not visible in Windows Explorer.

- **External hard disk**: If you store your backup on an external hard disk, you can recover files, folders, applications, and volumes, perform system state and operating system recoveries if the backup used contains all the critical volumes, and more easily move backups offsite for disaster protection. If you store your scheduled backups on an external hard disk, the disk is dedicated for storing your backups and is not visible in Windows Explorer. This enables users to move disks offsite for disaster protection and ensures backup integrity.

To create a backup schedule using the Windows Server Backup user interface, follow these steps:

1. Click Start, Administrative Tools, Windows Server Backup.

2. In the Actions pane of the snap-in default page, under Windows Server Backup, click Backup Schedule. This opens the Backup Schedule Wizard.

3. On the Getting Started page, click Next.

4. On the Select Backup Configuration page, select Full Server or Custom Backup and click Next. Choose Full Server to back up all volumes on the server. Choose Custom to back up just certain volumes and then click Next. On the Select Backup Items page, select the check boxes for the volumes that you want to back up and clear the check boxes for the volumes that you want to exclude.

5. On the Specify Backup Time page, click Once a Day or click More Than Once a Day. Then enter the time or times to start the backups. When completed, click Next.

6. On the Select Destination Disk page, select the check box for the disk that you attached for this purpose and then click Next.

7. On the Label Destination Disk page, the disk that you selected is listed. A label that includes your computer name, the current date, the current time, and a disk name is assigned to the disk. Click Next.

8. On the Confirmation page, review the details and then click Finish. The wizard formats the disk, which may take several minutes, depending on the size of the disk.

9. On the Summary page, click Close.

Using `wbadmin.exe`

The `wbadmin` command enables you to back up and restore your operating system, volumes, files, folders, and applications from a command prompt. The subcommands include

- **`wbadmin enable backup`**: Configures and enables a daily backup schedule.

- **`wbadmin disable backup`**: Disables your daily backups.

- **`wbadmin start backup`**: Runs a one-time backup. If used with no parameters, uses the settings from the daily backup schedule.

- **`wbadmin stop job`**: Stops the currently running backup or recovery operation.

- **`wbadmin get versions`**: Lists details of backups recoverable from the local computer or, if another location is specified, from another computer.

- **`wbadmin get items`**: Lists the items included in a specific backup.

- **`wbadmin start recovery`**: Runs a recovery of the volumes, applications, files, or folders specified.

- ► **wbadmin get status**: Shows the status of the currently running backup or recovery operation.

- ► **wbadmin get disks**: Lists disks that are currently online.

- ► **wbadmin start systemstaterecovery**: Runs a system state recovery.

- ► **wbadmin start systemstatebackup**: Runs a system state backup.

- ► **wbadmin delete systemstatebackup**: Deletes one or more system state backups.

- ► **wbadmin start sysrecovery**: Runs a recovery of the full system (at least all the volumes that contain the operating system's state). This subcommand applies only to Windows Server 2008, and it is only available if you are using the Windows Recovery Environment.

- ► **wbadmin restore catalog**: Recovers a backup catalog from a specified storage location in the case where the backup catalog on the local computer has been corrupted.

- ► **wbadmin delete catalog**: Deletes the backup catalog on the local computer. Use this subcommand only if the backup catalog on this computer is corrupted and you have no backups stored at another location that you can use to restore the catalog.

For example, to create a system state backup and save it to volume F, type

```
wbadmin start systemstatebackup -backupTarget:F
```

Backup Catalogs

Windows Server Backup stores the details about your backups (what volumes are backed up and where the backups are located) in a file called a *backup catalog*. The catalog is stored in the same place that you store your backups. If that file gets corrupted, you are alerted and an event is added to the event log (Event 514). To continue with future backups, you need to either restore the catalog, using an available backup, or delete the catalog.

If you have no backups that you can use to recover the catalog (so you need to delete the catalog), the information about previous backups will be lost and you will not be able to access the backups using the Windows Server Backup snap-in. In this case, you should create a new backup after your catalog is deleted.

You can use the Catalog Recovery Wizard to recover a local backup catalog that has been corrupted. To recover a backup catalog, follow these steps:

1. Click Start, Administrative Tools, Windows Server Backup.

2. In the Actions pane of the snap-in default page, under Windows Server Backup, click Recover Catalog. This opens the Catalog Recovery Wizard.

3. On the Specify Storage Type page, if you do not have a backup that you can use to recover the catalog, and just want to delete the catalog, click I Don't Have Any Usable Backups, Next, Finish. If you do have a backup that you can use, specify whether the backup is on a local drive or remote shared folder and then click Next.

4. If the backup is on a local drive (including DVDs), on the Select Backup Location page select the drive that contains the backup that you want to use from the drop-down list. If you are using DVDs, make sure the last DVD of the series is in the drive. Click Next.

5. If the backup is on a remote shared folder, on the Specify Remote Folder page, type the path to the folder that contains the backup that you want to use and then click Next.

6. You receive a message that you cannot access backups taken after the backup you are using for the recovery. Click Yes.

7. On the Confirmation page, review the details and then click Finish to recover the catalog.

8. On the Summary page, click Close.

After the catalog recovery is completed or you have deleted the catalog, you must close and then re-open Windows Server Backup to refresh the view.

NTFS Disk Quotas

NTFS *disk quotas* track and control disk usage on a per-user, per-drive letter (partition or volume) basis. You can apply disk quotas only to NTFS-formatted drive letters under Windows Server 2008. Quotas are tracked for each drive letter, even if the drive letters reside on the same physical disk. The per-user feature of quotas enables you to track every user's disk space usage, regardless of the folder in which the user stores files. To enable disk quotas, open Windows Explorer or My Computer, right-click a drive letter, and select Properties, click the Quota tab, and configure the options as shown in Figure 7.12.

EXAM ALERT

NTFS disk quotas do not use compression to measure disk-space usage, so users cannot obtain or use more space simply by compressing their own data.

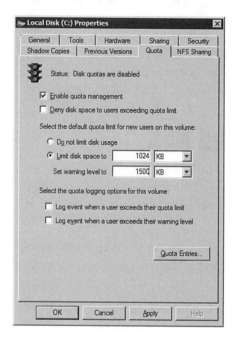

FIGURE 7.12 Configuring disk quotas.

After you turn on the disk quota system, you can establish individual disk-quota limits for each user by clicking the Quota Entries button at the bottom of the Quota tab. By default, only members of the Administrators group can view and change quota entries and settings. In addition, all members of the Administrators group inherit unlimited disk quotas by default. NTFS disk quotas are based on file ownership; operating system accounts are not immune to disk quotas. System accounts such as the local system are also susceptible to running out of disk space because of disk quotas having been set. From the Quota Entries window you can change an existing quota entry for a user by double-clicking the quota entry. To set up a new quota entry for a user, click the Quota menu and select the New Quota Entry option. When a user no longer stores data on a volume, you should delete the user's disk-quota entries. The catch is that you can delete the user's quota entries only after you remove all the files that the user owns or after another user takes ownership of the files.

File Server Resource Manager

File Server Resource Manager is a suite of tools for Windows Server 2008 that allows administrators to understand, control, and manage the quantity and type of data that is stored on their servers. By using File Server Resource Manager, administrators can place quotas on folders and volumes, actively screen files (such as blocking audio and video files, emails, pictures and executables), and generate comprehensive storage reports. This set of advanced instruments not only helps the administrator efficiently monitor existing storage resources, but it also aids in the planning and implementation of future policy changes.

Support for UNIX and NFS

Network File System (NFS) was developed by Sun Microsystems in the 1980s as a way for UNIX to share files and applications across the network. It enables you to attach a remote drive or directory to a virtual file system and work with it as if it were a local drive.

Windows Servers 2008 can share their files with NFS if they install the File Services Role. To start Client for NFS from the Windows interface, follow these steps:

1. Open Services for Network File System by clicking Start, Programs or All Programs, Administrative Tools, Services for Network File System (NFS).

2. If necessary, connect to the computer that you want to manage.

3. Right-click Client for NFS and then click Start Service.

To start Client for NFS from the command line,

1. Open an elevated privilege command prompt.

2. At a command prompt, type

```
nfsadmin client [ComputerName] start
```

To view NFS mount options using Windows Explorer,

1. Open Windows Explorer and click Start, Programs or All Programs, Accessories, Windows Explorer.

2. Right-click the name of the file or directory, right-click the drive that is assigned to a Network File System (NFS) mount, and then click Properties.

3. To view the NFS mount options for the drive, click NFS Mount Options.

4. To view the NFS properties for the mounted directory, click NFS Attributes.

To mount an NFS shared resource to a drive letter from the command line,

1. Open Windows Explorer and click Start, Programs or All Programs, Accessories, Windows Explorer.

2. Right-click the name of the file or directory, right-click the drive that is assigned to a Network File System (NFS) mount. and then click Properties.

3. Click the Manage NFS Sharing button.

4. Click the Share This Folder option.

5. Specify a share name and encoding.

6. To set the permissions, click Permissions.

To mount from the command prompt, use the mount command.

Exam Prep Questions

1. Which of the following are default hidden shares under Windows Server 2008? (Choose three.)

   ○ **A.** SYSVOL

   ○ **B.** ADMIN$

   ○ **C.** D$

   ○ **D.** PRINTER$

   ○ **E.** IPC$

   ○ **F.** C$

2. What does the Shared Folders snap-in provide, in terms of setting permissions for a new share, that the Sharing tab of a folder's properties sheet does not offer?

   ○ **A.** Setting share permissions

   ○ **B.** Publishing the share in Active Directory

   ○ **C.** Specifying offline settings

   ○ **D.** Specifying both share permissions and NTFS permissions

   ○ **E.** Specifying Web Sharing access permissions

3. When both share permissions and NTFS permissions exist on the same shared folder, how is access control to the shared folder affected for users trying to access the files stored in the shared folder over the network?

   ○ **A.** NTFS permissions take precedence.

   ○ **B.** Share permissions take precedence.

   ○ **C.** The most liberal permissions take precedence.

   ○ **D.** The most restrictive permissions take precedence.

4. Which of the following characteristics apply to NTFS inherited permissions? (Choose three.)

   ○ **A.** Special permissions are inherited by default.

   ○ **B.** Basic permissions are inherited by default.

   ○ **C.** Explicit permissions are the same as inherited permissions.

   ○ **D.** NTFS permissions are inherited by default.

   ○ **E.** NTFS explicit permissions are not inherited by default.

   ○ **F.** You cannot set explicit permissions on files.

5. The basic NTFS permission, Modify, when set on a folder, consists of which of the following special permissions? (Choose three.)

   ○ **A.** List Folder/Read Data

   ○ **B.** Create Files/Write Data

   ○ **C.** Change Permissions

   ○ **D.** Delete Subfolders and Files

   ○ **E.** Take Ownership

   ○ **F.** Write Extended Attributes

6. When you view NTFS effective permissions for a user or a group, which of the following permissions are displayed?

   ○ **A.** Basic permissions

   ○ **B.** Special permissions

   ○ **C.** Share permissions

   ○ **D.** Not inherited permissions

7. In which of the following ways can ownership of an NTFS file or folder change? (Choose three.)

   ○ **A.** Any user who is a member of the Domain Users group can take ownership of any folder or file whether or not she has permissions to the folder or file.

   ○ **B.** The current owner of a file or folder can assign the Take Ownership permission to another user for the file or folder; the other user must then take ownership of the object.

   ○ **C.** A member of the Administrators group can assign ownership of a file or folder to another user.

   ○ **D.** Any user who is granted the Restore Files and Directories user right can assign ownership of a file or folder to another user.

   ○ **E.** Any member of the Backup Operators group can take ownership of any file or folder at any time.

   ○ **F.** Any member of the Authenticated Users group can assign ownership of files or folders to another user at any time.

8. You have an APP1 folder on a Windows Server 2008 computer. User1 belongs to Group1 and Group2. User1 has no NTFS permissions assigned. Group1 has Allow Read NTFS permission, and Group2 has Allow Modify NTFS permission. What permission does User1 have for the APP1 folder?

   ◯ **A.** Allow Full Control NTFS permission

   ◯ **B.** Allow Modify NTFS permission

   ◯ **C.** Allow Read NTFS permission

   ◯ **D.** No access NTFS permission

9. You have an APP1 folder on a Windows Server 2008 computer. User1 belongs to Group1 and Group2. User1 has Allow Full Control NTFS permission, and Group2 has Allow Modify NTFS permission. Group1 has Deny Full Control NTFS permission. What permission does User1 have for the APP1 folder?

   ◯ **A.** Allow Full Control

   ◯ **B.** Allow Modify

   ◯ **C.** Allow Read

   ◯ **D.** No access

10. On a Windows Server 2008 computer, you have a shared folder called DATA1. You apply the default share permissions and NTFS permissions to DATA1. You then create a folder called DATA2 in DATA1. You apply the default NTFS permissions to DATA2. When GROUP1 tries to add files to DATA2, they get an `Access is denied` error message. What do you need to do so that GROUP1 can create, modify, and delete files in DATA1 and DATA2? All other users must be able to read the files in DATA1 and DATA2.

   ◯ **A.** For the DATA1 folder, assign the Change share permission to the Everyone group. For the DATA2 folder, assign the Allow Write NTFS permission for GROUP1 group.

   ◯ **B.** For the DATA1 folder, assign the Change share permission to the GROUP1 group and assign the Allow Write NTFS permissions to the GROUP1 group.

   ◯ **C.** For the DATA1 folder, assign the Change share permissions to the Everyone group and assign the Allow Modify NTFS permissions to the GROUP1 group.

   ◯ **D.** For the DATA1 folder, assign the Change share permissions to the GROUP1 and assign the Allow Modify NTFS permissions to the GROUP1 group.

11. On a Windows Server 2008 computer, you have a shared folder called APP1. At this time, Joe does not belong to the Sales, Marketing, or Executive group. You set the NTFS and APP1 as shown in the following table:

	NTFS Permission	**Share Permission**
Everyone	Read	Read
Sales group	Read and Execute	Change
Marketing group	Read/Write	Full Control
Executive group	Read and Execute	Read

You want Joe to be able to make changes to the files in the APP1 folder. What should you do?

- ○ **A.** Assign Joe to the Sales group and assign Allow Write NTFS permission to the Sales group.

- ○ **B.** Assign Joe to the Executive group and assign the Allow Write NTFS permission to the Executive group.

- ○ **C.** Assign Joe to the Executive group and assign the Change share permission to the Executive group.

- ○ **D.** Assign the Full Control share permission to Everyone.

12. You want to control the permissions of files and directories on an NTFS drive on the network. Which application must you use?

- ○ **A.** Windows Explorer

- ○ **B.** Active Directory Users and Computers console

- ○ **C.** Computer Management console

- ○ **D.** Disk Administrator console

13. You work as the desktop support technician at Acme.com. A Windows Vista computer contains a shared folder on an NTFS partition. Which one of the following statements concerning access to the folder is correct?

- ○ **A.** A user who is accessing the folder remotely has the same or more restrictive access permissions than if she accesses the folder locally.

- ○ **B.** A user who is accessing the folder remotely has less restrictive access permissions than if she accesses the folder locally.

○ **C.** A user who is accessing the folder remotely has the same access permissions than if she accesses the folder locally.

○ **D.** A user who is accessing the folder remotely has more restrictive access permissions than if she accesses the folder locally.

14. Which of the following characteristics of shadow copies are true? (Choose the best three answers.)

○ **A.** Previous versions of files stored as shadow copies are available under Windows 2000 Professional as long as you install the Previous Versions Client software.

○ **B.** You must store shadow copies on NTFS drive volumes.

○ **C.** You can make shadow copies only from files stored on NTFS drive volumes.

○ **D.** Shadow copies are enabled by default on the %systemdrive% volume.

○ **E.** You must store shadow copies on an NTFS drive volume other than the drive volume being shadowed.

○ **F.** You can schedule shadow copies to occur automatically, and you can create them manually.

15. How can you set disk quotas on an NTFS drive letter for the Remote Desktop Users group and for the Administrators group? (Choose the best answer.)

○ **A.** Right-click the drive letter in My Computer, select Properties, click the Quota tab, and mark the check boxes for Enable Quota Management and Deny Disk Space to Users Exceeding Quota Limit. Click Apply and click the Quota Entries button. Configure quota entries for the Remote Desktop Users group and for the Administrators group.

○ **B.** Right-click the drive letter in My Computer, select Properties, click the Quota tab, and mark the check boxes for Enable Quota Management and Deny Disk Space to Users Exceeding Quota Limit. Click Apply and click the Quota Entries button. Configure quota entries for the Remote Desktop Users group.

○ **C.** Right-click the drive letter in My Computer, select Properties, click the Quota tab, and mark the check boxes for Enable Quota Management and Deny Disk Space to Users Exceeding Quota Limit. Click Apply and click the Quota Entries button. Configure quota entries for each member of the Remote Desktop Users group.

○ **D.** Create a new local group named Super Users and make all the members of the Power Users group and the Administrators group members of this new group. Right-click the drive letter in My Computer, select Properties, click the Quota tab, and mark the check boxes for Enable Quota Management and Deny Disk Space to Users Exceeding Quota Limit. Click Apply and click the Quota Entries button. Configure quota entries for the Super Users group.

16. Brandy wants to move an NTFS-compressed file from NTFS drive D: to an uncompressed folder on NTFS drive F:. What will happen to the file when she performs this operation? (Choose the best answer.)

○ **A.** The compressed file will become uncompressed when it is moved to drive F:.

○ **B.** The compressed file will remain compressed when it is moved to drive F:.

○ **C.** Windows Server 2003 will prompt the user whether the file should remain compressed or should be uncompressed after it is moved.

○ **D.** Brandy will receive an error message when she attempts to move the file to an uncompressed folder.

17. Nicole encrypts an NTFS folder named SECRET DOCS on the hard drive of a Windows Server 2008 computer. Nicole is the only user with access to all the encrypted files in the SECRET DOCS folder (except for the DRA). Nicole shares the computer with her associate, Aaron. Aaron is not the DRA. Later, Aaron logs on to the same computer and attempts to copy one of the files stored inside of the SECRET DOCS folder, named Salaries.xls, to a floppy disk in drive A. After that, Aaron tries to move the same file to an unencrypted folder on the same NTFS drive volume named PUBLIC DOCS. What are the results of Aaron's file operations? (Choose the best answer.)

○ **A.** Aaron will receive an error message for trying to copy the encrypted file to a floppy disk, but he will be able to move the encrypted file to the PUBLIC DOCS unencrypted NTFS folder, where the file will remain encrypted.

○ **B.** Aaron will receive an error message for trying to copy the encrypted file to a floppy disk, and he will also receive an error message for attempting to move the encrypted file to the PUBLIC DOCS unencrypted NTFS folder.

○ **C.** Aaron will receive an error message for trying to copy the encrypted file to a floppy disk, but he will successfully move the encrypted file to the PUBLIC DOCS unencrypted NTFS folder, where it will lose its encryption attribute.

○ **D.** Aaron will successfully copy the encrypted file to a floppy disk, where it will remain encrypted, and he will successfully move the encrypted file to the PUBLIC DOCS unencrypted NTFS folder.

18. As a network administrator for her company, Alexis wants to create scripts that will automate the process of encrypting and decrypting files using the Encrypting File System (EFS). She may create `.bat` files for the scripts or she may use program scripts for use with the Windows Script Host (WSH). Which of the following commands can she use in a script file to encrypt and decrypt files? (Choose the best answer.)

- ○ **A.** `attrib.exe`
- ○ **B.** `cisvc.exe`
- ○ **C.** `cipher.exe`
- ○ **D.** `convert.exe`
- ○ **E.** `change.exe`
- ○ **F.** `compact.exe`

19. As a network administrator for his company, Brendan needs to set up Shadow Copies of Shared Folders on the D: drive of a newly installed Windows Server 2003 file server for the Sales division. Corporate management requires that the server must store at least two weeks' worth of previous versions of files. The managers of the Sales division want to maximize the number of shadow copies available on a daily basis. Given these constraints, how many times a day should Brendan schedule Shadow Copies to be created, assuming a five-day work week? (Choose the best answer.)

- ○ **A.** Eight times per day
- ○ **B.** Six times per day
- ○ **C.** Four times per day
- ○ **D.** Seven times per day
- ○ **E.** Five times per day
- ○ **F.** Eight days a week

20. Which of the following features are only supported by the NTFS file system? (Choose the best three answers.)

- ○ **A.** Shadow Copies of Shared Folders
- ○ **B.** Compressed (Zipped) Folders
- ○ **C.** Encrypting File System (EFS)
- ○ **D.** Disk quotas
- ○ **E.** Drive letter onto which you copy the previous version of a file
- ○ **F.** USB Storage Devices

21. Alison is an employee for XYZ Corporation in the Marketing department. Alison has been working on a very important Microsoft Excel worksheet that needs to be kept confidential. She encrypts the worksheet using EFS and she stores it in T:\data\alison. Her co-worker, Dan, notices the worksheet and tries to open the file to read it.

    Dan and Alison are both members of the same security groups, so both users have the same NTFS access permissions to the Excel file. Neither Alison nor Dan has administrator-level permissions. When Dan tries to open the file, Excel opens but the contents of the worksheet do not display because the file has been encrypted by Alison. Because Dan cannot read the file, he attempts to move the file to a folder named "Dan's Stuff" on the T: drive. The "Dan's Stuff" folder is not encrypted under EFS. What happens when Dan tries to move this file? (Choose the best answer.)

    ○ **A.** The file is moved and remains encrypted.

    ○ **B.** Dan receives an Access Is Denied error message.

    ○ **C.** The file is moved and becomes unencrypted.

    ○ **D.** The file is copied to T:\Dan's Stuff and remains encrypted.

22. You have a Windows Server 2008 computer configured as a domain controller. How would you back up Active Directory?

    ○ **A.** Back up the System State data.

    ○ **B.** Back up C:\windows\ntds.

    ○ **C.** Back up C:\windows\sysvol.

    ○ **D.** Back up C:\.

Answers to Exam Prep Questions

1. B, E, and F are correct. Default hidden shares include ADMIN$, IPC$, and the root of each available drive letter, such as C$. Answer A is incorrect because although SYSVOL is a default administrative share, it is not hidden. Answer C is incorrect because there is no default share named D$ for a CD drive. Answer D is incorrect because there is no default share named PRINTER$, but there is a default hidden share named PRINT$.

2. D is correct. By clicking the Customize button from the permissions window, you can specify both share permissions and NTFS permissions when you create a new share using the Share a Folder Wizard from the Shared Folders snap-in. Answer A is incorrect because the Shared Folder's snap-in and the Sharing tab of a folderallow you to set share permissions. Answer B is incorrect because publishing a share in Active Directory is not a permissions setting. Answer C is incorrect because the Shared Folder's snap-in

and the Sharing tab of a folder allow you to specify offline settings. Answer E is incorrect because you can set Web Sharing access permissions only from the Web Sharing tab of a folder's properties sheet.

3. Answer D is correct. The most restrictive permissions always override any other permissions, whether they are share permissions or NTFS permissions. Answer A is incorrect because NTFS permissions do not take precedence over share permissions unless they are the most restrictive. Answer B is incorrect because share permissions do not take precedence over NTFS permissions unless they are the most restrictive. Answer C is incorrect because the most restrictive permissions always override more liberal permissions.

4. A, B, and D are correct. Special permissions get inherited by child objects, basic permissions get inherited by child objects, and NTFS permissions (in general) all get inherited by default. Answer C is incorrect because explicit permissions are set by users; inherited permissions are set by parent containers. Answer E is incorrect because even explicit permissions set on parent containers (folders) are inherited by child objects (subfolders and files) by default. Answer F is incorrect because you can set explicit permissions on any object or container.

5. A, B, and F are correct. When set on a folder, the Modify Basic NTFS permission consists of the List Folder/Read Data, Create Files/Write Data, and Write Extended Attributes special permissions, among several others. Answer C is incorrect because the Change Permissions special permissions setting is not part of the Modify permission. Answer D is incorrect because the Delete Subfolders and Files special permission is not part of the Modify permission; however, the Delete special permission is included. Answer E is incorrect because the Take Ownership special permission is not part of the Modify permission.

6. Answer B is correct. NTFS special permissions appear in the Effective Permissions dialog box. Answer A is incorrect because basic permissions do not appear in the Effective Permissions dialog box. Answer C is incorrect because share permissions do not appear in the Effective Permissions dialog box. Answer D is incorrect because both inherited and explicit NTFS permissions appear in the Effective Permissions dialog box.

7. Answers B, C, and D are correct. A user who is the current owner of an object can assign the Take Ownership permission to another user, a member of the Administrators group can assign ownership, and any user who is assigned the Restore Files and Directories right can transfer ownership to another user. Answer A is incorrect because members of the Domain Users group cannot assign the Take Ownership permission to another user for an object. Answer E is incorrect because members of the Backup Operators group cannot take ownership of files or folders at any time. Answer F is incorrect because members of the Authenticated Users group cannot assign ownership of files to other users at any time.

8. Answer B is correct. When combining NTFS permissions on users and groups, you have to look at the least restrictive. In this case, Group2 has the least restrictive NTFS permission, which is the Allow Modify permission.

9. Answer D is correct. When combining NTFS permissions on users and groups, you have to look at the least restrictive. However, Deny permissions always take higher precedence. Therefore, because Group1 has Deny Full Control NTFS permission, User1 has no access because the user has been denied Full Control, including all permissions. Therefore, answers A, B and C are incorrect.

10. Answer D is correct. By default, Everyone is assigned the Read share permission. So for the users to be able to make changes, you have to assign the Change share permission to Group1. In addition, by default, Everyone has Read and Execute NTFS permission to the root of each drive. These permissions are not inherited by folder or file. Therefore, you also have to assign the Allow Modify NTFS permissions to Group1. therefore, answers A, B and C are incorrect.

11. Answer A is correct. To be able to make changes to the files, Joe needs the Read and Write (or Full Control) NTFS permission and the Change (or Full Control) Share permission. One way would be to add Joe to the Marketing group, but this is not one of the options. Of the options shown, you would assign Joe to the Sales group. This gives the Change Share permission, but not the NTFS permission. Therefore, you would also have to add the Write NTFS permission for the Sales group. Therefore, answers B, C and D are incorrect.

12. Answer A is correct. Folders and files and their NTFS permissions are managed by Windows Explorer. Answer B is incorrect because the Active Directory Users and Computers console is used to manage the user and computer accounts within Active Directory, not NTFS permissions. Answer C is incorrect because the Computer Management console, which includes the Disk Administrator console, can be used to look at the event viewer and the status of the disks and to manage the file system volumes, but has nothing to do with NTFS permissions. Answer D is incorrect because the Disk Administrator has nothing to do with NTFS permissions.

13. Answer A is correct. When you access a computer remotely through the share, you include the share permissions and the NTFS permissions, which can both restrict access. When you access the local folder directly, only the NTFS permissions apply. Therefore, you could have the same or more restrictive access if both are applied. Answers B and C are incorrect because if the user is accessing the folder remotely, share permissions may impose further restrictions. Answer D is incorrect because the share and NTFS permissions combined may also give the same access rather than just more restrictive access.

14. Answers B, C, and F are correct. You must store shadow copies on NTFS drive volumes, you can only make shadow copies from files stored on NTFS drive volumes, and you can schedule shadow copies to run automatically and create them manually. Answer A is incorrect because previous versions of files stored as shadow copies can be retrieved only under Windows XP, Windows Vista, Windows Server 2003, and Windows Server 2008 with the Previous Versions Client software installed. Answer D is incorrect because shadow copies are not enabled by default for any drive volume. Answer E is incorrect because you can store shadow copies on any available NTFS drive volume, including the drive volume being shadowed.

15. Answer C is correct. Windows Server 2008 supports disk quotas on NTFS drive volumes only for individual users, not for groups. Therefore, you would have to create a quota entry for each member of the Remote Desktop Users group—you cannot assign a quota limit to a group. All members of the Administrators group inherit a no-limit disk quota by default, so you cannot set quotas on members of this group. Answer A is incorrect for the reasons just cited. Answer B is incorrect because you cannot set quotas on groups. Answer D is incorrect for the same reason.

16. Answer A is correct. When you move a compressed file from one NTFS volume to a different NTFS volume, the file inherits the compression attribute from the target location. Answer B is incorrect because an NTFS compressed folder or file retains its compression attribute only when it is moved to another folder on the same NTFS volume. Answer C is incorrect because Windows Server 2008 never prompts the user as to whether a folder or file should remain compressed or uncompressed. Answer D is incorrect because Windows Server 2008 does not generate error messages for moving compressed files to an uncompressed folder.

17. Answer A is correct. Only the user who originally encrypted the file (or any users given shared access to the encrypted file) may copy the file to a non-NTFS drive volume or to any type of removable media. In addition, only the user who originally encrypted the file (or any users given shared access to the encrypted file) may copy the file or move it to a folder located on a different NTFS volume. A user without shared access to an encrypted file is permitted to move the file only to another folder located on the same NTFS volume, where the file remains encrypted. Answer B is incorrect because although Aaron will receive an error message when he attempts to copy the file to a floppy disk, he will not receive an error message when he attempts to move the encrypted file to an unencrypted NTFS folder located on the same NTFS volume. Answer C is incorrect because although Aaron will receive an error message when he attempts to copy the file to a floppy disk, he will be allowed to move the encrypted file to an unencrypted NTFS folder located on the same NTFS volume, but the file will not lose its encryption attribute. Answer D is incorrect because Aaron will receive an error message when he attempts to copy the encrypted file to a floppy disk.

18. Answer C is correct. The `cipher.exe` command enables you to encrypt and decrypt files from the command line for EFS. Answer A is incorrect because the `attrib.exe` command does not provide encryption or decryption features. Answer B is incorrect because `cisvc.exe` is used for the Content Index Service, not for EFS. Answer D is incorrect because the `convert.exe` command is used for converting a FAT or FAT32 partition or volume into an NTFS partition or volume. Answer E is incorrect because the `change.exe` command is used for terminal services only. Answer F is incorrect because the `compact.exe` tool is a command-line utility used to compress and uncompress files and folders stored on NTFS drive letters.

19. Answer B is correct. Because the maximum number of shadow copy snapshots that can be stored by a Windows Server 2003 computer is 64, six times a day is the best

answer. Six shadow copies multiplied by 10 work days (5 days per week multiplied by 2 weeks) equals 60 shadow copies—just beneath the maximum threshold of 64. Answer A is incorrect because if Brendan were to schedule eight shadow copies per day, 8 multiplied by 10 work days equals 80 shadow copies. Because the maximum number of stored shadow copies is 64, the oldest shadow copies would be overwritten during each previous two-week period and this would not provide for a full two weeks' worth of previous versions of data files. Answer C is incorrect because although 4 multiplied by 10 work days is less than the maximum of 64 shadow copies stored within a two week period, this schedule does not maximize the number of shadow copies that can be stored on a daily basis. Answer D is incorrect because if Brendan were to schedule seven shadow copies per day, 7 multiplied by 10 work days equals 70 shadow copies. Because the maximum number of stored shadow copies is 64, the oldest shadow copies would be overwritten during each previous two-week period and this would not provide for a full two weeks' worth of previous versions of data files. Answer E is incorrect because although 5 multiplied by 10 work days is less than the maximum of 64 shadow copies stored within a two-week period, this schedule does not maximize the number of shadow copies that can be stored on a daily basis. Answer F is incorrect because it is the title of a song by the Beatles—a joke answer.

20. Answers A, C, and D are correct. Shadow Copies of Shared Folders can be created only on NTFS drive letters; you can use EFS only on NTFS-formatted drive letters; and disk quotas are available only on NTFS partitions and volumes. Answer B is incorrect because Compressed (Zipped) Folders are supported under the FAT, FAT32, and NTFS file systems. Answer E is incorrect because you can copy the previous version of a file or folder onto a drive letter formatted as FAT, FAT32, or NTFS. Answer F is incorrect because USB storage devices can be formatted as FAT, FAT32, or NTFS.

21. Answer A is correct. Users who have the proper NTFS security permissions can move an EFS-encrypted file from one folder to another as long as the folder resides on the same NTFS partition or volume. Answer B is incorrect for the same reason as Answer A—Dan would have received an Access Is Denied error message if he had tried to copy the file. Answer C is incorrect because even though the file may be moved, it cannot be unencrypted when a user who does not have shared access to the encrypted file simply moves it to another location. Answer D is incorrect because the question stipulates that the file was moved, not copied, and an attempt to copy the file would result in an Access Is Denied error message.

22. Answer A is correct. To back up Active Directory, you need to back up the System State. Answers B and C are incorrect because much of the system data is inaccessible by normal means, including doing a normal file backup. Answer D is incorrect because if you backup the root of the C drive (C:\) it would back up all files and folders on the C drive, but it would not back up many of the system files that make up the system state.

Need to Know More?

For more information about File Services, visit the following:

▶ http://technet2.microsoft.com/windowsserver2008/en/servermanager/
  fileservices.mspx

For articles on NTFS and Shared Permissions, see the following:

▶ http://technet.microsoft.com/en-us/magazine/cc160775(TechNet.10).aspx

▶ http://technet.microsoft.com/en-us/magazine/cc161041(TechNet.10).aspx

For an overview of backup and recovery, including backup and recovery techniques, shadow copies of shared folders, Windows Server backups, and Windows Recovery environment, visit the following:

▶ http://technet2.microsoft.com/windowsserver2008/en/library/12d477a8-
  36db-4c26-aa9f-e85499545b5b1033.mspx?mfr=true

For more information about BitLocker Drive Encryption, see the following:

▶ http://technet.microsoft.com/en-us/windows/aa905065.aspx

CHAPTER EIGHT

Print Services

Terms you'll need to understand:

✓ Print device

✓ Printer

✓ Spooler

✓ Print driver

✓ Local printer

✓ Network printer

✓ Print queue

✓ Print spooler

✓ Print priority

✓ Print scheduling

✓ Printer pool

Techniques/concepts you'll need to master:

✓ Understanding the print process on Windows Server 2008 computers

✓ Installing local and network printers on the server

✓ Sharing printers on a Windows Server 2008 computer

✓ Configuring the properties of a printer on a Windows Server 2008 computer

✓ Implementing printer permissions

✓ Restarting the print service

✓ Changing the location of the spool file

✓ Changing the priority of printers and print jobs

✓ Creating a printer pool

✓ Managing print jobs

✓ Redirecting print jobs

✓ Enabling and analyzing the printer logs

✓ Monitoring print queue performance

✓ Troubleshooting common printer problems

Users in a home environment mostly print to a local printer directly attached to their home computer. In a business environment, client computers often print to a centralized print server that forwards the print jobs to a print device. Network printing or print sharing allows several people to send documents to a centrally located printer or similar device in an office so that you do not have to connect expensive printers to every single computer in the office. By using a print server, the network administrator can centrally manage all printers and print devices.

Printer Terminology

Microsoft defines the following terms as follows:

- **Print device (physical printer)**: The physical *print device*, such as a printer, copy machine, or plotter.

- **Printer (logical printer)**: The *printer* is the software interface between a print device and the print clients or applications. It is a logical representation of a printer device in Windows that has an assigned printer name and software that controls a printer device. When you print to the printer device, you print to the printer, which then prints to the printer device.

- **Spooler**: Often referred to as a *print queue*, the *spooler* accepts each document being printed, stores it, and sends it to the printer device when the printer device is ready.

- **Print driver**: The *print driver* is a program designed to enable other programs to work with a particular printer without concerning themselves with the specifics of the printer's hardware and internal language.

EXAM ALERT

Make sure you understand the difference between a printer and a print device. A printer is the logical representation and the printer device is the physical representation.

You can connect a print device (printer, plotter, copy machine, or similar device) to your Windows Server 2008 computer using a parallel (LPT) port, Universal Serial Bus (USB), or infrared (IR), similar to what you would do on a Windows XP computer. You can then print to the printer when running applications on the Windows Server 2008 computer, or you can share the printer so that other users and network applications can print to the printer over the network using Internet Protocol (IP), IPX, or AppleTalk. You can also connect the printer directly to the network by using a network interface card (such as an HP JetDirect card or similar technology) and use IP, IPX, or AppleTalk to communicate with the network device.

Local Versus Network Printing

As an administrator, you can install two types of printers: a local or a network printer. Both types of printers must be created before they can be shared for others to use. Table 8.1 lists the advantages and disadvantages of printing to a *local printer* and printing to a *network printer*.

TABLE 8.1   Comparing Local and Network Printers

	Local Printer	Network Printer
Advantages	The print device is usually in close proximity to the user's computer.	Many users can access print devices.
	Plug and Play can detect local printers and automatically install drivers.	Network printers support distributing updated printer drivers to multiple clients.
		The print server manages the printer driver settings.
		A single print queue appears on every computer connected to the printer, enabling each user to see the status of all pending print jobs, including their own jobs.
		All users can see the state of the printer.
		Some processing is passed from the client computer to the print server.
		You can generate a single log for administrators who want to audit the printer events.
		Network printers are easy to deploy centrally and manage.

continues

TABLE 8.1 *Continued*

	Local Printer	Network Printer
Disadvantages	A print device is needed for every computer.	The print device might not be physically close to the user.
	Drivers must be manually installed for every local printer.	Security is physically limited on the print device.
	A local printer takes more processing to print.	
	Having many local printers adds a lot of administrative overhead.	

NOTE

Whether you choose to print locally or on a network, make sure that your system has sufficient memory and free disk space to handle your print jobs.

When you print to a local or network printer, you must have a print driver that is compatible with the print device to which you are printing. The print driver is software used by computer programs to communicate with a specific printer or plotter, which translates the print jobs from a certain platform to information that the printer understands. The print driver also helps define the capabilities of the printer to the system.

NOTE

A computer running Microsoft Windows XP Professional and Windows Vista can also function as a print server. However, it cannot support Macintosh or NetWare services, and it is limited to only 10 network connections.

As with any driver that you load on a Windows system, it is strongly recommended that you use only device drivers with the Designed for Microsoft Windows Vista or Designed for Microsoft Windows 2008 Server logos. Installing device drivers that are not digitally signed by Microsoft might disable or impair the operation of the computer or allow viruses onto your computer.

EXAM ALERT

Whenever possible, you should use digitally signed device drivers. Having a digitally signed device driver means that the driver has been tested, verified, and signed by Microsoft so that it is safe for your computer.

Printing Process

When users print a document, most know only to click the print icon or select Print from the File menu and go grab their document from the printer. Of course, a lot happens in the background that gets the document out of the printer.

The following briefly describes the printer process:

1. If a printer is connected directly to its computer, you must load the appropriate driver so that it knows what commands to send to the printer. If a client computer connects to a printer, the print server downloads a print driver to the client computer automatically.

2. When users print from an application such as Microsoft Word, they select the Print option or button and a print job is created. The application calls up the graphical device interface (GDI), which calls the printer driver associated with the target print device. The GDI renders the print job in the printer language of the print device, such as HP's Printer Control Language or Adobe's Postscript, to create an enhanced metafile (EMF). The application then calls the client side of the spooler (Winspool.drv).

3. After it has been formatted, the print job is sent to the local spooler, which provides background printing. The print job is then forwarded based on if the print device is local or on the network:

   ▶ If the print job is being sent to the local print device, the print device saves it to the local hard drive's spool file. When the printer is available, it will print on the local print device.

   ▶ If the local spooler determines that the job is for a network print device, it sends the job to the print server's spooler. If the local printer is being sent to a shared printer (\\server\printer), the print job goes to the server message block (SMB) redirector on the client. UNIX or other line printer remote (LPR) clients can print to the Windows Serve 2008 line printer daemon (LPD) service. The print server's spooler saves it to the print server's hard drive spool file. When the network print device becomes available, it prints on the network print device.

The *print spooler* (`spoolsv.exe`) manages the printing process, which locates the correct print driver, loads the driver, spools (queues) the print job, and schedules the print job.

Installing a Printer on Windows Server 2008

If you have the correct permissions to add a local printer or a remote shared printer, use the Add Printer Wizard. The users that have the correct permission are defined by the following:

▶ On domain controllers, members of the Administrators and Print Operators groups can install local printers.

▶ On member servers, members of the Administrators and the local Print Operators groups can install local printers.

▶ On Windows XP Professional or Windows Vista, only Administrators can install local printers.

▶ Any authenticated user can connect and submit print jobs to a remote shared printer, assuming that the user has the proper printer permissions.

In a small workgroup that has only a few computers, each computer most likely connects to a local printer, a printer connected directly to the computer, or a printer connected directly to the network. They do not use a print server. All users on the network add the printer to their Printer and Faxes folders without sharing the printer and configure their own driver settings. Unfortunately, connecting to a local printer has the following disadvantages:

▶ Users do not know the actual state of the printer, including errors such as paper jams or empty paper trays.

▶ Users can view only their own print queue, which displays their own print jobs.

▶ All the processing of the document being printed is done on that one computer.

Installing Local Printer

To add a local printer to a Windows Server 2008 computer,

1. Click Start and open the Control Panel.

2. Under Hardware and Sound, click Printer.

3. To start the Add Printer Wizard, click Add a printer.

4. Select Add a Local Printer (see Figure 8.1).

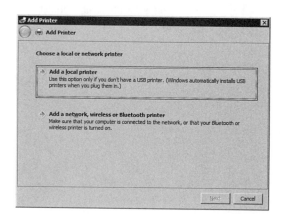

FIGURE 8.1 Choosing between local and network printing.

5. When the Add Printer dialog box appears (see Figure 8.2), you specify to which port the printer is connected. If the port already exists, such as an LPT1 or a network port specified by an IP address, select the port from the Use an Existing Port drop-down list. If the port does not exist, click Create a New Port, select Standard TCP/IP Port and click Next. For the device type, you can select Auto Detect, TCP/IP Device, or Web Services Device. Then specify the IP address or DNS name of the printer and the Port Name. If you type the address in the Hostname or IP Address box, the IP address is populated in the port name (see Figure 8.3). Windows then tries to communicate with the printer, using the address you specified.

NOTE

The TCP/IP printer port uses TCP port 9100 to communicate.

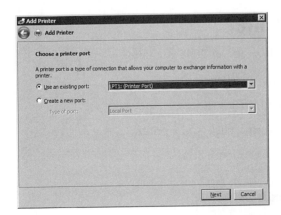

FIGURE 8.2 Choosing a printer port.

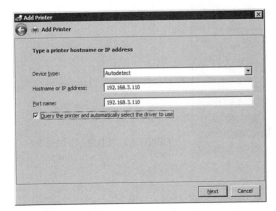

FIGURE 8.3 Creating a TCP/IP device port.

6. If Plug and Play does not detect and install the correct printer automatically, you are asked to specify the printer driver (printer manufacturer and printer model). If the printer is not listed, you have to use the Have Disk option (see Figure 8.4).

7. When the Type a Printer Name dialog box appears, specify the name of the printer. If you want this to be the default printer for the system on which you are installing the printer, select the Set as the Default Printer option. Click Next.

8. On the Printer Sharing dialog box, specify the share name. You can also specify the Location or Comments. Although Windows Server 2008 supports long printer names and share names including spaces and special characters, it is best to keep names short, simple, and descriptive. The entire qualified name, including the server name (for example, \\Server1\HP4100N-1), should be 32 characters or fewer.

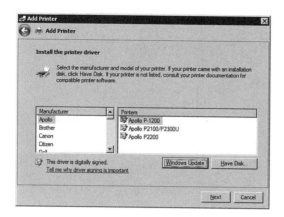

FIGURE 8.4 Installing the printer driver.

9. When the printer has been successfully added, you can print the standard Windows test page by clicking the Print a Test Page button. Click Finish.

Installing a Network Printer

To add a network printer to a Windows Server 2008, follow these steps:

1. Click Start and open the Control Panel.

2. Under Hardware and Sound, click Printer.

3. To start the Add Printer Wizard, click Add a Printer.

4. Select Add a Network, Wireless, or Bluetooth printer.

5. If the printer is not automatically found, click the The Printer That I Want Isn't Listed option.

6. If you have a printer published in Active Directory, you would choose Find a Printer in the Directory, Based on Location or Feature. If you know the UNC, select the Select a Shared Printer by Name option. If you know the TCP/IP address, choose the last option. Click Next (see Figure 8.5).

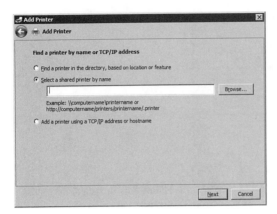

FIGURE 8.5 Specifying the location of the network printer.

7. In the Type a Printer Name dialog box, specify the printer name. If you want this to be the default printer for the system you are installing, select the Set as the Default Printer option. Click Next.

8. When the printer is successfully added, you can print the standard Windows test page by clicking the Print a Test Page button. Click Finish.

Deploying Printer Connections

To deploy printer connections to users or computers by using Group Policy, use the Deploy with Group Policy dialog box in Print Management. This adds the printer connections to a Group Policy Object (GPO). To deploy printers to users or computers by using Group Policy, follow these steps:

1. Open the Administrative Tools folder and double-click Print Management.

2. In the Print Management tree, under the appropriate print server, click Printers.

3. In the Results pane, right-click the printer that you want to deploy and click Deploy with Group Policy.

4. In the Deploy with Group Policy dialog box, click Browse and then choose or create a new GPO for storing the printer connections.

5. Click OK.

6. Specify whether to deploy the printer connections to users or to computers:

> ▶ To deploy to groups of computers so that all users of the computers can access the printers, select the The Computers That This GPO Applies To (Per Machine) check box.

> ▶ To deploy to groups of users so that the users can access the printers from any computer they log on to, select the The Users That This GPO Applies To (Per User) check box.

7. Click Add.

8. Repeat steps 3 through 6 to add the printer connection setting to another GPO, if necessary.

9. Click OK.

Listing printers in Active Directory Domain Services (AD DS) makes it easier for users to locate and install printers. After you install printers on a printer server, you can use Print Management to list them in AD DS.

Listing Printers in Active Directory

To make printers easier to find, you can publish them in Active Directory. To list or remove printers in Active Directory, follow these steps:

1. Open the Administrative Tools folder and double-click Print Management.

2. In the Print Management tree, under the appropriate print server, click Printers.

3. In the Results pane, right-click the printer that you want to list or remove and then click List in Directory or Remove from Directory.

Migrating Print Servers

You can use the Printer Migration Wizard or the `Printbrm.exe` command-line tool to export print queues, printer settings, printer ports, and language monitors, and then import them on another print server running a Windows operating system. This is an efficient way to consolidate multiple print servers or replace an older print server.

NOTE

The Printer Migration Wizard and the `Printbrm.exe` command-line tool were introduced in Windows Vista. They replace Print Migrator 3.1.

To migrate print servers by using Print Management, follow these steps:

1. Open the Administrative Tools folder and click Print Management.

2. In the Print Management tree, right-click the name of the computer that contains the printer queues that you want to export and then click Export Printers to a File. This launches the Printer Migration Wizard.

3. On the Select the File Location page, specify the location where you want to save the printer settings and then click Next to save the printers.

4. Right-click the destination computer on which you want to import the printers and then click Import Printers from a File. This launches the Printer Migration Wizard.

5. On the Select the File Location page, specify the location of the printer settings file and then click Next.

6. On the Select Import Options page, specify the following import options:

   ▶ **Import Mode**: Specifies what to do if a specific print queue already exists on the destination computer.

   ▶ **List in the Directory**: Specifies whether to publish the imported print queues in the Active Directory Domain Services.

   ▶ **Convert LPR Ports to Standard Port Monitors**: Specifies whether to convert Line Printer Remote (LPR) printer ports in the printer settings file to the faster Standard Port Monitor when importing printers.

7. Click Next to import the printers.

To migrate print servers by using a command prompt, follow these steps:

1. To open a Command Prompt window, click Start > All Programs > Accessories. Right-click Command Prompt and then click Run as administrator.

2. To export the printer configuration, type the following commands:

```
CD %WINDIR%\System32\Spool\Tools
Printbrm -s \\<sourcecomputername> -b -f <filename>.printerExport
```

3. To import the printer configuration, type the following command:

```
Printbrm -s \\<destinationcomputername> -r -f
➥<filename>.printerExport
```

Use the Universal Naming Convention (UNC) for the *sourcecomputername* and *destinationcomputername*.

Printer Properties

After installing the logical printer, you can right-click the printer and select Properties to configure numerous settings. The following tabs enable you to configure the settings:

- ▶ The General tab enables you to configure the printer name, location, and comments and to print a test page.

- ▶ The Sharing tab enables you to share a printer. You can also publish the printer in Active Directory if you chose the List in the Directory option. Because the printer on a server can be used by other clients connected to the network, you can add additional drivers by clicking the Additional Drivers button. By default, Windows Server 2008 includes drivers for 32-bit clients (x86 drivers), 64-bit clients (x64), and Itanium PCs.

- ▶ The Ports tab enables you to specify which port (physical or TCP/IP port) the printer will use, as well as create new TCP/IP ports (see Figure 8.6).

- ▶ The Advanced tab enables you to configure the driver to use with the printer, the priority of the printer, when the printer is available and how print jobs are spooled.

- ▶ The Security tab enables you to specify the permissions for the printer.

- ▶ The Device Settings tab enables you to configure the trays, font substitution, and other hardware settings.

- ▶ If you click the Printing Preferences button on the General tab, you can choose the default paper size, paper tray, print quality/resolution, pages per sheet, print order (such as front to back or back to front), and number of copies. The options that are available vary depending on your printer.

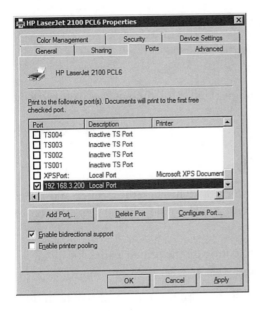

FIGURE 8.6 Configuring the printer ports.

Printer Permissions

To control who can use the printer and who can administer the print jobs and printers, use the Security tab to specify printer permissions for those who are not otherwise administrators (see Figure 8.7). Windows Server 2008 provides three levels of printer permissions:

- ▶ **Print**: Enables users to send documents to the printer.

- ▶ **Manage Printers**: Enables users to modify printer settings and configuration, including the ACL itself.

- ▶ **Manage Documents**: Provides the ability to cancel, pause, resume, or restart a print job.

By default, the Print permission is assigned to the Everyone group. If you need to restrict who can print to the printer, you need to remove the permission and assign Allow Print permission to other groups or individual users. Much like file permissions, you can deny print permissions.

The Creator Owner group is allowed Manage Documents permission. This means that when a user sends a print job to the printer, he can manage his own print job. Administrators, print operators, and server operators have the Manage Documents and the Manage Printers permission.

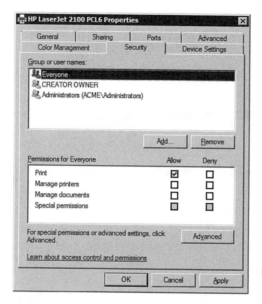

FIGURE 8.7 Printer permissions.

Internet Printing

Another way for a user to print to a printer is to connect to a printer using *Internet Print Protocol (IPP)*, which is transported by being encapsulated in Hypertext Transfer Protocol (HTTP) packets. To make the printer available via Internet Printing, you must install the TCP/IP Print Server role, which also installs Internet Information Services (IIS) web server with ASP.NET on the computer running Windows Server 2008.

> **EXAM ALERT**
>
> To print over the Internet using Internet Printing, you must install IIS with Internet Printing and enable Internet Printing in Web Service Extensions.

When you use Internet Printing, you can print or manage documents through a web browser, such as Internet Explorer 4.01 or later. You can then print over an intranet or the Internet by specifying the URL to the print server, such as http://server1/printers/ (see Figure 8.8).

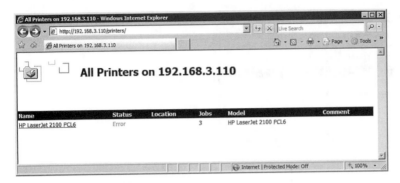

FIGURE 8.8 Managing the IPP printer.

When a user connects to the printer's web page, the server bundles the printer drivers and any other necessary files into a .cab file so that the files can be downloaded to the user's system. After the files are downloaded and installed, the printer is displayed in the Printers and Faxes folder.

To use Internet Printing from a client computer running Windows Server 2008, the Internet Printing Client optional feature must be installed. The Internet Printing Client is installed by default on Windows Vista, Windows XP, and Windows Server 2003.

To install the Internet Printing Client, use one of the following methods:

▸ **In Windows Vista**: In Control Panel, click Programs and Features, click Turn Windows Features On or Off, expand Print Services, select the Internet Printing Client check box, and then click OK.

▸ **In Windows Server 2008**: In Server Manager, click Add Features, select the Internet Printing Client check box, and then click OK.

Managing the Print Spooler

The *print spooler* is an executable file that manages the printing process, which includes retrieving the location of the correct print driver, loading the driver, creating the individual print jobs, and scheduling the print jobs for printing.

Typically, the print spooler is loaded during startup and continues to run until the operating system shuts down. You can restart the print spooler by following these steps:

1. Open the Services console located in Administrative Tools.

2. Right-click Print Spooler and select Restart (see Figure 8.9).

3. You can also stop the service, then start the service.

EXAM ALERT

If the print spooler becomes unresponsive or you have print jobs that you cannot delete, you should try to restart the Print Spooler service.

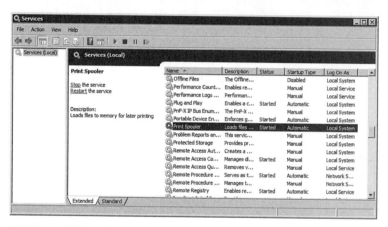

FIGURE 8.9 Print services in the Services console.

After the print jobs are created, they are stored as files on the hard drive. When the print device is available, the spooler retrieves the next print job and sends it to the print device. By default, the spool folder is located at %SystemRoot%\System32\Spool\Printers. So on most installations, this is the C:\Windows\System32\Spool\Printers folder. If the system drive becomes full, the server's performance might slow down dramatically, services and applications running on the server might degrade or not function at all, and the system can become unstable. Because the Print Spooler is on the same volume that holds the Windows system files, the administrator must ensure that spooling print jobs do not accidentally fill up the system volume.

If you have only a couple of printers with low traffic volumes, most likely the default location of the spool folder is sufficient. However, if you have a large number of printers or frequent large print jobs, you should move the spool folder to another location, preferably another volume that is on its own input/output (I/O) controller so that frequent disk reads and writes will not dramatically affect the overall performance of Windows. It is recommended that you use a RAID 1 or 5 volume.

> **NOTE**
>
> When you print a Word document or a PDF file, the actual print job sent to the printer is many times larger than the original Word or PDF file itself.

To change the location of the spool folder, follow these steps:

1. Click Start and open the Control Panel.

2. Under Hardware and Sound, click Printer.

3. Open the File menu and select Server Properties.

4. Select the Advanced tab.

5. Specify the full local drive letter and path of the new spool folder in the Spool Folder text box (see Figure 8.10).

6. Click OK to save the new settings.

7. Stop the Spooler service and then restart it for the changes to take effect.

> **NOTE**
>
> If you move the location of the spool folder while print jobs are waiting in the queue, those print jobs do not print. Therefore, it is recommended that you wait for documents in the queue to complete before moving the spool folder.

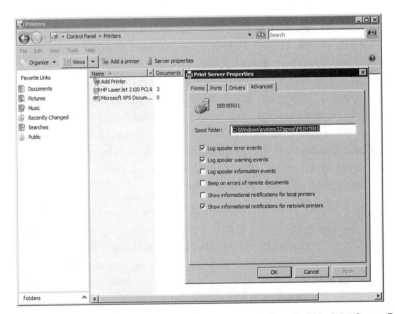

FIGURE 8.10 Specifying the location of the spool folder found within Print Server Properties.

Printers, Print Devices, and Printer Pools

When a user prints something, the user prints to a printer (logical representation), which then sends the print job to the print device (physical representation) after spooling. You can configure several printers to point to a single print device, or you can have a printer print to several print devices, known as a *printer pool*.

Priorities and Scheduling

By having multiple printers print to a single print device, you can configure a high print priority for one printer and a low print priority for the other printer. The print jobs sent to the printer with the high priority print before the printer with the lower priority, even though they are printing to the same print device. The priorities range from 1 to 99. To give some users preference when printing, you can assign those users to one printer that is assigned high priority and other users to another printer with low priority. You use permission to control who can print to which printer.

NOTE

When a printer with a higher priority receives a print job, it does not stop processing a job on which it is already working.

Follow these steps to set printer priorities:

1. Click Start and open the Control Panel.

2. Under Hardware and Sound, click Printer.

3. Right-click the printer and select Properties.

4. Select the Advanced tab.

5. Specify the priority (1–99): the higher the number, the higher the job (see Figure 8.11).

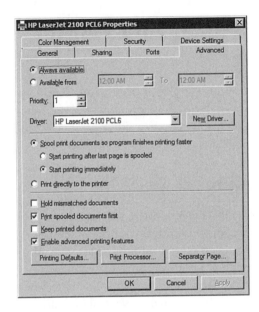

FIGURE 8.11 The Advanced tab showing printer priority.

Most printers are configured to print immediately when receiving the print job. In some situations, you might choose to print during certain times (print scheduling), such as at night or when the printer is not being used as much. By configuring a printer's schedule at night, print jobs created during the day are stored in the print queue until night. The jobs print during the night, and the user can pick them up in the morning. Of course, this is assuming that you did not run out of paper during the night.

To configure a printer to print to a printer device at certain times,

1. Click Start and open the Control Panel.

2. Under Hardware and Sound, click Printer.

3. Right-click the printer and select Properties.

4. Select the Advanced tab.

5. Select the Available From option and specify the time that the printer is to print.

By default, when the print job reaches the spool folder, it immediately starts feeding into the printer. You can configure the print jobs to be spooled entirely in the print queue before being sent to the print device. This comes in handy if you have large print jobs that delay the print device as it waits for the print job being processed on the print queue, minimizing the impact large print jobs have on the performance of the printer. You can do this by going into the Printer properties and selecting the Advanced tab. You can then use the default Start Printing Immediately option, or you can choose the Start Printing After Last Page Is Spooled option.

Printer Pools

A printer pool associates two or more identical print devices to the same printer. Although this allows for redundancy, it is mostly intended for when you have a high volume of printing that can be evenly distributed between print devices. When a document is sent to the printer pool, the first available printer receives the job and prints it. If one device within a pool stops printing, the current document is still held at that device. Print jobs arriving later are sent to the other print devices.

Although printers can use different ports (parallel, serial, and network), all printers in the pool should be the same model. In addition, it is recommended to have all print devices in the same location so that users don't have to run around the office trying to find their print jobs. Windows Server 2008 places no limit on the number of printers in a pool.

To set up such a pool, first use the Add Printer Wizard and assign the logical printer as many output ports as there are identical printers. Then when you go into the properties of the printer, select the Ports tab and select Enable Printer Pooling. Last, check the various ports that point to the different print devices that you want to include in the printer pool (see Figure 8.12).

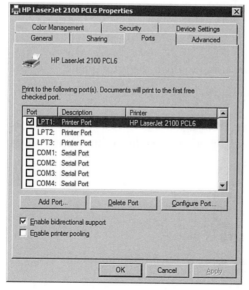

FIGURE 8.12 Creating a printer pool.

Managing Print Jobs

As a user or an administrator, at times you might need to manage individual print jobs or documents. To view documents waiting to print,

1. Click Start and open the Control Panel.

2. Under Hardware and Sound, click Printer.

3. Double-click the printers on which you want to view the print jobs waiting to print.

The print queue shows information about a document such as print status, owner, and number of pages to be printed. From the print queue, you can cancel or pause the printing of a document that you have sent to the printer. You also can open the print queue for the printer on which you are printing by double-clicking the small printer icon in the status area on the taskbar.

To pause a document,

1. Click Start and open the Control Panel.

2. Under Hardware and Sound, click Printer.

3. Double-click the printer you are using to open the print queue.

4. Right-click the document you want to pause and select the Pause option.

By default, all users can pause, resume, restart, and cancel their own documents. To manage documents that are printed by other users, however, you must have the Manage Documents permissions.

To cancel a print job,

1. Click Start and open the Control Panel.

2. Under Hardware and Sound, click Printer.

3. Double-click the printer you are using to open the print queue.

4. Right-click the document that you want to stop printing and select Cancel. You can cancel the printing of more than one document by holding down the Ctrl key and clicking each document that you want to cancel.

To change the printing priority of documents waiting to print within a print queue, follow these steps:

1. Click Start and open the Control Panel.

2. Under Hardware and Sound, click Printer.

3. Double-click the printer you are using to open the print queue.

4. Right-click the document that you want to move in the print order and click the Properties option.

5. Under the General tab, drag the Priority slider to raise or lower the document priority.

After a document has started printing, any printing priority change you make does not affect the document.

Line Printer Daemon (LPD) Service

The *Line Printer Daemon (LPD) Service* installs and starts the TCP/IP Print Server (LPDSVC) service, which enables UNIX-based computers or other computers that are using the Line Printer Remote (LPR) service to print to shared printers on this server. It also creates an inbound exception for port 515 in Windows Firewall with Advanced Security.

No configuration is necessary for this service. However, if you stop or restart the Print Spooler service, the TCP/IP Print Server service is also stopped, and it is not automatically restarted.

To use a computer that is running Windows Vista or Windows Server 2008 to print to a printer or print server that uses the LPD protocol, you can use the Network Printer Installation wizard and a Standard TCP/IP printer port. However you must install the Line Printer Remote (LPR) Port Monitor feature to print to a UNIX print server. Use one of the following methods:

▶ **In Windows Vista**: In Control Panel, click Programs and Features, click Turn Windows Features On or Off, expand Print Services, select the LPR Port Monitor check box, and then click OK.

▶ **In Windows Server 2008**: in Server Manager, click Add Features, select the LPR Port Monitor check box, and then click OK.

Redirecting Print Jobs

If a printer fails before printing and cannot be repaired quickly, you might want to transfer the documents to another printer:

1. Click Start and open the Control Panel.

2. Under Hardware and Sound, click Printer.

3. Double-click the printer that holds the document(s) that you want to redirect.

4. Open the Printer menu and select the Properties option.

5. To send the documents to a different print device on the same print server, click the port to which the other print device is assigned and click OK. To send documents to another printer on a different print server, click Add Port, select the Local Port option, and click New Port. Type the name of the other print server and the share name, using the UNC name. Click OK.

After the print jobs have been redirected, the check box of the malfunctioning printer's port is immediately cleared unless printer pooling is enabled. Because print jobs have already been formatted for a specific printer, the printer on the new port must be compatible with the driver used in the logical printer. It should also be noted that any documents currently printing cannot be redirected.

Looking at the Logs

To look at spooler and printer activity, you can use the logs shown in the Event Viewer to look at the logs that pertain to the printer and spooler activity. By default, the system logs show printer creation, deletion, and modification. You can also find entries for printer traffic, hard disk space, spooler errors, and other relevant maintenance issues.

To modify the event logging for the spooler,

1. Open the Printers and Faxes folder and choose Server Properties from the File menu.

2. Click the Advanced tab to access the properties.

3. You can then select to log errors, warnings, and information events; beep on errors of remote documents; and show information notifications for local and network printers.

Auditing Printer Access

Similar to file and folder access, you can also audit printers. You can specify which users or groups and which actions to audit for a particular printer. Before you can do printer auditing, you need to enable Audit Object Access policy, which is done through local or group policies (Computer Configuration\Windows Settings\Security Settings\Local Policies\Audit Policy). After the policy has taken effect, take these steps:

1. Open the Printer and Faxes folder.

2. Right-click the printer you want to audit and select Properties.

3. Choose the Security tab.

4. Click Advanced.

5. Choose the Auditing tab.

6. Select Add and then choose the groups or users you want to audit.

7. Check the boxes for auditing successful or failed events.

8. Click OK to close the Advanced Security Settings box.

9. Click OK to close the printer Properties box.

You would then look in the Security logs in the Event Viewer for inappropriate or unauthorized printing.

Monitoring Print Queue Performance

If you find that your print jobs are too slow to print or you want to see the overall performance of the printing system, you can monitor the performance of a print server's print queue by using the Performance Monitor snap-in. You can monitor real-time statistics using System Monitor, and you can log performance over time using Performance Logs and Alerts. The performance object to specify is Print Queue. The object instances are the printers installed on the local print server computer along with the _Total instance. The available counters include

▶ **Bytes/Printed/sec**: The number of bytes per second printed on a print queue.

▶ **Job errors**: The total number of job errors in a print queue since the last restart.

- ▶ **Jobs**: The current number of jobs in a print queue.

- ▶ **Job Spooling**: The current number of spooling jobs in a print queue.

- ▶ **Not Ready Errors (since last restart)**: The total number of printer-not-ready errors in a print queue since the last restart.

- ▶ **Out of Paper Errors (since last restart)**: The total number of out-of-paper errors in a print queue since the last restart.

- ▶ **Total Jobs Printed (since last restart)**: The total number of jobs printed on a print queue since the last restart.

- ▶ **Total Pages Printed (since last restart)**: The total number of pages printed through GDI on a print queue since the last restart.

Print Management Console

The Print Services role in Windows Server 2008 includes three role services:

- ▶ Print Server
- ▶ LPD Service
- ▶ Internet Printing

Together, these role services provide all the functionality of a Windows print server. You can add these role services while you are installing the Print Services role with the Add Roles Wizard of Server Manager. Or you can install them at a later time by using the Add Role Services Wizard of Server Manager.

Print Management console, installed with the Print Services role, provides a single interface that administrators can use to efficiently administer multiple printers and print servers. You can use Print Management to manage printers on computers that are running Microsoft Windows 2000, Windows XP, Windows Server 2003, Windows Vista, or Windows Server 2008.

The Print Management console is installed as the Print Service role. The Print Management console provides current details about the status of printers and print servers on the network. You can use Print Management to install printer connections to a group of client computers simultaneously and to monitor print queues remotely. Print Management can help you find printers that have an error condition by using filters. It can also send email notifications or run scripts when a printer or print server needs attention. On printers that provide a web-based management interface, Print Management can display more data, such as toner and paper levels.

Filters display only those printers that meet a certain set of criteria. For example, it might be helpful to filter for printers with certain error conditions or those printers in a group of buildings regardless of the print server they use. Filters are stored in the Custom Printer Filters folder in the Print Management tree and are dynamic, so the data is always current.

Two default filters are provided with Print Management (`Printmanagement.msc`). For each filter that you create, you have the option to set up an email notification or to run a script when the conditions of the filter are met. This is useful when you want to be alerted about printer problems, particularly in an organization with multiple buildings and administrators.

For example, you can set up a filter of all printers managed by a particular print server where the status does not equal Ready. Then, if a printer changes from the Ready status to any other status, the administrator could receive a notification email from Print Management.

To set up and save a filtered view,

1. Open the Administrative Tools folder and double-click Print Management.

2. In the Print Management tree, right-click the Custom Printer Filters folder and then click Add New Printer Filter. This launches the New Printer Filter Wizard.

3. On the Printer Filter Name and Description wizard page, type a name for the printer filter. The name appears in the Custom Printer Filters folder in the Print Management tree.

4. In Description, type an optional description.

5. To display the number of printers that satisfy the conditions of a filter, select the Display the Total Number of Printers option next to the name of the Printer Filter check box.

6. Click Next.

7. On the Define a Printer Filter wizard page:

   ▶ In the Field list, click the print queue or printer status characteristic.

   ▶ In the Condition list, click the condition.

   ▶ In the Value box, type a value.

   ▶ Continue adding criteria until your filter is complete and then click Next.

8. On the Set Notifications (Optional) wizard page, select one or both of the following:

    ▶ To set an email notification, select the Send Email Notification check box and type one or more recipient and sender email addresses. An SMTP server must be specified to route the message. Use the format account@domain and semicolons to separate multiple accounts.

    ▶ To set a script to run, select the Run Script check box and then type the path where the script file is located. To add more arguments, type them in Additional Arguments.

9. Click Finish.

To set notifications on existing printer filters, right-click a filtered view and then click Set Notifications.

Troubleshooting Printing Problems

When problems occur, you must be ready to troubleshoot those problems. Of course, when looking at what is causing the problem, you need to look at everything that can cause the problems. When it comes to printing, this includes

▶ The application attempting to print

▶ The logical printer on the local computer

▶ The network connection between the local computer and the print server

▶ The logical printer on the server

▶ The network connection between the print server and the print device

▶ The print device itself, including hardware, configuration, and status

The first step is to identify the scope of the failure; in other words, determine what is working and what is failing. For example, if a user can print from one application but not another on the same computer, the problem is most likely related to the application that is having problems printing. If the user can print to other printers with no problem, you would then try to print from another system in an attempt to duplicate the problem. If the problem occurs on multiple computers, you need to focus on the logical printer on the server or the print device. Of course, one place to give you insight into some problems is the logs in the Event Viewer, specifically whether the spooler has written any errors to the event logs.

You can confirm connectivity between the print client and the print server by opening the Printer and Faxes folder and double-clicking the printer to open the printer window. If the printer window opens and it shows documents in the print queue, the client is communicating with the print server. If you cannot open the printer window, the problem is with authentication, security permissions, or a network connectivity problem. You can test connectivity further by trying to ping the print server or by clicking Start, selecting run, and typing `\\printservername`. Also, make sure that the printer has not been disabled or taken offline within Windows.

If you suspect that the print server cannot connect to the printer, you should first check to see whether the print device is in operation. (Make sure that the printer is on and online, make sure that it is connected to the server or network, and make sure that the printer is not showing any errors.) Next, from the print server, make sure that the print server can access the print device. You can also make sure that the IP address on the logical printer port matches the address of the print device. You could test network connectivity by pinging the address of the print device.

If you suspect a problem with the print server itself, you need to make sure that the print service and the remote procedure call (RPC) service is running. You might also try to restart the print service and make sure that you have sufficient disk space on the drive where the spool folder is located.

If pages are only partially printed, check that there is sufficient memory on the printer to print the document. If text is missing, verify whether the missing text uses a font that is valid and installed. Of course, another reason might be that you need to replace the printer's toner cartridge.

If your printed documents have garbled data or strange characters, you should verify that you have the correct print driver loaded for the printer. You might also consider reinstalling the drivers because they could be corrupt. Finally, check for bad cables or electromagnetic interference. See Table 8.2 for a list of common printing problems and how to fix them.

EXAM ALERT

Anytime you have garbled data or strange characters, you should always suspect that you have the wrong print driver installed.

Table 8.2   Troubleshooting Common Printing Problems

If You Encounter This Problem	Do This
Printer server cannot connect to the printer.	Make sure print device is operation (printer is on and online, printer is connected to the server or network, and printer is not showing any errors).
	Make sure the IP address on the logical printer port matches the address of the print device.
	Try pinging the address of the print device.
Print server is having problems.	Make sure that the printer services and remote procedure call (RPC) service is running.
	Restart the print spooler service.
	Make sure you have sufficient disk space on the drive where the spool folder is located.
Pages are partially printed.	Check that there is sufficient memory on the printer.
	Check to see whether the printer's toner or ink cartridge needs to be replaced.
Text is missing.	Verify wither the missing text uses a font that is valid and installed.
	Check to see whetherthe printer's toner or ink cartridge needs to be replaced.
Documents have garbled data or strange characters.	Verify that the correct print driver is loaded on the printer.
	Reinstall the drivers because they could be corrupt.
	Check for bad cables.
	Check for electromagnetic interference.

Exam Prep Questions

1. In Windows Server 2008, the printer is defined as

    ○ **A.** The logical device that represents the print device

    ○ **B.** The physical print device

    ○ **C.** The network IP address located in DNS

    ○ **D.** The print driver

2. Which of the following can install a printer on a server that is part of the domain? (Choose all that apply.)

    ○ **A.** Domain administrators

    ○ **B.** Local administrators

    ○ **C.** Domain print operators

    ○ **D.** Power users

3. You add a printer directly to the network, using a built-in Ethernet card. Now you want to load the printer onto the server. Which of the following is true?

    ○ **A.** The printer is considered a local printer.

    ○ **B.** The printer is considered a network printer.

    ○ **C.** The printer needs to be moved so that it can be plugged directly into the Windows Server 2003 acting as a print server.

    ○ **D.** The printer needs to be assigned a name such as http://servername/ printername.

4. What do you need to load if you want to print to a UNIX computer?

    ○ **A.** LPR and LDP

    ○ **B.** IIS and IPP

    ○ **C.** Appletalk redirector

    ○ **D.** NetWare redirector

5. You are the network administrator for Acme.com. You have a Windows Server 2008 named Server1 with a printer named Printer1. John prints several large print jobs before he is called away from the office. Because these print jobs are so large, they prevent other users from printing important documents. How can you allow Jane, the office manager, to delete those print jobs?

    ○ **A.** Configure the printer permissions to give Jane the Allow Manage Printers permission.

    ○ **B.** Configure the printer permission to assign the Allow Manage Documents permission.

    ○ **C.** Create a new print queue that points to the same print device and assigns full permission to Jane.

    ○ **D.** Configure the Allow Manage Queue permission.

6. What permission do you have to give a user to change a printer's configuration?

    ○ **A.** Allow Manage Printers

    ○ **B.** Allow Manage Documents

    ○ **C.** Full Control for Documents

    ○ **D.** Modify permission for Printers

7. A user sent a large print job to the printer and realized that some changes had to be made. Therefore, the user wants to delete the print job. What do you need to do for that user to delete the print job?

    ○ **A.** Give the user the Allow Manage Printer permission.

    ○ **B.** Give the user the Allow Manage Documents permission.

    ○ **C.** Give the user both Allow Manage Printer permission and Allow Manage Documents permission.

    ○ **D.** Give the Allow Delete Print Jobs permission.

    ○ **E.** You don't have to do anything because the user can already delete his own print job.

8. You are the network administrator for Acme.com. You have a Windows Server 2008 named Server1 with a printer named Printer1. You instruct users to connect to the printer by using the following address: http://Server1/Printer1. However, users cannot connect to the printer when using HTTP. What must you do?

    ○ **A.** Install IIS on the server and install the Internet Printing component of IIS.

    ○ **B.** Stop and restart the print spooler.

    ○ **C.** Make sure that you have sufficient disk space for the print jobs.

    ○ **D.** Create a virtual directory called Printer1.

9. You are a network administrator for Acme.com. You have a Windows Server 2008 computer that functions as a print server. You have a couple of groups that print large documents. When they print large documents, the server becomes extremely slow. You decide to use System Monitor to view the server's performance. You determine that the average disk queue increases and that the hard drive becomes full. What should you do? (Choose the best answer.)

○ **A.** Increase the amount of physical RAM on the server.

○ **B.** Upgrade to a faster processor or install a second processor on the server.

○ **C.** Install an additional hard drive on the server and move the spool folder to the new hard drive.

○ **D.** Configure a printer pool so that you can print faster.

10. You are the administrator for Acme.com. You have a Printer1 connected to a Windows Server 2008 called Server1. You assign the Everyone group the Allow Print permission. When a user tries to print to \\Server1\Printer1, the user is unable to print. You soon discover that a few other users also cannot print to the same printer. You log on to a computer that has been mapped to the share printer and try to print several documents to the printer, but none will print. You soon discover the following message when you try to access the print queue:

Printer1 on Server1 is unable to connect.

You are able to ping the server. What do you need to do to ensure that the print jobs will be printed? (Choose the best answer.)

○ **A.** On the domain controller, create a share printer that is published in Active Directory that points to \\Server1\Printer1.

○ **B.** From a command prompt, run the `net print \\Server1\printer1` command.

○ **C.** You restart the Print Spooler service on the local computer.

○ **D.** You restart the Print Spooler service on the print server.

11. You have a Windows Server 2008 sever called Server1. Connected to that printer, you have Printer1 configured with the default settings. You want the accounting department to have exclusive use of the printer between 9 a.m. and 3 p.m. During the rest of the time, anyone can use the printer. What should you do? (Choose two answers.)

○ **A.** Modify Printer1 to be available from only 3 p.m. to 9 a.m.

○ **B.** Modify Printer1 to be available from only 9 a.m. to 3 p.m.

○ **C.** Share and configure a Printer2 to be available from 3 p.m. to 9 a.m. For the second printer, assign the Everyone group the Deny Print permission and assign the accounting department to the second printer.

    ○ **D.** Share and configure a Printer2 to be available from 9 a.m. to 3 p.m. For the second printer, remove permissions for the Everyone group and assign the accounting department to the second printer. Instruct the users in the accounting group to use the second printer.

    ○ **E.** Create a printer pool. Assign the Accounting group to the pool.

12. You are a network administrator for Acme.com. You have a Windows Server 2008 named Server1 with a printer named Printer1. You get reports that print jobs for Printer1 are failing. You try to delete the print jobs, but cannot. What do you do to overcome this problem?

    ○ **A.** Increase the priority of Printer1.

    ○ **B.** Increase the priority of the print jobs.

    ○ **C.** Delete the files in the C:\Windows\System32\Spool folder.

    ○ **D.** Restart the spooler server on Server1.

    ○ **E.** Make sure that the printer has the correct driver.

13. You are the network administrator for Acme.com. You have a Windows Server 2008 named Server1 with a printer named Printer1. The president of the company wants his documents to take precedence over documents sent by other users. Of course, if a document is already printing, he wants the document to finish. What do you need to do?

    ○ **A.** Configure the printer permissions to take ownership of the print jobs.

    ○ **B.** Give full control to the president of the company.

    ○ **C.** Create a new printer and configure it to print to the print device. Assign a high priority to that printer. Configure the president's computer to the new printer.

    ○ **D.** Make the printer into a printer pool. Have the president print to one printer of the pool and everyone else print to the other one.

14. You are the network administrator for Acme.com. You have a Windows Server 2008 named Server1 with a printer named Printer1. The marketing department complains that when they print large files that contain multiple complex graphics, document printing is very slow and the print device pauses for several seconds between each page. How can you minimize the impact that large print jobs with complex graphics have while performing the least administrative effort?

    ○ **A.** Configure the printer to start printing after the last page is spooled.

    ○ **B.** Create a printer pool with two or more printers.

    ○ **C.** Increase the priority of the print job.

    ○ **D.** Increase the priority of the printer.

15. You are the network administrator for Acme.com. You have a Windows Server 2008 named Server1 with a printer named Printer1. Users report that print jobs being sent to the printer take a long time to print. You want to make sure that the server is performing well. So what would be your next step in identifying the problem?

    ○ **A.** Use Task Manager to look at the processor and memory usage.

    ○ **B.** Use Windows Explorer to look at the free disk space.

    ○ **C.** Use System Monitor to view the Print Queue\Jobs counter.

    ○ **D.** Use System Monitor to view the Disk\Disk Queue counter.

Answers to Exam Prep Questions

1. Answer A is correct. According to Microsoft, the printer is the logical representation of the points to the physical print device. Answer B is incorrect because the physical printer is known as a print device. Answer C is incorrect because DNS entries for printers are only for our convenience; they assign a name to an IP address so that we can remember it more easily. Answer D is incorrect because the print driver is the component that is used to translate the documents into a language that is understood by the printer.

2. Answers A, B, and C are correct. On domain controllers, members of the Administrators and Print Operators groups can install local printers. On member servers, members of the Administrators and the local Print Operators groups can install local printers. On Windows XP Professional or Windows 2000 Professional, only Administrators can install local printers. Any authenticated user can connect to and submit print jobs to a remote shared printer, assuming that the user has the proper printer permissions. Answer D is incorrect because power users are not assigned printer permissions, although the users in power users maybe assigned to other groups that give them permissions for the printer.

3. Answer A is correct. When you connect a printer to the network, you install it as a local printer and use the Create a New Port Wizard to create a standard TCP/IP port. Answer B is incorrect because the printer is not connected directly to the server. Answer C is incorrect because you do not have to connect it directly to the printer to use it. Answer D is incorrect because it is not necessary for a printer to use IPP.

4. Answer A is correct. UNIX and Linux computers use Line Printer Remote (LPR) and Line Printer Daemon (LPD) to print to a print device. Answer B is incorrect because IIS and IPP are necessary for Internet printing. Answer C is incorrect because Appletalk redirector is used for older Apple computers. Answer D is incorrect because Netware redirector is used for printing with Novell NetWare.

5. Answer B is correct. By default, a user can delete his own print jobs. To be able to delete any print job, the user must have the Manage Documents permission for the printer. Answer A is incorrect because Allow Manage Printers enables Jane to configure settings on the printer itself but does not enable her to manage the documents being sent to the printer. Answer C is a long-term solution but the question asks how to delete these print jobs. Answer D is incorrect because there is no Allow Manage Queue permission.

6. Answer A is correct. To change the printer configuration, the user needs the Allow Manage Printers permission. Answer B is incorrect because if a user has to manage documents, he can manage only documents sent to the print queue. Answer C is incorrect because it would give additional permissions that the question does not ask, including managing the print jobs. Answer D is incorrect because there is no Modify permission for printers.

7. Answer E is correct. Users can delete their own print jobs, so no additional permissions must be given. Therefore, answers A, B, C, and D are incorrect.

8. Answer A is correct. To make sure that you can print with HTTP, you must have IIS to service the HTTP calls. In addition, you must install the Internet Printing components of IIS. Answer B is incorrect because restarting the print spooler would have no effect. Answer C is incorrect because although you need sufficient disk space to print, it has no bearing on Internet printing. Answer D is incorrect because IIS does not require a virtual directory to print.

9. Answer C is correct. When the large print jobs are being printed, the print jobs stored within the spool folder are filling up the hard drive. As a result, performance of the entire machine slows down. Adding RAM (answer A) or increasing the processor speed (answer B) do not increase the performance of the system when the hard drive fills up. Therefore, you need to move the spool folder to a different hard drive so that the system drive does not fill up. Answer D is incorrect because the server does not slow down because the printers cannot keep up, but because the hard drive is full.

10. Answer D is correct. If the print spooler stalls, you need to stop and restart the service. After the queues have been deleted, the users need to resubmit their print jobs. Of course, because this affects more than one user, the problem is with one server and not the local computer. Therefore, answer C is incorrect. Answer A is incorrect because creating a share printer and publishing it in Active Directory does not fix the real problem. Answer B is incorrect because running a net command does not fix any printer problems.

11. Answer D is correct. You already have a printer that allows everyone to print to it at any time. First, you need to modify the first printer so that it is available from only 3 p.m. to 9 a.m. You then need to create a new printer that is available from 9 a.m. to 3 p.m. and that only the accountants can print to it. You then have to instruct the accounting department to print to the printer. Answers A and B do not configure a second printer for the accountants to use. Answer C is incorrect because the printer needs to be available from 9 a.m. to 3 p.m., not 3 p.m. to 9 a.m. Answer E is incorrect because creating a printer pool is used for servicing heavy loads by using two or more printers working together to service a queue.

12. Answer D is correct. The print spooler service loads files to memory for printing from the print queue. Sometimes, you need to stop and restart the service to delete the queue. Answers A and B are incorrect because changing priorities does not fix the problem when the print spooler is having problems. Answer C is incorrect because deleting files does not restart the print spooler, which is the main problem. Answer E is incorrect because the incorrect driver give strange characters and the like.

13. Answer C is correct. By assigning two different printers that point to the same print device, you can assign different priorities to each one. By assigning different users to the two printers, you can have one group of people with a higher priority than other users. Answer A is incorrect because there is no permission to take ownership of a print job, only a print device. Answer B is incorrect because giving full control enables him to manage print devices and print jobs but does not give a higher priority. Of course, with those permissions, he could assign himself a higher priority, but that's something you typically don't want to give full permissions to any of your users. Answer D is incorrect because it requires two printers. Printer pools are used to split a busy print queue among multiple printers.

14. Answer A is correct. When you configure spooling options, you specify whether print jobs are spooled or sent directly to the printer. Spooling means that the print jobs are saved to disk in a queue before they are sent to the printer. In the Advanced tab, you can keep the Start Printing Immediately option selected or you can choose the Start Printing After Last Page Is Spooled option. If you choose the latter option, a smaller print job that finishes spooling first prints before the large print job. Answer B is not the best answer because having multiple large print jobs would also cause problems on multiple printer pools. It is also not cost effective. Answer C is incorrect because increasing the priority of a print job would not help on every print job in the future. Answer D is incorrect because you cannot increase the priority of the printer.

15. Answer C is correct. The Print Queue\Jobs counter specifies the current number of print jobs that are pending in the print queue. If processor, memory, or disk usage is high, your entire system would be slow, not just in printing. You have to look at the free disk space only if the performance is slow or print jobs are having problems. Answer A is incorrect because processor and memory usage gives only overall performance, not performance measures specific to printing. Answer B is incorrect

because although lack of free disk space may cause problems, it is not the best indicator for performance. Answer D is incorrect because these settings give you only disk performance.

Need to Know More?

For more information about print services, visit the following website:

► http://technet2.microsoft.com/windowsserver2008/en/servermanager/printservices.mspx

CHAPTER NINE

Monitoring and Managing a Network Infrastructure

Terms you'll need to understand:

✓ Microsoft updates

✓ Windows Server Update Services (WSUS)

✓ Downstream server

✓ Upstream server

✓ Microsoft Baseline Security Analyzer (MBSA)

✓ Simple Network Management Protocol (SNMP)

✓ SNMP community

✓ Community name

✓ SNMP trap

✓ Protocol analyzer

✓ Network Monitor

Techniques/concepts you'll need to master:

✓ Install and configure Windows Server Update Services (WSUS).

✓ Use group policies to configure clients to use WSUS.

✓ Use SNMP to monitor network devices and systems.

✓ Use Microsoft Baseline Security Analyzer to find potential security holes.

✓ Use Network Monitor to capture packets.

To keep your network and servers running smoothly, you must learn to use various components and tools to keep your computers up to date, to find and fix problems, and to make your network as secure as possible.

Microsoft Updates

It is important that you keep your systems up to date with *Microsoft updates* and security patches. If your system is not kept up to date, it may not run as reliably as it should and it is not as resistant against viruses and other forms of Denial of Service (DoS) attacks.

You could manually log in into each computer within your organization and go to the http://update.microsoft.com website to download and install the updates. Unfortunately, if you have hundreds of computers, this approach is impractical because of the labor involved and because hundreds of computers downloading patches also use valuable bandwidth. In addition, you often want a way to control what updates get applied because updates may cause problems with certain applications.

Another option is to configure each computer for automatic updates. To enable automatic updates, use the Control Panel to open the System Properties and select the Automatic Updates tab. Select Automatic (Recommended). You can also use group policies to configure these options automatically so that you don't have to configure each computer manually.

Unfortunately, if you have hundreds of computers downloaded patches and security fixes, the downloads may use valuable bandwidth and you do not have a way to control which updates get applied. To overcome these problems, you can set up a *Windows Server Update Services (WSUS)* server to provide a central point for client computers and servers to acquire updates. With WSUS, you can also update Microsoft Office, Microsoft SQL, Microsoft Exchange, and other Microsoft applications.

Installing Windows Server Update Services (WSUS)

WSUS is provided for free from Microsoft. The software and step-by-step guides can be found at http://www.microsoft.com/windowsserversystem/updateservices/default.mspx.

To install WSUS 3.0, the file system of the server must meet the following requirements:

- ▶ Both the system partition and the partition on which you install WSUS 3.0 must be formatted with the NTFS file system.

- ▶ A minimum of 1GB of free space is recommended for the system partition.

- ▶ A minimum of 20GB of free space is recommended for the volume where WSUS stores content; 30GB of free space is recommended.

- ▶ You also need a SQL server. If you do not have a dedicated SQL server, WSUS installs Windows Internal Database. A minimum of 2GB of free space is recommended on the volume where WSUS Setup installs Windows Internal Database.

After WSUS is installed, the WSUS server needs to be able to communicate with the Microsoft update sites so that it can download the updates.

Using Downstream Servers

If you have multiple sites and you have limited bandwidth between sites, you can create a more complicated multiple-server WSUS deployment. The first server (or *upstream server*) is used to download the updates from the Internet and distribute those updates to the various remote sites that have downstream servers. The *downstream servers* then distribute the updates to the individual clients.

To connect a downstream server to an upstream server,

1. On the WSUS console toolbar, click Options, Synchronization Options.

2. In the Update Source box, click Synchronize from an Upstream Windows Server Update Services Server and then enter the server name and port number in the corresponding boxes.

3. Under Tasks, click Save Settings and then click OK when the confirmation box appears.

When configured this way, WSUS shares only updates and metadata with its downstream servers during synchronization; it does not share computer group information or information about which updates are approved. If you want to set up WSUS to distribute information about which updates are approved, look into using replica mode:

▶ **Distributed management**: An administrator at each site is given full control over update approvals and which computers get updated by the WSUS server. Distributed management is the default installation option for all WSUS installations. You do not have to do anything to enable this mode.

▶ **Centralized management**: Utilizes the replica server role, which features a single administered server and one or more subordinate replicas. The approvals and targeting groups created on the master server are replicated throughout the entire organization. Remember that computer group membership is not distributed throughout the replica group, only to the computer groups themselves. In other words, you always have to load client computers into computer groups.

Managing WSUS

To configure WSUS, you need to use the WSUS administration website located at http://*servername*/WSUSAdmin, where *servername* is the DNS name of the server on which WSUS is installed. You can also open Administrative Tools and click Microsoft Windows Server Update Services. To run the WSUS console, you must be a member of the WSUS Administrators or the local Administrators security groups on the server on which WSUS is installed.

These are the five primary administrative tasks for managing WSUS:

▶ Review status information, such as computers requiring updates.

▶ Review and approve updates for distribution to clients.

▶ Generate reports on the status of updates, computers, synchronization, and WSUS settings.

▶ Manage computers and computer groups.

▶ Configure WSUS options for synchronization, automatic approval, and assigning computers to groups.

By default, only critical updates and security updates are downloaded. You can select specific products and update classifications such as Microsoft Office, Microsoft Exchange, Microsoft SQL, and so on. You can also limit the versions of Windows that it will update and the languages that are available to limit the size of the database and archive of the updates (see Figure 9.1).

FIGURE 9.1   Using the WSUS 3.0 console.

Configuring Clients to Use WSUS

To limit which computers get updates and which updates these computers get, you define computer groups. This enables you to configure test computers for updates before rolling out updates to all computers. After a client computer makes contact with the WSUS server for the first time, it is listed on the Computers page of the WSUS administration site. You must approve the computers to get updates to initiate deployment of updates.

After the updates have been downloaded from Microsoft or another WSUS server, you need to approve which updates will be propagated to the client computers. When you approve updates, you can choose to install, detect only, remove, or decline. After detection, you can view how many computers do not have the update installed and need it. If the number needed for an update is zero, then all client computers are up to date. When you right-click an update and select the Install Approval option, you then select which computer groups get the update. By default, updates are not downloaded until they are approved for installation. Using the WSUS console, you can run reports to show how many computers have been updated, a list of those computers updated, the status of the computers, and synchronization results (see Figure 9.2).

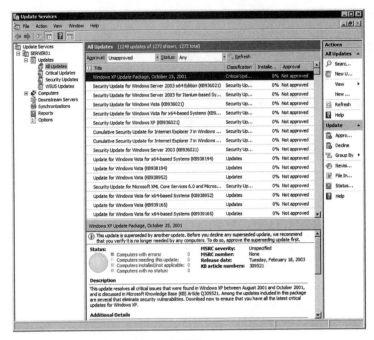

FIGURE 9.2 Approving updates in WSUS.

To configure the client computers to use the WSUS server, you can configure the Registry or you can use group policies. To use group policies, follow these steps:

1. In Group Policy Management Editor, expand Computer Configuration, expand Administrative Templates, expand Windows Components, and then click Windows Update (see Figure 9.3).

2. In the details pane, double-click Specify Intranet Microsoft Update Service Location.

3. Click Enabled, and type the HTTP URL of the same WSUS server in the Set the Intranet Update Service for Detecting Updates box and in the Set the Intranet Statistics Server box. For example, type `http://servername` in both boxes.

4. Click OK.

5. Double-click Configure Automatic Updates.

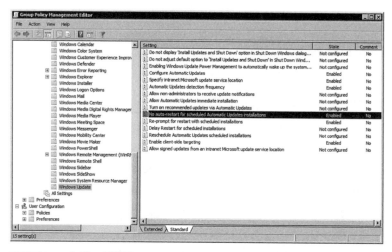

FIGURE 9.3 Setting WSUS group policies.

6. Click Enabled and specify the type of updates and type of the install (see Figure 9.4). The type of updates include

  ▶ 2—Notify for Download and Notify for Install

  ▶ 3—Auto Download and Notify for Install

  ▶ 4—Auto Download and Schedule the Install

7. Click OK.

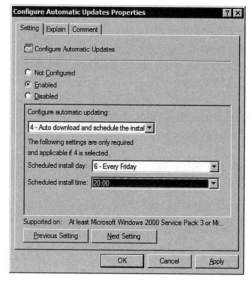

FIGURE 9.4 Using Group Polices to specify when and how updates will be installed.

After you establish a group policy, it may take a few minutes for it to take effect. Therefore, you may want to refresh the group policy by using gpudpate /force if you want more immediate results.

To manually initiate detection by the WSUS server, follow these steps:

1. On the client computer click Start, Run.

2. Type **cmd** and then click OK.

3. At the command prompt, type **wuauclt.exe /detectnow**. This command-line option instructs Automatic Updates to contact the WSUS server immediately.

If you are having issues getting updates, run the following command to force the workstation to download a new certificate from the WSUS serer and then download the updates from WSUS:

```
wuauclt.exe /resetauthorization /detectnow
```

Although WSUS does not provide built-in backup tools, you can use normal backup tools, such as the backup utility that comes with Microsoft Windows, to back up and restore the WSUS database and update the file storage folder. It is recommended that when you back up the database (MSSQL$WSUS), you should stop the database to prevent inconsistencies.

Baseline Security Analyzer

As part of Microsoft's Strategic Technology Protection Program, and in response to direct customer need for a streamlined method of identifying common security misconfigurations, Microsoft developed the *Microsoft Baseline Security Analyzer (MBSA)*. The MBSA includes a graphical and command-line interface that can perform local or remote scans of Windows systems. MBSA scans for missing hot fixes and vulnerabilities in Windows, IIS, SQL Server, Internet Explorer, and Office. MBSA creates and stores individual XML security reports for each computer scanned and displays the reports in the graphical user interface in HTML (see Figure 9.5).

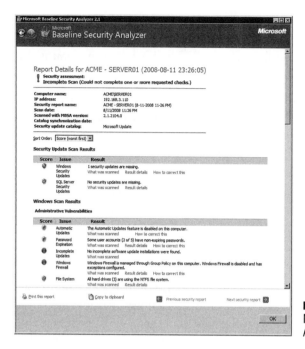

FIGURE 9.5 Using the Microsoft Baseline Security Analyzer (MBSA).

To download MBSA, visit the following website:

http://www.microsoft.com/technet/security/tools/mbsahome.mspx

Simple Network Management Protocol (SNMP)

The *Simple Network Management Protocol (SNMP)* has become the de facto standard for internetwork management. It enables you to configure remote devices, monitor network performance, detect network faults, detect inappropriate access, and audit network usage. Remote devices include hubs, bridges, routers, and servers.

SNMP Overview

SNMP contains two primary elements, a manager and agents. The SNMP manager is the console through which the network administrator performs network management functions. The SNMP works by sending messages called protocol data units (PDUs) to different parts of a network. Agents store data about themselves in Management Information Bases (MIB). The manager, which is the console through which the network administrator performs network management functions, requests the information from the MIB. The SNMP agent returns the appropriate information to the manager.

A *SNMP trap* is an unsolicited message sent by an SNMP agent to an SNMP management system when the agent detects that a certain type of event has occurred locally on the managed host. The SNMP management console receives a trap message known as a trap destination. For example, a trap message might be sent when a system restarts or when a router's links go down.

Each SNMP management host and agent belongs to an SNMP community. An *SNMP community* is a collection of hosts grouped together for administrative purposes. What computers should belong to the same community is generally, but not always, determined by the physical proximity of the computers. Communities are identified by the names you assign to them.

Although most networks use a username and a password for authentication, SNMP messages are authenticated by only the *community name*. Although a host can belong to several communities at the same time, an SNMP agent does not accept requests from a management system in a community that is not on its list of acceptable community names. If the community name is incorrect, the agent sends an "authentication failure" trap to its trap destination. Therefore, it is the responsibility of the administrator to set hard-to-guess community names.

After the SNMP authenticates a message, the request is evaluated against the agent's list of access permissions for that community. The types of permissions that can be granted to a community are

▶ **None**: The SNMP agent does not process the request. When the agent receives an SNMP message from a management system in this community, it discards the request and generates an authentication trap.

▶ **Notify**: This is currently identical to the permission of None.

▶ **Read Only**: The agent does not process SET requests from this community. It processes only GET, GET-NEXT, and GET-BULK requests. The agent discards SET requests from managment systems in this community and generates an authentication trap.

▶ **Read Create**: The SNMP agent processes or creates all requests from this community. It processes SET, GET, GET-NEXT, and GET-BULK requests, including SET requests that require the addition of a new object to an MIB table.

▶ **Read Write**: Currently identical to Read Create.

Community names are transmitted as clear text (that is, without encryption). Because unencrypted transmissions are vulnerable to attacks by hackers with network analysis software, the use of SNMP community names represents a potential security risk. However, Windows 2008 IP Security can be configured to help protect SNMP messages from these attacks.

The SNMP service requires the configuration of at least one default community name. The name Public is generally used as the community name because it is the common name that is universally accepted in all SNMP implementations. You can delete or change the default community name or add multiple community names. If no community names are defined, the SNMP agent denies all incoming SNMP requests.

When an SNMP agent receives a message, the community name contained in the packet is verified against the agent's list of acceptable community names. After the name is determined to be acceptable, the request is evaluated against the agent's list of access permissions for that community.

There are two versions of SNMP. SNMP 1 reports only whether a device is functioning properly. The industry has attempted to define a new set of protocols called SNMP 2 that would provide additional information, but the standardization efforts have not been successful. Instead, network managers have turned to a related technology called RMON that provides more detailed information about network usage.

Installing and Configuring SNMP

By default, SNMP is not installed on Windows Server 2008. To install it, open the Server Management console and install SNMP as a feature. Then access the Services Console to configure the SNMP.

To configure agent properties, follow these steps:

1. Under Administrative Tools, open Computer Management.

2. In the console tree, click Services, which is located under Services and Applications.

3. In the details pane, click to highlight SNMP Service.

4. Right-click the SNMP service in the details pane and select the Properties option.

5. On the Agent tab, in Contact, type the name of the user or administrator for this computer (see Figure 9.6).

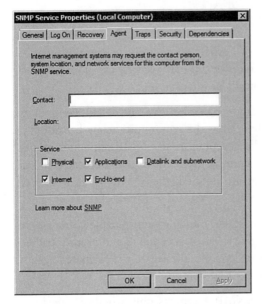

FIGURE 9.6 Configuring the SNMP Agent Properties.

6. In Location, type the physical location of the computer or the contact.

7. Under Service, select the appropriate check boxes for this computer:

   ▶ **Physical**: Manages physical devices, such as a hard disk partition.

   ▶ **Applications**: Uses any applications that send data using the TCP/IP protocol suite. This service should always be enabled.

   ▶ **Datalink and Subnetwork**: Manages a bridge.

   ▶ **Internet**: Is an IP gateway (router).

   ▶ **End-to-end**: Is an IP host. This service should always be enabled.

8. Click OK.

To configure traps,

1. Under Administrative Tools, open Computer Management.

2. In the console tree, click Services, which is located under Services and Applications.

3. In the details pane, click to highlight SNMP Service.

4. Right-click the SNMP service in the details pane and select the Properties option.

5. On the Traps tab, under Community Name, type the case-sensitive community name to which this computer will send trap messages. Click Add to List (see Figure 9.7).

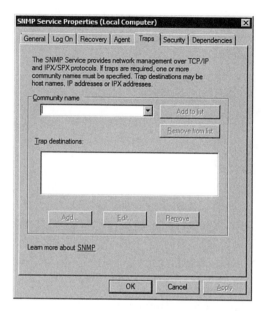

FIGURE 9.7 Setting SNMP trap properties.

6. In Trap Destinations, click Add.

7. In Host Name, IP, type information for the host, and click Add.

8. Repeat steps 5 through 7 until you have added all the communities and trap destinations you want.

To configure security,

1. Under Administrative Tools, open Computer Management.

2. In the console tree, click Services, which is located under Services and Applications.

3. In the details pane, click to highlight SNMP Service.

4. Right-click the SNMP service in the details pane and select the Properties option.

5. On the Security tab, select Send Authentication Trap if you want a trap message sent whenever authentication fails (see Figure 9.8).

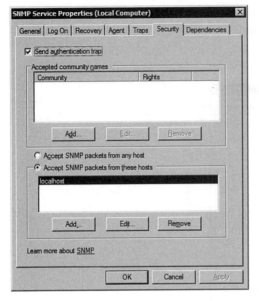

FIGURE 9.8 Setting SNMP security properties.

6. Under Accepted Community Names, click Add.

7. Under Community Rights, select a permission level for which this host processes SNMP requests from the selected community.

8. In Community Name, type a case-sensitive community name and then click Add.

9. In SNMP Service Properties, specify whether or not to accept SNMP packets from a host:

   ▶ To accept SNMP requests from any host on the network, regardless of identity, click Accept SNMP Packets from Any Host.

   ▶ To limit acceptance of SNMP packets, click Accept SNMP Packets from These Hosts, click Add, type the appropriate hostname or IP or IPX address, and then click Add again.

You can make changes to an entry by clicking the entry and then clicking the Edit button. You can delete a selected entry by clicking the Remove button.

Network Monitor

Sometimes when you have to troubleshoot some network problems, you need to take a good look on what is being sent through your network to determine the cause. This is where protocol analyzers come in. A *protocol analyzer*, also known as a network analyzer or packet analyzer, is software or a hardware/software device that enables you capture or receive every packet on your media, store it in a trace buffer, and then see a breakdown of each of the packets by protocol in the order in which they appeared. Therefore, it can help you analyze all levels of the OSI model to determine the cause of the problem. Network analysis is the art of listening in on the network communications to examine how devices communicate and determine the health of that network. Microsoft's protocol analyzer is *Network Monitor*.

Introduction to Protocol Analyzers

The operation of a protocol analyzer is actually quite simple:

1. Receive a copy of every packet on a piece of wire by operating in a promiscuous capture mode (a mode that captures all packets on the wire, not just broadcast packets and packets addressed to the analyzer's adapter).

2. Timestamp the packets.

3. Filter out the items of no interest.

4. Show a breakdown of the various layers of protocols, bit by bit.

These packet traces can be saved and retrieved for further analysis. After a packet has been captured from the wire, the analyzer breaks down the headers and describes each bit of every header in detail.

Although it is easy to capture and timestamp the packets, novice users tend to capture every packet on a segment when trying to troubleshoot a specific problem. The only problem with that approach is the sheer volume of traffic sent over a network medium. When you analyze the packets, you easily can become overwhelmed. Therefore, by setting up filters and doing some basic statistical analysis, you can isolate the problem with more quickly and easily.

The problem that you are trying to troubleshoot determines what to filter. You also need to be familiar with the protocols (so you know what to look for). For example, if you are trying to troubleshoot a DHCP problem, you have a client who is requesting from the server. That should help determine the source and destination computers. You also know that the DHCP should perform a four-way handshake. Therefore, this should help you determine the packetsanalyzer for which you should be looking.

Placing a Protocol Analyzer

For these analyzersanalyzer to capture all the traffic, you must have a network interface card and driver that supports promiscuous mode operations. A promiscuous mode card is able to capture error packets and packets that are not addressed to the local card. Of course, broadcast and multicast traffic should be visible to the analyzer also.

Most current analyzers require NDIS version 3.0+ drivers to support promiscuous mode operations. In some cases, the analyzer manufacturer offers a specialized driver to enhance the card and provide error reporting. This does not mean that all cards can run in promiscuous mode. Some cards use special functionality to enhance performance at the expense of promiscuous mode operations. For example, although some cards support promiscuous mode operation, those same cards, in an attempt to increase network performance, do not report bad packets.

To analyze multiple LAN and/or WAN segments simultaneously, you have to figure where you want to place your network analyzers. You don't necessarily need an analyzer on every network segment. Of course, having multiple analyzers also has its advantages. The network devices that connect your network and the layout of the network affect where you need to place the routers:

▸ Because a hub is a multi-port repeater, the traffic generated or received by one computer can be seen by all computers connected to the hub. Therefore, if you have a hub, you can connect your protocol analyzer to any port on the hub.

▸ Because a bridge isolates and localizes traffic, you should consider placing protocol analyzers on both sides of the bridge.

▸ If you have a switch (a *switch* is a multi-port bridge that isolates and localizes traffic), you have to use a hub to connect the switch port, the PC, or the host that you want to analyze, and the protocol analyzer. This way you can see all the traffic being sent or received by the PC or host. You can also use analyzer agents or configure your switch for port spanning or mirroring (if your switch supports it). Port spanning or mirroring configures the switch to send a copy of any port's traffic to another port.

▶ Because routers isolate and direct traffic based on the network address, if you place an analyzer on one side of the router, you see only traffic that is destined to that network. Therefore, you should consider placing an analyzer on each side of the router or load analyzer agents on the router.

NOTE

The analyzer agent should be a multi-segment agent that can capture packets from both connected networks.

▶ To test WAN links, you can connect analyzers or agents to both sides of the WAN links and you can also connect analyzers or agents to the IP router. Of course, you may need assistance from your WAN link provider on how to make the physical connection to your WAN link.

Analyzer agents are typically configuration options or software programs that are loaded on switches or PCs to enable them to capture traffic from the wire and send the data to a management console. This way, you can set up the agents and tap into them as needed without actually being there. This enables you analyze all the traffic from a central location.

Using Microsoft's Network Monitor

To install Network Monitor, you must first download Network Monitor 3.1 from the following website:

http://www.microsoft.com/Downloads/details.aspx?familyid=1801D59D-F4D8-4213-8D17-2F6DDE7D7AAC+displaylang=en

Double-click the `.msi` file and step through the wizard.

After it is installed, you can use the GUI interface or you can use `nmcap.exe` (located in the Network Monitor 3.1 installation directory). For sample usage for `nmcap.exe`, just execute the `nmcap /?` or `nmcap /example` commands. You can also use `nmcap` to sweep through saved capture files, filter out frames, and store them in new capture files.

Creating and Saving a Capture Session

To start a capture session, follow these steps:

1. From the start page, click Create a New Capture Tab (or on the File menu, click New, Capture). A new Capture workspace tab opens.

2. In the Select Networks window, select the network or networks from which you want to capture frames.

3. In the Filter window, set up any filters you want to apply during this capture session.

4. On the Capture menu, click Start.

When you have the packets that you want, click Stop Capture or open the Capture menu and click Stop. The packets are then listed in the Frame Summary pane. As you click each packet, the contents of the packets are displayed in the Frame Details pane.

To save a capture so that you can compare it to other captures later or analyze it later, follow these steps:

1. Click the Save icon on the main toolbar (or select File, Save).

2. Browse to the location where you want to save the file (the default location is Microsoft Network Monitor_3\Captures under your Documents directory).

3. Select Displayed Frames, All Frames, or specify a range of frames.

4. Click Save.

To load a capture,

1. Click the Open Folder icon on the main toolbar (or select File, Open, Capture).

2. Browse to the file's location.

3. Click Open.

Using Aliases

Aliases in Network Monitor 3.1 enable you to replace IPv4, IPv6, and Ethernet addresses displayed in the Frame Summary with meaningful user-defined names. For example, you could create the alias localhost to replace the IP address of the local machine. If you apply the alias, the local IP address is replaced with the text localhost everywhere it appears in the Frame Summary.

To create and apply an alias, follow these steps:

1. Create or open a Capture tab.

2. Select the Aliases tab.

3. Click the Create New Alias icon.

4. Enter the address you want to replace and the name with which you want to replace it. Optionally, provide a comment for the alias. The address, name, and comment will appear in the aliases table.

5. Click the stick-pin Apply button in the aliases toolbar to apply the alias. Click the Set Aliases as Default icon to set the aliases as default for all captures.

To save aliases,

1. Click the Save icon on the aliases toolbar.

2. (Optional) Navigate to the folder in which you want to save the aliases.

3. Type the filename for the aliases.

4. Click Save.

To load saved aliases,

1. Click the Open Folder icon on the aliases toolbar.

2. Navigate to the folder containing the saved aliases file (with the extension .nma).

3. Select the aliases file. The aliases table is populated with information from the saved file.

4. Apply the aliases by clicking the stick-pin button.

Using Filters

Filtering is one of the most powerful features of Network Monitor 3.1. Using filters, you can capture or display only those frames that meet the criteria you specify. You can filter on any protocol, protocol element, or property. For example, you can choose to capture only frames that originate from a particular IP address.

Network Monitor 3.1 enables you to select from standard built-in filters or create your own. You can build filters directly from network capture data by right-clicking a protocol property in the Frame Details window and creating a filter for the displayed data.

Filters are text strings that can be typed or pasted into the capture or display filter windows. You can append filters to each other by using keywords such as AND and OR. Examples include

▶ TCP: Pass frames containing the TCP protocol (only).

▶ TCP or UDP: Pass frames containing TCP or frames containing UDP.

▶ `IPv4.sourceaddress==10.1.1.1`: Pass only frames with an IPv4 source address of 10.1.1.1.

▶ `IPv4.address==10.1.1.1`: Pass only frames with an IPv4 source or destination address of 10.1.1.1

To insert one of the standard filters into a capture or display filter pane,

1. From a capture tab, select the Capture or Display Filter window.

2. Select the folder icon or the down-arrow adjacent to it in the filter toolbar.

3. Select Standard Filters.

4. Choose a filter from the cascading menu.

5. The filter is inserted at the current cursor location.

To apply the filter, click the Apply Filter icon on the filter toolbar or press the keyboard shortcut CTRL+ENTER. When a filter is applied, the text box to the right of the Remove Filter button shows the currently applied filter. To remove the filter, press the Remove Filter icon on the filter toolbar.

To make custom filters easier, Network Monitor enables you to use Intellisense to see available options. You can start Intellisense by typing a period (.) in the filter window. You can also shorten things by typing a known keyword (such as `protocol`) and then typing a period. For example, if you type **protocol.**, you see a list of available protocols. If you type **TCP.**, you see a list of TCP protocol elements on which you can filter. In addition, the filter window supports standard windows cut/copy/paste shortcuts. When a filter is typed, you can use the Verify Filter button to check the validity of the filter in the Filter Expression box.

To create and apply a filter,

1. Create or open a Capture tab.

2. Select the Capture Filter window or the Display Filter window by clicking the respective tab according to the type of filter you want to create.

3. Type the filter in the Filter Expression box.

4. Click the Apply Filter button on the filter toolbar (or press Ctrl+Enter) to apply the filter.

To see an example of creating your own filter using Intellisense, follow these steps:

1. Create or open a capture session.

2. Select the Capture Filter window or the Display Filter window according to the type of filter you want to create.

3. Type `protocol.`.

4. Select IPv4 from the drop-down menu and then type a period.

5. Select Address from the drop-down menu.

6. Type `==10.1.1.1`.

7. You will see `IPv4.address==10.1.1.1` in the Filter window.

8. Click the Apply Filter button on the filter toolbar or press Ctrl+Enter to apply the filter.

Capture Options

Network Monitor copies frames to the capture buffer, a resizable storage area in memory. The default size is 20MB. As Network Monitor 3.1 captures network frames, it creates temporary files to store captured data for each capture session running. By default, these files are stored in the temporary directory that is defined in your user profile. You can also customize the maximum size of each of these temporary files. The default is 20MB.

To avoid consuming all available disk space, you can also select the point at which Network Monitor 3.1 stops capturing data. This can be expressed as either a total file size or as a percentage of remaining available disk space. The default is two percent (2%) remaining.

To change any of these file preferences, go to the Tools menu, select Options, and select the Capture tab. They are listed in the Temporary Capture File section.

Looking at a Packet

Data is encapsulated at the transport layer, which is encapsulated at the network layer, which is encapsulated at the data link layer, converted to bits, and sent over some form of media. Of course, when the packet is received at the destination device, the packet is received and processed by the network interface card, and the data is stripped out as you go through the data link layer, the network layer, and the transport layer. The protocol analyzer typically shows the data and the headers that were added by each layer.

Most packets captured by a protocol analyzer have up to four parts (simplified OSI model):

- ▶ Ethernet (data link layer) header includes the destination and source MAC addresses
- ▶ IP header shows the packet as an IPv4 or IPv6 packet and the source and destination IP addresses
- ▶ TCP header or UDP header, including the source and destination ports
- ▶ Protocol payload

Exam Prep Questions

1. For what would SNMP be used?

   ○ **A.** To provide a simple mail delivery system

   ○ **B.** To enable you to read and write to a Trivial File Transfer Protocol server

   ○ **C.** To enable you to activate Windows on your network

   ○ **D.** To monitor network-attached devices in network management systems for conditions that warrant administrative attention

2. You want the SNMP service on the Windows Server 2008 computer to send trap messages to an SNMP trap destination. Which of the following must be supplied? (Select two answers.)

   ○ **A.** SNMP management station's community

   ○ **B.** SNMP management station's IP address

   ○ **C.** SNMP management's scope ID

   ○ **D.** SNMP management station's subnet mask

3. You have a Windows Server 2008 computer. You have 25 computers to which you need push out Windows updates. What would be the easiest way to configure the workstations to get the updates automatically?

   ○ **A.** Configure the Windows Update Settings on each server by using the Control Panel.

   ○ **B.** Run the wuauclt.exe /detectnow command on each server.

   ○ **C.** Run the wuauclt.exe /reauthorization /detectnow command on each server.

   ○ **D.** Use group policies to configure that each computer is to get updates automatically through Windows Updates.

4. Why is it important to have the most up-to-date service packs and security patches? (Choose two answers.)

   ○ **A.** To make your machine more resistant against viruses and other forms of malware

   ○ **B.** To help keep hackers out of your system

   ○ **C.** To make your system legal

   ○ **D.** To test your machine against RPC attacks

5. You have a Windows Server 2008 computer with WSUS. You soon discover that you need to add another server with WSUS to help keep up with the workload. You want the new server to receive updates from the old server. How should you configure the new server?

   ○ **A.** Configure it to communicate with a proxy server.

   ○ **B.** Configure it to communicate with upstream server.

   ○ **C.** Configure it as a WSUS client.

   ○ **D.** Create a new computer group on the upstream server that contains the downstream computer.

6. You are your company's network administrator. You have Windows Server 2008 and Windows XP computers. You would like to verify the security settings to make sure that your systems are secure. What tool can you use to quickly scan the systems you manage?

   ○ **A.** Microsoft Baseline Security Analyzer (MBSA)

   ○ **B.** Security Configuration and Analysis console

   ○ **C.** gpresult.exe

   ○ **D.** Resultant Set of Policy console in planning mode

7. Which of the following is a packet analyzer?

   ○ **A.** Performance Monitor

   ○ **B.** Server Manager

   ○ **C.** Network Monitor

   ○ **D.** MBSA

8. You have Microsoft Network Monitor 3.0 installed on a Windows Server 2008 computer. You capture some packets. However, although some frames show the source and destination computer as names, others display them with IP addresses. You prefer to use names instead of IP addresses. What should you do?

   ○ **A.** Create a new capture filter and apply the filter to the capture.

   ○ **B.** Populate the Aliases table and apply the aliases to the capture.

   ○ **C.** Right-click an IP address and select Convert to Name.

   ○ **D.** Right-click an IP address and select nslookup.

9. You used Network Monitor to capture traffic for four hours. Unfortunately, the captured file called `traffic.cap` ended up being approximately 500MB. You need to create a smaller file from `traffic.cap` called `http.cap` that contains only HTTP-related data. What should you do?

   - ○ **A.** Apply the filter that shows only HTTP traffic and save the file as `ftp.cap`.
   - ○ **B.** Run the `nmcap.exe /inputcapture traffic.cap /capture HTTP /file ftp.cap` command.
   - ○ **C.** Sort the traffic by protocol. Then highlight the unwanted protocols and click Delete from the Action menu.
   - ○ **D.** Open the display option and select port 80 and 443 only. Then save the file as `ftp.cap`.

10. You have a Windows Server 2008 computer that is configured as a DHCP server. You are trying to figure out why a client (MAC address is 0323040A3231) cannot get a DHCP address from the server. What filter can you use?

    - ○ **A.** `IPv4.Address == 0x0323040A3231 && DHCP`
    - ○ **B.** `IPv4.address == 0323040A3231 && DHCP`
    - ○ **C.** `Ethernet.Address == 0x0323040A3231 && DHCP`
    - ○ **D.** `Ethernet.Address == 0323040A3231 && DHCP`

Answers to Exam Prep Questions

1. Answer D is correct. Simple Network Management Protocol (SNMP) enables you to manage and monitor network hosts such as workstation or server computers, routers, bridges, and hubs from a centrally located computer running network management software. Answer A is incorrect because the Simple Mail Transfer (SMTP) is used provide a simiple mail delivery system, not SNMP. Answer B is incorrect because the TFTP client enables you to read and write to a TFTP server. Answer C is incorrect because SNMP has nothing to do with activating Windows.

2. Answers A and B are correct. You need specify the community name (which is the closest to a username and password) and the IP address of the destination. Answers C and D are incorrect because neither a scope ID nor subnet mask is required to send a trap.

3. Answer D is correct. You would use group policies to automatically configure the 25 computers to get updates automatically through Windows Updates. Answer A is incorrect because using group policies would be much easier then configuring each server individually. Answers B and C are incorrect because the `wuauclt.exe` command would not help get updates automatically.

4. Answers A and B are correct. Security patches are essential to keep your system secure. They make your system more resistant against viruses and prevent intruders from accessing your machine. Answer C is incorrect because service packs and security patches do not make a system legal. Answer D is incorrect because although it might make your system more resistant against RPC attacks, service packs and security patches do not test your machine.

5. Answer B is correct. You need to configure the new server to get downloads from the upstream server. Answer A is incorrect because the proxy server allows and filters access to the Internet, which does not help get data from the old server. Answer C is incorrect because the WSUS client is for update installations, not to get downloads from the server to distribute to other servers. Answer D is incorrect because a new computer group does not help get updates from the old server.

6. Answer A is correct. MBSA can be used to scan your own computer or other remote computers for any kind of security problem, including password security, disk security, account security, and security patches. Answer B is incorrect because the Security Configuration and Analysis console is used to compare security settings within group policies. MBSA does more in checking security settings and weaknesses. Answers C and D are incorrect because `gpresult.exe` and Resultant Set of Policy are used to give you the overall effect of group policies.

7. Answer C is correct. Network Monitor is a packet analyzer/protocol analyzer. Answer A is incorrect because Performance Monitor is used to identify bottlenecks on an individual computer. Answer B is incorrect because the Server Manager is used to configure and manage the server. Answer D is incorrect because the Microsoft Baseline Security Analyzer is used to find security holes on a computer.

8. Answer B is correct. You can use aliases to convert the IP addresses to names. Answer A is incorrect because a filter is to help you narrow down the problem. Answers C and D are incorrect because you cannot convert an IP address by right-clicking it and picking an option.

9. Answer B is correct. You need to use the `nmcap.exe` command to isolate the packets. Answer A is incorrect because if you apply the filter, the other packets are still there but only the HTTP is being displayed at the moment. So when you save it, it will still be a large file. Answer C is incorrect because you cannot delete the unwanted packets. Answer D is incorrect because you can not use the display to isolate the packets.

10. Answer C is correct. When figuring out a DHCP problem, you need to start with the MAC address because the IP address has not been assigned yet. So you need to specify `Ethernet.Address`. In addition, the MAC address must begin with 0x. You then use the `&&` DHCP to specify the `AND` DHCP protocol. Answers A and B are incorrect because you need to specify `Ethernet.address` instead of `IPv4.Address`. Answer D is incorrect because the MAC address needs to begin with 0x.

Need to Know More?

For more information about Windows Updates and security, visit the following website:

▸ http://www.microsoft.com/protect/computer/updates/mu.mspx

For more information about WSUS 3.0, visit the following website:

▸ http://technet.2microsoft.com/windowsserver/en/library/
bc61fb16-13d4-4b3e-b547-fae6a0d5b7bc1033.mspx?mfr=true

For more information about MBSA, visit the following website:

▸ http://technet.microsoft.com/en-us/security/cc184924.aspx

CHAPTER TEN

Practice Exam I

1. You have one server at the corporate office and a server at each of the two remote sites. You want to configure the Event Logs subscription at the corporate office to collect events from the other two servers. What do you need to do?

   ○ **A.** Create an event collector subscription configuration file named `subscription.xml`. Then run the `wecutil cs subscription.xml` command on the server1.

   ○ **B.** Create a custom view on server1. Then export the custom view to a file named `subscription.xml`. Then run the `wecutil cs subscription.xml` command on server1.

   ○ **C.** Create an event collector subscription configuration file named `subscription.xml`. Then run the `wecutil im subscription.xml` command on server1.

   ○ **D.** Save the configuration from the `ForwardedEvents.log` and save it as `subscription.xml`. Then run the `wecutil cs subscription.xml` command on server1.

2. You have a computer with Windows Server 2008 Server Core installed. You need to configure the server to point to 172.24.1.10 as the preferred DNS server. What should you do?

   ○ **A.** Open the Network and Sharing Center. Click Manage Network Connections. Double-click the network card and open the TCP/IP properties. Change the DNS to point 172.24.1.10.

   ○ **B.** Execute the `netsh interface ipv4 add dnsserver "LAN" static 172.24.1.10 index=1` command.

   ○ **C.** Execute the `ipconfig /dnsserver:172.24.1.10 index=1` command.

   ○ **D.** Execute the `netsh interface ipv4 set address name "LAN" source=static address=172.24.1.10` command.

3. You have a server that runs the Server Core installation of Windows Server 2008. The server runs the DHCP server role and the DNS server role. How would you configure the server to use Server2 (IP address 192.168.0.254) as the preferred DNS server?

○ **A.** Execute the `netsh interface ipv4 set dnsserver "LAN" static 192.168.0.254 primary` command and the `netsh interface ipv4 set dnsserver "LAN" static 192.168.0.1` commands.

○ **B.** Execute the `netsh interface ipv4 set address name="Local Area Connection" source=static address=192.168.0.254 mask=255.255.255.0 gateway=172.24.1.1` command.

○ **C.** Execute the `netsh interface ipv4 Name="Local Area Connection" add 192.168.0.254 255.255.255.0 gateway=172.24.1.1` command.

○ **D.** Execute the `netsh interface ipv4 add dnsserver "LAN" static 192.168.0.254 index=1` command.

4. For your company, you have decided to segment your class B address. The location has three buildings and each building contains no more than 175 unique hosts. You want to make each building its own subnet, and you want to utilize your address space the best way possible. Which subnet mask meets your needs in this situation?

○ **A.** 255.0.0.0

○ **B.** 255.255.255.0

○ **C.** 255.255.0.0

○ **D.** 255.255.255.240

5. You want to send packets to a group of PCs but you want only one PC to respond. Which kind of address would you use?

○ **A.** Unicast

○ **B.** Broadcast

○ **C.** Multicast

○ **D.** Anycast

6. What can be said about the address 224.20.0.20?

○ **A.** Because it starts with 224, it is a class B address with a subnet mask for 255.255.0.0.

○ **B.** Because it starts with 224, it is a class C address with a subnet mask for
255.255.255.0

○ **C.** Because it starts with 244, it is a class D address used for multicasting.

○ **D.** It is a reserved address that is used for broadcast all class C addresses.

7. You have several Windows Server 2008 computers that act as DNS servers. You make
changes on the primary DNS server. You want the secondary DNS servers to be updated
immediately. What should you do?

○ **A.** Run the `dnscmd /ZoneUpdateFromDs` command on the other servers
where the change was made.

○ **B.** Run the `dnscmd /ZoneUpdateFromDs` command on the server where
the change was made.

○ **C.** Decrease the Minimum (default) TTL option to 15 minutes on the Start of
Authority (SOA) record for the zone.

○ **D.** Run the `dnscmd /zonerefresh` command on the other servers where
the changes were made.

8. You have two Windows Server 2008 computers with DNS. Server1 handles your external
DNS for your corporation and Server2 handles your internal DNS for your corporation.
The users of your corporation use Server2 as their primary DNS server. Server2 then
forwards requests to Server1. You find a problem with your external DNS and you
therefore make the appropriate changes on Server1 to correct the problem. However,
the internal users cannot see the new IP address assigned to the problem hostname.
What should you do?

○ **A.** Run the `dnscmd /clearcache` on Server1.

○ **B.** Run the `dnscmd /clearcache` on Server2.

○ **C.** Run the `ipconfig /flushdns` on Server1.

○ **D.** Run the `ipconfig /flushdns` on Server2.

○ **E.** Run the `ipconfig /flushdns` on the workstation.

9. You have a primary DNS server hosted at your corporate office. You also have several
secondary DNS servers hosted at your various remote sites. You need to minimize
DNS zone transfer traffic over the WAN links. What should you do?

○ **A.** Decrease the Retry Interval setting in the Start of Authority (SOA) record
for the zone.

○ **B.** Decrease the Refresh Interval setting in the Start of Authority (SOA) record
for the zone.

○ **C.** Increase the Retry Interval setting in the Start of Authority (SOA) record for the zone.

○ **D.** Increase the Refresh Interval setting in the Start of Authority (SOA) record for the zone.

10. You have a server application that will be placed on a Windows Server 2008 member server. This server is not a member of the corporate domain. Users will access the server application by running a client application that will access the server. However, when the users run the client connection, it fails frequently. You discover that it has no problem converting from the hostname to the IP address but has problems converting from the IP address to the hostname. What do you need to do?

○ **A.** On each client computer, add a HOSTS file entry for the application server.

○ **B.** Create a host (A) record for the application server.

○ **C.** Create a pointer (ptr) record for the application server.

○ **D.** Modify each client computer to use the application server as the primary DNS server.

11. You are the administrator for your domain. You have two DNS servers. Server1 handles your external DNS and Server2 handles your internal DNS. You discover your email server is not receiving email from the Internet. What do you need to do?

○ **A.** Make sure that you have an MX record for your mail server on Server1.

○ **B.** Make sure that you have an MX record for your mail server on Server2.

○ **C.** Make sure that you have an SRV record for your mail server on Server1.

○ **D.** Make sure that you have an SRV record for your mail server on Server2.

12. You have a Windows Server 2008 computer called Server1 configured as a DNS server. You have a VPN connection to a partner company. The partner company has a DNS server called Oscar. You decide to create a stub zone on Server1 for the partner domain. However, when Oscar fails, users cannot perform name resolution for the partner website. What can you do?

○ **A.** Change the stub zone to a primary zone on Server1.

○ **B.** Change the stub zone to a secondary zone on Server1.

○ **C.** Open the SOA record for the stub zone. Change the Minimum (default) TTL setting to 12 hours.

○ **D.** Increase the TTL for the SOA on Oscar.

13. You have a Windows Server 2008 computer with a DNS secondary zone. You need to reconfigure the server as a caching-only DNS server. What should you do?

    ○ **A.** Uninstall and reinstall the DNS role.

    ○ **B.** Change the DNS zone to a stub zone.

    ○ **C.** Delete the zone and re-create the zone.

    ○ **D.** Change the zone type to a caching-only DNS zone.

14. You are the network administrator for your company. All servers are running Microsoft Windows Server 2008. The network currently consists of a single subnet. You need to subnet the existing network to optimize network traffic. You plan to use a class C network ID of 192.168.0.0. The network will be subdivided into 12 different subnets. There may be future plans to add an additional 2 subnets. Which subnet mask should you choose?

    ○ **A.** 255.255.255.224

    ○ **B.** 255.255.255.240

    ○ **C.** 255.255.255.248

    ○ **D.** 255.255.255.252

15. You have several Windows Server 2008 computers that host your Active Directory domain acme.com. Your clients receive their IP addresses from a DHCP server. You decide to create a second DHCP server. You therefore configure the servers using the 80-20 rule. You have a workstation called XPPR that needs to have a DHCP reservation. What should you do?

    ○ **A.** Run the `ipconfig /renew` command on XPPR.

    ○ **B.** Run the `netsh add helper` command on XPPR.

    ○ **C.** Add the DHCP reservation for XPPR to both DHCP servers.

    ○ **D.** Add a host record to the DNS server for the XPPR host.

16. You are the network administrator for your company. All servers are running Microsoft Windows Server 2008. You have been using Network Monitor to capture and analyze DHCP-related traffic. You notice a large amount of traffic from IP address lease requests, and the frequency of the requests is high. You verify that there are more IP addresses in the scope than DHCP clients on the network. You want to reduce network traffic. What should you do?

    ○ **A.** Configure half of the clients with static IP addresses.

    ○ **B.** Increase the lease duration for the scope.

    ○ **C.** Configure another DHCP server on the network.

    ○ **D.** Add a DHCP relay agent to the network.

17. You have a configured DHCP scope to hand out IP configuration to the DHCP addresses. By default, how long does it wait before it attempts to renew its lease?

    ○　**A.**　Four hours

    ○　**B.**　Eight hours

    ○　**C.**　Three days

    ○　**D.**　Four days

    ○　**E.**　Eight days

18. You have a computer running Windows Server 2008. You need to configure the printer to support both Windows and UNIX users. What you need to do?

    ○　**A.**　Install the Line Printer Daemon (LPD) Services role service on SRV1.

    ○　**B.**　Configure the printers on SRV1 to use Line Printer Remote printing.

    ○　**C.**　Install the File Server role on SRV1 and activate the services for the NFS Role Service option.

    ○　**D.**　Install the Subsystem for UNIX-based Applications role on the SRV1.

19. You have multiple print servers. You decide to use the Print Management console to manage your print servers. You need to send automatic notification when a printer is not available. What should you do?

    ○　**A.**　Configure an email notification for the Printers with Jobs printer filter.

    ○　**B.**　Configure an email notification for the Printers Not Ready printer filter.

    ○　**C.**　Enable the Show Informational Notifications for Local Printers option on the print servers.

    ○　**D.**　Enable the Show Informational Notifications for Network Printers option on the print servers.

20. Which of the following authentication protocols send information in clear text?

    ○　**A.**　PAP

    ○　**B.**　EAP

    ○　**C.**　MS-CHAP

    ○　**D.**　SPAP

21. Which authentication method would you use to create an encrypted channel between an 801.11 wireless client computer and a RADIUS server?

    ○ **A.** PAP

    ○ **B.** CHAP

    ○ **C.** MS-CHAP

    ○ **D.** PEAP

22. You are the network administrator for your company. All servers are running Microsoft Windows Server 2008. You discover that the IPSec policy configured for domain controllers is not behaving normally. You suspect that a configuration change was made by another administrator. You need to determine whether a change was made. What should you do?

    ○ **A.** Open the IP Security Monitor tool and select the Active Policy container.

    ○ **B.** Launch the Security Configuration and Analysis tool. Analyze the IPSec settings on the server.

    ○ **C.** Open the Windows Event Viewer and view the contents of the Security log.

    ○ **D.** Execute the `ipsecpol` command from the command prompt.

23. You are the network administrator for your company. All servers are running Microsoft Windows Server 2008. You are configuring IPSec between two servers in a workgroup. You assign Client (Respond Only) to each of the servers, but you notice that IP packets being sent between the two servers are not being secured. What is causing the problem?

    ○ **A.** Both are configured with the Client (Respond Only) policy.

    ○ **B.** IPSec can be used only with Active Directory.

    ○ **C.** One of the servers must be configured as an IPSec client.

    ○ **D.** The servers cannot be members of the same workgroup.

24. You have a Windows Server 2008 computer configured as a VPN server. When users trying to connect to your network using PPTP, they get the following error message:

    Error 721: The remote computer is not responding

    What do you need to do to overcome this problem?

    ○ **A.** Open port 443 on the firewall.

    ○ **B.** Open port 500 on the firewall.

    ○ **C.** Open port 1723 on the firewall.

    ○ **D.** Open port 1701 on the firewall.

25. You have a network with all servers running Microsoft Windows Server 2008. You need to implement Routing and Remote Access to enable users to access resources from other locations while still maintaining a high level of security. The company president needs to be able to access resources from his home office and other locations. You need to configure callback for the user accounts. What should you do?

   ○ **A.** Choose No Callback for the president's account and Set by Caller for the other accounts.

   ○ **B.** Choose Set by Caller for the president's account and No Callback for the other accounts.

   ○ **C.** Choose Always Callback To for the president's account and Set by Caller for the other accounts.

   ○ **D.** Choose Set by Caller for the president's account and Always Callback To for the other accounts.

26. You have Windows Server 2008 with the Network Access Protection (NAP) role installed. You want the NAP policies to enforce all wireless connections. What should you do?

   ○ **A.** Configure all portable computers to use PAP authentication.

   ○ **B.** Configure all portable computers to have the Security Center enabled.

   ○ **C.** Configure all access points to use 802.1X authentication.

   ○ **D.** Configure all portal computers to have the Windows Firewall enabled.

27. You have the domain-based DFS namespace called \\acme.com\data. The namespace hierarchy is updated frequently. How can you reduce the workload put on the PDC emulator?

   ○ **A.** Enable the Optimize for Consistency option.

   ○ **B.** Enable the Optimize for Scalability option.

   ○ **C.** Set the Ordering Method option to Lowest Cost.

   ○ **D.** Change the Ordering method option to Random Order.

   ○ **E.** Increase the cache duration.

28. You have a Windows Server 2008 computer with WSUS 3.0 installed. You want to make sure that the traffic is encrypted when administrators access the WSUS administrative website. What should you do?

   ○ **A.** Install a digital certificate and configure SSL encryption.

   ○ **B.** Configure WSUS to use MS-CHAP version 2.

○   **C.** Configure the WSUS folder to use EFS.

○   **D.** Require the server to use IPSec.

29. Which of the backups are available in Windows Server Backups? (Choose all that apply.)

    ○   **A.** Full backups

    ○   **B.** Incremental backups

    ○   **C.** Differential backups

    ○   **D.** Copy backups

30. Which group enables you to back up and restore all files even if they do not have NTFS permissions to the files and folders?

    ○   **A.** Power Users group

    ○   **B.** Replicator group

    ○   **C.** Backup Operators group

    ○   **D.** Authenticated Users group

31. What occurs if you move a file from one folder to another within the same NTFS volume?

    ○   **A.** The file retains its permissions.

    ○   **B.** The file inherits the permissions of the source folder.

    ○   **C.** The file inherits the permissions of the target folder.

    ○   **D.** The file permissions are lost.

32. You have a computer with Windows Server 2008. You have a folder called Data. Pat is a member of the Sales group and the Management group. The Sales group is given the Read NTFS permission to the Data folder and the Management group is given the Manage NTFS permission. The Pat user is not assigned any permissions. What is Pat's effective permission for the files in the Data folder?

    ○   **A.** Read

    ○   **B.** Modify

    ○   **C.** Full Control

    ○   **D.** No permissions

33. You have a computer with Windows Server 2008. You have a folder called C:\Data. Pat is a member of the Sales group. The Sales group is given the Reader shared permission and the Full Control NTFS permission. What is Pat's effective permission when he tries to access the C:\Data\report.doc document while sitting in front of the computer?

    ○ **A.** Read

    ○ **B.** Modify

    ○ **C.** Full Control

    ○ **D.** No permission

34. You have a laptop that will be used by the vice president of your company. You want to encrypt the C drive and all the data files in case the laptop is stolen. What should you do?

    ○ **A.** Use EFS.

    ○ **B.** Use BitLocker.

    ○ **C.** Use NTFS volume encryption.

    ○ **D.** Use NTFS permissions.

35. Which of the following is not part of the system state?

    ○ **A.** Registry

    ○ **B.** Boot files

    ○ **C.** The INI files for the various applications

    ○ **D.** The SYSVOL folder

    ○ **E.** IIS Metadirectory

36. What command can be used to run the Windows Server backups?

    ○ **A.** backup

    ○ **B.** ntbackup

    ○ **C.** sysbackup

    ○ **D.** wbadmin

37. You have a computer running Windows Server 2008. You have folder called C:\SalesData that contains confidential information. You want to make sure that when users are not connected to the network, the file is not available as an offline file. What do you need to do?

   ○ **A.** You can use group policies to stop this folder from being available offline.

   ○ **B.** Open the folder properties and select Offline Settings. Then specify that the folder is not available offline.

   ○ **C.** Open the folder properties and select Offline Settings. Set the cache to 0MB.

   ○ **D.** Remove the shared folder.

38. A printer has documents you cannot delete from the printer queue. What can you do?

   ○ **A.** Shut off and turn on the printer.

   ○ **B.** Restart the print spooler.

   ○ **C.** Delete the C:\Windows\Spooler folder.

   ○ **D.** Open the printer queue and select Clear Print Queue. Be sure to also select the Force option.

39. When you want to connect directly to a printer that is connected directly to the network, what do you have to do?

   ○ **A.** Install the printer as a local printer.

   ○ **B.** Install the printer as a network printer.

   ○ **C.** Install the printer as a remote printer.

   ○ **D.** Install the printer as a hybrid printer.

40. What command would you use to migrate printers from one Windows Server 2008 to another?

   ○ **A.** The `printmig.exe` command

   ○ **B.** The `printbrm.exe` command

   ○ **C.** The `wbadmin.exe` command

   ○ **D.** The `print.exe` command

41. How do you install WSUS?

   ○ **A.** Install it as a server role.

   ○ **B.** Install it as a feature.

   ○ **C.** Download it from Microsoft and install it.

   ○ **D.** Use Add/Remove Programs to install it from the Windows Server 2008 DVD.

42. Which of the following describes an unsolicited message sent by an SNMP agent to an SNMP management system when the agent detects that a certain type of event has occurred locally on the managed host?

- ○ **A.** SNMP trap
- ○ **B.** SNMP agent
- ○ **C.** SNMP community
- ○ **D.** SNMP MIB

43. You have a class B network that has been subnetted. Its subnet mask is 255.255.224.0. How many subnets can you have?

- ○ **A.** 6
- ○ **B.** 8
- ○ **C.** 14
- ○ **D.** 16
- ○ **E.** 30

44. You have a subnet mask of 255.255.240.0. What is the CIDR for this subnet mask?

- ○ **A.** \20
- ○ **B.** \22
- ○ **C.** \24
- ○ **D.** \26

45. What allows multiple computers to share a single external IP address?

- ○ **A.** CIDR
- ○ **B.** NFS
- ○ **C.** NAT
- ○ **D.** IPv6

46. Ping and tracert use which protocol?

- ○ **A.** ARP
- ○ **B.** ICMP
- ○ **C.** TCP
- ○ **D.** UDP

47. To access a shared folder, you would use what?

   ○ **A.** UNC

   ○ **B.** FQDN

   ○ **C.** SOA

   ○ **D.** Root hint

48. How do you compress the WINS database?

   ○ **A.** Use the `jetpack` command.

   ○ **B.** Use the `nbtstat` command.

   ○ **C.** Use `nslookup` command.

   ○ **D.** Use the `compress` command.

49. Which resource record is used to translate a hostname to an IPv6 address?

   ○ **A.** A

   ○ **B.** AAAA

   ○ **C.** ptr

   ○ **D.** CNAME

50. What tool can you use to help you find a rogue DHCP server?

   ○ **A.** DHCP console

   ○ **B.** `nslookup` command

   ○ **C.** `dhcploc` command

   ○ **D.** `jetpack` command

11

Answers to Practice Exam I

Answers at a Glance

1. A	**18.** A	**35.** C
2. B	**19.** B	**36.** D
3. D	**20.** A	**37.** B
4. B	**21.** D	**38.** B
5. D	**22.** C	**39.** A
6. C	**23.** A	**40.** B
7. D	**24.** C	**41.** C
8. B	**25.** D	**42.** A
9. D	**26.** C	**43.** A
10. C	**27.** B	**44.** A
11. A	**28.** A	**45.** C
12. B	**29.** A, B	**46.** B
13. A	**30.** C	**47.** A
14. B	**31.** A	**48.** A
15. C	**32.** B	**49.** B
16. B	**33.** C	**50.** C
17. D	**34.** B	

Answers with Explanations

1. Answer A is correct. `Wecutil.exe` is a Windows Event Collector utility that enables an administrator to create and manage subscriptions to events forwarded from remote event sources that support the WS-Management protocol. After creating the configuration XML file, you then use the `wecutil cs` command to create the subscription. Answer B is incorrect because you do not export the configuration file. Answer C is incorrect because it should be `wecutil cs`, not `wecutil im`. Answer D is incorrect because you need to create the XML file, not save the configuration from the `forwardedevents.log`.

2. Answer B is correct. You need to use the `netsh interface ipv4 add dnsserver` command. Because it specifies the preferred DNS server, you specify `index=1`. Answer A is incorrect because the Network and Sharing Center is not available on a Server Core. Answer C is incorrect because `ipconfig.exe` cannot be used to configure static addresses. Answer D is incorrect because the `netsh` command needs to use the add `dnsserver` option.

3. Answer D is correct. You need to use the `netsh interface` command add `dnsserver` command to configure the DNS serer. The `index=1` specifies the first DNS server or the preferred server.

4. Answer B is correct. With 175 hosts, you need to use 8 bits to represent the hosts (Remember $2^8-2=254$). Out of the 16 bits that are pre-designated for a class B address, that leaves 8 bits for the subnets and 8 bits for the hosts computers, which shows a subnet mask of 255.255.255.0. Answers A and C are incorrect because 255.0.0.0 is the default subnet mask for a class A and 255.255.0.0 is the default subnet mask for a class B. Answer D is incorrect because a 255.255.255.240 subnet mask means that there are only 4 host bits ($2^4-2=14$), nowhere near enough to cover the 175 hosts for each building.

5. Answer D is correct. Anycast is a one-to-many routing topology. However, the data stream is not transmitted to all receivers, just the one that the router decides is the "closest" in the network. Answer A is incorrect because a unicast address is sent to a single host. Answer B is incorrect because broadcasts are sent to all hosts within a subnet. Answer C is incorrect because a multicast has the sender send a single transmission (from the sender's unicast address) to the multicast address, and the routers take care of making copies and sending them to all receivers that have registered their interest in data from that sender.

6. Answer C is correct. Multicast addresses are defined as a class D, which are from 224.0.0.0 to 239.255.255.255. Answer A is incorrect because a class B starts from 128 to 191. Answer B is incorrect because a class C starts from 192 to 223. Answer D is incorrect because a broadcast address has all host bits set to 1.

7. Answer D is correct. The dnscmd /zonerefresh command forces a secondary DNS zone to update from the master. Answer A is incorrect because the dnscmd /ZoneUdpateFromDs command updates the specified Active Directory–integrated zone from Active Directory. Answer B is incorrect because you need to run the dnscmd /ZoneUpdatefromDs command from the servers that still need the change. Answer C is incorrect because decreasing the TTL does not force changes to propagate immediately.

8. Answer B is correct. Because entries are cached on the user's primary server, you need to clear the cache so that it can get the new value from Server1. Answer A is incorrect because you already made the change on Server1. Answers C and D are incorrect because they will not clear the cache generated by the DNS servers, just the cache generated for their own DNS resolution. Answer E is incorrect because as long it is cached in Server2, the users will keep getting the same value back.

9. Answer D is correct. You need to increase the Refresh Interval settings so that updates are not sent as often. Answers A and C are incorrect because the retry interval determines how often other DNS servers that load and host the zone are to retry a request for update of the zone each time the refresh interval occurs. Answer B is incorrect because decreasing the Refresh Interval setting would generate more traffic.

10. Answer C is correct. The ptr record is to translate from IP address to hostname. Answer A is incorrect because although this may be a possible solution, you have to modify every client computer to complete it. Adding an entry to the DNS server is a much better option. Answer B is incorrect because the A record translates hostname to the IP address. Answer D is incorrect because the application server has never been stated as a DNS server and therefore would cause other name resolution problems if a client tries to use it as a DNS server and it is not a DNS server.

11. Answer A is correct. For users to be able to send email, they must find the location of your email server. This is done by the MX record, which must be placed on the external DNS server. Answer B is incorrect because the MX record needs to be placed on the external DNS server and not the internal DNS server. Answers C and D are incorrect because the SRV records are not needed for your email to work.

12. Answer B is correct. The secondary zone has all information for the zone. The stub zone has only the minimum information to redirect people to the DNS server for the partner zone. Answer A is incorrect because a zone can have only one primary DNS server. Answers C and D are incorrect because the TTL specifies only how long a record remains in the DNS cache. It does not help if the server fails.

13. Answer A is correct. The caching-only DNS server has no preconfigured DNS zones. Therefore, to get rid of the DNS configuration, you need to uninstall and reinstall the DNS role. Answer B is incorrect because the stub zone only directs users to a specific zone. Answer C is incorrect because deleting the zones and re-creating a zone does not make a caching-only DNS server. Answer D is incorrect there is no caching-only DNS zone.

14. Answer B is correct. You should use a subnet mask of 255.255.255.240. This will allow for a total of 14 subnets. You can determine the number of subnets by using the formula of 2^x-2 where x is the number of bits taken from the host IDs and used for the subnet mask. With a subnet mask of 255.255.255.240, 4 bits have been used and 2^4-2 is equal to 14. Therefore, a total of 14 subnets can be created. Answers A, C, and D are incorrect. You should not use a subnet mask of 255.255.255.224 because it only allows you to create a maximum of 6 subnets. The remaining subnets should not be selected because they support far more subnets than will ever be required..

15. Answer C is correct. You need to add the DHCP reservation to both DHCP servers so that if one server fails, the other one can still hand out the reservation. Answer A is incorrect because the `ipconfig /renew` command would not create reservations on both servers. Answer B is incorrect because the `netsh` command would not create reservations on both servers. Answer D is incorrect because adding a host record to the DNS server would not create reservations on the DHCP server.

16. Answer B is correct. If you increase the lease duration, clients do not have to renew their IP address leases with the DHCP server as often. Answer A is incorrect because although this would reduce the amount of DHCP traffic, it does not really address the problem at hand and decentralizes IP address administration. Answer C is incorrect because placing a second DHCP server on the network would provide load balancing but would not address the amount of traffic being generated. Answer D is incorrect because a DHCP relay agent is used to forward DHCP requests from one subnet to the DHCP server located on another subnet.

17. Answer D is correct. By default, the lease duration is eight days. In addition, by default, a DHCP client tries to renew the DHCP lease by half of the lease duration. Therefore, the lease attempt would be four days. Therefore, answers, A, B, C, and E are incorrect.

18. Answer A is correct. You need to install the LPD Services role on the server so that the UNIX computers can print with the server. Answer B is incorrect because you don't have to reconfigure the printers to communicate with the UNIX users. Answer C is incorrect because NFS is to support file sharing for UNIX users, not to print. Answer D is incorrect because the subsystem for UNIX-based applications is used to run certain UNIX applications, not for printing.

19. Answer B is correct. You can configure an email notification for the printer by using the Print Management console. Answer A is incorrect because you don't want to be notified when printers have jobs. Answers C and D are incorrect because you don't want to be sent information notifications for the printers; you want only notifications of when the printer is not available.

20. Answer A is correct. Password Authentication Protocol (PAP) is not recommended as an authentication protocol because information is sent in unencrypted clear text. Answers B, C, and D are incorrect because they do not sent passwords in clear text.

21. Answer D is correct. The Protected Extensible Authentication Protocol (PEAP) uses Transport Layer Security (TLS) to create an encrypted channel between an authenticating EAP client, such as a wireless computer, and an EAP authenticator, such as the RADIUS server. Answers A, B, and C are incorrect because PAP, CHAP, and MS-CHAP are not used for wireless authentication.

22. Answer C is correct. As long as auditing of policy changes has been enabled, you can monitor when changes are made to an IPSec policy by using the Event Viewer. Audited events are written to the Security log. Therefore answers A, B, and D are incorrect because these tools cannot be used to monitor whether an IPSec policy change was made. The `ipsecpol` command is used in Windows 2000 to configure IPSec policies, filters, and filter actions.

23. Answer A is correct. If both servers are configured with the Client (Respond Only) policy, they respond only to requests for secure communications. One of the servers must be configured with Server (Request Security). Answer B is incorrect because IPSec can be configured through Active Directory or on the local computer. Answer C is incorrect because computers are not configured as IPSec clients. Answer D is incorrect because the workgroup membership has no impact on how servers respond to security.

24. Answer C is correct. Because the Windows firewall is enabled by default, you need to disable the firewall or open port 1723 for PPTP to function. Answer A is incorrect because port 443 is used for SSL and SSTP. Answers B and D are incorrect because port 500 and 1701 are needed for L2TP with IPSec.

25. Answer D is correct. Because the president needs remote access from various locations, you should select the Set by Caller option. To limit the locations from which network administrators can dial in, select Always Callback To. In this way, the remote access server always calls them back at the configured phone numbers, ensuring they are attempting remote access from authorized locations. Selecting No Callback disables this feature. Therefore, answers A, B, and C are incorrect.

26. Answer C is correct. For you to enforce all wireless connections, you must have 802.1X authentication. Answer A is incorrect because PAP is an unencrypted authentication and is not recommended for any authentication. Answers B and D are incorrect because neither the Security Center nor the Windows Firewall are a factor in wireless connections.

27. Answer B is correct. By default, DFS namespace is optimized for consistency, which attempts to poll the PDC every hour. To reduce the workload on the PDC emulator, you can select Optimize for Scalability, which polls the closest domain controller every hour. Answer A is incorrect because enabling the Optimize for Consistency option polls the PDC emulator every hour. Answers C, D, and E are incorrect because ordering and cache do not configure how the DFS namespace communicates with the PDC.

28. Answer A is correct. You need to install a digital certificate and configure SSL to encrypt the traffic when accessing the administrative website. Answer B is incorrect because the MS-CHAP version 2 is for authentication, not for encryption. Answer C is incorrect because encrypting the WSUS folder does not encrypt the traffic. Answer D is incorrect because if you require IPSec, all traffic is encrypted.

29. Answers A and B are correct. Windows Server Backups provide only full and incremental backups. Therefore, answers C and D are incorrect.

30. Answer C is incorrect. Members of the Backup Operators group can back up and restore all files and folders even if they are not owners of the file and do not have permissions to the file. Answer A is incorrect because the Power Users group gives a user a little more ability on a server, but it does not give additional ability to back up and restore files. Answer B incorrect because the Replicator group is for directory replication functions. Answer D is incorrect because the Authenticated Users group is anyone who successfully authenticates in Windows.

31. Answer A is correct. If you move a file within the volume, the file retains the same permissions. Therefore, answers B, C, and D are incorrect.

32. Answer B is correct. When figuring out the effective NTFS permissions, permissions are cumulative and least restrictive (except denied permissions). Therefore, the least restrictive is the Modify permission. Therefore answers A, C, and D are incorrect.

33. Answer C is correct. Because Pat accesses the document directly without accessing the shared folder, Pat has Full Control. Share permissions do not matter if they are accessed directly. Therefore, answers A, B, and D are incorrect.

34. Answer B is incorrect. To encrypt an entire drive, you can use BitLocker. Answer A is incorrect because EFS should be used only to encrypt individual files and folders. Answer C is incorrect because there is no such thing as NTFS volume encryption. Answer D is incorrect because you cannot use NTFS permission to encrypt a volume, folder, or file.

35. Answer C is correct. The INI files for the varousapplications are not part of the system state. Therefore, these INI files willhave to be backed up as part of a normal file backup. Answers A, B, D, and E are incorrect because the Registry, boot files, the SYSVOL folder, and IIS Metadirectory are part of the system state.

36. Answer D is correct. In Windows Server 2008, backups are done with the wbadmin command. Therefore, answers A, B, and C are incorrect.

37. Answer B is correct. You can specify a folder to not be available offline. Answer A is incorrect because you can specify only whether offline files are available, not which folder is available offline. Answer C is incorrect because there are no cache settings for a shared folder. Answer D is incorrect because you don't want to remove the shared folder because it would not be available when users are connected to the network.

38. Answer B is correct. If the print spooler becomes unresponsive or you have print jobs that you cannot delete, you should try to restart the Print Spooler service. Answer A is incorrect because shutting off and turning on the printer does not clear the queue on

the server. Answer C is incorrect because you cannot fix the problem by manually deleting the spooler folder. Answer D is incorrect because there is no Clear Print Queue or Force option.

39. Answer A is correct. When you connect to a printer that is connected through a TCP/IP port, you install the printer as a local printer. Answer B is incorrect because the network printer is used to access a shared printer. Answers C and D are incorrect because these options do not exist when installing a printer.

40. Answer B is correct. To migrate printers from one server to another, you would use the `printbrm.exe` command. Answer A is incorrect because the `printmig.exe` command was used to migrate printers in Windows Server 2003. Answer C is incorrect because the `wbadmin.exe` command is used to back up files and folders. Answer D is incorrect because the `print.exe` command is not used to migrate printers.

41. Answer C is correct. WSUS is only available from Microsoft as an executable. Answers A, B, and D are incorrect because WSUS is not available within Windows Server 2008 itself.

42. Answer A is correct. A trap is an unsolicited message sent by an SNMP agent to a SNMP management system when the agent detects that a certain type of event has occurred. Answer B is incorrect because the SNMP agent is used monitor for SNMP traps. Answer C is incorrect because the SNMP community is used to manage the SNMP security. Answer D is incorrect because the SNMP Management Information Base is used to store data used by the agents.

43. Answer A is correct. Because it is a class B network, the third octet was split. 224 translates to 1110 0000. Because 3 bits are used for hosts, $2^3-2=6$. Therefore, answers B, C, D, and E are incorrect.

44. Answer A is correct. 255.255.240.0 translates to 1111 1111.1111 1111.1111 0000.0000 0000. Because there are 20 1s, the CIDR is \20. Therefore, answers B, C, and D are incorrect.

45. Answer C is correct. Network address translation (NAT) enables multiple computers to share a single public IP address. Answer A is incorrect because CIDR is used with classless networks. Answer B is incorrect because NFS is used by UNIX computers to share files. Answer D is incorrect because IPv6 does not enable you to use a single IP address for multiple computers.

46. Answer B is correct. `Ping` and `tracert` use the ICMP. Answer A is incorrect because ARP is used to translate IP addresses to MAC addresses. Answers C and D are incorrect because ICMP does not use TCP and UDP.

47. Answer A is correct. A UNC is used to connect to a shared folder via the \\servername\ sharename format. Answer B is incorrect because the FQDN is used to access a web page. Answer C is incorrect because the Start of Authority (SOA) is used to define a DNS domain. Answer D is incorrect because the root hint is used by DNS to find the top-level DNS servers when performing name resolution.

48. Answer A is correct. The `jetpack` command can be used to compress both the WINS and DHCP databases. Answer B is incorrect because `nbtstat` is used to troubleshoot WINS resolution. Answer C is incorrect because `nslookup` is used to troubleshoot DNS name resolution. Answer D is incorrect because the `compress` command cannot be used to compress a WINS database.

49. Answer B is correct. AAAA resource records are used to translate hostnames to IPv6 addresses. Answer A is incorrect because the A records translate hostnames to IPv4 addresses. Answer C is incorrect because the ptr record is used to translate from IP address to hostname. Answer D is incorrect because the CNAME is used as an alias.

50. Answer C is correct. The `dhcploc` command can be used to locate all DHCP servers, including rogue DHCP servers. Answers A and B are incorrect because they cannot help you find a rogue DHCP server. Answer D is incorrect because the `jetpack` command is used to compact a DHCP database.

CHAPTER TWELVE

Practice Exam 2

1. You have computer with Windows Server 2008 Server Core installed. You need to configure the Local Area Connection interface to the IPv4 address 172.24.1.10 and a subnet mask of 255.255.255.0. In addition, you need to assign the default gateway of 172.24.1.1. What should you do?

   ○ **A.** Open the Network and Sharing Center. Click Manage Network Connections. Double-click the network card and open the TCP/IP properties. Change the DNS to point 172.24.1.10.

   ○ **B.** Execute the `netsh interface ipv4 Name="Local Area Connection" add 172.24.1.1 255.255.255.0 gateway=172.24.1.1` command.

   ○ **C.** Execute the `ipconfig /dnsserver:172.24.1.10 index=1` command.

   ○ **D.** Execute `netsh interface ipv4 set address name="Local Area Connection" source=static address=172.24.1.10 mask=255.255.255.0 gateway=172.24.1.1` command.

2. You want to send packets to a single PC. Which kind of address would you use?

   ○ **A.** Unicast

   ○ **B.** Broadcast

   ○ **C.** Multicast

   ○ **D.** Anycast

3. You have several Windows Server 2008 computers that act as domain controllers and DNS servers. You make a change to an IP address of one of your member servers. You need the other DNS servers to reflect the changes immediately. What should you do?

   ○ **A.** Run the dnscmd /ZoneUpdateFromDs command on the others servers where the change was made.

   ○ **B.** Run the dnscmd /ZoneUpdateFromDs command on the server where the change was made.

   ○ **C.** Decrease the Minimum (Default) TTL option to 15 minutes on the Start of Authority (SOA) record for the zone.

   ○ **D.** Run the dnscmd /zonerefresh command on the other servers where the change were made.

4. You have a Windows Server 2008 that hosts a domain called Acme.com. Acme.com has a VPN connection with a partner company, that also use Windows Server 2008 that hosts a domain called CatandMouse.com. You need to allow users in your corporation to resolve hostnames in CatandMouse.com. What should you do?

   ○ **A.** Create a stub zone for acme.com on each DNS server in CatandMouse.com.

   ○ **B.** Create a stub zone for CatandMouse.com on each DNS server in acme.com.

   ○ **C.** Create a forwarder to CatandMouse.com on each of the DNS servers in acme.com.

   ○ **D.** Create a forwarder to acme.com on each of the DNS servers in CatandMouse.com.

5. You have three domain controllers with Active Directory integrated zones for your domain acme.com. You add another Windows Server 2008 computer configured with a secondary DNS zone. However, the zone transfers fail. What do you need to do to overcome this problem? (Choose two answers.)

   ○ **A.** Execute the dnscmd Server4 /zonerefresh acme.com command.

   ○ **B.** Add the computer name for the new DNS server to the DNSTransfer group.

   ○ **C.** Add the new DNS server to the Zone Transfers tab on one of the other DNS servers.

   ○ **D.** Open the firewall to DNS transfers.

6. You have a Windows Server 2008 computer with the DNS role installed. You need to ensure that inquires for the acme.com DNS domain are sent to administrator@acme.com. What should you do?

- ○ **A.** Modify the A record for the domain controller.

- ○ **B.** Modify the Name Server (NS) record for the domain controller.

- ○ **C.** Modify the Service Locator (SRV) record for the domain controller that points to your corporate email server.

- ○ **D.** Modify the Start of Authority (SOA) record on the domain controller.

7. You have placed a server application on a Windows Server 2008 member server. This server is not a member of the corporate domain. Users access the server application by running a client application that accesses the server. However, when the users run the client connection, it cannot connect to the member server by name. What do you need to do?

- ○ **A.** On each client computer, add a HOST file entry for the application server.

- ○ **B.** Create a host (A) record for the application server.

- ○ **C.** Create a pointer (ptr) record for the application server.

- ○ **D.** Modify the client's computer to use the application server as the primary DNS server.

8. You have an Active Directory forest with multiple domains. You want all users to be able to access several application servers, using just their hostname instead of an FQDN. What should you do?

- ○ **A.** Create a host (AAAA) record for the applications in the DNS zone for the forest root domain.

- ○ **B.** Create a zone named GlobalNames on a DNS server. Replicate the GlobalNames zone to all domain controllers in the forest. Create a host (A) record for all the application servers in the zone.

- ○ **C.** Create a zone named LegacyWINS on a DNS server. Replicate the LegacyWINS zone to all domain controllers in the forest. Create a host (A) record for the Appl1 Web server in the zone.

- ○ **D.** Create an SRV record for the application in the DNS zone for the forest root domain.

9. You are the network administrator for the Acme Corporation. Your domain controllers are running Windows Server 2008 with Active Directory integrated zones. You verify that changes have recently been made to some resource records in the zone file. You suspect there are outdated entries in the client resolver cache. The problem is not affecting any other clients on the network. What should you do?

◯   **A.**   Uninstall the DNS server service.

◯   **B.**   Delete the cache.dns file.

◯   **C.**   Use the `ipconfig /flushdns` command on the client computer.

◯   **D.**   Use the Clear Cache option from the Action menu within the DHCP console.

10. You are the network administrator for your organization. You have installed the DNS service on all the Windows Server 2008 domain controllers in the company domain. Zone information is stored within Active Directory. You want to verify that zone data is being updated between DNS servers. Which tool can you use to verify this?

◯   **A.**   System Monitor

◯   **B.**   Replication Monitor

◯   **C.**   DNS management console

◯   **D.**   DNS debug logging

11. You are the network administrator for your company. All servers have been upgraded to Microsoft Windows Server 2008. Client computers are running Microsoft Windows XP Professional and Windows Vista. You have installed the DNS service on DNSSRV01. You want to configure this DNS server to forward queries that it cannot resolve to another DNS server on the network.

You log on to DNSSRV01, using a user account that belongs to the DNS Admins group. When you display the Forwarders tab in the properties of SRV1 in the DNS console, the option to enable forwarders is unavailable. What should you do?

◯   **A.**   Add your user account to the Enterprise Admins group.

◯   **B.**   Configure DNSSRV01 as a secondary DNS server.

◯   **C.**   Enable round robin on DNSSRV01.

◯   **D.**   Delete the root DNS zone on DNSSRV01.

12. You are the network administrator for the Acme Corporation. You have upgraded all servers to Microsoft Windows Server 2008. Client computers are running Microsoft Windows XP Professional and Windows Vista. All computers are members of a single Active Directory domain called acme.com. The company website is hosted on three

different web servers. The web servers are configured with identical hardware and each one is assigned a unique IP address. You want traffic to the company website distributed evenly across all three web servers. You open the properties windows for the DNS server. Which option should you select?

- ○ **A.** Disable Recursion
- ○ **B.** Bind Secondaries
- ○ **C.** Enable Round Robin
- ○ **D.** Enable Netmask Ordering

13. What is used to resolve computer names/NetBIOS names to IP addresses? (Choose two answers.)

- ○ **A.** DNS
- ○ **B.** WINS
- ○ **C.** LMHOSTS files
- ○ **D.** HOSTS files
- ○ **E.** Active Directory

14. You have a network with Windows Server 2008 computers. Your UNIX hosts cannot resolve the NetBIOS names of the legacy clients. What should you do?

- ○ **A.** Enable DNS for WINS lookup.
- ○ **B.** Configure replication between DNS and WINS.
- ○ **C.** Install a WINS proxy agent on the network.
- ○ **D.** Configure DHCP to register NetBIOS names with the DNS server.

15. You are the network administrator for your company. Servers are running Microsoft Windows Server 2008. Client computers have been upgraded to Windows XP Professional or have new Windows Vista computers. You are planning the subnet configuration for the network. The network currently needs to support 12 subnets with 12 hosts per subnet. The number of subnets is expected to reach 16 within the next year. You need to choose a subnet mask that will support this configuration. What should you do?

- ○ **A.** Use a subnet mask of 255.255.255.192.
- ○ **B.** Use a subnet mask of 255.255.255.224.
- ○ **C.** Use a subnet mask of 255.255.255.240.
- ○ **D.** Use a subnet mask of 255.255.255.248.

16. You have a DHCP server named Server1 running Windows Server 2008. You need to ensure that Server2 always receives the same IP address while ensuring that the DNS and WINS settings are received from the DHCP server. What should you do?

○ **A.** Create a multicast scope.

○ **B.** Assign a Static IP address to Server2.

○ **C.** Create an exclusion range in the DHCP scope.

○ **D.** Create a DHCP reservation in the DHCP scope.

17. DHCP is deployed on the network, and all clients are configured to automatically obtain an IP address. If the DHCP server is unavailable, clients use an IP address from which of the following address ranges?

○ **A.** 192.168.0.1 to 192.168.255.254

○ **B.** 192.168.0.1 to 192.168.0.254

○ **C.** 127.0.0.1 to 127.255.255.154

○ **D.** 169.254.0.0 to 169.254.255.255

18. You have a Windows Server 2008 computer that is hosting your DHCP services located at the corporate office. Your remote offices are separated by a router and a WAN link. You discover that remote users cannot get a DHCP address. What can you do to overcome this problem? (Choose two answers.)

○ **A.** Configure the router between the offices to forward BOOTP broadcasts.

○ **B.** Configure the DHCP server in each office with a DHCP scope that includes the same IP addresses as the DHCP server in the other office. Activate the scope.

○ **C.** Configure the DHCP server in each office with an additional network adapter. Connect each new network adapter to the local network. Assign an IP address from the other office's network to each new network adapter.

○ **D.** Install and configure a DHCP relay agent in each office.

19. You are the network administrator for your company. All servers have been upgraded to Microsoft Windows Server 2008. You have configured Routing and Remote Access on an existing server. The remote access server is configured with the default settings.

You are still using WINS on the internal network because you are still in the process of upgrading workstations. Clients using a UNC path report that they can successfully connect but cannot access network resources. Network resources are accessible to clients connected to the LAN. Remote access clients need to be able to access network resources. What should you do?

   ○ **A.** Configure a range of IP addresses on the RAS server, as well as assign any optional IP parameters to clients.

   ○ **B.** Manually configure the IP settings on the remote access clients.

   ○ **C.** Configure the DHCP server to assign DHCP clients the IP address of the WINS server.

   ○ **D.** Install the DHCP Relay Agent on the RAS server.

20. You are the network administrator for an investment company. All servers have been upgraded to Microsoft Windows Server 2008. Client computers are running Microsoft Windows XP Professional and Windows Vista. Some of the company employees require remote access to the network. The company's new security policy now requires all remote access users to use smart cards. You need to configure the remote access server to use the correct authentication protocol. Which of the following protocols should you enable?

   ○ **A.** PAP

   ○ **B.** EAP

   ○ **C.** MS-CHAP

   ○ **D.** SPAP

21. You have a Windows Server 2008 with Routing and Remote Access Service (RRAS). To connect to the server, you use smart cards. What do you need to do to make sure that users with smart cards can connect with a dial-up connection?

   ○ **A.** Install the Network Policy Server (NPS) on the server.

   ○ **B.** Create a remote access policy that requires users to authenticate by using PAP.

   ○ **C.** Create a remote access policy that requires users to authenticate by using MS-CHAP v2.

   ○ **D.** Create a remote access policy that requires users to authenticate by using EAP-TLS.

22. You have a domain controller with an enterprise root certificate authority on a Windows Server 2008 computer. You want to use the Network Access Protection (NAP) to protect the VPN connection. You therefore use Server1 with Windows Server 2008 configured as a Network Policy Server and System Health Validation Server. Your VPN server, Server2, is also a Windows Server 2008 computer with Router and Remote Access Server installed. What do you need to do to ensure that the system health policy is applied to all client computers that attempt VPN connections?

- ○ **A.** Reconfigure Server1 as a RADIUS client.

- ○ **B.** Reconfigure Server2 as a RADIUS client.

- ○ **C.** Reconfigure the domain controller as a RADIUS client.

- ○ **D.** Add the Server2 computer account to the local Administrator group on Server1.

23. You are the network administrator for an accounting firm. You have recently upgraded the servers to Microsoft Windows Server 2008. The network consists of three subnets: Subnet A, Subnet B, and Subnet C. There is an RRAS server on Subnet C configured with a range of IP addresses to assign to remote access clients. There are two DNS servers on the network, DNS01 and DNS02. You want remote access clients to use DNS02. What should you do?

- ○ **A.** Configure the RRAS server to use DHCP. Install a DHCP server on Subnet C. Configure a scope on the DHCP server for the remote access clients. Configure the DHCP relay agent on the DNS server.

- ○ **B.** Install a DHCP server on the network and configure the RRAS server to use DHCP for IP address assignment. Configure a scope on the DHCP server for the remote access clients.

- ○ **C.** Install a DHCP server on the network. Configure a scope on the DHCP server for remote access clients. Configure RRAS to use DHCP. Configure the relay agent on the DHCP server.

- ○ **D.** Install a DHCP server on Subnet C. Configure a scope on the DHCP server for remote access clients. Configure RRAS to use DHCP. Configure the relay agent on the RRAS server.

24. You are the network administrator for your company. All servers are running Microsoft Windows Server 2008. You are implementing an IP security policy for your network. SRV1 requires the highest level of security because it hosts sensitive company data. SRV2 does not require this level of security but should respond to any requests for secure communication. How should you proceed? (Choose two answers.)

- ○ **A.** Assign the Server (Request Security) policy on SRV1.

- ○ **B.** Assign the Secure Server (Require Security) policy on SRV1.

- ○ **C.** Assign the Client (Respond Only) policy on SRV2.

- ○ **D.** Assign the Server (Request Security) policy on SRV2.

- ○ **E.** Assign the Secure Server (Require Security) policy on SRV2.

- ○ **F.** Assign the Client (Respond Only) policy on SRV1.

25. You have configured Network Access Protection (NAP) to enforce policies on client computers that connect to the network. You also use a WSUS server to install Windows updates. You have a company policy that requires that critical updates are installed on the Windows Vista computer before the client computers can access network resources. What can you do to enforce this policy?

- ○ **A.** Enable automatic updates on each client.
- ○ **B.** Enable the Security Center on each client.
- ○ **C.** Quarantine clients that do not have all available security updates installed.
- ○ **D.** Disconnect the remote connection until the required updates are installed.

26. You have a Windows Server 2008 computer with Network Access Protection (NAP) enforcement for VPNs. You need to ensure that the health of all clients can be monitored and reported. What should you do?

- ○ **A.** Create a Group Policy object (GPO) that enables Security Center and links the policy to the domain.
- ○ **B.** Create a Group Policy object (GPO) that enables the Windows firewall.
- ○ **C.** Create a Group Policy object (GPO) that enables Automatic Updates.
- ○ **D.** Create a Group Policy object (BPO) that enables Windows Defender.

27. You have a computer running Windows Server 2008. You have a shared folder. A user uses the Previous Version tab to restore a large file. How can you view the progress of the file restoration?

- ○ **A.** From the command prompt, run the `vssadmin query reverts` command.
- ○ **B.** Right-click the shared folder and select the Previous Versions tab.
- ○ **C.** From Computer Management console, click the Shared Folders node and then click Sessions.
- ○ **D.** From the command prompt, run the `vssadmin revert status` command.

28. You have a file server that runs Windows Server 2008. You want to configure a shared folder that notifies you when a user uses more then 250MB of data. What should you do?

- ○ **A.** Create a soft quota.
- ○ **B.** Create a hard quota.
- ○ **C.** Create a file sharing filter.
- ○ **D.** Create an Alert Viewer filter.

29. You have a computer with Windows Server 2008. You configure quotas on the server. You want to view each user's quota usage on a per-folder basis. What should you do?

   ○ **A.** From the command prompt, execute the `frs /query` command.

   ○ **B.** Right-click the properties of each volume and review the Quota Entries list.

   ○ **C.** From File Server Resource Manager, create a Storage Management report.

   ○ **D.** Right-click the `vssadmin.exe /query` command.

30. Which type of backup can you perform using the Windows Server 2008 Windows Server Backup program if you only want to back up files that have their archive bits set and you want the backup job to clear each file's archive bit after each file has been backed up?

   ○ **A.** Incremental

   ○ **B.** Differential

   ○ **C.** Normal

   ○ **D.** Copy

31. You need to create a static route on your server to the 10.128.4.0/24 network by going through the 10.128.6.1 network interface. In addition, you also need configure the system so that when you reboot the system, the static route will stay. What command should you use?

   ○ **A.** `Route add 10.128.4.0 255.255.255.0 10.128.6.1`

   ○ **B.** `Route add -p 10.128.4.0 255.255.255.0 10.128.6.1`

   ○ **C.** `Route add 10.128.4.0 mask 255.255.255.0 192 10.12.6.1`

   ○ **D.** `Route add -p 10.128.4.0 mask 255.255.255.0 192 10.128.6.1`

32. You are sharing a folder called Download. You want the share to be hidden from the network browse list. What should you name the share?

   ○ **A.** download

   ○ **B.** %download

   ○ **C.** download$

   ○ **D.** %download%

33. You have created an uncompressed file called `MyPaper.doc` in the Documents folder on an NTFS volume. The Documents folder is not compressed. Now you move the file

MyPaper.doc to a compressed folder called TermPaper on a different NTFS volume. Which of the following will occur?

- ○ **A.** The file stays uncompressed.
- ○ **B.** The file inherits the compression attribute from the target partition.
- ○ **C.** The file inherits the compression attribute from the target volume.
- ○ **D.** A dialog box appears, asking you whether you want to compress the file in the target folder.

34. What command do you use to display the routes on a computer running Windows Server 2008?

- ○ **A.** route
- ○ **B.** route show
- ○ **C.** route print
- ○ **D.** route display
- ○ **E.** route /showall

35. You have a Windows Server 2008 computer file called reports.doc. Pat is a domain administrator and is also a member of the Sales group. Pat is given Full Control NTFS permission. The Sales group is given the denied Full Control NTFS permission. What is Pat's effective permission when he tries to access the file?

- ○ **A.** Full Control
- ○ **B.** Modify
- ○ **C.** Read
- ○ **D.** No permission

36. You have a computer with Windows Server 2008 called Server1. You have a folder called C:\Data. Pat is a member of the Sales group. The Sales group is given the Reader shared permission and the Full Control NTFS permission. What is Pat's effective permission when he tries to access the \\Server1\Data\report.doc document?

- ○ **A.** Read
- ○ **B.** Modify
- ○ **C.** Full Control
- ○ **D.** No permission

37. Your corporation has several remote sites. Each remote site has a server running Windows Server 2008. Each site server contains data files for the site users. You want to copy all these files to a centralized server so that you can back them up more efficiently. What should you use to accomplish this?

- ○ **A.** Shadow copy
- ○ **B.** DFS
- ○ **C.** EFS
- ○ **D.** NFS

38. You have a computer running Windows Server 2008. You have a file called `reports.doc`. As a domain administrator, you discover that you do not have any NTFS permissions to access the folder. Unfortunately, the person who created the folder has left the company. What can you do?

- ○ **A.** Give yourself Full Control NTFS permission to the file.
- ○ **B.** Give yourself Full Control NTFS permission to the folder where the file is located.
- ○ **C.** Remove all NTFS assigned permissions from the NTFS properties dialog box.
- ○ **D.** Take ownership of the file and reassign the permissions.

39. You have several remote sites. Each site has its own Windows Server 2008 computer. You want to assign permissions to the local manager to delete print jobs as necessary. What is the least permission you can give the manager to complete this task?

- ○ **A.** Print
- ○ **B.** Manage Printers
- ○ **C.** Manage Documents
- ○ **D.** Full Control

40. If you need to enable Internet printing, you need what Windows component?

- ○ **A.** CertSrv
- ○ **B.** IIS
- ○ **C.** Wbadmin
- ○ **D.** DFS

41. You have a Windows Server 2008 computer with several printers. One printer failed. You want to redirect to another printer connected to the server. What can you do?

   ○ **A.** Within Printer Properties, click the port to which the other print device is assigned.

   ○ **B.** Within Printer Properties, create a new port that points to the print device.

   ○ **C.** Right-click the print queue and select Redirect. Then specify the UNC for a working printer.

   ○ **D.** Open the print queue. Right-click each print job and select Redirect. Then specify the UNC for a working printer.

42. You are the network administrator for Acme.com. You have a Windows Server 2008 named Server1 with a printer named Printer1. You want to connect two additional printers so that all three printers can operate as one to handle a larger workload. What can you do?

   ○ **A.** Create a printer pool.

   ○ **B.** Share each individual printer.

   ○ **C.** Share each individual printer but use the same port.

   ○ **D.** Share each printer but assign each printer the same shared name.

43. What does SNMP use for security?

   ○ **A.** Username and password

   ○ **B.** A PIN

   ○ **C.** A community name

   ○ **D.** A digital certificate

44. What command would you use to renew the DHCP IPv6 addresses?

   ○ **A.** `ipconfig`

   ○ **B.** `ipconfig /renew`

   ○ **C.** `ipconfig /renew6`

   ○ **D.** `ipconfig /release_and_renew`

   ○ **E.** `ipconfig /registerdns`

45. You work as the desktop support technician at Acme.com. You want to assign an address to a computer that will be available on the Internet and will have the same address for both IPv4 and IPv6. What kind of address is this?

○ **A.** A site-local address

○ **B.** A global unicast address

○ **C.** A unique private address

○ **D.** A multicast local address

46. You connect to a network and notice that the IP address is 172.24.43.27. What can be said about this address?

○ **A.** It is a private network address.

○ **B.** It is a multicast network address.

○ **C.** It is a class B public address.

○ **D.** It is a class C public address.

47. You have a class C network that has been subnetted. Its subnet mask is 255.255.255.240. How many hosts are available per subnet?

○ **A.** 6

○ **B.** 8

○ **C.** 14

○ **D.** 16

○ **E.** 30

48. What type of resource records do you find in the in-addr-arpa zone?

○ **A.** A

○ **B.** AAAA

○ **C.** PTR

○ **D.** NS

49. What command do you use to manually force a refresh of the client-named registration in DNS?

○ **A.** `ipconfig /renew`

○ **B.** `ipconfig /release`

    ○ **C.** `ipconfig /registerdns`

    ○ **D.** `arp -a`

50. You have 20 DHCP scopes defined on your DHCP server. You want to define the DNS and WINS servers with the least administrative effort. What should you do?

    ○ **A.** Define the DNS and WINS at the server level.

    ○ **B.** Define the DNS and WINS at the scope level.

    ○ **C.** Define the DNS and WINS at the class level.

    ○ **D.** Define the DNS and WINS at the client level.

13

Answers to Practice Exam 2

Answers at a Glance

1. D	**18.** A and D	**35.** D
2. A	**19.** D	**36.** A
3. A	**20.** B	**37.** B
4. B	**21.** D	**38.** D
5. C, D	**22.** B	**39.** C
6. D	**23.** D	**40.** B
7. B	**24.** B, C	**41.** A
8. B	**25.** C	**42.** A
9. C	**26.** A	**43.** C
10. B	**27.** A	**44.** C
11. D	**28.** A	**45.** B
12. C	**29.** C	**46.** A
13. B, C	**30.** A	**47.** C
14. A	**31.** D	**48.** C
15. C	**32.** C	**49.** C
16. D	**33.** C	**50.** A
17. D	**34.** C	

Answers with Explanations

1. Answer D is correct. You need to use the `netsh interface ipv4 set address` command. Because it specifies the preferred DNS server, you need to use `index=1`. Answer A is incorrect because the Network and Sharing Center is not available on a Server Core. Answer B is incorrect because you need to use the `netsh interface ipv4 add` command. Answer C is incorrect because `ipconfig.exe` cannot be used to configure static addresses.

2. Answer A is correct. A unicast address is sent to a single host. Answer B is incorrect because broadcast are sent to all hosts within a subnet. Answer C is incorrect because a multicast has the sender send a single transmission (from the sender's unicast address) to the multicast address, and to the routers taking care of making copies and sending them to all receivers that have registered their interest in data from that sender. Answer D is incorrect because anycast is a one-to-many routing topology. However, the data stream is not transmitted to all receivers, just the one that the router decides is the "closest" in the network.

3. Answer A is correct. The `dnscmd /ZoneUdpateFromDs` command updates the specified Active Directory integrated zone from Active Directory. Answer B is incorrect because you need to run the `dnscmd /ZoneUpdatefromDs` command from the servers that still need the change. Answer C is incorrect because decreasing the TTL would not force changes to propagate immediately. Answer D is incorrect because the `dnscmd /zonerefresh` command forces a secondary DNS zone to update from the master.

4. Answer B is correct. A stub zone lists information about the authoritative name servers of a zone so that the DNS server knows directly which server is the authority for a par-ticular zone. This enables it to perform recursive queries using the stub zone's list of name servers without having to query the Internet or an internal root server for the DNS namespace. Answers B and D are incorrect because the name resolution needs to go in the opposite direction. C is incorrect because you want to forward only requests for CatandMouse.com, not all DNS requests.

5. Answers C and D are correct. You need to add the new DNS server to the Zone Transfer tab so that zone updates are allowed to be sent. In addition, the firewall is on by default and needs to be opened for DNS update traffic to flow. Answer A is incorrect because the `dnsmcd /zonerefresh` command forces a secondary DNS zone to update from the master. However, the updates are not allowed until you add to DNS servers on the Zone Transfer tab. Answer B is incorrect because there is no such thing as the DNS Transfer group.

6. Answer D is correct. One of the fields in the SOA record includes the email address for the domain. Answers A, B, and C are incorrect because the A, NS, and SRV records do not include email address fields for the zone.

7. Answer B is correct. The A record translates host name to the IP address. Answer A is incorrect because although this may be a possible solution, you have to modify every client computer to complete it. Adding an entry to the DNS server is a much better option. Answer C is incorrect because the ptr record is to translate from IP address to hostname. Answer D is incorrect because the application server has never been stated that it is a DNS server and therefore modifying the client's computer would cause other name resolution problems.

8. Answer B is correct. The GlobalNames zone can be used for single-label names instead of the fully qualified domain names that DNS uses. Answer A is incorrect because the AAAA records are used to translate hostnames to IPv6 addresses. Answer C is incorrect because the LegacyWins domain does not do anything to resolve single-label names. Answer D is incorrect because the SRV record specifies where certain services, such as LDAP, are located.

9. Answer C is correct. By executing the `ipconfig/flushdns` command, you can delete the contents of the client resolver cache on the client computer. Although uninstalling the service clears the contents of the cache, it's not the easiest way to perform the task; therefore, answer A is incorrect. Answer B is incorrect because deleting the file completely removes it. Answer D is incorrect because this option is used to clear the contents of the cache file on the DNS server. However, the problem is not affecting any other DNS clients, which indicates that the problem likely resides with the cache on the DNS client.

10. Answer B is correct. If the support tools have been installed, you can use Replication Monitor to ensure that replication between DNS servers is occurring on a regular basis. Answer A is incorrect because System Monitor is used to monitor the real-time performance of a DNS server. Answer C is incorrect because the DNS management console is used to configure and manage a DNS server but cannot be used to monitor DNS replication. Answer D is incorrect because DNS debug logging is used to collect detailed information about how a DNS server is operating.

11. Answer D is correct. If a root DNS zone exists on the DNS server, you cannot configure a DNS forwarder. You must delete this file before you can proceed. Answer A is incorrect because you do not need to be a member of the Enterprise Admins group to manage a DNS server. Answer B is incorrect because changing the server's DNS role does not determine whether the DNS server can be a forwarder. Answer C is incorrect because the round robin feature is used to load-balance queries across multiple DNS servers.

12. Answer C is correct. If you select the Round Robin option, the DNS server can distribute queries across the web servers. It does so by rotating the list of web servers so a different web server is returned to a client. Answer A is incorrect because the Disable Recursion option determines whether the DNS server uses recursion. If recursion is disabled, the DNS server will always use referrals, regardless of the type of request from clients. Answer B is incorrect because the BIND Secondaries option determines whether fast transfers are used when zone data is transferred to a BIND DNS server. Answer D is incorrect because the Enable Netmask Ordering option determines

whether the DNS server reorders host (A) records so that when a client is trying to resolve a hostname with multiple IP addresses, an address is chosen based on the client's IP address in an attempt to get the closest server to the host.

13. Answers B and C are correct. WINS and LMHOSTS files are used to translate NetBIOS/computer names to IP address. Answers A and D are incorrect because DNS is a service that resolves hostnames to IP addresses. HOSTS files can also be used to resolve hostnames, located on each server. Answer E is incorrect because Active Directory is a directory service.

14. Answer A is correct. If the UNIX hosts do not support NetBIOS, WINS lookup can be enabled on the DNS server. The DNS server can query the WINS server if it cannot resolve the hostname. Answer B is incorrect because you cannot configure replication between DNS and WINS. Answer C is incorrect because a WINS proxy forwards NetBIOS broadcasts to a WINS server. Answer D is incorrect because a DHCP server cannot update NetBIOS names with a DNS server.

15. Answer C is correct. The subnet mask of 255.255.255.240 allows for a maximum number of 16 subnets. This meets the requirements for 12 subnets. Answers A and B are incorrect because these subnet masks do not allow for enough subnets. Answer D is incorrect because this subnet mask allows for more subnets that will ever be required. It also does not allow for the required number of hosts per subnet.

16. Answer D is correct. A DHCP reservation makes sure that the computer gets the same IP address. Answer A is incorrect because a multicast scope does not assign an IP address to the server. Answer B is incorrect because the static IP does not assign DNS and WINS settings from the DHCP server. Answer C is incorrect because creating an exclusion range does not assign IP addresses in the exclusion range.

17. Answer D is correct. If a DHCP server is unavailable, clients use Automatic Private IP Addressing and use an IP address in the range of 169.254.0.0 to 169.254.255.255. Therefore, answers A, B, and C are incorrect.

18. Answers A and D are correct. Broadcasts typically are not allowed to go through routers and WAN links. Because DHCP lease requests are broadcast, the lease request cannot traverse routers. To overcome this problem, you need to either configure the routers to forward the BOOTP broadcast or install DHCP relay agents at each site, which forwards the BOOTP broadcast to the DHCP server. Answers B and C are incorrect because you want to centralize the DHCP administration.

19. Answer D is correct. The clients need to be configured with the IP address of the WINS server. To do this, the DHCP Relay Agent must be installed on the RAS server so that it can forward DHCP Inform messages between the clients and the DHCP server. Answer A is incorrect because optional parameters cannot be configured on the RAS server. Clients can be configured with the IP address of the WINS server; however, it's easier from a management perspective to centralize IP address assignment and use a relay agent instead. Therefore, answer B is incorrect. Answer C is incorrect because the

DHCP server is already assigning the IP address of the WINS server to DHCP clients because the scenario indicates this problem is not affecting clients connected to the LAN.

20. Answer B is correct. The Extensible Authentication Protocol is required to support smart card authentication. Answers A, C, and D are incorrect because they do not support smart card authentication.

21. Answer D is correct. You need to create a remote access policy to control access and the access must specify EAP, which is required by the smart cards. Answer A is incorrect because NPS is the Microsoft RADIUS server. Answers B and C are incorrect because the smart cards require EAP.

22. Answer B is correct. The VPN server needs to communicate with the RADIUS server for authentication. Therefore, you need to configure Server2 as the RADIUS client. Answer A is incorrect because Server1 is the RADIUS server. Answer C is incorrect because the RADIUS server is configured to communicate with the domain controller for authentication. Answer D is incorrect because you do not have to add computer accounts to the Administrators group to use RADIUS.

23. Answer D is correct. Install a DHCP server on Subnet C and configure it with a scope for remote access clients. The scope should assign the clients the IP address of the DHCP server. Configure RRAS to use DHCP and configure it as a relay agent. This step ensures that remote users are assigned the IP address of the DNS server. Therefore, answers A, B, and C are incorrect.

24. Answers B and C are correct. SRV1 should be using the Secure Server (Require Security) policy. This policy ensures that only secure communications are permitted. SRV2 should be using the Client (Respond Only) policy. This policy ensures that the server does not require secure communication but responds to any requests for it. Therefore, answers A, D, E, and F are incorrect.

25. Answer C is correct. You need to quarantine the clients until they can get the critical updates. Answer A is incorrect because although automatic updates help the client get updated, if the critical update has not been installed, they still need to be stopped from accessing resources. Answer B is incorrect because the Security Center does not keep users from accessing resources. Answer D is incorrect because a user that is disconnected would not be able to get updates from your WSUS server.

26. Answer A is correct. With the Security Center, NAP can figure out whether the system has a firewall, up-to-date antivirus protection, or the necessary updates. Answers B, C, and D are incorrect because Windows Firewall, Automatic Updates, and Windows Defender do not report status of Windows Defender back to NAP.

27. Answer A is correct. You can use the `vssadmin query revert` command to get the status of a restored file. Answer B is incorrect because the Previous Versions tab does not display the status of a file restoration. Answer C is incorrect because the Computer Management console does not show the status. Answer D is incorrect because `revert status` is an invalid parameter for the `vssadmin` command.

28. Answer A is correct. A soft quota can be used to warn when the quota is met or exceeded. Answer B is incorrect because a hard quota prevents the user from saving files to the shared folder. Answer C is incorrect because there is no such thing as a file sharing filter. Answer D is incorrect because the Alert Viewer filter does not automatically send email notifications.

29. Answer C is correct. You can use the File Server Resource Manager console to get a detailed report. Answer A is incorrect because the `frs` is used for file replication service, not file server resources. Answer B is incorrect because you can not use the properties of each volume to get how a volume is being used. Answer D is incorrect because the `vssadmin` command is used to manage the volume shadow copies (previous versions).

30. Answer A is correct. When you complete an incremental backup, you are backing all new and changed files since the last backup. Answer B is incorrect because differential backups do not shut off the archive attribute. Answer C is incorrect because the normal or full backup copies all files regardless of the archive attribute. Answer D is incorrect because the Copy command backs up all files but does not shut off the archive attribute.

31. Answer D is correct. You need to use the `route add` command and you need to specify the word mask. The `-p` makes the route persistent so that it will be reloaded when the server is rebooted. Therefore answers A, B, and C are incorrect.

32. Answer C is correct. Hidden shares have the $ at the end of their name. Therefore answers A, B, and D are incorrect.

33. Answer C is correct. If you move a file from one volume to another, it inherits the compression attribute from the target volume. Therefore answers A, B, and D are incorrect.

34. Answer C is correct. To display all routes execute the `route print` command. Therefore all other answers are incorrect.

35. Answer D is correct. Because the Sales group, of which Pat is a member, was given the denied Full Control permission, Denied permissions always win out. Therefore, the other answers are incorrect.

36. Answer A is correct. When you combine NTFS permissions and Shared permissions, you need to take the most restrictive. Therefore, Pat has only the read permission. Because Pat has the read permission, answers B, C, and D are incorrect.

37. Answer B is correct. DFS replication can be used to copy all the files from one server to another server. Answer A is incorrect because shadow copies make copies only within an individual volume, so users can access previous versions of a file. Answer C in incorrect because EFS is for encrypting a file or folder. Answer D is incorrect because NFS is used for UNIX users to access a shared folder.

38. Answer D is correct. You need to take ownership of the file. As a domain administrator, the user can take ownership of any file or folder on the server. Answers A, B, and C are incorrect because you have no permissions to access the file and therefore you cannot modify the access control list for the NTFS permissions.

39. Answer C is correct. For the manager to manage the documents in the print queue, you just need to give the Manage Documents permission. Answer A is incorrect because the Print permission enables users to print to the printer. Answer B is incorrect because the Manage Printer permission is used to configure printer options. Answer D is incorrect because there is no Full Control print permission.

40. Answer B is correct. Because Internet printing allows printing with a browser or FQDN, you need IIS, which is Microsoft's web server. Answer A is incorrect because you do not need a certificate server. Answer C is incorrect because the wbadmin is the Windows Server backup utility. Answer D is incorrect because DFS is for replication or for creating a DFS namespace.

41. Answer A is correct. If the printer is located on the same server as the print job, you just need to redirect to a port where the printer is assigned. Answer B is incorrect because this would describe how to redirect to a printer that is connected to another server. Answers C and D are incorrect because there are no Redirect options to select.

42. Answer A is correct. For a set of printers to work together is to create a printer pool. Answers B and C are incorrect because sharing the printers does not allow the printers to work together as one identity. Answer D is incorrect because you cannot have multiple printers with the same share name on the same printer.

43. Answer C is correct. To manage or configure SNMP, you use community names. Answers A, C, and D are incorrect because these are not used by SNMP.

44. Answer C is correct. The /renew6 option renews IPv6 IP addresses. Answer A is incorrect because the ipconfig command without any options displays only basic IP configuration information. Answer B is incorrect because the /renew option is used to renew IPv4 IP addresses. Answer D is incorrect because the /release_and_renew option does not exist. Answer E is incorrect because the /registerdns option is how to get the computer to register itself with the DNS server.

45. Answer B is correct. If you want an address to be available from the Internet and be the same address for both IPv4 and IPv6, the address must be a global one that can be seen on the Internet. Answer A is incorrect because a local address cannot be seen on the outside. Answer C is incorrect because private addresses cannot be used on a public network such as the Internet. Answer D is incorrect because it has to be a single address assigned to a single computer, not a multicast that is used to broadcast to multiple addresses at the same time.

46. Answer A is correct. Private addresses include 10.x.x.x, 172.16.x.x, 172.31.x.x, 192.168.0.x, and 192.168.255.x. Answer B is incorrect because multicast network addresses are class D, and start with 224–239. Answers C and D are incorrect because this is a private address, not a public address.

47. Answer C is correct. Because it is a class C, the last octet is split. 240 translates to 1111 0000. Because four bits are used for hosts, $2^4-2=14$. Therefore, answers A, B, D, and E are incorrect.

48. Answer C is correct. In-addr-arpa is used as reverse lookup zones. Therefore, they contain PTR records, which provide IP address-to-hostname resolution. Answers A and B are incorrect because they are found in forward lookup zones to translate from hostnames to IP addresses. The NS resource record defines name servers.

49. Answer C is correct. To force a refresh of the DNS registry, execute the `ipconfig /registerdns` command. Answers A and B are incorrect because the `ipconfig /renew` and `ipcofnig /release` commands are used to renew and release the DHCP addresses. Answer D is incorrect because `arp -a` is used to display the ARP cache, which consists of IP addresses and their corresponding MAC addresses.

50. Answer A is correct. If you define the DNS and WINS server at the server level, you have to do it only once. Answer B is incorrect because you would have to define the DNS and WINS 20 times, once for each defined scope. Answers C and D are incorrect for customized settings, based on the operating system or type of computer.

Number Systems

The most commonly used numbering system and the one that you use every day is the decimal number system. In a decimal numbering system, each position contains 10 different possible digits. Because there are 10 different possible digits, the decimal number system are numbers with base 10. These digits are 0, 1, 2, 3, 4, 5, 6, 7, 8 and 9. To count values larger than 9, each position away from the decimal point in a decimal number increases in value by a multiple of 10. See Table A.1.

TABLE A.1   Decimal Number System

7ᵗʰPlace	6ᵗʰPlace	5ᵗʰPlace	4ᵗʰPlace	3ʳᵈPlace	2ⁿᵈPlace	1ˢᵗPlace
10^6	10^5	10^4	10^3	10^2	10^1	10^0
1,000,000	100,000	10,000	1,000	100	10	1

Example:

Decimal Number: 234

2	3	4
2×10^2	3×10^1	4×10^0
200	30	4

Therefore, the value is 200+30+4=234.

Binary Number System

The binary number system, used heavily in computer systems, is another way to count. The binary system is less complicated than the decimal system because it has only two digits, a zero (0) and a one (1). A computer represents a binary value with an electronic switch known as a transistor. If the switch is on, it allows current to flow through a wire or metal trace to represent a binary value of one (1). If the switch is off, it does not allow current to flow through a wire, representing a value of zero (0). See Table A.2. The on switch is also referred to as a high signal, whereas the off switch is referred to as a low signal.

TABLE A.2 One-Digit Binary Number

Wire #1	Binary Equivalent	Decimal Equivalent
Off	0	0
On	1	1

If you use two wires to represent data, the first switch can be on or off and the second switch can be on or off, giving you a total of four combinations or four binary values. See Table A.3. If you use four wires to represent data, you can represent 16 different binary values. See Table A.4.

TABLE A.3 Two-Digit Binary Number

Wire 1	Wire 2	Binary Equivalent	Decimal Equivalent
Off	Off	0 0	0
Off	On	0 1	1
On	Off	1 0	2
On	On	1 1	3

TABLE A.4 Four-Digit Binary Number

Wire1	Wire2	Wire3	Wire4	Binary Equivalent	Decimal Equivalent
Off	Off	Off	Off	0 0 0 0	0
Off	Off	Off	On	0 0 0 1	1
Off	Off	On	Off	0 0 1 0	2
Off	Off	On	On	0 0 1 1	3
Off	On	Off	Off	0 1 0 0	4
Off	On	Off	On	0 1 0 1	5
Off	On	On	Off	0 1 1 0	6
Off	On	On	On	0 1 1 1	7
On	Off	Off	Off	1 0 0 0	8
On	Off	Off	On	1 0 0 1	9
On	Off	On	Off	1 0 1 0	10

TABLE A.4 *Continued*

Wire1	Wire2	Wire3	Wire4	Binary Equivalent	Decimal Equivalent
On	Off	On	On	1 0 1 1	11
On	On	Off	Off	1 1 0 0	12
On	On	Off	On	1 1 0 1	13
On	On	On	Off	1 1 1 0	14
On	On	On	On	1 1 1 1	15

Because each switch represents two values, each switch used doubles the number of binary values. Therefore, the number of binary values can be expressed with the following equation:

Number of Binary Numbers=$2^{\text{numbers of Binary digits}}$

Therefore one wire allows 2^1=2 binary numbers, 0 and 1. Two wires allow 2^2=4 binary numbers, 0, 1, 2 and 3. Four wires allows 2^4=16 binary numbers. So how many values does 8 bits represent? Because a byte has 8 binary digits, a byte can represent 2^8=256 characters.

Much like decimal numbers, the binary digits have placeholders that represent certain values, as shown in Table A.5.

Table A.5   Binary Number System

8th Place	7th Place	6th Place	5th Place	4th Place	3rd Place	2nd Place	1st Place
2^7	2^6	2^5	2^4	2^3	2^2	2^1	2^0
128	64	32	16	8	4	2	1

Example:

Convert the binary number 11101010 to a decimal number.

1	1	1	0	1	0	1	0
1×2^7	1×2^6	1×2^5	0×2^4	1×2^3	0×2^2	1×2^1	0×2^0
128	64	32	0	8	0	2	0

Therefore, the binary number of 11101010 is equal to the decimal number of 128+64+32+8+2=234.

Example:

Convert the decimal number 234 to a binary number.

Referring to Table A.5, you can see that the largest power of 2 that will fit into 234 is 2^7 (128). This leaves the value of 234-128=106. The next largest power of 2 that will fit into 106 is 2^6 (64). This leaves a value of 106-64=42. The next largest power of 2 that will fit into 42 is 2^5 (32), which gives us 42-32=10. The next largest power of 2 that will fit into 10 is 2^3 (8), which gives us 10-8=2. The next largest power of 2 that will fit into 2 is 2^1 (2), which gives us 2-2=0.

$$
\begin{array}{rl}
234 & \\
-128 & \quad 2^7 \\
\hline
106 & \\
-64 & \quad 2^6 \\
\hline
42 & \\
-32 & \quad 2^5 \\
\hline
10 & \\
-8 & \quad 2^3 \\
\hline
2 & \\
-2 & \quad 2^1 \\
\hline
0 &
\end{array}
$$

Therefore, the binary equivalent is 11101010 as shown by:

1	1	1	0	1	0	1	0
2^7	2^6	2^5	2^4	2^3	2^2	2^1	2^0

In computers, one of these switches is known as a bit. When several bits are combined together, they can signify a letter, a digit, a punctuation mark, a special graphical character or a computer instruction. Eight bits make up a byte.

Because bytes are such a small unit, kilobytes (KB), megabytes (MB) and gigabytes (GB) are used. The kilo prefix indicates a thousand, mega indicates a million, giga indicates a billion, and tera indicates a trillion. With computers, the measurement is not exact. A kilobyte is actually 1,024 bytes, not a 1,000 because 2^{10} is equal to 1,024. Like the kilobyte, a megabyte is 1,024 kilobytes, a gigabyte is 1,024 megabytes, and a terabyte is 1,024 gigabytes.

1 kilobyte = 1,024 bytes

1 megabyte = 1,024 kilobytes = 1,048,576 bytes

1 gigabyte = 1024 megabytes = 1,048,576 kilobytes = 1,073,741,824 bytes

Hexadecimal Number System

The hexadecimal number system has 16 digits. One hexadecimal digit is equivalent to a four-digit binary number (4 bits or a nibble), and two hexadecimal digits are used to represent a byte (8 bits). Therefore, it is very easy to translate between hexadecimal and binary, and hexadecimal is used primarily as a "shorthand" way of displaying binary numbers. See Table A.6.

TABLE A.6   Hexadecimal Digits

Decimal	Binary	Hexadecimal
0	0000	0
1	0001	1
2	0010	2
3	0011	3
4	0100	4
5	0101	5
6	0110	6
7	0111	7
8	1000	8
9	1001	9
10	1010	A
11	1011	B
12	1100	C
13	1101	D
14	1110	E
15	1111	F

To designate a number as a hexadecimal number, it often ends with the letter H. To count values larger than 15, each position away from the decimal point in a decimal number increases in value by a multiple of 16. See Table A.7.

TABLE A.7   Hexadecimal Number System

7thPlace	6thPlace	5thPlace	4thPlace	3rdPlace	2ndPlace	1stPlace
16^6	16^5	16^4	16^3	16^2	16^1	16^0
16777216	1048576	65536	4096	256	16	1

Question:

What is the hexadecimal representation of the binary number 1001 1010?

Answer:

Because 1001 is equivalent to 9 and 1010 is equivalent to A, the hexadecimal equivalent is 9AH.

To convert a hexadecimal number to decimal number, you could first could convert the hexadecimal number to binary and then convert the binary number to decimal. Another way to convert is to multiply the decimal value of each hexadecimal digit by its weight and then take the sum of these products.

Example:

To convert EAH to a decimal number, you would multiply the A by the 1s and E by 16 and then add them up.

E	A
Ex16^1	Ax16^0
14x16^1	10x16^0
14x16	10x1
224	10

Therefore, the hexadecimal number of EA is equal to the decimal number of 224+10=234.

Example:

To convert the decimal number of 234 to a hexadecimal number, you would refer to Table 2.9 to see that largest power of 16 that will fit into 234 is 16^1 (16). 16 goes into 234 14 (E) times, leaving a 10 (A).

234/16=14.625

234(14x16)=10

14=EH

10=AH

This can be broken down as follows:

16^1	16^0
14×16^1	10×16^0
E	A

IPv4 addresses are based on 32 bits divided as four groups of 8 bits. The groupings of 8 bits are sometimes referred to as an octet. Of course, because a hexadecimal digit consists of 4 bits, it takes two hexadecimal digits to express an octet. IPv6 addresses are based on 128 bits, usually expressed in 32 hexadecimal digits.

Using Microsoft Calculator

On any Windows computer, you can use the Microsoft Calculator to perform quick conversions between the binary, decimal, and hexadecimal number systems. When you start the Microsoft Calculator, you first need to open the View menu and select Scientific mode. You then select the number system that you are starting with (Hex, Dec, Oct, and Bin, short for hexadecimal, decimal, octal, and binary). Octal is a fourth-number system based on 0–7. You then enter the starting value. When the number is entered, you then select the number system to which you want to convert. Figure A.1 shows converting from 124 to 1111100. To make binary and decimal digits easier to read, you can also select digit grouping from the View menu, which adds commas (,) to decimal numbers and groups binary numbers into sets of four bits. Therefore, the binary number 1111100 would be expressed as 111 1100 and the decimal number 105245 would be expressed in 105,245.

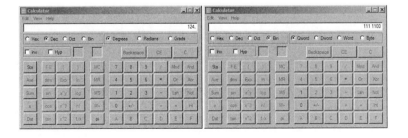

APPENDIX B

What's on the CD-ROM

The CD-ROM features an innovative practice test engine powered by MeasureUp™, giving you yet another effective tool to assess your readiness for the exam.

Multiple Test Modes

MeasureUp practice tests can be used in Study, Certification, or Custom Modes.

Study Mode

Tests administered in Study Mode enable you to request the correct answer(s) and the explanation for each question during the test. These tests are not timed. You can modify the testing environment during the test by selecting the Options button.

You may also specify the objectives or missed questions you want to include in your test, the timer length, and other test properties. You can also modify the testing environment during the test by selecting the Options button.

In Study Mode, you receive automatic feedback on all correct and incorrect answers. The detailed answer explanations are a superb learning tool in their own right.

Certification Mode

Tests administered in Certification Mode closely simulate the actual testing environment you will encounter when taking a certification exam and are timed. These tests do not allow you to request the answer(s) and/or explanation for each question until after the exam.

Custom Mode

Custom Mode enables you to specify your preferred testing environment. Use this mode to specify the objectives you want to include in your test, the timer length, number of questions, and other test properties. You can also modify the testing environment during the test by selecting the Options button.

Attention to Exam Objectives

MeasureUp practice tests are designed to appropriately balance the questions over each technical area covered by a specific exam. All concepts from the actual exam are covered thoroughly to ensure you're prepared for the exam.

Installing the CD

System Requirements:

- ▶ Windows 95, 98, ME, NT4, 2000, XP or Vista
- ▶ 7MB disk space for the testing engine
- ▶ An average of 1MB disk space for each individual test
- ▶ Control Panel Regional Settings must be set to English (United States)
- ▶ PC only

To install the CD-ROM, follow these instructions:

1. Close all applications before beginning this installation.

2. Insert the CD into your CD-ROM drive. If the setup starts automatically, go to step 6. If the setup does not start automatically, continue with step 3.

3. From the Start menu, select Run.

4. Click Browse to locate the MeasureUp CD. In the Browse dialog box, from the Look In drop-down list, select the CD-ROM drive.

5. In the Browse dialog box, double-click Setup.exe. In the Run dialog box, click OK to begin the installation.

6. On the Welcome screen, click MeasureUp Practice Questions to begin installation.

7. Follow the Certification Prep Wizard by clicking Next.

8. To agree to the Software License Agreement, click Yes.

9. On the Choose Destination Location screen, click Next to install the software to C:\Program Files\Certification Preparation. If you cannot locate MeasureUp Practice Tests through the Start menu, see the section titled "Creating a Shortcut to the MeasureUp Practice Tests," later in this appendix.

10. On the Setup Type screen, select Typical Setup. Click Next to continue.

11. In the Select Program Folder screen, you can name the program folder where your tests will be located. To select the default, simply click Next and the installation continues.

12. After the installation is complete, verify that Yes, I Want to Restart My Computer Now is selected. If you select No, I Will Restart My Computer Later, you cannot use the program until you restart your computer.

13. Click Finish.

14. After restarting your computer, choose Start, Programs, Certification Preparation, Certification Preparation, MeasureUp Practice Tests.

15. On the MeasureUp Welcome Screen, click Create User Profile.

16. In the User Profile dialog box, complete the mandatory fields and click Create Profile.

17. Select the practice test you want to access and click Start Test.

Creating a Shortcut to the MeasureUp Practice Tests

To create a shortcut to the MeasureUp Practice Tests, follow these steps:

1. Right-click on your Desktop.

2. From the shortcut menu, select New, Shortcut.

3. Browse to C:\Program Files\MeasureUp Practice Tests and select the `MeasureUpCertification.exe` or `Localware.exe` file.

4. Click OK.

5. Click Next.

6. Rename the shortcut MeasureUp.

7. Click Finish.

After you complete step 7, use the MeasureUp shortcut on your Desktop to access the MeasureUp products you ordered.

Technical Support

If you encounter problems with the MeasureUp test engine on the CD-ROM, please contact MeasureUp at (800) 649-1687 or email support@measureup.com. Support hours of operation are 7:30 a.m. to 4:30 p.m., EST. Additionally, you can find Frequently Asked Questions (FAQ) in the Support area at www.measureup.com. If you would like to purchase additional MeasureUp products, call 678-356-5050 or 800-649-1687 or visit www.measureup.com.

Glossary

Numerics

802.1X authentication   A standard authentication protocol for passing EAP over a wired or wireless LAN.

A

access control list (ACL)   A list of who can access an object and the type of access granted.

Active Directory (AD)   A directory service that uses the "tree" concept for managing resources on a Windows network. It stores all information about the network resources and services, such as user data, printers, servers, databases, groups, computers, and security policies. In addition, it identifies all resources on a network and makes them accessible to users and applications.

Active Directory integrated zone
A DNS zone that has the zone data stored as an Active Directory object and is replicated as part of the domain replication.

address resolution protocol (ARP)
A TCP/IP protocol used to obtain hardware addresses (MAC addresses) of hosts located on the same physical network.

administrative shares   Special shared volumes or folders that do not show when a user browses the computer resources using Network Neighborhood, My Network Place, or similar software. The administrative shares end with a dollar sign ($).

Administrative Tools   A folder in Control Panel that contains tools for system administrators and advanced users.

anycast   A one-to-many routing topology. However, the data stream is not transmitted to all receivers, just the one the router decides is the "closest" in the network. Anycast is useful for balancing data loads.

arp command   A command that enables you to view and configure the ARP cache.

authentication   The process by which the system validates the user's logon information.

B

backup   An extra copy of data and/or programs.

backup catalog   A file that stores the details about your backups (what volumes are backed up and where the backups are located).

BitLocker Drive Encryption   New technology that is used to encrypt an entire drive, which is designed to protect computers from attackers who have physical access to a computer.

Bootstrap Protocol (BOOTP)
A UDP network protocol used by a network client to obtain its IP address automatically. This is usually done during the bootstrap process when a computer is starting up.

broadcast   A routing topology that sends data or broadcasting to all possible destinations. This permits the sender to send the data only once and all receivers can copy it.

C

caching-only server   A DNS server that does not contain any zone information, used to build the cache file as names are resolved.

Challenge Handshake Authentication Protocol (CHAP)   A commonly used dial-up authentication protocol that uses an industry Message Digest 5 (MD5) hashing scheme to encrypt authentication.

classful address   The traditional IPv4 addresses based on classes (Class A, B, C, and D).

Classless Interdomain Routing (CIDR) address   An IPv4 address scheme that is based on the classful address but does not use the traditional classes (Class A, B, C, and D).

client reservation   A DHCP mechanism that ensures that a client always gets the same reserved IP address.

community name   Used in SNMP, a collection of hosts grouped together for administrative purposes.

compression   Storing data in a format that requires less space than usual.

Computer Management
Management of local or remote computers by using a single, consolidated desktop tool. Using Computer Management, you can perform many tasks, such as monitoring system events, configuring hard disks, and managing system performance.

conflict detection   A DHCP mechanism that checks to make sure that an IP address being handed out is not already in use.

Connection Manager Administration Kit (CMAK)   A versatile client dialer and connection software that can be used to create an executable program. The executable program can then be used to install on client computers to provide a a preconfigured network connection for a VPN.

Control Panel   A graphical tool used to configure the Windows environment and hardware devices.

D

default gateway   The defined nearest router that allows a host to communicate with other networks.

DFS namespace   Technology that enables you to group shared folders that are located on different servers into one or more logically structured namespaces.

DFS replicated folder An efficient, multiple-master replication engine that you can use to keep folders synchronized between servers across limited bandwidth network connections.

DHCP options Options that a DHCP server configures, such as the addresses of the DNS and WINS servers.

DHCP relay agent A computer that relays DHCP and BOOTP messages between clients and servers on different subnets. This way, you can have a single DHCP server handle several subnets without the DHCP server being connected directly to those subnets.

DHCP scope A range of IP addresses on a DHCP server, which defines a single physical subnet on a network.

dial-up networking The technology that allows a remote access client to make a nonpermanent, dial-up connection to a physical port on a remote access server by using the service of a telecommunications provider, such as an analog phone or ISDN.

differential backup A backup that backs up the files selected only if the archive file attribute is on (files since the last full backup). Different from the incremental backup, it does not shut off/reset the archive attribute/bit.

directory service A network service that identifies all resources on a network and makes those resources accessible to users and applications.

disk quota A mechanism that tracks and controls disk usage on a per-user, per–drive letter (partition or volume) basis.

distance vector–based routing protocols Routing protocols that periodically advertise or broadcast the routes in their routing tables, but send them to only their neighboring routers.

distributed file system (DFS) A set of client and server services that enable a large enterprise to organize many distributed SMB file shares into a distributed file system.

DNS zone A portion of the DNS namespace whose database records exist and are managed in a particular DNS database file.

domain controller The computer that stores a replica (copy) of the account and security information of the domain and defines the domain.

Domain Name System (DNS) A hierarchical client-server-based distributed database management system that translates Internet domain names to an IP address. It is used because domain names are easier to remember than IP addresses. The DNS clients are called resolvers and the NS servers are called name servers.

downstream server The second server in a multiple tier system.

dynamic DNS A mechanism where a hostname and its associated IP address is automatically registered in the DNS server.

Dynamic Host Configuration Protocol (DHCP) A mechanism used to automatically configure a host during boot up on a TCP/IP network and to change settings while the host is attached. Before your DHCP server can provide IP address leases to clients, you have to provide a range of IP addresses at the DHCP server. This range, known as a scope, defines a single physical subnet on your network to which DHCP services are offered.

dynamic routes Routes that are automatically calculated and created.

E

encrypting file system (EFS) Technology built into the NTFS that enables a user to encrypt and decrypt files that are stored on an NTFS volume.

encryption The process of disguising a message or data in what appears to be meaningless data (cipher text) to hide and protect the sensitive data from unauthorized access.

Event Collector A component that forward events from one Windows computer to another.

Event Viewer A management console that allows you to view information about significant events, such as a program starting or stopping, or a security error, that are recorded in event logs.

explicit permission Permissions given to a user and applied directly to an object.

Extensible Authentication Protocol (EAP) An open-ended authentication mechanism that allows new authentication schemes to be plugged in as needed.

F

features Software programs that are not directly part of a role or can support or augment the functionality of one or more roles, or enhance the functionality of the entire server.

File Server Resource Manager A suite of tools for Windows Server 2008 that allows administrators to understand, control, and manage the quantity and type of data that is stored on their servers.

firewall A system designed to prevent unauthorized access to or from a private network.

forwarder A DNS configuration where a DNS server forwards a query to a specific DNS server for resolution.

Fully Qualified Domain Names (FQDNs) Names used to identify computers on a TCP/IP network; sometimes referred to as just domain names.

G

GlobalNames zone A special DNS zone used for single-name instead of Fully Qualified Domain Names.

group policy A feature of the Microsoft Windows NT family of operating systems that provides centralized management and configuration of computers and remote users in an Active Directory environment. Group Policy can control a target object's Registry, NTFS security, audit and security policy, software installation, logon/logoff scripts, folder redirection, and Internet Explorer settings. The policy settings are stored in Group Policy Objects (GPOs).

group policy object (GPO) The component in which the group policies are stored. Each GPO may be linked to multiple websites, domains, or organizational units. This allows for multiple machines or users to be updated via a change to a single GPO, in turn reducing the administrative burden and costs associated with managing these resources.

H

hop The trip a data packet takes from one router to another router or a router to another intermediate point to another in the network.

host A connection on a TCP/IP network that is assigned an IP address. It includes the network's interface cards or a network printer that connects directly onto the network.

host (A or AAAA) records A DNS resource record that translates from hostname to IP address.

HOSTS file A configuration file used to translate hostnames to IP addresses.

I

incremental backup A backup that backs up the files selected if the archive file attribute is on (file since the last full backup or incremental backup). After the file has been backed up, it shuts off/resets the file archive attribute/bit, indicating that the file has been backed up.

inherited permission Permissions that are granted because they flow down from another object.

Initial Configuration Tasks A feature launched automatically after the installation of Windows Server 2008. As the name implies, it is designed to finish the setup and configuration of a new server, including performing many security-related tasks, such as setting the administrator password, changing the name of the administrator account, running Windows updates, and configuring the Windows firewall. It also enables you to add roles and features.

Internet Control-Message Protocol (ICMP) A TCP/IP protocol that sends messages and reports errors regarding the delivery of a packet. ICMP is used by the ping and tracert commands to test network connectivity.

Internet Information Services (IIS) Microsoft's web server.

Internet Print Protocol (IPP) Printing that is encapsulated in Hypertext Transfer Protocol (HTTP) packets.

Internet Protocol (IP)   A protocol that is primarily responsible for addressing and routing packets between hosts.

IP Security (IPSec)   A suite of protocols that provide a mechanism for data integrity, authentication, and privacy for the Internet Protocol. IPSec can provide either message authentication and/or encryption.

ipconfig command   A utility used to view and configure the IP configuration.

IPv4   The traditional version of the TCP/IP protocol.

IPv4 address   The traditional logical address that identifies a host on a TCP/IP network. The format of the IPv4 address is four 8-bit numbers (an octet) divided by a period (.). Each number can be 0 to 255.

IPv6   The upgraded version of the TCP/IP protocol.

iterative query   A DNS query that gives the best answer it currently has back as a response. The best answer is the address being sought or an address of a server that would have a better idea of its address.

L

Layer 2 Forwarding (L2F)   A protocol developed by Cisco that enables a server to frame dial-up traffic using PPP and transmit over WAN links to an L2F server or router, which then unwraps the packets before releasing them to the network.

Layer 2 Tunneling Protocol (L2TP) A VPN protocol that combines L2F and PPTP so remote users can access networks in a secure fashion. Typically, L2TP is combined with IPSec to provide security.

Lightweight Directory Access Protocol (LDAP)   A set of protocols for accessing information directories. LDAP is based on the standards contained within the X.500 standard, but is significantly simpler; unlike X.500, LDAP supports TCP/IP, which is necessary for any type of Internet access. Because it is a simpler version of X.500, LDAP is sometimes called X.500-lite.

Line Printer Daemon (LPD)   A set of programs that provide printer spooling and network print server functionality for UNIX-like systems.

link-local multicast name resolution (LLMNR)   A mechanism that allows IPv4 and IPv6 hosts on a single subnet without a Domain Name System (DNS) server to resolve each other's names.

link-state algorithms   Also known as shortest path first algorithms, a routing algorithm that has routers send updates directly (or by using multicast traffic) to all routers within the network. Each router, however, sends only the portion of the routing table that describes the state of its own links.

LMHOSTS file   A configuration file used to translate NetBIOS names to IP addresses.

local printer   A printer that is connected directly to a computer.

M

media access control (MAC) address
The physical device address, which is 48 bits (6 bytes) in length. Because many network devices share the same transmission channel, each node on the network must have some way to identify itself from the other nodes. The physical device address or media access control (MAC) address is a unique hardware address (unique on the LAN) burned onto a ROM chip assigned by the hardware vendors.

metric A standard of measurement, such as hop count, that is used by routing algorithms to determine the optimal path to a destination.

Microsoft Baseline Security Analyzer (MBSA) A graphical and command-line interface that can perform local or remote scans of Windows systems and that is used to identify common security misconfigurations.

Microsoft Challenge Handshake Authentication Protocol Version (MS-CHAP) An authentication mechanism that has strong security for remote access connections and that allows for mutual authentication where the client authenticates the server.

Microsoft Management Console (MMC) A fully customizable administrative console used as a common interface for most administrative tasks.

Microsoft Remote Server Administration Tools (RSAT) Enables administrators to remotely manage roles and features in Windows Server 2008 from a computer that is running Windows Vista with Service Pack 1 (SP1).

Microsoft updates Updates that are available from Microsoft to make systems more reliable or secure or to fix a problem or bug.

multicast The technology that allows the sender to send a single transmission (from the sender's unicast address) to the multicast address, and the routers take care of making copies and sending them to all receivers that have registered their interest in data from that sender.

Multicast Address Dynamic Client Allocation Protocol (MADCAP) The technology that performs multicast address assignment in a DHCP environment. When registered clients are dynamically assigned IP addresses through MADCAP, they can participate efficiently in the data stream process, such as for real-time video or audio network transmissions.

N

Network Access Protection (NAP) Microsoft technology for controlling a computer host's network access, based on the host's system health. With NAP, system administrators of an organization's computer network can define policies for system health requirements.

network address translation (NAT) A method of connecting multiple computers to the Internet (or any other IP network), using one IP address. It is often used to translate public addresses to internal private IP addresses.

network file system (NFS)
Technology that enables UNIX to share files and applications across the network.

Network Monitor   Microsoft's protocol analyzer.

network policies   A sets of conditions, constraints, and settings that enable you to designate who is authorized to connect to the network and the circumstances under which they can, or cannot, connect. It limits network access of computers based on predefined health requirements.

Network Policy Server (NPS)
Microsoft's Radius server used in Windows Server 2008.

network printer   A printer that is connected to the network.

nslookup   A diagnostic tool that displays information from the DNS servers.

NTFS   The preferred file system that supports larger hard disks, enhanced recovery, and better security.

O

offline folder   A shared folder that is available to users when they are not connected to the network where the share folder exists.

Open Shortest Path First (OSPF)   A link-state routing protocol used in medium-sized and large networks that calculates routing table entries by constructing a shortest-path tree. OSPF is designed for large internetworks (especially those spanning more than 15 router hops).

P

Password Authentication Protocol (PAP)   A authentication mechanism that is the least secure because it uses clear text/plain text (unencrypted) passwords.

permission   Defines the type of access granted to an object or object attribute.

ping command   A utility used to test network connectivity based on the ICMP protocol.

pointer (PTR) records   A DNS resource record that translates IP address to hostname.

Point-to-Point Protocol (PPP)   The predominant protocol for modem-based access to the Internet, which provides full-duplex, bi-directional operations between the host and the private network.

Point-to-Point Tunneling Protocol (PPTP)   A VPN protocol that is based on the point-to-point protocol.

port   A logical connection used by client programs to specify a particular server program running on a computer on the network defined at the transport layer.

primary name server   A name server (DNS) that stores and maintains the zone file locally. Changes to a zone, such as adding domains or hosts, are made by changing files at the primary name server. You can have only one primary name server for each domain.

print device   The physical print device, such as a printer, copy machine, or plotter.

print driver   A program designed to enable other programs to work with a particular printer without concerning themselves with the specifics of the printer's hardware and internal language.

print job   Data that is set to a printer to be printed.

print priority   A prioritizing of print jobs so that certain print jobs can be printed before other print jobs.

print queues   A location where print jobs are held until they can be printed by the print device.

print scheduling   The scheduling of printers so that print jobs can be printed when they are less used.

printer   The software interface between a print device and the print clients or applications. It is a logical representation of a print device in Windows that has an assigned printer name and software that controls a print device. When you print to the print device, you print to the printer, which then prints to the print device.

printer pools   Two or more identical print devices belonging to the same printer, associated together as one.

private network   Networks that can be accessed only within a corporation and that cannot be accessed from public network.

Protected Extensible Authentication Protocol (PEAP)   A method to securely transmit authentication information, including passwords, over wired or wireless networks.

protocol analyzer   Also known as a network analyzer or packet analyzer, software or a hardware/software device that enables you to capture or receive every packet on your media, store it in a trace buffer, and then show a breakdown of each of the packets by protocol in the order in which they appeared.

proxy server   Any device that acts on behalf of another.

public folder   A folder sharing that is designed to enable users to share files and folders from a single location quickly and easily.

R

recursive query   A DNS query that asks the DNS server to respond with the requested data or with an error stating that the requested data doesn't exist or that the domain name specified doesn't exist.

remote access service (RAS)   A service that enables users to connect remotely, using various protocols and connection types. A RAS is the computer and associated software that is set up to handle users seeking access to the network remotely. Sometimes called a communication server, a RAS usually includes or is associated with a firewall server to ensure security and a router that can forward the remote access request to another part of the corporate network.

Remote Authentication Dial-In User Service (RADIUS)   The industry standard client/server protocol and software that enables remote access servers to communicate with a central server and database to authenticate dial-in and remote users and authorize their access to the requested system or service.

right   A user's authorization to perform certain actions on a computer, such as logging on to a system interactively, logging on locally to the computer, backing up files and directories, performing a system shutdown, or adding/removing a device driver.

root hints   A file that provides a list of IP addresses of DNS servers that are considered to be authoritative at the root level of the DNS hierarchy.

round robin   A mechanism to share and distribute loads for network resources.

router   A Layer 3 device that manages the flow of data between network segments, or subnets.

Router Information Protocol (RIP)   A popular distance-vector routing protocol designed for exchanging routing information within a small-to medium-size network.

Routing and Remote Access (RRAS)   A Windows server component that enables a Windows Server 2008 server to function as a network router and remote access server.

S

secondary name server   A name server (DNS) that gets the data for its zone from another name server, either a primary name server or another secondary name server.

Secure Socket Tunneling Protocol (SSTP)   A VPN protocol that uses HTTPS protocol over TCP port 443 to pass traffic through firewalls and web proxies that might block PPTP and L2TP/IPsec traffic.

secured dynamic updates   A mechanism where only those clients authorized within the domain are permitted to update resource records.

server   A specialized computer that is designed to provide services.

server core   A Windows Server 2008 installation that provides a minimal environment with no Windows Explorer shell for running specific server roles and no Start button.

Server Manager console   An MMC console designed to simplify the task of managing and securing server roles.

server message block (SMB)   A mature protocol that enables Windows and other operating systems to share folders and printers and access those shared folders and printers.

server role   A set of software programs that enable a computer to perform a specific function for multiple users or other computers within a network.

service   A program, routine, or process that performs a specific system function to support other programs.

shadow copy   Technology that automatically creates backup copies of the data stored in shared folders on specific drive volumes at scheduled times.

shared folder   A folder available for others to use on the network. A shared drive on a computer makes the entire drive available for others to use on the network.

Simple Network Management Protocol (SNMP) A de facto standard for internetwork management that makes it possible to configure remote devices, monitor network performance, detect network faults, detect inappropriate access, and audit network usage. Remote devices include hubs, bridges, routers, and servers.

smart card A pocket-sized card with embedded integrated circuits that can process information, often used for authentication.

SNMP trap An unsolicited message sent by an SNMP agent to a SNMP management system when the agent detects that a certain type of event has occurred locally on the managed host.

split horizon A mechanism that ensures that routing loops do not occur because the routes learned from a router are not rebroadcast to that network.

spooler Often referred to as a queue, the spooler accepts each document being printed, stores it, and sends it to the printer device when the printer device is ready.

Start of authority (SOA) A DNS resource record that indicates the starting point or original point of authority for information stored in a zone.

stateful firewall A firewall that monitors the state of active connections and uses the information gained to determine which network packets are allowed through the firewall. Typically, if the user starts communicating with an outside computer, it remembers the conversation and allows the appropriate packets back in. If an outside computer tries to start communicating with a computer protected by a stateful firewall, those packets are automatically dropped unless the packet or protocol was granted access by an access control list (ACL).

statement of health (SoH) A report of the client configuration state.

static route An administrator-defined route that does not change and that defines the pathway from one network to another network.

stub zone Lists information about the authoritative name servers of a zone so that the DNS server knows directly which server is the authority for a particular zone. This enables it to perform recursive queries using the stub zone's list of name servers without having to query the Internet or an internal root server for the DNS namespace. Stub zones contain the Start of Authority (SOA) resource records of the zone.

subnet A smaller part of network.

subnet mask Used to define which bits represent the network address (including the subnet number) and which bits represent the host address.

superscope A group of multiple scopes (child scopes) as a single administrative entity used on DHCP servers.

system health validators (SHVs) Defined client computer configuration requirements for the NAP-capable computers that attempt to connect to your network.

system state   A collection of system-specific data, including the following: the Registry, COM+ Class Registration database, boot files, including the system files, Certificate Services database, Active Directory directory service if it is a domain controller, the SYSVOL directory, the Cluster Service information, IIS Metadirectory, and system files that are under Windows File Protection.

T

TCP/IP protocol suite   An industry suite of protocols on which the Internet is based. It is supported by most versions of Windows and virtually all modern operating systems.

tombstoning   A WINS mechanism that marks a record that it considers no longer active to be deleted.

Trusted Platform Module (TPM)   A microchip that is built into a computer. It is used to store cryptographic information, such as encryption keys.

U

unicast   The most commonly used IP address. It refers to a single sender or a single receiver, and can be used for both sending and receiving. Usually, a unicast address is associated with a single device or host.

Universal Naming Convention (UNC)   Naming scheme used on TCP/IP networks, using the NetBIOS names

(such as that used to identify share names for files and printers: \\COMPUTERNAME\ SHARENAME).

upstream server   The first server in a multiple-tier system.

usage profile   A firewall profile that groups settings such as firewall rules and connection security rules that are applied to the computer, depending on where the computer is connected.

V–W

virtual private networking (VPN)   The creation of secured, point-to-point connections across a private network or a public network, such as the Internet. A VPN client uses special TCP/IP-based protocols called tunneling protocols to make a virtual call to a virtual port on a virtual private networking server.

wbadmin.exe   The Windows Server 2008 command prompt backup program.

web server   A computer equipped with the server software that uses Internet protocols such as HTTP and FTP to respond to web client requests on a TCP/IP network via web browsers.

WiFi Protected Access (WPA)   A Wi-Fi standard that was designed to improve upon the security features of WEP and that includes improved data encryption through the temporal key integrity protocol (TKIP) and user authentication.

Wi-Fi Protected Access Version 2 (WPA2)   A security method for wireless networks that provides stronger data protection and network access control than Wireless Equivalency Proteciton (WEP). It is based on the IEEE 802.11i standard and uses AES encryption.

Windows Firewall   A packet filter and stateful host-based firewall that allows or blocks network traffic according to the configuration.

Windows Firewall with Advanced Security   An enhanced firewall found on Windows Server 2008 that enables you to also manage IPSec.

Windows Internet Name Service (WINS)   A service that resolves NetBIOS/computer names to IP addresses.

Windows PowerShell   A command-line shell and scripting language.

Windows Reliability and Performance Monitor   A Microsoft Management Console snap-in that provides tools for analyzing system performance.

Windows Server 2008   A network operating system and server that is successor to Windows Server 2003. The client version of Windows Server 2008 is Windows Vista, on which Windows Server 2008 is partially based.

Windows Server Updates Services   A service that can install Microsoft updates automatically.

WINS proxy agent   A WINS-enabled computer configured to act on behalf of other host computers that cannot use WINS directly.

Wireless Equivalency Protection (WEP)   The most basic wireless encryption scheme.

Z

zone file   A file that defines a zone and is kept on the DNS name server.

zone transfers   A mechanism that replicates and synchronizes all copies of the zone files between DNS name servers.

Index

EXAM CRAM

The Smart Way to Study™

Exam 70-642

MCTS

Windows Server 2008
Network Infrastructure,
Configuring

CD features Test Engine
Powered by MeasureUp!

Patrick Regan

FREE Online Edition

Your purchase of **MCTS 70-642 Exam Cram: Windows Server 2008 Network Infrastructure, Configuring** includes access to a free online edition for 45 days through the Safari Books Online subscription service. Nearly every Que book is available online through Safari Books Online, along with more than 5,000 other technical books and videos from publishers such as Addison-Wesley Professional, Cisco Press, Exam Cram, IBM Press, O'Reilly, Prentice Hall, and Sams.

SAFARI BOOKS ONLINE allows you to search for a specific answer, cut and

Activate your FREE Online Edition at www.informit.com/safarifree

> **STEP 1:** Enter the coupon code: HGFWGCB.

> **STEP 2:** New Safari users, complete the brief registration form. Safari subscribers, just log in.

If you have difficulty registering on Safari or accessing the online edition, please e-mail customer-service@safaribooksonline.com